Color in Three-Dimensional Design

Jeanne Kopacz

McGraw-Hill

New York   Chicago   San Francisco   Lisbon   London   Madrid
Mexico City   Milan   New Delhi   San Juan   Seoul
Singapore   Sydney   Toronto

Library of Congress Cataloging-in-Publication Data
Kopacz, Jeanne.
    Color in three-dimensional design / Jeanne Kopacz.
        p.   cm.
    Includes bibliographical references and index.
    ISBN 0-07-141170-4 (alk. paper)
    1. Color in design.   2. Color vision.   3. Space perception.   I. Title.

    NK1548.K66   2003
    701'.85—dc21
                                                2003052786

1 2 3 4 5 6 7 8 9 0 DOC/DOC 0 9 8 7 6 5 4 3

ISBN 0-07-141170-4

The sponsoring editor for this book was Cary Sullivan and the
production supervisor was Pamela A. Pelton. It was set in
Times Roman by North Market Street Graphics.

Printed and bound by RR Donnelley.

This book was printed on acid-free paper.

McGraw-Hill books are available at special quantity discounts to use as
premiums and sales promotions, or for use in corporate training programs.
For more information, please write to the Director of Special Sales,
Professional Publishing, McGraw-Hill, Two Penn Plaza, New York, NY
10121-2298. Or contact your local bookstore.

This book is dedicated to designers learning about color.

Contents

x *Contents*

Acknowledgments

The expression "it takes a village" can be applied to many efforts, and this book is certainly one of them. While researching data on the subject of color in three-dimensional design over the past seven or eight years, I've been amazed to see so many people come forward to share their own findings on the same subject. Some spoke from experience, others shared an observation or a project case study. A few offered published materials or pointed me to people more knowledgeable than myself. This book would not be as complete as it is if were not for some of the generous people who surround me.

Karen Vagts is the person who first showed me how to make the transition from teacher to writer. Without her inspiration and advice, this might still be a lecture series. I appreciate her efforts to help me initiate the project as a structured document. Other people gave helpful feedback on the document in draft form. They include Elissa Gotha and Jon Richmond. And of course, Cary Sullivan, the editor for this book, was instrumental in showing me how it's done and encouraging me to keep going.

While the people who shared color stories are too numerous to mention, I would like to credit the design teams who helped with images. They are Bergmeyer Associates, Inc., Flansburgh Associates, Inc., ADD Inc, and Perry, Dean, Rogers & Partners. In addition, the people at Griswold, Heckel & Kelly Associates, Inc. (GHK), Ellenzweig Associates, Inc., Cubellis Associates, Inc., and CBT/Childs, Bertman, Tseckares Inc., willingly contributed key projects from their extensive portfolios. New England School of Art & Design, at Suffolk University also provided me with a strong design team in the form of students who not only produced good work, but who asked challenging questions.

Individuals who made contributions relative to their area of expertise include Bob Ponzini of Osram Sylvania; Barbara Jacobs, Color & Design; and Diane Facteau of Shaw Industries, Inc. Deborah Szwarce of Inter Fashion Concepts, Ltd., was instrumental in the discussion on color forecasting; and Anne Robinson of Parsons Brinckerhoff was particularly generous in her review of the lighting chapter. Designers who provided knowledge based on application experience are Valerie Curtis and Laurie Barton on educational work, Irene Elsinovsky on medical applications, and Jeff Ornstein in the area of hospitality. Marg Dion was especially helpful given her strong expertise in historic preservation, and John Rafuse provided instructive insight on bioscience facilities.

I would like to acknowledge a few other professionals. Chris Indoe helped me to see the value of electronic color tools. Sheila Selby and Diane Richmond provided their Photoshop skills, which are evident in some of the graphic material included in this book. Of course, no one can manage graphic material without the support of a good technology person. In this case, Mike Andrea was a tremendous resource when the technology gods were unkind.

Finally, I would like to thank my better half, Karol Kopacz, who seized the opportunity to redefine the concept of supportive spouse so that I could stay focused on this project. For this I am truly grateful.

My thanks to all the villagers who supported this project.

Introduction

A wealth of information is available today concerning color in three-dimensional applications. Some comes from the scientific arena where conclusions surface through methodical analysis in the search for proof. Other insights are derived from artistic intuition, observation of human response, and personal knowledge, all of which depend on experience. Together these sources contribute to our understanding of color and its impact on design in the twenty-first century.

Each conclusion we reach regarding a design solution is based on what we know at a specific point in time. The more insight we have from our own experience and the collective wisdom of others, the more effective we are at anticipating results in the context of something new. We consider conclusions shared by others, and we evaluate their potential in the context of our own challenges. Many theorists and practitioners have documented their findings on color response. However, access to all the information is limited for one simple reason. We just don't have the time for research. In addition, the printing life cycle of each colorist's thesis is frequently short-lived due to a limited audience. This means some meaningful color work comes to light and recedes as a historic record before many design practitioners are even aware it exists. How much more effective we might be if we could selectively capture the wisdom of the past generations of colorists in a concise document.

This text is offered as that document. It's intended to arm practicing designers with tools for successful color implementation in three-dimensional work. Aesthetic debates are subjective and plentiful, but rarely do they address issues of physical consequence. Such results are realized only through a commitment to rational criteria as the basis for color selection. This approach allows us to anticipate results and ensure success on the basis of known color relationships. The impact of depth perception, the sense of balance, the psychological response of users, and the emphasis of contrast—these are the things we use intuitively to make our color decisions more powerful in the realm of spatial work. This book offers traditional (and some nontraditional) color theory so that it can be evaluated for its potential in the context of individual practice. In addition, this document explores contemporary practice. It asks the questions, "What are designers doing with the information?" and "How is color being used to effect positive results?"

The organization of this book is meant to be academic: a linear progression of conceptual to practical subject matter. Theoretical issues are explained first. Then each section builds on information that precedes it, beginning with perception and psychology issues, exploring three-dimensional concepts, and adding more detailed aspects of technical issues that impact color selection. Finally, we close by identifying specific matters of professional practice in environmental design. The attempt is to keep the focus on color concepts. Of course, other aspects combine naturally, and, where appropriate, supplemental comments are offered. Suggestions are also included for those who are using this as a tool for personal development. Since color expertise is acquired through experimentation, those who are exploring the subject in depth for the first time may find it valuable to replicate some experiments firsthand.

By reading this book you will, at the very least, increase your exposure to possibilities for three-dimensional color expression. At best, you will assemble your own set of useful conclusions and enhance your ability to control color and its three-dimensional effects. Good information is a valuable tool. How we use the information is limited only by our creativity.

PART 1

Color Theory and Observation

1

Color Basics

Each unique color can be described by a variety of individual characteristics. As the eye views a collection of colors, it visually merges those that appear similar and accentuates the characteristics that make dissimilar colors different. This is what makes a red barn stand out in a field of green or a black reveal recede into a finished walnut panel.

Design captures color effects in ways that enhance the physical world. The more we can predict color behavior and our reactions to it, the greater will be our ability to use naturally occurring color phenomena to enhance designed form. We do this by taking advantage of the insights color theorists have uncovered over the past 400 years. Their collective wisdom has been documented and taught in ways that provide us a framework, a systematic basis of the complex color experience, which we can use to anticipate visual experiences.

The first step to understanding color theory and its use in design practice is to develop a familiarity with the basic characteristics of color as they contribute to visual perception. These characteristics are the tools used to discriminate color and establish common language for collaboration. They form the basis of many color theories and methods of color measurement. This chapter summarizes the key elements of color, establishing the three characteristics that define all color. Applying this knowledge is how visual color effects are created.

▨ BASIC COLOR TERMS

The term *color* refers to all visual sensations. It includes the emptiness of white and the darkness of black, as well as the intensity of lipstick red and the subtlety of red brick. For color analysis we use definitive terms to address distinctions of color, either as precise measurements or in relative terms.

Colorimetry is the combination of color measurements used to identify color for precise communication. Three main color attributes—hue, value, and saturation—together can be used to determine any individual color visible to the human eye. In science, precise tools are used to mathematically define each of these three attributes. Numerical scales identify the dominant wavelength (hue) and relative gray-scale reference (value), and the degree of purity (saturation) is measured by a percentage calculation. In design, individual colors are described in comparison to each other and in association with the full palette of colors.

Other terms, such as *brightness, complement,* and *temperature,* are also used to articulate relative aspects of colors used in combination. Various professionals use these terms, not always consistently, to identify issues of color for the purpose of their practice. The following sections define key color attributes *as they're used in design practice.*

► Hue: Color Quality

The attribute of color experienced first in the course of human development is *hue*. Hue is sometimes described as the primary character, or the pure essence, of color. It refers to the wavelength of the color and its relative position in a two-dimensional color circle—in other words, the redness, yellowness, or blueness of the color. We identify hue by distinguishing one chromatic color from another, such as red-orange from orange, or blue from greenish-blue. There are an infinite number of definable hues, all of which may be described in relative terms according to six familiar primary and secondary colors: violet, blue, green, yellow, orange, and red. The color circle shown in Figure 1.1 includes 24 individual hues.

The term *quality* is similarly used to describe color. When we say a color has a blue quality, we're describing its position relative to other hues as occurring between green and violet. If a blue quality, or cast, is noted in a green color, this

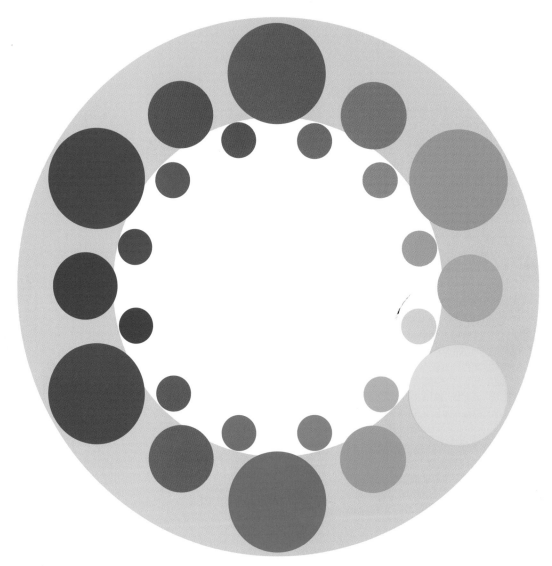

FIGURE 1.1 This color circle has 24 different hues, but additional distinguishable hues do exist between those shown. *(Illustration by author.)*

places it in the green family, relatively closer to blue than to yellow.

► Value: Lightness and Darkness

Value is the term used to describe how light or dark a color is. When two colors differ in terms of their relative lightness or darkness, they are of different values. Traditionally speaking, the lighter the color, the higher its value. Relative value is most easily recognized between two shades of a neutral color or between two colors of a similar hue. However, differences in value are also visible between dissimilar hues. For example, it's easy to recognize that a cream-colored wall (of yellow hue) has a higher value than the color of an adjacent mahogany door (which has a red hue).

The value of a given color changes by adding either black or white to it. Mixing with white increases the value of a basic hue, creating *tints*. Tints are successively lighter as they approach white. For instance, pink is a tint of the color red. When black is added to a color, *shades* of that hue are created. Maroon is a shade that occurs when the same red used to create pink is mixed with black. An infinite number of incremental shades and tints can be developed through the mixing of one hue with either black or white. Figure 1.2 displays two value scales—one is a gray scale, the other shows the same number of value steps in a pale red.

Value is adjusted in a variety of ways depending on the media used. With solid pigments, white pigment can be added to make a color lighter, but with watercolors, the color of hue is diluted with water to reduce its value. In print, dots of color may be spaced farther apart to lighten an area if the underlying paper is white. On the computer, the quantities of light from all three light guns (red, green, and blue) are increased to lighten the color on the monitor.

Value in Colors of Hue

Most people can comfortably distinguish comparative values in shades of gray. However, when colors of similar value are presented in contrasting hue or saturation, it's more difficult to determine which is lighter or darker. A photographic process is not completely reliable as a value gauge because pho-

FIGURE 1.2 Differences in value can occur between colors with or without obvious hue characteristics.

tography tends to exaggerate the lightness and darkness of gray values, distorting the value of what the eye really sees. It also reduces the differences between the middle values slightly. There are more effective shortcuts.

Colors of hue can be distinguished in value by their corresponding gray scale. A simple reference tool for designers is a strip of gray color samples, incrementally adjusted in value from white to black, as shown in Figure 1.3. If a hole is punched in each gray-scale sample, they can be placed over a saturated color sample to find the closest value. The lighter color is the one with a lighter corresponding gray. A large area of gray relative to the size of the hole helps to avoid influence from the color being evaluated. No tinge of hue should appear—the scale is a better reference if it's completely hue-neutral.

When a color becomes more saturated, our perception of its value becomes dependent on the inherent value of that hue. Highly saturated colors of hue that are very close in value may be difficult

FIGURE 1.3 A good reference gray scale for value studies has evenly spaced steps, using a geometric progression, with a gray of medium value at the center of the scale.

to distinguish along a value scale. We are easily influenced by the contrast of hue and may make incorrect assumptions based on the relationship of the colors at full saturation. For example, a specific orange may be presumed to be lighter than a particular violet color, because in a fully saturated state orange is lighter than violet. However, if the orange has been reduced in saturation by mixing with a darker brown, and the violet has been lightened by combination with white, the violet may in fact be lighter in value.

In a comparison of chartreuse and fuchsia, the differences in hue are readily apparent, but determining the lighter value may be troublesome. Artist Josef Albers offers a simple approach (*Interaction of Color,* page 12) to establish the relative value of two colors. Place a sample of one color so that it overlaps the other, as shown in Figure 1.4. Then focus on the upper sample for several minutes, and subsequently remove it while you continue looking at the area of overlap. If it appears lighter than the lower sample, the upper sample is darker. If the previously overlapped area is darker, then the upper sample is lighter. If it's difficult to ascertain, then reverse the position of the two samples and repeat the experiment.

▶ Saturation: Chroma

Saturation refers to the amount of hue, or the degree of fullness of the hue, that exists in a color. To reduce the saturation level of any color, it can be mixed either with a gray equal in value to the original hue or with the complement of the original color. The word *intensity* is another term used to describe the relative proportion of hue saturation versus neutrality as it exists in color. A very intense

color is one closer to a full hue. When we decrease the intensity of a color, only its saturation is reduced.

Chroma is often used as a synonym for saturation. A color that has full chroma is one that is fully saturated or has a significant amount of color strength. When we talk about adjusting the amount of chroma, we mean changing the saturation level of the color. Chroma is also used to describe hue

FIGURE 1.4 The overlapping sample technique is a handy way to determine the relative value of two colors.

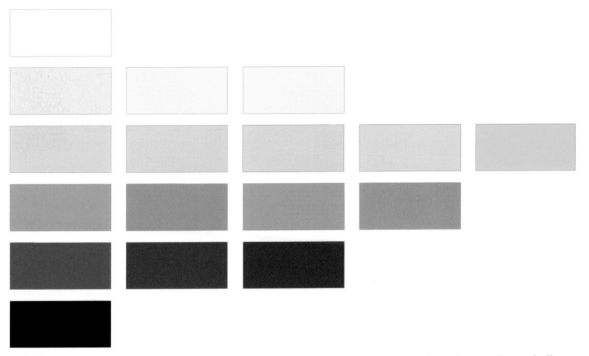

FIGURE 1.5 In this color matrix, rectangles are uniform in value horizontally and consistent in saturation vertically.

characteristics, as in the expression "a shift in chroma," which describes a change in relative hue. The overall quality of a color is known as its *chromacity* and is described in terms of hue and saturation only (i.e., the particular hue and the amount of chroma). Chromacity can be described in general terms, such as a lilac, which is moderate in saturation and falls halfway between blue and red, or it can be scientifically defined using numerical references.

To demonstrate the difference between value and saturation, a matrix has been developed in Figure 1.5 for a single yellow hue. When a given color is changed by mixing it with a gray of equal value, the result is a *tone* of the original color. Many tones can be created from one hue and one gray simply by varying the amounts of each. In the diagram, the band to the left is simply a gray scale showing a range of value without any chroma applied. In the second vertical band, equal amounts of chroma are visible in each established column 2 value. The resulting colors are consistent in saturation, but unequal in value. Each horizontal band shows a range of colors equal in value, but which vary in their level of saturation, or the amount of chroma.

The most saturated colors in this example are on the right-hand side of the color matrix.

▶ Brightness: Brilliance

Brightness and *brilliance* are synonymous words whose meaning varies slightly according to their use. In design, these terms are usually associated with the strength of a color. A strong color is one that first catches the eye of the observer. The greater the tendency for a color to draw attention to itself, the greater is its strength. The more strength a color has, the brighter or more brilliant it seems. In environmental forms of design, brightness can also be augmented through an increase in light: as light is added, the brightness of a colored surface will increase. The same surface will appear darker and less saturated as the general light level is reduced.

Brightness is measured as a combination of two things: value and saturation. An increase in either value or saturation level will cause a color to be stronger, brighter, more brilliant. In Figure 1.6, the left column shows a range of selected colors. In the second column, the saturation level of each is

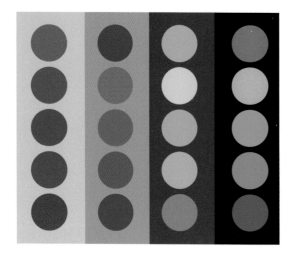

FIGURE 1.6   The brightest colors are those of great saturation and high value.

color that catches the viewer's attention first will be considered the stronger of the two, or the brightest. If both colors are equal in value, the more saturated of the two draws our attention. If they're equal in saturation, the lighter of the two has the greater strength, or drawing power. As an example, if a fully saturated orange is shown with a fully saturated blue, the orange will be more brilliant due to its lighter value. The comparison changes if the orange is significantly neutral, closer to a spice tone or a shade of umber. In this case, the fully saturated blue will be brighter by virtue of its saturation as the intensity of the bright blue gives it greater strength than the neutral orange. Many creative color combinations have been developed using uncommon variations of a color's value and saturation level.

▶ **Color Complement**

Every hue has an opposite on the color circle that's called its *complement*. This relationship is shown in Figure 1.7. To find the complement of any color, use a well-balanced color circle for reference. Draw a line directly through the center of the circle from the first color, and you'll find it's complement on the opposite site. This relationship is frequently used

increased, but the value is maintained. The third column shows the colors with increased value and a saturation level similar to the first column. Finally, the fourth band shows each color with both value and saturation increased. Of all the selections, those in the last vertical band appear brightest. When comparing two different colors to each other, the

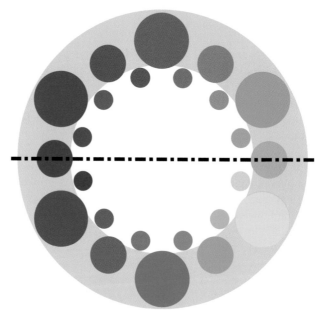

FIGURE 1.7   A true diagonal through the circle's center consistently connects two complementary colors. *(Illustration by author.)*

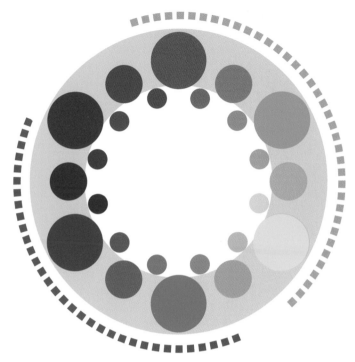

FIGURE 1.8 The hues along the orange band are considered warm; those along the blue band are cool. *(Illustration by author.)*

when working with contrasts and harmonies in pigmentary material. Since the color circle for additive color systems (colors of light) and subtractive color systems (colors of pigment) differ from each other, their complements differ as well. (The conditions of additive and subtractive color will be explained in more detail later in this chapter.)

▶ Color Temperature

Color establishes an impression of temperature according to its hue characteristics. Many believe this impression can be powerful enough to impact physical response. In her book, *The Ancient Art of Color Therapy,* Linda Clark cites an example in which occupants complain a room is too hot or too cold at a given temperature, and their perception is managed by a change of room color without a change in air temperature (page 35). Most colorists accept the idea that humans associate temperature with certain hues. Figure 1.8 illustrates those associations. Hues in the yellow, orange, and red range are considered warm, while colors ranging from blue to green are considered cool. Yellow-green and violet

can seem either warm or cool depending on the relative temperature of the adjacent colors in view. In spatial applications, we tend to favor warm colors in colder climates and cool ones in hot climates.

■ COLOR VISION

The visual sensory process involves two steps. First there's a source of stimulation, the eye; then there's a point of recognition, which is in the brain. The eye is the sense organ for vision. It enables us to distinguish both forms and colors and to recognize movements as they occur. Simply speaking, as the eye is stimulated, the visual image comes into being in the brain. This process of recognition is similar to the experience of dreaming. In a dream state most people can see a significant number of three-dimensional images in living color, even though the eyes are closed.

Our reactions to light stimuli and ability to process them determine what we see. A person with normal color-sensitive vision and a person whose sense of color deviates from the norm may have different impressions of an object. The object is constant, but each viewer's image is impacted by his or her physiological ability to distinguish color. Some variations in color perception are measurable. Others are much more subjective, but just as real. Because of our individual uniqueness, there is no true absolute vision of our surroundings. Instead, we collectively see a range of personal pictures, and for each of us our own image is the only "real" one. Our descriptions may sound the same, however, because each observation is in the context of our own experience. For the moment, let's focus on strictly physical aspects of color recognition.

▶ The Human Camera

The simplest way to explain the functions of the human eye is to compare it to a photographic camera. Assume that the camera body is essentially a hollow box. It has a round opening of adjustable size in front of the camera—the stop. In front of the stop are several optical lenses, which together bundle the light rays, directing them into the camera. At the rear wall of the camera is a light-sensitive material with a foil backing—the film.

Figure 1.9 is a graphic illustration of this idea. Four components in the eye perform roles similar to the camera box, lens, stop, and film. The eyeball itself serves as the camera box. The *pupil* of the eye is an adjustable stop, a hole in the center of the iris. The *iris* is the colored part of the eye that we see from the outside. As light passes through the hole (the pupil) the iris dilates and constricts to compensate for changes in the level of available light. The lower the light level, the more the pupil is dilated. The *cornea,* a bowed transparent layer at the outermost front of the eye, and the *lens,* positioned just behind the iris, bundle light rays the way that the camera lens functions. Together they form a small inverted image on the *retina* that lines the back of the eyeball. In this discussion, we can consider the retina our "film." It contains light-sensitive nerve cells, which send signals to the brain through the optic nerve behind the eye.

Three-dimensional perception is made possible during this process, as the lens alters the optical image gathered in the cornea, making more distant objects smaller and closer objects larger. To take in larger images, camera lenses have been developed that adjust for the effects of perspective. A printed

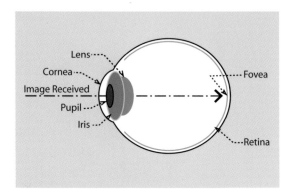

FIGURE 1.9 Here we have a very simplified illustration of a very complex organ—the eye.

picture is usually consistent, both in color and form, all the way to the edges of the image. In contrast, the retina is spherical in form, which means that the image it contains is curved. This causes those portions of the picture closest to the edges to be slightly distorted, affecting both the shape of the forms and the clarity of their colors. Color vision is strongest at the *fovea,* the sensitive center of the retina. The closer an object image is to the visual axis, the greater the clarity of color. The exception is a *blind spot* on the eye, where the nerve fibers connecting the retina to the brain pass through the surface of the eyeball. The blind spot has no sensitivity to light. Instead the brain fills in the spot with whatever is in the surrounding environment to complete the picture as we see it.

Dimensional Range

Human beings experience space as a series of images with outer limits. These limits affect our impression of the forms we see. For most of us, our field of vision includes a vertical range of about 140 degrees in one position. That range may be reduced for some individuals depending on the position of facial features. Each eye has its own horizontal field of vision, and the two overlap in the middle, as shown in Figure 1.10. Both eyes together can encompass more than 180 degrees. The area seen by both eyes simultaneously, known as the *binocular area,* is a little more than 90 degrees. What we can clearly see three-dimensionally falls within the binocular area. Beyond it, images flatten out, similar to the outer limits of a photograph taken with a wide-

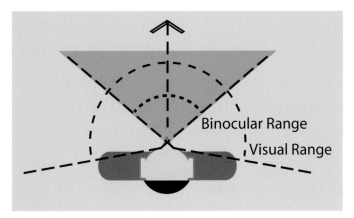

FIGURE 1.10 Our range of vision extends beyond our binocular range, which is shown in orange.

angle lens. Our ability to distinguish color diminishes in the outer visual range.

Colorific Range

It's generally assumed that under the best conditions, humans are capable of distinguishing between 7 and 12 million different colors. We recognize as many as 300 variations of hue. What we see as color is the result of electromagnetic energy in the form of light. Electromagnetic energy is generated in waves traveling at about 186,000 miles per second. Variation in hue is due to variation in the wavelengths, which are measured in meters, nanometers (nm), and angstrom units (Å). A nanometer equals one-millionth of a millimeter or one-billionth of a meter. One angstrom equals one ten-billionth of a meter. The range of electromagnetic wavelengths to which the eye is sensitive determines our color visibility. As humans, we're not sensitive to the same range of electromagnetic wavelengths as all other animals. For example, the bee is able to detect ultraviolet rays that are invisible to humans (shorter wavelengths than the human spectrum), yet the eye of a bee cannot perceive the longer-wave rays (what we know as red).

The range of electromagnetic radiation to which the human eye is sensitive is known as *light*. We realize the presence of light in the form of color. Human beings recognize light in wavelengths that occur between 400 nm (violet) and 750 nm (red). Ultraviolet light rays, known as UV light, have a slightly shorter wavelength, with a correspondingly higher frequency, than what we distinguish as violet light. Infrared rays are slightly longer, with lower frequency, than visible red light. The recognizable colors of light in order of their corresponding wavelengths are shown in Figure 1.11.

Other forms of electromagnetic energy create nonvisible waves in the universe. The shortest wavelengths, measured at less than one-millionth of a nanometer, are the dangerous cosmic rays that come to earth from the outer universe. They're reflected away from the earth by the outer layers of the earth's atmosphere. These are followed by gamma rays, which are released during nuclear explosions and are also life-threatening. Extremely long wavelengths occur when electric current is altered. This type of current is carried via conductive wiring and facilitates radar, television, and radio waves. Microwaves fall somewhere between the wavelengths we can see (color) and those we use for communications.

Cones and Rods

The retina of the eye has two types of receptor cells that receive light: *rods* and *cones.* Cones have primary responsibility for our daylight vision. They contain the pigments that are sensitive to chromatic distinctions (i.e., they recognize variation in spectral wavelength, establishing our sense of color saturation and characteristics of hue). Although scientists have not reached full consensus on the mechanics of color vision, most believe that we

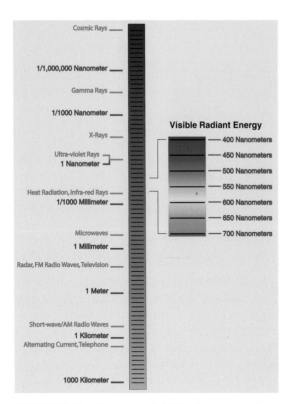

Visible Radiant Energy

Cosmic Rays

1/1,000,000 Nanometer

Gamma Rays

1/1000 Nanometer

X-Rays — 400 Nanometers

Ultra-violet Rays — 450 Nanometers
1 Nanometer — 500 Nanometers

— 550 Nanometers

Heat Radiation, Infra-red Rays — 600 Nanometers
1/1000 Millimeter — 650 Nanometers

Microwaves — 700 Nanometers
1 Millimeter

Radar, FM Radio Waves, Television

1 Meter

Short-wave/AM Radio Waves
1 Kilometer
Alternating Current, Telephone

1000 Kilometer

FIGURE 1.11 The range of visible electromagnetic waves is a small portion of the electromagnetic waves we know to exist.

have three types of cones, each sensitive to a different range of the spectrum. Identified as red, green, and blue cones, all three are stimulated together in the presence of white light. Cones receive signals sent as small dots and provide individual sensations to the brain, where the dots are reassembled into a complete image. Physiological differences in individual color perception are attributed to variations in this area of color function.

Rods, which are slightly smaller, contain visual pigment, called *rhodopsin,* and work in dim light. The image they produce is somewhat achromatic, providing us greater distinctions of lightness and darkness than that of hue. It's interesting to note that the retinas of nocturnal animals, which are effectively color blind, contain rods almost exclusively. Alternatively, the retinas of certain birds that are most active during daylight predominantly use cones. Creatures whose lives are spent in the sun tend to have better color vision than those living in the shade, and they tend to be more brightly colored.

▶ Color Spectrum

The color spectrum we experience is a product of the range of colors that make up white light. To see these colors distinctly, one must observe light through a prism—a transparent glass body with a triangular cross section. Truly neutral-colored light, or white light, consists of rays of all wavelengths from 380 to 760 nm (nanometers). As a reminder, we see violet in shortwave light and all other colors in increasingly longer wavelengths, up to the longest-wave light, which is red.

Colored light of one uniform wavelength is called *monochrome light.* It can be separated from the other wavelengths in white light by using prismatic lenses. Laser light is a common example of monochrome light. Laser is essentially a tight bunch of monochrome light rays of high intensity. By mixing monochrome light rays from the short-, middle-, and long-wave areas of the light spectrum, we can re-create a balanced light source.

Additive Color

One condition that has caused confusion for many generations of color theorists is the difference between colors as they behave in light and in pigment. The color of light is *additive color,* also called *spectral* color in reference to the light spectrum just discussed. The color of solid objects and surfaces using physical media is known as *subtractive color.* Within each realm, color mixing and methods of control vary significantly. Artists, scientists, and philosophers have come to conclusions about color in the course of their work; however, their statements occasionally appear to conflict due to differences in their chosen media. Fortunately, today's colorists recognize the distinctions between these two forms of color and have documented independent methods for dealing with each application. Visible color in any three-dimensional situation is the result of both our handling of subtractive colors in tangible forms (e.g., print, dyes, paint, and other types of pigment) and the manipulation of additive color in the form of light. Light enables us to experience color—there is no color without light. Light can be mixed or modified. The same is possible with pigments. In the context of three-dimensional design,

Isaac Newton

No color reference is complete without mention of the significant contributions by physicist Sir Isaac Newton (1642–1727). His experimental work in the science of light and color, performed in 1666 at Trinity College, Cambridge, in Great Britain, forms the basis of current color theory. Newton is best known for directing rays of sunlight through a prism, causing the light to fan out into several distinct colors, like a rainbow. This fan of light included the colors red, orange, yellow, green, blue, indigo, and violet in order of appearance. Newton identified this range as the full spectrum of light. He then passed light of each individual color through a prism to find its derivative and found he could not break down the individually colored lights further. He also observed that if one of these colors is missing, a true white light cannot be formed. Instead, the remaining six combine to form the complementary color of the missing one.

complements contain all the light colors contained in white light. Pair mixing with primary light colors is useful in some applications, but the results are not always what we expect. The rays from the middle (green) and long (red) waves of the spectrum combine to produce yellow light. The rays from the short (violet-blue) and middle (green) waves of the spectrum together create cyan-blue. Rays from the long (red) and short (violet-blue) waves of the spectrum look like magenta-red color to the eye. These relationships are illustrated in Figure 1.12.

Additive color mixing is handled a number of ways. The most common is with light filters. A red filter lets only long-wave radiation through, visible as red. A green filter allows only medium-wave light to pass and a blue filter only shortwave light. Color can be mixed by overlapping two beams of light or by showing two colors in rapid succession. Experiments once done by projecting light against a wall are now more accurately performed using computer graphics to blend the light. Video monitors have three electronic guns, corresponding to the light primaries, and these are labeled red, green, and blue. In today's experiments, all the colors we see are created on the screen surface by varying the combinations and intensity of these three sources. Several computer graphics programs are available that offer

we use practical knowledge of both types of color to anticipate their interaction with each other.

The principles of additive color are focused on the concept of white light. To create a true white light, all other colors of light must be combined. The greater the number of colors combined in the form of light, the lighter the color created. For practical purposes, humans use three primary colors of light to create a full range of distinguishable color. These are a red with an orange tendency (700 nm), green (546 nm), and a blue that has a violet cast to it similar to indigo (435 nm). Together they form white light. By adjusting the intensity of one or more of the three primary light colors we can create all other colors of light.

Yellow, cyan blue, and magenta are secondary additive colors. Secondary colors tend to be more luminous than primaries. A mix of two complementary monochrome light rays, such as red and cyan, produces the same white light as a mix of three primaries. This is true because, together, two

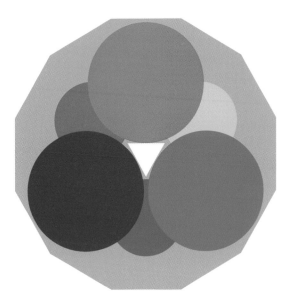

FIGURE 1.12 This color circle shows primary and secondary additive colors.

the ability to create very complicated additive color combinations with mechanical precision.

Subtractive Color

Color that is visible on the surface of solid objects is properly known as *subtractive* color. It refers to color mixed in solid media, such as paint pigment or dye. Subtractive color is recognized when light strikes an object and that object absorbs certain wavelengths, thus subtracting them from our view, while others are reflected. The reflected wavelengths form the color we see. For example, a green leaf absorbs all wavelengths except those that create the sensation of green, which are reflected back into the eye. Another term often used to describe subtractive color is *colorant,* the chemically definable and analyzable pigment source.

Generally speaking, the more subtractive colors that are combined to create a new color, the darker the final mixture will appear. This is the opposite of additive color behavior. There are three primary pigments of subtractive color: red, yellow, and blue, as shown in Figure 1.13. As with additive color, these primaries form the basis of all other colors throughout the mixing process. Primaries cannot be created by any combination of other colors. When all three subtractive primaries are combined, the result is a dark brown, gray, or black, depending on the media used. It's this opposition of color-mixing behavior that makes color difficult to command when both additive and subtractive sources are in use. Secondary subtractive colors are those formed by mixing two primary colors together. When yellow and red subtractive colors are combined, the result is orange; a combination of red and blue yield violet; and green is the blending of yellow and blue. Theoretically, a stark white piece of paper is reflecting almost all wavelengths. An object that appears black absorbs almost all wavelengths. Carbon black is the darkest color known. This color absorbs 97 percent of the daylight that reaches it.

▶ Visualizing Color

Color is often difficult to visualize, even for experts. We know color preferences are frequently stated while looking at samples in the abstract; however, many people cannot visualize such examples in the context of an object or a room. Many of us have also had the experience of shopping for an article of clothing only to realize a color mismatch when we place the item next to something we have at home. There are a few human conditions that contribute to our ability, or lack of ability, to foresee color in its

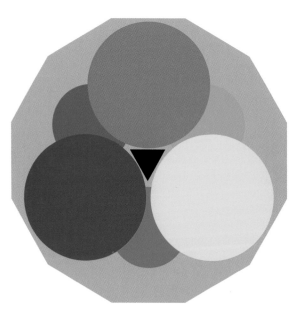

FIGURE 1.13   This color circle shows subtractive color relationships. Note the differences in comparison to Figure 1.12.

Johann Goethe

Johann Wolfgang von Goethe (1749–1832) was a German poet, novelist, and natural philosopher best known as a leading force in the Romantic movement through his writings, which include *The Sorrows of Young Werther* (1774 fiction) and *Faust* (1808 theatrical drama). Goethe deserves recognition as a colorist for the more physiological and psychological aspects of color he observed and documented. If Newton's color analysis can be described as driven by science, Goethe was driven by the human condition. In 1791, he published *Contributions to Optics,* which addressed artistic issues such as harmony and temperature, and *Theory of Colours,* which included value contrasts and emotional associations with color. Goethe's focus on human perception of color and color phenomenon, such as afterimages, proved valuable to contemporary painters of his day. His concern for subtractive color behavior offered variation from the additive color analysis done by his predecessor, Newton. To our benefit, both theorists' writings have been preserved and translated into many languages.

intended context. Two such conditions set our individual limitations. The first, *color memory,* is a predictable handicap that affects all of us as humans. The second, *color deficiency,* is somewhat random, conditional, and less predictable. Both impact our spectral view of the world.

Color Memory

We have said that human beings have the ability to distinguish thousands of distinct colors. We recognize the differences between any two colors according to their respective hue (redness, blueness, yellowness), changes in value (lightness or darkness), or variations in intensity (saturation) levels. This ability can be increased over time with concentrated training, as often occurs with artists and designers. What we cannot improve upon is our color memory. Humans have a fairly limited capac-

ity to retain color images accurately. Although many of us have excellent auditory capacity and can whistle a tune heard only once or twice, we are rarely able to accurately re-create a color seen many times. Even when the color is present in the midst of several similar colors, we may not be able to discern it. This can be demonstrated by showing a range of red samples to a group of people and asking them to choose the color used by Coca-Cola. Each person will select a red according to personal recollection. All of them may seem reasonably credible, but collectively these selections often show a broad range of reds. **Accurate color matching is best managed with samples in hand, permitting us to trust our visual judgment rather than rely on memory alone.**

A lack of color memory is a slight handicap to visualization because we tend to compare new information to what is already known. A client's impression of a new color or a unique combination of colors is in many ways influenced by his or her recollection of similar color experiences. The fact that this memory is imperfect only serves to complicate matters. A proposed color may in fact be quite different from one associated with a negative connotation. However, the lack of proper recall establishes a categorical nonpreference for the color in question. When colors are presented in the abstract, random association based on memory is more likely to occur. Context is the key to reducing memory deficiency influence. Colors proposed for a new design are selected in the context of a specific application. To help a client distinguish this mental picture from the influence of prior experience, we establish our visions as clearly as possible through drawings, samples, and photographic images. Within the new framework, proposed colors can be evaluated more clearly according to their intended use.

Color Deficiency

Each person has some ability to distinguish colors as a mix of the three primary colors. However, we may not see colors the same as each other due to genetics, the aging process, or a medical condition. Such limitations—what we commonly refer to as *color blindness*—are more accurately termed *color deficiencies.* Defective color vision can result from several physiological conditions, which are usually present at birth. Less common, but also possible, are color vision defects due to diseases of the liver and eye, multiple sclerosis, and diabetes, as well as the aging process itself. Regardless of the cause, the effect on the individual is a reduction in color discrimination in comparison to the majority of the population.

The tendency toward color deficiency is highest in many parts of North America and most of Europe. The rate of occurrence is about 1 in 12 people according to the reference *Colour* (edited by Helen Varley, page 36), compared to a 1 in 20 occurrence in most of Asia and a 1 in 50 occurrence rate in large areas of South America, Africa, and New Guinea. One possible explanation for this is the evolution of the eye based on need. In areas where we are less dependent on color clarity for basic survival, our abilities may be gradually reduced from one generation to the next. Another theory is that our visual abilities depend on our access to sunlight. Statistically speaking, the incidence of defective color vision is more common in men. This is because the genes that determine color blindness lie on the X chromosome. A woman will inherit the condition only if the X chromosomes from both parents carry a gene for color-defective vision. She will be a carrier if only one chromosome holds the gene. Since a man has only one X chromosome, he can inherit color deficiency as long as one parent carries such a gene.

There are several categories of color defective vision, but the main categories as explained by the team of Bartleson, Burnham, and Hanes are as follows (*Color: A Guide to Basic Facts and Concepts,* Chapter 4):

- *Anomalous trichromatism.* This is the least severe color blindness and the most common. For this viewer, color is recognizable in three ranges: from blue to yellow, red to green, and light to dark. However, the individual's ability to discriminate does not coincide with the normal range.
- *Dichromatism.* Individuals with this condition perceive color according to only two distinctions: light to dark and one range of hue. The hue range is either red to green or blue to yellow. In their eyes, all colors are a mixture of these two scales.
- *Monochromatism.* This is the least common and most severe form of color defective vision. This viewer sees only achromatic (colorless) vision, images that resemble a black-and-white movie.

For a designer with some color deficiency, knowing one's personal limits will enable him or her to solicit a second opinion when appropriate. For instance, a designer who has some limits in distinguishing subtle shades of green may involve a colleague in the resolution of a cool color palette. If a client is aware of personal color limitations, or exhibits the possibility, this may be taken into consideration during development of the color concept. In this case, it's best to avoid subtle shifts in color that fall within the client's nonvisible range to ensure that the end product will be fully appreciated, because the palette is within the client's range of visual experience.

At this point we've identified the processes used to experience color. We've also established some baseline terms that are used to explore more complex aspects of color. The next step is to consider the tools available for color experimentation and palette development for their usefulness in design practice.

2

Color Models

Historically, color experts have developed their own reference tools. Each tool served a practical purpose, enabling its creator to categorize color options systematically. New colors could be uncovered through methodical exploration and a logical cataloging process.

This chapter deals with the theoretical approaches to organizing color for reference, including an in-depth look at the methods used by two well-known colorists, Ostwald and Munsell. The purpose of this assessment is twofold. One is to provide a basis for consideration of standard reference systems available to designers. The second is to outline methods developed by others for consideration of one's own training. As with any learned process, the student of color will learn the most by undertaking each process personally. What we gain through firsthand application of these principles is color experience. As we explore each model, consider re-creating a prototype of that model, or a portion of it, to see what the theorist saw. By replicating as many color characteristic models as possible, you'll expand the color capabilities of your own eyes. To support experimentation, we also look briefly at the benefits of color-mixing tools presently in use.

COLOR CIRCLES

The color circle is a basic reference tool that most colorists of the past two centuries have relied upon.

It quickly relates the hue relationship of any color to another and is usually organized to illustrate dominant color relationships. Its value in design practice is tied to reasonably accurate hue rendition. In color circles that function as a design tool, each color represented is diametrically opposite its complementary color. Historically, differences in hue placement have occurred according to what was believed about color at the time. Some theorists placed blue opposite yellow, particularly if their interest was scientific in nature. For practical purposes, color circles currently used in art and design locate yellow opposite violet, orange opposite blue, and red diametrically opposed to green. In a high-quality color circle, all the colors that are equidistant from the center are equal in their level of saturation. Figures 2.1 through 2.6 illustrate a few popular circle diagrams.

▶ Developing a Color Circle

One of the best ways to train the eye to recognize incremental distinctions in color hue is to develop one's own color circle with at least 12 different hues at full saturation. (See the example in Figure 2.4.) Consistency is the measure of quality in a color circle. Incremental color shifts around the circle should be in even degrees of change as much as possible. If you are developing your own color circle, color samples will be easier to read against a neutral background. A true gray is ideal, particularly

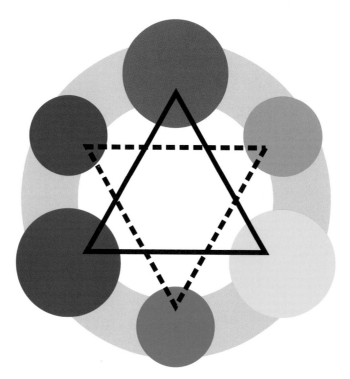

FIGURE 2.1   In most modern subtractive color circles, the primary colors (yellow, red, and blue) are equidistant from each other, forming an equilateral triangle within the circle. Secondary colors (orange, green, and violet) are at the midpoints of the primaries, forming a second equilateral triangle. Jacques Christophe Le Blon (English, 1670–1741), a painter and engraver who originated full-color printing, is often credited with the discovery that all hues can be created using the three primaries.

one that's temperature-neutral, neither warm nor cool. In the absence of a gray ground, either black or white may be used. However, be aware that value contrasts will influence samples somewhat. Lighter hues may appear to increase in value against a black background. Darker hues may appear darker against white.

It's ideal to start with a red paint that is neither yellowish nor bluish; a yellow that is neither bluish nor reddish; and a blue that has no red or yellow apparent in it. Some manufacturers offer such colored pigments; usually described as "primary red" or "true blue." If these are not available, primaries can be mixed from a combination of warm and cool reds, blues, and yellows, respectively. Most oil, acrylic, and watercolor paints from the tube have either a warm or cool tone to them (a warm yellow

and a cool yellow, etc.) A mixing guide is helpful with traditional paints, such as Michael Wilcox's book, *Blue and Yellow Don't Make Green.* After the primary colors have been selected, the secondary colors are developed by finding the hue at the true midpoint between each of the two primaries. After all secondary colors are resolved, it's safe to mix the hues between each pair of primary and secondary colors. These are the *tertiary* colors. Each incremental step around the circle will be more consistent if the circle is developed properly in the order of first primary, then secondary, then tertiary colors. If the circle is developed in sections, there's a tendency for the steps within each section to be uniform, but the overall circle may not be balanced due to an inconsistent break between sections. The last step in a 24-hue circle is to find the midpoint

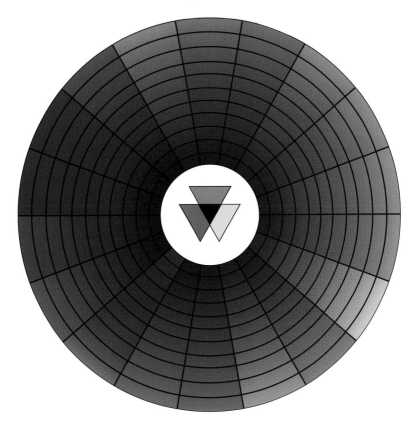

FIGURE 2.2   Moses Harris (1731–1785), an English engraver and entomologist (a zoologist who specializes in insects), first published a complete color circle using three primaries in 1766. Few copies of this were made available, but his work provided basic tools for color theorists for over 100 years thereafter. His model uses three equidistant primary colors with secondary colors positioned at their midpoints. Two intermediate colors were developed between each primary and its adjacent secondary color. Harris broke his circle into a series of concentric rings, with the strongest hues positioned at the perimeter of the circle. Each hue was shaded in stages (by adding black) working toward the center. His color circle appeared in the appendix of his book, *The Natural System of Colours.*

between each primary or secondary color and its adjacent tertiary, which is called a *quarternary.* These are shown in Figure 2.5.

The next logical step in development of a color circle is to incorporate variations in value. To explore variations in lightness and darkness for each hue, several theorists associated with the Bauhaus school in early-twentieth-century Germany extended their circles into other forms. Johannes Itten used a 12-pointed star, and Herbert Schumann used a series of squares in a circle formation, to name a few. In Figure 2.6, an example of an expanded color circle shows lighter tints of each color at the center of the circle, with darker shades of each hue successively reaching outer points. The fully saturated hues occur at the third position out from center.

■ COLOR SOLIDS

The theory of the color solid is that the entire range of visible colors may be organized neatly into one three-dimensional form according to hue, value, and saturation. Access to such a model allows us to select each color relative to all others by attribute. It

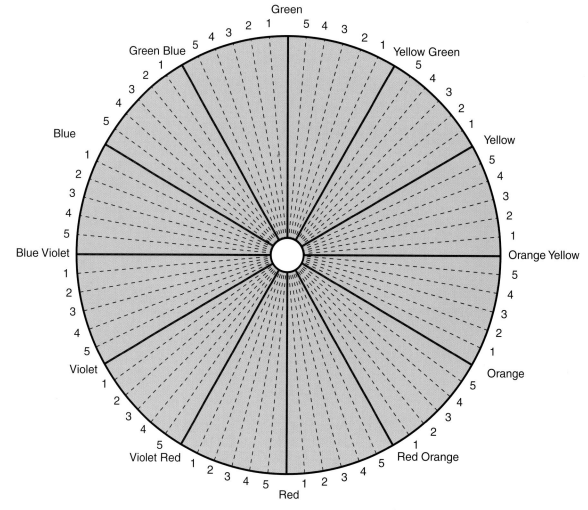

FIGURE 2.3 The complexity of each theorist's reference circle increased over time. In his book, *The Principles of Harmony and Contrast of Colors,* M. E. Chevreul (1786–1889) used a color circle with 5 intermediate colors between each primary and secondary, for a total of 72 hues. His circle included a numbering system so each color could be cataloged, similar to the diagram shown here.

also serves as a tool for comparing any two specific colors. The relative value and saturation levels of two colors are quickly established by their position in the model. Comparative hue relationships can also be established for any color regardless of the amount of chroma it contains.

Color-solid reference forms have a distinct advantage over color circles, triangles, and stars. Two-dimensional models can take into account a full range of only one or two characteristics. Most establish color relationships according to hue only, or in some cases hue and value, or hue and saturation. The third dimension allows exploration of all

three color characteristics in the same reference system. Many color reference solids have been developed over the past four centuries. Generally speaking, they fall into two categories: (1) two-dimensional references expressed over a three-dimensional form and (2) solid models, which are composed of both surfaces and sections of organized colors.

▶ Matrix Models

A color matrix is a two-dimensional reference tool commonly used to compare two aspects of color

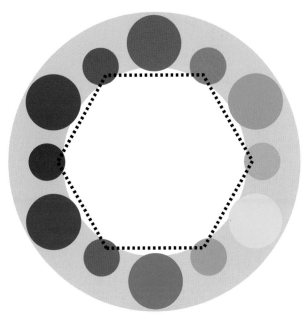

FIGURE 2.4   The colors between each primary and secondary color are called *tertiaries*. (*Illustration by author.*)

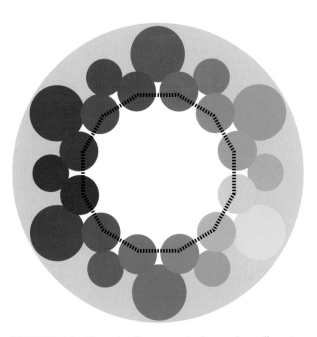

FIGURE 2.5   The colors between a tertiary and an adjacent primary or secondary color are called *quaternaries*. (*Illustration by author.*)

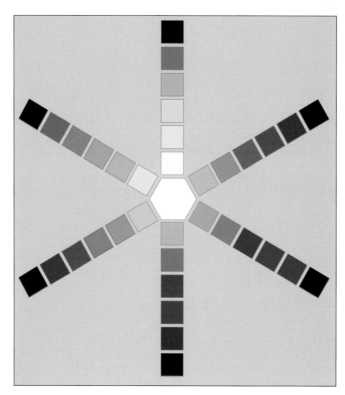

FIGURE 2.6   This color circle has been extended to include a range of values for each hue.

simultaneously. In its simplest form, a grid of colored geometries is set up using rows and columns. Saturation-value grids are popular to distinguish between incremental shifts in one or both. An example is shown in Figure 2.7.

To expand the matrix and demonstrate the continuum of colors by hue, the two-dimensional color matrix can be applied to the surface of a three-dimensional form, such as a sphere, cylinder, or pyramid. The simplicity of these geometries offers a logical organization to the colors. By organizing the matrix three-dimensionally, there is an increased continuous surface area, allowing greater exploration of color according to two key characteristics. Colors may be organized along one axis relative to hue and along another according to value or saturation. For the purpose of this discussion, we call these *matrix models,* or two-dimensional models, since they essentially consist of a matrix applied to a three-dimensional form for expansion purposes.

Several color theorists attempted to work with a hemispheric model of some type to represent color physically in space. The advantage of a sphere is that it allows light values and dark values to be explored at the same time. Full hues in this case occur at the horizontal center, or equator, and less saturated tints and tones work their way to the top and bottom. The difficulty with this form is that the incremental changes in hue between extremely light or dark values are smaller than those taken at the equator and can appear to be duplicates. The struggle to use three-dimensional forms effectively led to true three-dimensional models, which we call *solid models.*

▶ Solid Models

Three-dimensional solid models were developed to simultaneously illustrate all three characteristics of color. Solid models are more complex to allow for more definitive color selection. Each solid model is a three-dimensional form made up of a series of flat planes. Each plane is a two-dimensional color matrix organized along two key characteristics, such as hue and value or value and saturation. The

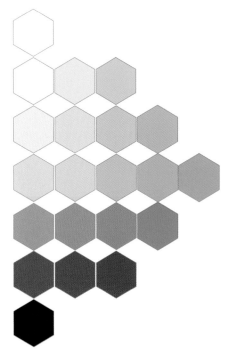

FIGURE 2.7 In this example of a color matrix, a single color of hue is developed in a range of value and saturation. Value decreases from top to bottom and saturation increases from left to right.

function, Runge draws on a horizontal section through the widest point to locate the circle of full hues. The medium-gray values and intermediate levels of saturation are described as occurring within the overall form.

Two other theorists attempted to use the cone as a form for their three-dimensional models. Wilhelm von Bezold (German, 1837–1907) described a cone in 1876 that essentially reversed the black-and-white positioning used by Lambert. Bezold's circle included full hues at the perimeter working toward white at the center. His model extended upward

planes are organized according to the remaining third characteristic. Each solid model is therefore a collection of matrices that may be read horizontally or vertically. Altogether, the collection of matrices offers the colorist a valuable tool for finding and comparing a large range of colors according to their respective characteristics of hue, value, and saturation. Like many matrix models, most solid models have taken the form of either a sphere or a pyramid. The Lambert model illustrated in Figure 2.8 is an example of a pyramid form. The Runge model in Figure 2.9 is a sphere.

Runge's theoretical model resembled a globe with fully saturated hues at the outermost edge of the equator and a conceptual neutral center. Tones of each hue were located between the equator and the center of the sphere. All colors adjusted progressively toward white when positioned north of the equator (tints) and toward black south of it (shades). His model was published in 1810 in *The Color Sphere (Die Farbenkugel)*. Although it appears to be a matrix model, the Runge model is considered three-dimensional, because in his explanation of its

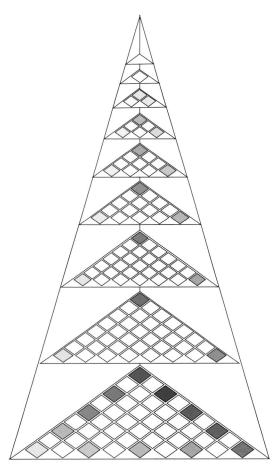

FIGURE 2.8 Johann Heinrich Lambert (German, 1728–1777) was a physicist and a philosopher who worked with a pyramid as his color model. The pyramid had a base triangle of yellow, red and blue on the angles, with shades of black toward the center. Subsequent triangles were positioned above the first, each smaller in dimension with lighter shades of color until they formed a white apex.

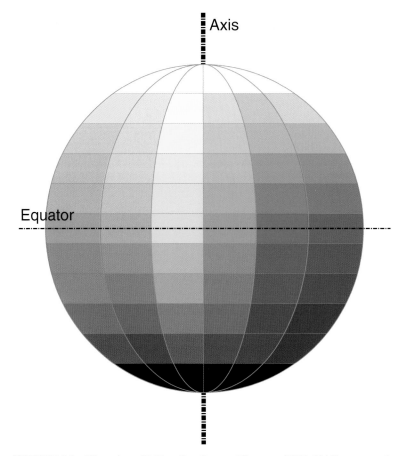

FIGURE 2.9 The painter Philipp Otto Runge (German, 1777–1810) attempted to give equal development to the light and dark values of the colors on his 12-part circle by using a solid sphere.

from the circle into a cone with a black apex. A few years later, Ogden Rood (American, 1831–1902) expanded this form into a double cone with one black and one white peak. Rood was instrumental in articulating the differences between hue, value, and purity (saturation) through his double-cone theory. Until this time, colorists often saw value and intensity as the same effect. It is Rood's effort to catalog color by all three characteristics and his ability to explain color differences that led to more complete models described next.

Axis and Equator

To visualize model forms used by Runge and several other colorists, consider the concept of an axis and an equator. The equator is the outer radial edge taken at widest horizontal section of the sphere, halfway between the top and bottom of the model, or the North and South Poles. In the Runge model, the equator is a circle of all hues represented, each in full saturation, his original color circle. A slice taken horizontally through the solid model would yield an outer ring of these fully saturated colors, with concentric rings of tones placed progressively near the center point, the value pole. The tones would also represent the full range of hue and are progressively reduced in saturation until they reach a true gray at the center. In the Runge model, all the colors within the equator are presumed to be of medium value.

The truly three-dimensional or solid color models developed by Rood, Runge, and others who succeeded them make use of these two basic solid-model components: an *axis* of neutral color range and an *equator* of full hue. The outward shape of these models may vary, but the consistent characteristic about them is their three-dimensionality as a necessity to mapping color for three characteristics: hue, value, and saturation. Fully saturated hues are placed on the outer edge of the equator, forming a color circle with a fixed number of hues. The axis is a vertical pole, running north to south through the form, to establish a hue-neutral center. It's made up of evenly distributed shades of gray, from white most often positioned at the top to black at the bottom. At each hue position, a vertical section is configured with incremental adjustments in value and saturation. These are cataloged using a series of flat matrices, which make up the model's interior. Each matrix is organized with lighter values at the top and darker ones at the bottom to correspond to equivalent gray values at the axis.

A vertical section at each hue position along the equator shows the various grades of color, using a combination of white, black, and each hue. With each step closer to the axis, the colors become less intense, more neutral. With each step closer to the equator, a color becomes more saturated, closer to full chroma. The tint scale for each color is considered the range of colors along the model, from the full-hue position at the equator to white in the northern hemisphere. The shade scale is the range of colors along the model, from the full hue to black in the southern hemisphere. And the tone scale is a horizontal plane from the full hue (the equator) to the true gray at the center (at the axis).

■ COLOR REFERENCE SYSTEMS

Practitioners often use three-dimensional models, or develop their own, as the basis for color reference systems. Reference systems, also known as *atlases,* use a solid model as a basis for organization and apply alphanumeric keys. Each key is a definitive reference for one, and only one, color sample. In atlas form, the model as reference system makes it easier to test adjustments in color without extensive searching. The atlas creator can also record formulas for each sample so that they may be duplicated. Some colorists do this as a way of record keeping; some use reference systems to

Reference Systems

Far more color reference systems have been developed than are mentioned in this text. However, the following deserve notation, as they may serve as a resource in design context:

- The *Pantone Matching System* is a specification system developed in 1985 that catalogs color using numeric references. Graphic designers and those in the fashion industry use it, and it has other retail and design applications as well.
- The *CIE System* is an internationally recognized scientific reference methodology established in 1931 by the International Commission on Illumination (CIE stands for Commission Internationale de l'Eclairage). This technically derived system without reference samples relies on additive color mixing.
- The *Coloroid System* was developed in Hungary specifically for use by architects in the 1980s. It uses a three-part numbering system to represent hue, chromatic content, and lightness, in that order.

control the quality of printed media; others, in manufacturing, do this to establish standards for their products.

The main advantage to established color reference systems is clarity. Without reference tools, we have a tendency to describe color by stylistic names, such as "dusty rose" or "Pompeii red." Such descriptive language has connotations that vary with each generation, locale, and individual experience. A naturalist would not rely on the common name of "largemouth bass" to identify a particular freshwater fish. Instead, the genus and species, *Micropterus salmoides,* would be used. With a color reference system, the same level of distinction can be communicated between colorists through the assignment of an alphanumeric code to the specific shade of red intended. The code controls the hue, value, and saturation levels of the chosen color. New colors can be created and added to the reference tool by establishing these three characteristics relative to those already referenced. In

Wilhelm Ostwald

Friedrich Wilhelm Ostwald (German, 1853–1932) established himself as a color expert by working at length with a three-dimensional double-conical model. His background was in chemistry and biology, and in 1909 he won the Nobel Prize for his achievements in physical chemistry. Ostwald was one of the first color theorists to consciously distinguish between spectral color and surface color in his experiments. He reasoned that a difference existed between light, which the human eye receives, and the sensation of color, recognized by the brain. Through his search for these distinctions Ostwald was able to differentiate chromatic character from value. His color system, published in 1916 as the *Colour Primer,* has been summarized by others and translated into several languages. (For an overview in English, refer to *Basic Color: An Interpretation of the Ostwald Color System,* by Egbert Jacobson.)

other words, newly developed colors fall between those already established according to characteristic measurements. The reference tool can also be used to establish color tolerances where they are needed. If fading has occurred, or is likely to occur, in a material, the reference system can be used to monitor this condition in quantitative terms.

In the early twentieth century, two color theorists, Friedrich Wilhelm Ostwald and Albert Munsell, developed very complete color models and documented their findings in the form of a color reference atlas. While there are many others we might consider, the work produced by these two contemporaries serves to illustrate the key considerations relative to reference models. We'll explore them both briefly for their respective advantages.

▶ Ostwald Model

Friedrich Ostwald tried to produce numerically predetermined colors according to the six funda-

mental color sensations he could describe. These sensations were achromatic (the whiteness and blackness of a color) and chromatic hue relative to four fundamental complements (yellow, red, blue, and green). Using his systematic approach, the formula for any color could be expressed in terms of its full color content (hue), its black content, and its white content.

Because it derived from four primary hues, Ostwald's color circle showed more green increments and fewer red than many artists' circles contain. These hues were numbered and divided into eight groups, or ranges: the yellow, the orange, the red, the purple, the blue, the turquoise, the seagreen, and the leafgreen. Each hue position was assigned a number. Ostwald then established an eight-position gray scale, with white at the top of the scale and black at the bottom, forming the axis of his color solid.

The beauty in this model is the ease with which a user can reference harmonic color combinations. Its consistency is tied to the pigment formulas themselves, which were established as percentages of black, white, and chroma. For each of the 24 positions in his color circle equator, Ostwald developed a value-saturation triangle similar to the versions shown in Figures 2.7 and 2.10, with a consistent lettering convention for each position within it. This means that a pale apricot (yellow-orange) sample 3GA has the same proportions of white and black as a light teal 16GA. Similarly, the two samples are allocated equal amounts of hue pigment, one in yellow-orange and one in blue-green. Every color around the solid model in position GA has the same proportions of color: 67 percent chroma, 22 percent white, and 11 percent black. This consistency was used to establish color harmony relationships within either one range of hue or across several. All colors with the same reference position GA are harmonious because they are similar in value and saturation levels. All colors along a common vertical are harmonious because of their consistent percent of hue. Colors along any diagonal share other characteristic consistencies.

When the triangle exercise was complete for all 24 hues, they were assembled into a three-dimensional double-cone model. All colors of maximum saturation aligned at the circumference, or equator. Each horizontal circle of samples within this model contains colors that are harmonic

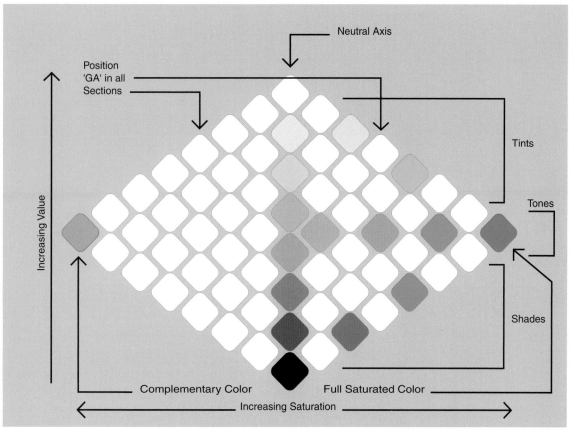

FIGURE 2.10 This matrix is organized to illustrate the Ostwald model concept where two triangles meet at the axis. For a color triangle modeled after Ostwald's method, refer to Figure 2.7.

because of their consistent value. Those above the equator are successively lighter tints until they approach white. The horizontal circles below the equator become progressively darker shades until they reach black. A vertical section yields a diamond shape made up of two color triangles bound at the neutral axis. Each triangle offers the full range of value and saturation for that hue. Colors to the left of the neutral axis are the complements of the colors on the right. Colors at the same height in the model contain the same amount of black and white. Colors at the same position relative to the axis and equator have the same amount of hue content. In solid form, this model resembles a two-pointed, spinning top.

The criticism of solid-color models established in uniformly geometric shapes such as Ostwald's is this: To keep the form consistent, all colors of full hue must be placed in the same horizontal position

regardless of their relative value. The result is a model that is elegant in its simplicity and consistent in its form, but it implies that a fully saturated yellow is equal in value to a blue at full chroma. This inequity causes the color triangle of a hue with inherently darker value to have larger incremental shifts in tints, while the shades in the lower half of the triangle show small incremental value changes. Lighter-hue triangles exhibit the opposite characteristics.

▶ Munsell Model

The Munsell system is another well-organized alphanumeric reference tool, but with a unique three-dimensional form. Called a *tree,* its structure was established under the premise that some fully saturated hues are inherently lighter than others and that their position within the model should reflect this. Using this approach, true parity is ensured from hue to hue across the value bands. Colors at full saturation are farther out on the equator, while tonal variations drop off somewhere within the volume at a vertical level equal to the corresponding gray and in a horizontal position appropriate to its saturation. This means that the horizontal center yields an inconsistent outer form, as illustrated in Figure 2.11. Increments of color shift are uniform, regardless of hue character. The Munsell form does not dictate color composition, but is the result of consistent color positioning relative to the three key elements, as shown in Figure 2.12.

In the Munsell model, incremental consistency determines the number of steps from the central axis to a color of hue. As a result, some hues (e.g., true red) have more incremental steps between their equivalent gray neutral and full saturation, placing them further from the axis than others (e.g., the color aqua). A fully saturated yellow (value step 8) is positioned higher in the model than true red (step 5) or true blue (step 4) and has more tints. However, yellow has very few steps in the shade range because it turns greenish as it darkens. While the Ostwald arrangement may be comparatively easier to replicate given the more consistent proportions of hue, black, and white, the Munsell system

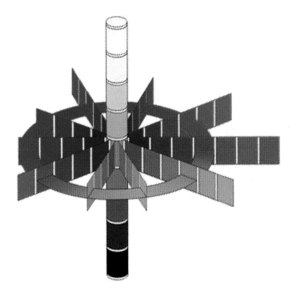

FIGURE 2.11   The Munsell model is characteristically color-consistent, but highly inconsistent in form. Here the tonal bands shown at the equator have inconsistent length, since some fully saturated hues fall above or below. For a color section modeled after Munsell's method, refer to Figure 1.5. (*Courtesy of GretagMacbeth.*)

allows for more consistent cross-hue referencing by alphanumeric assignment.

▶ Complex Models

Many three-dimensional models have been developed that provide the designer with systematic ways to organize, find, and compare various colors, but no system can ideally address all circumstances. Many more models are available for use. Access to one makes for quick decision making because of the quantity of specific colors displayed and the logic of its organization, whether the model is purchased or developed by our own hands. Despite their grace, each three-dimensional color model that uses a central axis may have some shortcomings. Often there are large differences between hues approaching full chroma, but a vanishingly small difference as the chroma approaches zero (the axis), which means fewer samples may be needed in this range. In many industries and in graphic design, the colors of greatest chroma are used more frequently than those of low chroma, but in architecture and interior design, where harmony and reduced intensity are more

---

Albert Henry Munsell

Albert Henry Munsell (American, 1858–1918) was an artist working with paint and a color theorist. He taught color and anatomy from 1890 to 1915 at the Massachusetts Normal Art School, which is now the Massachusetts College of Art. He also invented a photometer, which measures the light reflected from a color, and developed an extensive three-dimensional color model known as the *Color Atlas,* in 1915. This model was later updated by his son, Alexander, as the *Munsell Book of Color* and is still in use today. In 1918 he formed the Munsell Color Company and produced color reference materials for distribution to educators and professionals. (Today the Munsell Color Company is a part of Gretag-Macbeth.)

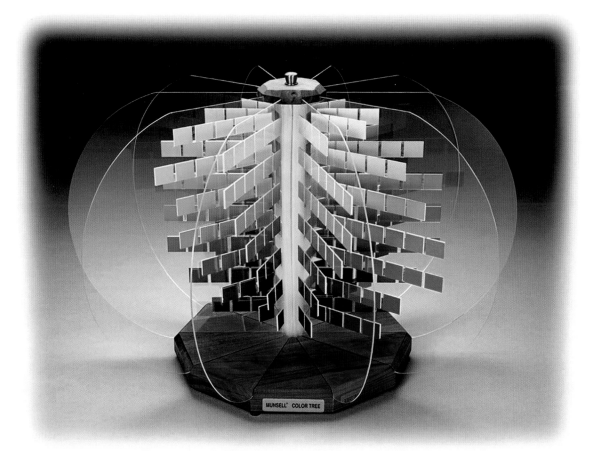

FIGURE 2.12—This photograph shows the Munsell system and its characteristic irregularity of shape along matrix sections. (*Courtesy of GretagMacbeth.*)

often the goal, less intense, desaturated colors prevail over clear colors. Manufacturers tend to develop their own reference standards to suit the specific purpose of their products.

Color models also tend to address colors on an individual and abstract basis. As new tools are developed to address our increased knowledge and added complexity of color applications, colorists continue to create more complex models to address such issues. In one color theory, published as the *Planetary Color System* in 1983, Michel Albert-Vanel (French, 1935–) attempts to account for the additional levels of color complexity associated with three-dimensional design by categorizing color in groups, not as isolated individual colors. His ideal model recognizes not only individual color positions relative to hue, value, and saturation, but also according to the amount of contrast apparent between colors in combination and

the texture of their applied materials. In the most complete color system, Albert-Vanel tells us, one would plot scales showing the range of pigment and light, opacity and transparency, and matte and gloss surfaces. Rather than a single solid, a planetary model shows ranges for each group of colors, with moons orbiting each planet and related colors positioned in the same solar system.

The Albert-Vanel concept is challenging. As a planetary model it is more difficult to visualize and document. But it does offer hypotheses on some of the physiological issues of color applications that manifest themselves in three-dimensional design. Many of those issues will be addressed in the next sections, along with guidelines for color interaction. Variations may be complex, but as each aspect of color response is isolated and analyzed, our ability to control color response is increased.

■ MODELS AND EXPERIMENTS

Many professionals who work with color develop their own reference tools and perform color experimentation to increase color expertise. As continuous testing is performed, color sense is improved by increasing the observer's ability to distinguish between hue, value, and saturation. The result is a more discriminating eye, one that recognizes subtle differences between colors much more quickly and with greater accuracy. Often, experimentation begins with color circles or value/saturation matrices as described in this chapter and is followed by exercises in color influence, which are addressed in Chapter 4, "Color Harmony."

Color experiments can also help us see the effects of specific color combinations simply, without the complications of form, by working with color as solid blocks rather than as outlines to be filled in. Uniform squares or bands of color are effective for keeping the focus on pigments. Once the desired color combination has been determined, then the forms of the color samples may be modified to enhance the color effect that has been established for each exercise.

The way that colors behave during mixing varies with each media. The color that results from mixing yellow and red paint, for example, will not be the same as the one we get from mixing yellow and red printers' ink, textile dyes, or beams of light. This is something to consider when shifting between materials. The ideal media is the one that offers the greatest efficiency in resolving key issues specific to the design process. Most people initially dabble in each of a few mediums to ascertain their advantages and disadvantages firsthand. Eventually, we each migrate to personal preferences. For example, a graphic designer may be better off using a computer, specifically one with CMYK color matching, which is based on printers' inks. (CMYK is an acronym that loosely stands for cyan, magenta, yellow, and black, the colors combined in a four-color printing process.) An architect may find cut paper to be desirable, given the consistency and the ease with which large forms may be roughed out. For those looking for greater subtlety, paint is a practical media. Since mixed paint, preprinted colored paper, and computer software are the most common tools used for color experiments, we'll compare them briefly for consideration as mixing tools.

▶ Paint

Paint is the traditional medium of choice for color experts. Its use is well established in the fine arts, and as such, it's readily available in a variety of consistencies and hues. As a fluid material, it allows us to develop an infinite number of specific colors through the mixing process. Small adjustments are easily obtained.

There are some disadvantages to working with paint in color experimentation. Because the medium is fluid, its consistency cannot be controlled. Variations in translucency or textures resulting from brush

Tips with Paint

When paint colors are combined, the combination of two colors will always be darker than the lightest of the two original colors, and it may be darker than either original. This means that when mixing two colors to create an equidistant third, the amounts should not be equal. It takes much more of the lighter color to result in a true middle tone.

Value is adjusted in a variety of ways according to each material used. With solid pigments, white will make a color lighter. In watercolors this is accomplished by diluting with water, which simultaneously changes the consistency. Gray added to any color reduces the intensity of it without changing value. The color gray can be created in three ways. Any color will move toward gray as its complementary color is added. Gray is also the result of a mix of yellow, blue, and red, the three primary colors. In addition, mixing black and white forms gray. Keep in mind that due to differences in the type of pigment used for each color of hue, the grays that result from each mix will vary.

If you're developing a color matrix of value and saturation, start with a large mixture of the hue being used, since it will be extremely difficult to mix more to match if you run out. Since you'll be looking at it intensively for a very long time, choose a color you enjoy. For the matrix exercise, yellow is not recommended for a first-time effort, since it tends toward green very quickly in shades.

strokes can detract from the focus on the colors themselves. In addition, it's impossible to duplicate a given color selection after the fact. One cannot hope to re-create a yellow-green that precisely matches the one developed in a previous experiment. Paint also requires that the designer obtain a number of tools (brushes, containers, palettes, etc.), which can quickly become expensive unless the tools are used for illustrative purposes as well. When mixing colors in paint, one thing to consider is the fact that there really are no true primaries in pigment. This is due to impurities in the paint itself, which results in color biases. Some manufacturers have gone to great lengths to offer yellow, red, and blue pigments as close to true primary colors as possible, but as a practical matter, pure primary color pigments do not exist. Each red tends to be very slightly orange or violet in nature; each blue leans slightly to green or purple; and yellows have a minor tendency toward orange or green. Although these variations are very subtle in some products, their cumulative effect causes significant concern for professional artists. Those experienced with paint usually keep a warm and cool version of each primary color on hand.

For basic first-time experiments, gouache paint is suggested, because reasonable primary pigments are available and it can be used as an opaque medium in very thin layers, reducing the impact of texture or transparency. It's the traditional pigment for designers who do formal renderings. It can be used to create very smooth, completely opaque blocks of color; and it can also be watered down to perform more like watercolors for rendering perspective drawings.

▶ Paper

There has been a strong shift toward paper as a tool for color work over the two most recent generations, due in part to production of reliable supplies of consistently colored material. Paper manufacturers now provide a countless number of colors, an extensive range of shades (dark neutrals), tints (light neutrals), and tones (medium neutrals). They are purchased ready to use, saving us time from the more traditional process of mixing paint until the desirable color is found. Paper products can be consistent in texture and opacity, or decidedly inconsistent, and offer uniformity from sample to sample. This is helpful, because a successful color combination can

Tips with Paper

Those who prefer paper often find inexpensive sources for it, such as cut paper from magazines or posters, discarded stationery sample books, or the waste materials from printers or bookbinders. Wrapping paper can be used, as well as wallpapers and paint samples. Due to the growing popularity of origami, a craft that involves folded colored paper, many lightweight papers in both solid color and small-scale patterns are available.

It may be difficult to find a specific color when subtle nuances are preferred. This can be resolved through texture. Many glossy papers reflect more light, and therefore appear lighter, than the same color in a matte finish. More textured materials may cause shadowing and will change in value when turned due to the direction of the light hitting the surface. This may be advantageous if slight variations of one tone are desired. Combinations with layers of transparent papers may also suffice. With printed material, the spacing of the dots affects the overall value. Dots spaced farther apart result in a lighter overall tone.

be duplicated precisely on demand, even after significant time has passed. Paper requires fewer tools than paint, but it is limited as a resource. Occasionally the exact color must be substituted with something "close enough." For some applications, paper is an expensive tool because of the inventory that must be accumulated. Alternatively, there are several large atlas-type reference collections available, which are extremely extensive. *Color-aid* is one popular brand of silk-screened colored papers, sold both as collections and in individual sheets.

▶ Computer

The computer is quickly gaining popularity as the color tool of choice. It involves basic hardware (a personal computer with monitor, keyboard, mouse, and peripherals), a software application that offers a color picker for mixing, and the use of a color printer for the output (hard copy). The computer

Two drawbacks still exist concerning the computer as a color tool. The most obvious is cost. Computer workstations remain one of the designer's most expensive tools, and graphic applications make them more costly due to the increased memory and processing capacity they require. Fortunately, hourly workstations are available through several retailers for occasional color work.

The second difficulty with computer work is the reconciliation between what is visible on the screen and its printed counterpart. This occurs partly because two different mixing methods are involved. Screen colors are produced by additive color mixing, which is created with the color of light. The printer uses subtractive color mixing, which is created with ink, a solid material. Incre-mental mixing is managed differently in each case, often resulting in slightly different output. Color calibration also varies from application to application, and some adjustments are experienced as files change electronic format. The situation is improving, but at the time of this writing, discrepancies between tools and between output devices remain a handicap for most of us seeking accurate color rendition. The tip here is to use the same workstation and output device consistently so that minor adjustments can be based on experience with that combination of equipment. For example, experience may suggest that greens on the screen need to be mixed a little on the cool side to match the desired green produced by the printer.

monitor has three light guns, one each to project red, blue, and green additive color on the screen's surface. When used in combination, they create the full range of color available. Lighter colors are created by allowing more light to shine on the surface of the monitor, darker ones by reducing light emission.

The obvious advantage to computer-driven color experiments is the unlimited number of color variation available combined with a significant increase in control over those variations. Colors can be reproduced to exacting specifications. Successful color formulas can be recorded for re-creation. Hue, value, and saturation can be adjusted in small increments, and these can be calibrated to matching specifications in other media. When computer color work first began, there were some technical limitations. Since color is created by light rather than pigment, lighter colors could be created at higher saturation levels. Black and other very dark colors were more difficult, since they could be produced only by reducing the amount of light from the monitor's light guns. The darkest color possible was limited to the natural color of the screen in the off state, which in the early years was not black, but more of a dull green. Recent technology seems to have accommodated for this, as any web surfer can attest, given the popularity of black to produce high-contrast images.

Now that we've explored the various tools and reference materials readily available, let's put them to good use. In the next two chapters we examine color theories of contrast and harmony. Together, these theories give us a broad range of opportunity for spatial color management.

3

Color Contrast

Characteristic differences between individual colors cause stimulation, excitement in the extreme, or at the very least, interest in a color composition. Collectively, these differences are known as *contrasts*. When two or more colors together display distinct variation, they are in contrast. Their relationship establishes a complexity that is unique to the combination of colors in view. The degree of our response corresponds to the strength of each contrast as it registers in the brain.

Color contrasts can be created between two or more colors in seven ways—eight if you work three-dimensionally. Through these characteristics, each color can be adjusted to enhance its dissimilarity with the others. Or surrounding colors may be selected to enhance conspicuous discrepancies between central colors. Contrast effects tend to enhance the individual colors by strengthening their differences, motivating a response in the individual who experiences them. When the intention is to stimulate the viewer, color contrasts are increased. When subtlety is the goal, contrasts are minimized.

In this chapter, we explore effective ways to create contrast between colors. More challenging contrasts are shown first in two-dimensional form for clarity. Applied examples of each are included in three-dimensional context.

■ DYNAMIC CONTRASTS

Not all contrasts are created equal. Some are highly dramatic, while others are much more subtle, discovered only after considerable observation. To distinguish contrast effects from one another, they've been separated here into three groups: dynamic contrasts that are readily recognized by most people; subtle ones reserved for more sophisticated situations; and complex contrasts, which offer the greatest creative challenges. We begin with the strongest of these effects—what I call the *dynamic contrasts*.

▶ Contrast of Value

The most forceful color contrast we have is that of value, also referred to as *light-dark contrast. Contrasts of value* involve the interaction of light and dark colors in combination with each other. Almost everyone with sight, regardless of any defective color vision, can recognize this contrast. The effect can be done in shades of neutral color, such as gray, black, and white, with some limited hue, or with a full range of hue. To make the contrast stronger, the edges of the lightest and darkest values in the composition share common boundaries. Value contrast is probably the most common one used in design

Usage

In art, the contrasting effect of light and shade in combination is known as *chiaroscuro.* Many well-known works of art take advantage of chiaroscuro effects without using any colors of hue at all. Etchings, Asian ink drawings, and modern cartoons are examples. Despite the dominance of many tints and shades, Impressionist paintings often relied on value contrast for impact. In architecture, white is often used to accentuate the form of a structure, allowing the contrasts of shadow to offer the color effect. Black is often applied to surfaces to make them "disappear," such as with reveals and exposed ceiling structures above an open grid.

practice because of its strength and the ease with which it can be developed.

The phenomenon of value contrast results from different levels of light reflected or absorbed by the image surface. Its greatest extreme is in black-and-white combinations, a comparison so intense that very dynamic compositions can be formed using a limited number of colors. Black-and-white contrasts are strongest because the effect

on the retina is one of opposing reactions. White excites the retina, while black reposes it. By viewing the two simultaneously, the eye is forced to dilate and contract rapidly as it compares the two extremes. Images high in value leave an impression on the eye according to their intensity of lightness, which appears as a dark afterimage, while black's afterimage is one of lightness.

Less extreme value contrasts are possible with comparatively lighter and darker grays. The number of distinguishable grays possible varies with each viewer. With practice, anyone can increase the number of grays he or she is able to differentiate. However, humans are more sensitive to value differences between light colors than dark ones. In order for value gradations to appear consistent from the lightest to the darkest, the percentage of change must increase with each shift to dark. This means that in a visually consistent gray scale, the increase in the amount of gray between the lightest two samples will be about half that of the increase between the second and third. The increase in gray from the third to the fourth sample must be four times as much as the increase from the first to the second if the progression of grays is to appear consistent. This comparison is shown in Figure 3.1. An *arithmetic gray scale,* on the left, shows four grays whose amount of color is increased in even percentages, even though

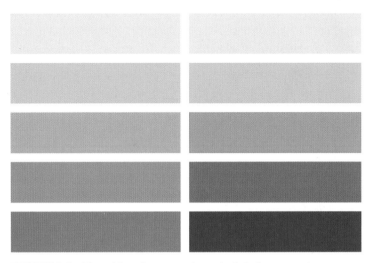

FIGURE 3.1 The arithmetic gray scale on the left shows consistent changes in value measured on a percentage basis. The geometric gray scale on the right appears to be much more consistent in value changes, even though each increase in darkness is actually twice that of its predecessor.

the difference between the top two appears greater than that of those below them. A *geometric gray scale,* on the right, includes five grays whose amount of color has been adjusted geometrically to account for human perception of value.

Ranges in value are easier to distinguish when achromatic colors (colors without chroma) are used or when a range of value is presented in one chromatic hue. As dissimilar hues are presented, value comparisons become less obvious, especially if the selected colors are also unequal in saturation level. The greater the number of hues in the composition, the less distinct the range of value will appear as the eye is influenced by other conditions. In the example in Figure 3.2, the value contrast is allowed to dominate because the range of hue and saturation is controlled.

▶ Contrast of Hue

Another form of color contrast that is immediately recognizable to most is *contrast of hue.* Hue contrast involves a combination of colors in which the distinctions of hue character are most pronounced. Here colors in at least two, but more often three or more different hues are used in combination. The effect is increased as colors are positioned farther apart on the color circle, as long as they are not complementary. This effect of hue contrast is also stronger when more heavily saturated colors are used. Physical proportions of the hues creating a contrast do not need to be equal to be effective. Neither does their intensity of chroma. Some combinations in hue contrast are arranged so that one hue is

Usage

Contrast of hue can be found frequently in costuming, embroidery, and synthetic jewelry. Art from the Middle Ages includes a large amount of hue contrast. In the modern world, hue contrast has been used heavily by several artists—Piet Mondrian (1872–1944) and Kandinsky (1866–1944) to name a few. In the architectural arena, contrast of hue is often called upon for spaces with little textural distinction where color provides dramatic emphasis, such as the example in Figure 3.4.

Johannes Itten

Swiss painter Johannes Itten (1888–1967) probably developed some of the best explanations of color contrast. Itten began his career as a painter, and in 1919 he became an instructor at the Weimar Bauhaus school in Germany. Fellow faculty members included architects Walter Gropius and Ludwig Mies van der Rohe and painters Paul Klee and Wassily Kandinsky. This group of contemporaries espoused two very different approaches to color: Architectural training focused on intrinsic color expression through the selection of materials; fine artists explored color behavior and psychology. Being of the latter camp, Itten treated both physical attributes and physiological color behavior as essential elements of design and developed the first basic course on form and color integration, including elements of color contrast and color harmony. In 1924 he left the Bauhaus and directed his own school in Berlin until 1934.

given a larger percentage of area in the composition, while other colors serve a secondary role, that of enhancing the key color. Other compositions create greater tension by maintaining a balance of all the colors in the composition, as shown in Figure 3.3.

Another way to increase the effect of this contrast is to separate the colors with either black or white. White has the effect of making the colors of hue appear richer, while black will give them a greater luminosity. Either can increase the effectiveness of the hue contrast depending on the selection of colors in use. This is the net effect of black lead on a stained-glass window.

▶ Contrast of Extent

All colors have some degree of inherent strength, or tendency to attract the eye. The amount of strength naturally exhibited by each color varies according to its relative lightness and its level of saturation. When two colors are shown at full saturation, in their greatest intensity, the lighter of the two will have greater strength. When two colors are of equal value, the more saturated of the two has greater

FIGURE 3.2 The contrast of value in this interior composition is dramatic, allowing the edges of each form to be read more distinctly. (*Design by Flansburgh Associates, Inc. Photo: Greg Premru.*)

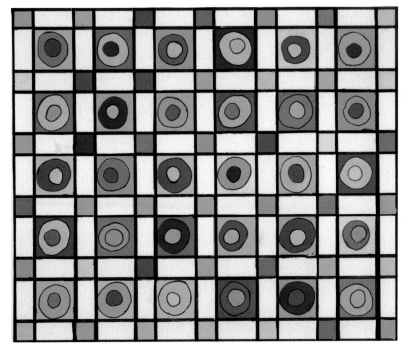

FIGURE 3.3 This composition is an example of a contrast of hue. (*Design by Sarah Hewins.*)

FIGURE 3.4 In this color scheme contrast of hue helps draw attention to key features of space. Its placement becomes an orienting device. (*Interior design by GHK. Photo: © Thomas Lingner/The Able Lens.*)

strength. To test this, refer to the extended circle shown in Chapter 2, Figure 2.6. Which colored squares catch your eye first? *Contrast of extent,* or *contrast of extension,* is the conscious attempt to shift the balance of strength between colors of unequal strength to create tension or excitement or to place emphasis within a color composition. Two attributes contribute to the dramatic effect of a color—its comparative strength, driven by value and saturation, and its extent, the amount of area it occupies. To create drama, unequal amounts of colors are used to accentuate their differences in strength. To maintain balance between any two colors in a composition, a smaller amount of the stronger color must be used. When the amount of each color is adjusted so that an overall balance of strength is achieved, there is a *balance of extent.* In this case the proportionate area of each color reflects its relative

level of strength—the stronger color occupies a smaller proportion within the composition. As the relative amounts of each color are adjusted, the balance is upset. When the six basic primary and secondary colors are compared at full saturation, we find that yellow can exist in much smaller quantities than violet or blue and still maintain its strength due to its inherent lightness. Red and green are fairly equal in their levels of brilliance. Goethe established numerical values for the relative brightness of colors at full saturation, which he called *light values.* A contemporary of his, Arthur Schopenhauer (Polish, 1788–1860), established what he called *harmonious areas* by using reciprocal numbers to Goethe's, reflecting the proportionate area each color must occupy to maintain its balance with the others. The ratios suggested by Goethe and Schopenhauer are illustrated in Figure 3.5.

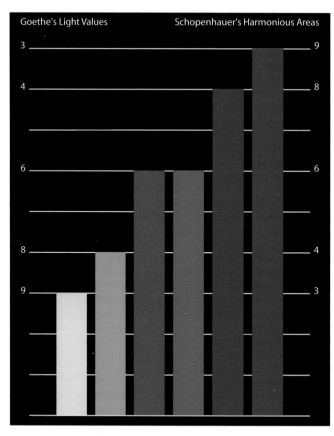

FIGURE 3.5 This diagram shows the six fully saturated basic hues in proportion to their strength. For balance, three times as much violet is needed as yellow (Schopenhauer). In other words, yellow is three times as strong as violet (Goethe).

Knowledge of extent is valuable when color is the only tool available to direct attention. One example is an oversized living room with a very high ceiling. Such a space will often have an overall tone that is light to medium in value in a neutral or low-intensity hue. As a counterbalance to the large expanse of a single color, small accent pillows in a strong color of hue will bring the focus to the seating area by drawing the eye down. It's also advantageous for getting attention in graphic design, exhibit functions, and some industrial design applications. Contrast of extent is frequently used to draw attention to a single focal point—a corporate logo, a key entry, or a valuable pendant. In the contrast-of-extent example in Figure 3.6, a retail space has been deliberately neutralized to allow the highly saturated objects to capture all the attention.

In extreme cases of extent contrast, the minority color will appear to react defensively and the colors may visually vibrate, as shown in the two examples in Figure 3.7. This can be an irritant in the case of written text. The movements caused by severely unequal color can also be disruptive to one's sense of place and is therefore uncommon in interior design and architectural environments, except in nightclubs or amusement centers.

FIGURE 3.6 This situation shows dramatic contrast of extent at work to ensure that the retail objects capture and hold buyers' attention. (*Carlos-Bergmeyer Associates, Inc., architect. Photo: © Lucy Chen.*)

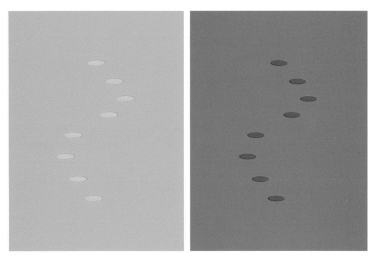

FIGURE 3.7 These compositions show the vibration that can occur when contrast of extent is used. To experience the effect, cover one rectangle while looking at the other. Then switch. To most eyes, one combination (or both) will offer movement.

SUBTLE CONTRASTS

Not all color contrasts are as imposing as the ones just discussed. Some express themselves best in moderation, making them useful in more reserved palettes. These contrasts are just as distinct as their dynamic counterparts, but are more difficult to recognize. For the sake of identity, I call these *subtle contrasts.*

▶ Contrast of Temperature

Colors appear in contrast when warm and cool colors are used in combination. This is *contrast of temperature,* also referred to as *warm-cool contrast.* As a reminder, warm colors fall in the yellow, yellow-orange, orange, red-orange, and red range; cool colors include green, blue-green, blue, and blue-violet. The apparent temperature of yellow-green and violet as warm or cool depends on the temperature of immediately adjacent colors, as illustrated in Figure 3.8. Blue and orange are the extremes in color temperature and influence our perception of color temperature the most. Colors near them appear warmer or cooler by contrast.

Warm-cool contrasts are most effective when a limited number of different hues are used in the

Usage

Temperature contrast was frequently used by the artists Renoir, Monet, and Cézanne to inspire emotion and engage the viewer. Many practical uses of warm and cool contrasts exist in contemporary society as well. The immediate effect of color temperature has some bearing on our selection of major colors in large spaces and in health, athletic, and similar therapeutic environments. Consider plumbing fixtures of the 1950s, when water temperature was designated by color—hot was red and cold was blue. A very intense red is usually used to designate all fire apparatus, and the traditional contrasting color of blankets on newborn babies (pink and blue) serves to designate gender. As a spatial composition, temperature contrasts are frequently found in large-volume spaces that serve the public. In the examples in Figures 3.10 and 3.11, the architects painted one face of the walls warm and the opposite face cool as an orientation device in a main walkway. The warmer colors lead to active functional areas, while the cooler ones lead to a library.

FIGURE 3.8 These two color combinations demonstrate the effects of color temperature. Both compositions use the same warm green; however, they diverge in color temperature across each composition, making the same greens appear different from each other. The top left and bottom right greens are the same color.

composition. It's also advantageous to use colors of similar value, maintaining the brilliance of both warm and cool tones so that any value contrast does not dominate. Like contrast of hue, the temperature contrast effect is heightened by an increase in saturation level. However, it can be equally effective as a subtle contrast in neutral versions of warm and cool colors, as shown in the example in Figure 3.9.

Most individuals are sensitive to the contrast that is created by a temperature contrast. This is probably due to physiological response. When the eye focuses on long wavelengths (red) rather than on short wavelengths (blue), the lens becomes slightly fatter and more curved. The condition is similar to what happens when the eye focuses on nearby objects. The muscles of the eye relax when looking at the horizon, similar to the adjustment made in the lens when it's focused on cool colors. This physical adjustment draws attention to the visual temperature shift and, in extreme cases,

can cause a vibrating edge, such as between a strong red and a strong adjacent blue or green color.

▶ Contrast of Complement

When two complements are used in combination, it is considered a *contrast of complement,* or *complementary contrast.* This is essentially a contrast of hue using diametrically opposing colors. Because complements are harmonically balanced, the effect tends to be dramatic yet easier on the eyes than other hue contrasts, making it popular in many design applications. The more saturated the colors and the larger the areas of complements, the stronger the contrast effect, particularly where direct complements touch. Added depth and complexity in contrast of complement occurs when colors of several saturation levels or value levels are used. Keep in mind that each color has one and only one hue complement, but neutralized versions and lighter or darker tones are still complementary.

Additive color, or the spectral color of light, behaves differently from pigment, in that **the combined light of two complementary colors yields a true white light.** To find the additive complement of any color, an afterimage approach can be used. In the presence of any color, particularly those strong of hue, the human eye naturally

Usage

In three-dimensional compositions where contrast of complement is used, colors are usually coordinated with an emphasis on one of the two hues, since the effect of the contrast is more apparent with complements in unequal amounts. For instance, a palette of gray-greens might be used with a small amount of red as an accent. Complements are often used in fashion to highlight key features or in design to add definition to form. In the example in Figure 3.12, the architects used complementary orange and blue with a neutral light gray to delineate the exterior building components.

FIGURE 3.9   Here temperature contrast is handled in warm and cool neutrals, creating a more sophisticated combination. (*Design by Flansburgh Associates, Inc. Photo: © Richard Mandelkorn.*)

FIGURE 3.10 This warm scheme and the cool one in Figure 3.11 are different views of the same public space. (*Design by Perry Dean Rogers, Partners Architects. Photo: © Steve Rosenthal.*)

FIGURE 3.11 See Figure 3.10. (*Design by Perry Dean Rogers, Partners Architects. Photo: © Steve Rosenthal.*)

seeks its additive complement, resulting in the projection of its afterimage. We see the complement in the mind's eye, even if it does not technically exist within view. The complement that relaxes the cones that have just been stimulated is a biological one. This means that it's not the same as the complement observed on a subtractive color wheel, but shifts more to an additive complement. Examples are yellow, which often generates a bluish-violet afterimage, and green, which produces a magenta afterimage. To experience afterimaging, have someone hold a sample of a highly saturated color against a white wall surface. Focus on this color for a few minutes and then remove the sample while continuing to look at the wall. In the place where the sample previously existed, a complementary color will appear in a shape similar to the original sample. As the eye becomes fatigued from concentrating on one color, an afterimage is projected to allow the cones to relax.

(Hint: If you do not see the effect the first time, try a very different hue. Like other body parts, not all cones have the same strength of response.)

▶ Contrast of Saturation

Contrast of saturation encompasses the use of both intense and diluted colors in association with each other, usually working within one hue. The contrast is created only in subtractive color, because it depends on the ability to manipulate saturation quantitatively. The spectral hues found in white light are uniformly of maximum saturation. This means the only way to reduce the intensity of an additive color is to reduce the amount of light allocated to it.

There are a number of ways to make a subtractive color less saturated. One is to dilute it with white. This causes it to soften, as in pastel colors. Color can also be diluted with black, creating rich

FIGURE 3.12 Color contrasts were used extensively in this science center to articulate building systems. Those shown on the exterior form a complementary contrast. (*Design by Perry Dean Rogers/Partners Architects. Photo: Edward Jacoby.*)

Usage

In art, a shift in saturation is often used in combination with other contrasts to draw attention from the background to the foreground or vice versa. Subtle contrasts of saturation are found in more expensive interiors where a change of materials offers textural variation. The nuances of saturation contrast don't distract the eye from characteristic details, but rather tend to enhance them. Textiles are often woven with saturation contrasts to express textural depth, since more dynamic contrasts will make a textile appear flattened. Saturation contrast is also used on building facades or interior spaces with more complex form to give order to the structure. In the example in Figure 3.14, a more exaggerated contrast of saturation is used for emphasis.

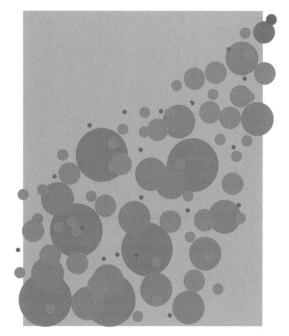

FIGURE 3.13 This composition uses contrast of saturation to vary the color of the circles. The presence of the color in its reduced intensity has the effect of softening the strong hues.

jewel tones. Of course, mixing with either black or white will also affect the value of the color. To maintain consistent value, a mixture of gray in equal value to the hue at hand can be used to create a color that is decidedly less intense. In the composition in Figure 3.13, the saturation level of the circles varies to create the color contrast, but the value stays the same. The only value shift is the lighter background color. (Hint: If you want to confirm that your composition is about saturation and not value, try photocopying it on a black-and-white copier. Like values will appear the same regardless of their saturation.)

Michel Chevreul

Michel-Eugène Chevreul (1786–1889) was a French Renaissance man with many interests, color being among them. He studied languages, mathematics, physics, chemistry, and mineralogy, as well as natural history, philosophy, archaeology, astrology, magic, and psychic phenomena. Chevreul held the position of Director of Dyes for the Royal Manufacturers at the Gobelins—a distinction given him by King Louis XVIII in 1824. In this capacity, he discovered issues of environmental influence in color perception while trying to resolve customer complaints about quality of the Gobelins dyegoods. To resolve issues of influence, he systematically analyzed the effects of color on the eye and published his findings in atlas form. His documentation included color samples produced by lithography, hand printing, and dyeing. Chevreul's explanations had a tremendous influence on the French schools of art, including Impressionists and Neo-Impressionists. Chevreul further illustrated the effects of value and hue contrast, color harmony, and conditions of color influence, particularly simultaneous contrast, and the occurrence of afterimages, which he referred to as *successive contrast*.

FIGURE 3.14   While many projects using contrast of saturation involve more subtle levels of contrast, the designers of this space used saturation contrast in the extreme to draw attention to key objects such as signage and furniture. (*Design by ADD Inc. Photo: © Lucy Chen.*)

■ COMPLEX CONTRASTS

Some conditions of color contrast cannot be captured photographically but must be experienced by the human eye. These are described here as *complex contrasts,* because they are more difficult to employ and in some cases occur without our intention. To understand these contrasts, the active effect of spontaneous afterimaging must be experienced. (Refer to the exercise described under "Contrast of Complement" to create this consequence.) The concept is simply that greater color stimuli generate a greater need for relief. When strong colors are used, the retina of the eye reacts to each color stimulus, looking for relief in an equal but opposite form. This strength can be one of fullness in satura-

tion, such as a highly saturated red, or it can be an extreme in value, such as black and white. The tendency for the eye to find relief influences one's perception of adjacent colors and causes the following two contrast effects.

▶ Contrast of Simultaneity

Simultaneous contrast, or *contrast of simultaneity,* occurs when a strong color influences another. When more than one strong color is present, colors in simultaneous contrast influence each other. In strong stimulation, the eye seeks repose in the form of a complement to colors strong in hue and in the form of an inverse value for colors of extreme value. This search for relief causes the eye to spontaneously generate an afterimage where the desired colors are not present. As the eye generates an afterimage of complementary color, the hue of the color it's projected onto appears to shift. As the eye shifts from one strong color to another, perception of each is impacted according to the strength of adjacent colors. If a neutral gray square is surrounded by a very warm color, it will appear to have an undertone of the complementary cool color, just as it will appear lighter if surrounded by a very dark color. However, if two intense colors are present, as in the example in Figure 3.15, they tend to influence each other. In this example, the eyes' search for blue, as a complementary relief to the orange, causes the blue-green to appear cooler, while the strong green causes the orange to seem more reddish. This is simultaneous contrast.

Contrast of simultaneity will occur between any two colors of hue that are not true complements. The projection of the afterimage is most effective in the less intense of the two colors—gray is particularly susceptible to the influence of simultaneous contrast. Two colors of equal strength will also exhibit the slight color imposition associated with afterimaging. Each color affects the other in a complementary way, changing the aesthetics of both. To intensify a simultaneous contrast, one of three things can be increased: the saturation level

Usage

The art world includes many individual examples of simultaneous contrasts in painted works. As a group, perhaps the portraits from seventeenth-century Europe include the best examples. To give the skin tones of their patrons a healthy glow, artists often added an undertone to the background color. Because of its large area, the understated color would cause a simultaneous contrast with the facial tones, breathing life into the subject. In architectural design, simultaneous contrast goes in and out of fashion as an intentional effect. It's a device used in small-scale patterns to give punch; or it is used on an edge trim to make a focal object pop. The biggest reason we try to understand this effect in design is to be able to control it when it occurs unintentionally. Sometimes the contrast surfaces at the point where the two disparate colors meet. To eliminate it, the hue of one color can be adjusted to bring them closer, the saturation level can be reduced, or a neutral color can be placed between the offending colors. Simultaneous contrast is minimized when colors are outlined with a neutral color, such as black, white, or gray, since the outline allows the eye to rest between strong contiguous colors.

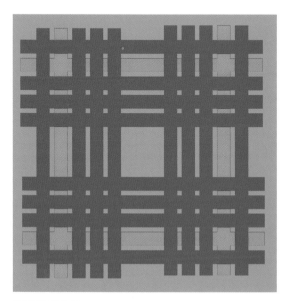

FIGURE 3.15 The orange and green hues in this composition are intensified due to simultaneous contrast at work.

of the imposing color, the relative proportions of the imposing color, or the amount of edge where the two colors touch in proportion to the solid form. Why? Higher saturation means more work for the cones. A large area of color leads to simultaneous contrast more readily than a small incidental amount. And the influence of this contrast occurs mostly along the edges where two colors meet—more edge means more of a sensation. The graphic diagram in Figure 3.16 demonstrates this effect. At first glance it is difficult to determine the number of colors in this composition because of the contrast effect.

M. E. Chevreul was the first to explain the concept of simultaneous contrast in universally acceptable terms, primarily through his text, *The Principles of Harmony and Contrast of Colors* (originally *De la Loi du Contraste Simultane des Couleurs*, Paris,

FIGURE 3.16 How many different colors appear to exist in this composition? In actuality there are three: an orange, a warm green, and a dark blue.

Although simultaneous contrast was identified by Chevreul as early as the mid-1800s, it is underutilized compared to other contrasts. It's most often employed to highlight a change in overall color tone. Filmmakers use contrast of succession when generating a change of mood from one scene to another, such as a shift from a seedy, after-hours nightclub scene to a bright, sunlit beach at dawn. One image serves as a predecessor to increase the impact of the next scene. Successive contrast can add impact between a series of rooms if the progression is consistent. A cool room can make the next space feel warmer; a dark passage can increase the feeling of the next light, voluminous space. In other projects, moving light sources with colored gels are used to change the color composition in a room. As a multicolored disc rotates, the colors projected change, causing successive contrast within the room.

1839). He pointed out that afterimages give vision a dynamic quality. They shift and fade; they appear larger or smaller depending on where the eye focuses. When they fade, they can be recovered by blinking, by shifting the eye, or by adjusting the light level within the field of vision. He also believed that simultaneous contrast is most effective between colors of similar value. Again, to fully experience this condition, it must be seen in person: **Simultaneous contrasts are the result of physiological phenomena captured only by the eye.**

▶ Contrast of Succession

The final contrast to be discussed is one that has its impact strictly in three-dimensional design applications. It is *successive contrast,* or *contrast of succession,* which is generated similar to simultaneous contrast. The difference is that successive contrast involves effects that depend on movement of the objects or the eye. When viewing two-dimensional work, it occurs as the eye moves across the surface to contiguous shapes of color. In three-dimensional work, this movement can involve physical shifts from room to room. With simultaneous contrast the impact is seen immediately. Contrast of succession occurs with the passage of time, albeit very short in duration. As with simultaneous contrast, the effect occurs most readily with colors that are extreme in saturation level or value level. The eye adapts to one color, and this adaptation impacts the perception of those colors that come into view immediately after-

ward, often by the projection of complementary afterimages. If the viewer looks at a given color with great intensity and immediately follows that observation by viewing a background of a different color, perception of that background color will be influenced by the first. Successive contrast can be one of significant temperature, hue, or value change. To experience this effect, refer to the two-part illustration in Figure 3.17.

▶ Resolving Contrasts

Each color contrast can be used to enhance a color combination, adding to its complexity and causing subtle adjustments in the perception of each individual color. To ensure the effectiveness of contrast as a tool, two conditions deserve some attention to detail. One is the tendency for contrasting colors to influence each other. The other is the tendency for contrasts in combination to become too extreme or to cancel each other out. A few words of caution are offered here.

FIGURE 3.17 This illustration is meant to demonstrate successive contrast. Stare at the image in the left square for several moments, focusing on the X at the center. Then shift your eye to the X in the square on the right. A successive image will appear in the void offered by the white square.

Color Influence

We know that the eye involuntarily compares adjacent colors for differences in character. In the absence of common characteristics, each intense color proceeds to project its complement on the other color, causing an increase in intensity for both if they are complements and simultaneous contrast if they are not. Here are a few reminders relative to managing contrasts.

- **Contrast effects are strengthened** when the colors of greatest impact share common boundaries. In other words, to influence an existing color, place a large amount of an influential color immediately adjacent to it. The closer two colors are physically to each other, the greater the strength of their contrast.
- Between two dissimilar colors, the **greater the area of edge** (imposing surface) in relationship to the overall area, the stronger the contrast. A series of small areas of the two colors is more potent than two large blocks of color since they have more edge in proportion to form. Contrasts can be reduced by increasing the solid area of the impacted color(s) or by placing

another color between them. Neutral borders are the most effective.

- To **reduce the influence** of one color over another without adjusting the colors themselves, the area of the imposing color can be reduced.
- In terms of **value**, any color will look lighter when placed in front of a very dark background and darker when placed before a very light background color. This is true of neutral colors, as well as colors of hue. White will make a color of hue appear deeper, while black will make it appear brighter, more luminous. (See Chapter 4, Figure 4.17.)
- A **temperature-neutral color** will seem cool in the presence of a warm color and warm in the presence of a cool one (refer to Figure 3.8). Temperature shifts are less effective in the presence of a stronger contrast, such as value. In combinations, the more dynamic contrast takes over, reducing the relationship of temperature between colors.
- When a background color has more **chroma** than the foreground object, the intensity of the object will be reduced (see Chapter 4, Figure

FIGURE 3.18 In this composition, *January Nocturne,* value contrast gives the image a dramatic effect. The store window draws the eye in by its comparative brightness. While variations in hue and saturation may account for some of the visible differences, value contrast has the strongest impact. (*Courtesy of Simie Maryles Gallery, Provincetown, Massachusetts.*)

4.17). Conversely, if the background is more neutral than the sample, the object will grow in its intensity. Gray makes a color of hue appear richer and more pure and exhibits the least amount of value influence by its neutrality.

■ If two colors are far from each other on the color circle but not diametrically opposed, they will influence each other. **To minimize the tendency to influence,** the saturation level of both colors should be reduced.

Each color contrast discussed has many applications in design practice, and often contrasts are used in combination with each other for more sophisticated contrast effects. **When two or more contrasts are combined, usually one stands out to the viewer first.** For instance, moderately saturated versions of yellow and violet together may read more as a value contrast than contrast of hue or complement. A combination of orange and blue is considered a complementary contrast, but the temperature contrast they form may be more obvious depending on the particular selections. In most cases, a contrast of value will dominate a coexisting contrast of saturation because of its greater impact on the eye. A contrast of hue can, but won't always, obscure a coexisting contrast of extension. Contrast of extension has a tendency to intensify the effect of other preexisting contrasts. Consequently, it is

often used with other forms of contrast, such as temperature or simultaneity.

The artist Simie Maryles is known for developing very complex color combinations. Her pastels and paintings often display multiple contrasts of hue when viewed at close range, but when seen from a distance other tonal contrasts become far more apparent, as evident in the example, Figure 3.18. This work demonstrates that a greater range of color is possible within one form if the values are kept close together. This way they do not compete with the drama of the larger contrast, which in this example is value. The key is to be cognizant of which contrasts support the overall intent and which ones are secondary, adding to the complexity of the color composition. If the secondary contrast starts to compete with the intended overall color effect, then adjustments are needed to keep it in check.

Each of the contrast effects described here has its place in the context of design opportunities. They are the tools we use to establish emphasis, create drama, and illustrate depth in the forms we compose. In its own way, each color contrast can increase the level of interest in any color composition. In the absence of balance, however, too much contrast can be overwhelming. In addition to tools of contrast, there are several ways to maintain unity in a color composition by making the visual experience easy on the eyes. Those are the tools we address in the next chapter.

4

Color Harmony

Color is used in design to evoke a mood or sentiment. When the goal is stimulation, contrast effects are used in greater quantity and to their extreme. When a more soothing environment is desired, contrast effects are reduced, and colors with more common characteristics are chosen. The goals shift to that of visual comfort, or a sense of aesthetic tranquility, which we call *harmony*.

To generate a state of harmony we focus on the total effect of the color combination on the eye, regardless of the individual color attributes. In a harmonic color composition, colors are observed easily, and the eyes do not work very hard to communicate to the brain what is seen. The cones are not stressed, and the constant comparison between colors adds visual interest without significant taxation. The eyes are relaxed, but not completely inactive.

Two methods are used to make colors harmonious. The first is to choose colors that are very similar to each other. The second is to select hues that together form a spectral balance. Both methods are explored in this chapter.

▨ HARMONIES OF CONSISTENCY

If color combinations can be made more stimulating by using colors that are different from each other, then it stands to reason that reducing contrasts makes a palette more cohesive. The easiest

way to effect harmony, then, is to choose colors with inherent similarities. The more consistent they are, the more harmonic the result, because the eye does less work to read the overall palette. When colors are more consistent with each other, the objects that contain them are grouped together in the mind's eye, read as one block of forms. For the purpose of this text, we'll call these approaches *harmonies of consistency*. In each situation, the sense of harmony comes from a synthesis between colors that are most like each other. Four types of harmony can be developed through strong characteristic consistencies: achromatic, monochromatic, adjacent, and polychromatic. They are relatively straightforward solutions that depend on a reasonable level of color control.

▶ Achromatic Harmony

The use of a single neutral color, or versions of a single nonchromatic color, is an *achromatic harmony*. This is also known as a *neutral scheme*. Examples of colors used in achromatic harmonies are gray, beige, black, and white. Variation between elements is established through value contrasts only, which can be introduced through changes in surface color or by positioning lighting to cast shadows.

Achromatic harmonies are one of the easiest to understand because of their elegant simplicity. In some cases they are developed to draw attention to

FIGURE 4.1   The classic simplicity of the achromatic color scheme in this executive reception area allows each modification in plane or change of material to be seen more easily. Effects of daylight are more apparent as it reaches large neutral surfaces. (*Interior Design by GHK. Photo: Jim Westphalen, Westphalen Photography.*)

differences in surface materials, as shown in the example in Figure 4.1. In other cases they're used as a backdrop in places where objects of transitory color will appear, such as galleries and food service areas. The risk with such a color scheme is that it can easily become too simple, losing the viewer's interest if a richness of form detail is not available. Another difficulty in this scheme is that a great level of control is needed to refine the final palette. Nothing can be left to chance, since the slightest color imperfection may easily draw attention to itself.

▶ Monochromatic Harmony

Monochromatic harmonies involve a selection of colors within a single hue, with some variation in the range of value, saturation, or both. Complexity is developed through a mixture of tones, tints, and/or shades, often arranged in gradual increments. As in the achromatic harmony, this one is visually simple to comprehend, but can lose the viewer's interest over time if it is too limited. Contrasts in value make it easier to distinguish form, either through surface color or variation in light level. Contrasts in saturation add interest without deformation of form. In three-dimensional design, monochromatic schemes sometimes include a small amount of an accent color to add interest, such as the one in Figure 4.2.

▶ Adjacent Harmony

There are several ways to produce color harmonies using more than one hue. One is to combine hues that are immediately adjacent to each other on the color circle, or at least within very close proximity.

This is known as an *adjacent harmony* or, as some colorists refer to it, an *analogous harmony*. In terms of complexity, this is the next step in development of a congruent color scheme. Its success comes from the realization that when two or more colors are close together in hue, the eye has a tendency to recognize them with greater similarity, allowing them to blend harmoniously. Chevreul suggested that simultaneous contrast of two adjacent hues will cause them to essentially neutralize each other. In any case, the net effect is that the eye reads them as more similar than they might otherwise appear.

FIGURE 4.2   A cool undertone and a range of value contrasts give this monochromatic palette its appeal, while a single accent color is used to draw the eye's attention to one point of focus. (*Interior Design by GHK. Photo: Steve Hall © Hedrich Blessing.*)

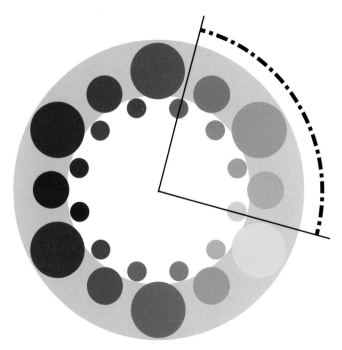

FIGURE 4.3 Adjacent harmonies are effective as long as the range of adjacency is small. (*Illustration by author.*)

Two or three hues are enough to create a range of hue without exceeding the appropriate limits of adjacency. The combination of any primary and secondary color, with the tertiary that occurs between them, is considered adjacent. These harmonies are commonly organized around a dominant hue in combination with a smaller amount of two hues either to one side or both on the color circle. **The key is to limit the number of hues and to include hue increments that occur between the dominant colors,** as suggested by the diagram in Figure 4.3. John Pile, a well-known educator and author in the field of interior design, recommends limiting analogous color schemes to a 90-degree range on the color circle (*Color in Interior Design,* page 90). Beyond this range, the effects of simultaneous contrast add to the complexity of the composition, resulting in more work for the eyes. Variations of value and saturation can be included within an adjacent scheme, but they're usually limited so as not to compete with the composition. The building exterior in Figure 4.4 is an example of an adjacent scheme.

Neutral spacing is one technique used with adjacent colors to make mismatched items appear similar. When two colors look the same but are not a true equal, their difference is intensified along the edge where they touch. If the same two colors are separated by a neutral color, they will more likely appear to match. The example used frequently in fashion is coordinating a dress or sweater with someone's eye color. Separation of the two by the neck's skin tone or a contrasting scarf allows the clothing to enhance eye color by approximating it. The wearer's eyes appear to have more color because of the adjacent cloth.

▶ Polychromatic Harmony

The last harmony of consistency is the *polychromatic harmony,* which is sometimes referred to as a *harmony of nuance.* In this approach, several different hues may be used regardless of their position on the color circle. Contrast is limited to hue only. This is what sets up the consistency. It means only a small range of value and a small range of saturation

FIGURE 4.4 An adjacent harmony can include a few colors or several colors, provided they are within a small range of hue. Here brickwork patterns are used to establish a residential scale for a large building through variation of color. The result is pleasing to look at, in part because of the small range of hue. (*Design by Flansburgh Associates, Inc. Photo: © Robert Benson.*)

can be used. When overall brightness is maintained, a wider range of hues can be combined without apparent discord. **The sense of harmony comes from the consistency in nonhue characteristics.** Polychromatic harmonies are most often, but not always, developed using low or medium saturation and light or medium values, such as the project shown in Figure 4.5.

Sometimes a polychromatic scheme is tied together by using a consistent *undertone.* This gives the selected hues some similarity without total limitation of hue. Undertones are created by the base color in a textured application, by the paper color in printed media, or by the warp and weft yarns in a complex textile. When all the colors in a composition have the same undertone, the range of visible hue is reduced. Another common application of polychromatic harmony is the use of pastels: several hues at very light value and reduced intensity. Less common but also harmonic

FIGURE 4.5   This interior space has a richness of complexity without confusion, which is due to the polychromatic harmony of the colors selected. Several hues are used, but the small range of value and saturation allows for effective integration with more complex forms. (*Design by ADD Inc. Photo: © Lucy Chen.*)

are combinations of darker values such as rich jewel tones. Full-intensity versions of polychromatic harmonies are also possible, such as those used frequently in children's play areas. However, in highly saturated color combinations, the guidelines for balanced color harmonies should be observed to ensure harmonious results. This is important because at greater intensities the cones of the eye are more readily taxed. To enable them some repose, a balance of hue is needed. This is explored in more detail in the next section.

■ HARMONIES OF BALANCE

The next color group is called *harmonies of balance* because it depends on a balance of spectral color. We've already mentioned that cones do the work of registering color in the human eye and that under stress they seek the relief of colors in opposition to those observed. **The idea of a balanced spectral harmony involves selecting colors in combination that offer comfort to our eyes, by relaxing the cones.** A chromatic balance is pleasing to the eye because it is experienced effortlessly. The observer senses a visual state of equilibrium through overall spectral balance. Hue selections are made across the full color circle with a focus toward harmony in the aggregate combination. This harmony occurs when all the colors of the composition are positioned according to a balance of the chromatic scale. Put another way, the theory is that if all the colors in a combination could be mixed together, and the aggregate mix forms a neutral gray, then the combination is a balanced harmony. This type of harmony is sometimes called *contrast harmony,* because the colors are drawn from different parts of the color circle, forming inherent contrasts. However, by choosing harmonic hues, the net effect is a balanced harmony possible in more complex combinations than those previously discussed.

A color circle is a handy tool for developing harmonies of balance. Generally speaking, when a diagonal is drawn across the color circle, any collection of hues that position themselves symmetrically along that diagonal will be more harmonious. The premise is that by balancing the selections of hues according to their respective wavelengths, the resulting color combination will always be aesthetically pleasing. You can test this by mapping any color combination with aesthetic appeal. If the scheme is too complex to be considered a harmony of consistency, try locating each color within it by a dot on a color circle. By connecting these dots, you can see the polygon the combination creates. If the combination seems a little off, adjust one color to align the polygon over a centerline. Proportionate amounts of each color do not need to balance— only their relative wavelengths do.

▶ Dyad Harmony

The most effective harmonies involve a combination of complementary hues. Two complementary hues create a *dyad harmony,* also known as a *complementary harmony.* In this case, several values and intensities of each complement may be included as long as each color is a derivative of one of the two hues represented. In more intricate versions, the quantitative balance of color is shifted to give dominance to one hue over the other. The result is still harmonious according to its balance of hue.

A dyad harmony can be developed into dramatic combinations without causing discord. One option is to use an area of strong, pure hues that are limited in size and surround them with larger areas of a complementary shade, tint, or tone. Dyads are also effective when two low-saturation complements are used. Using the full contrast of two fully saturated colors makes a strong statement, but one that is spectrally balanced, provided they are diametrically opposed on the color circle, as shown in the diagram in Figure 4.6, with the three-dimensional example shown in Figure 4.7. When working with dyad harmonies in interior space, it's better not to give complementary colors equal weight. The presence of a dominant color's complement will give needed respite from a highly saturated color. However, if distributed equally, focus cannot be on both colors at the same time, and they tend to compete. The preferred solution is to allow one color to dominate in scale, subduing the secondary color.

▶ Triad Harmony

The next balanced harmony on the scale of difficulty is the *triad.* As the name implies, this one involves three hues positioned around the color circle such that a line connecting all three would result in an equilateral triangle. This harmony only occurs when the three colors are equally spaced. Triad color schemes are most dramatic when primaries are used, as shown in the diagram in Figure 4.8 and the photograph in Figure 4.9. Secondary colors in combination form a somewhat less intense, balanced triad. Any equally spaced combination that falls between the primaries and secondaries will offer balance as a hue contrast with less strength. Generally speaking, triad harmonies do not rely on uniformity of value or saturation. Like the dyad scheme, this is a spectral balance. Colors may be similar in value and saturation or different. Or two of the three colors may be reduced in intensity, allowing the third to have a greater saturation level and serve as an accent without disturbing the visual balance.

▶ Split Complement Harmony

A *split complement harmony* is built on the concept of complementary colors. It follows the same premise as a dyad in that colors directly opposite each other on the circle are combined to form a balance of hue. The difference here is that one color is combined with the two hues on either side of its oppo-

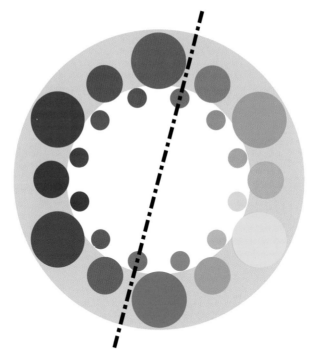

FIGURE 4.6 A dyad harmony is diagrammatically the simplest form of spectrally balanced harmonies. (*Illustration by author.*)

FIGURE 4.7 A dyad or complementary color scheme can include fairly saturated hues. It's pleasing to the eye due to the condition of harmony, in this case a balance of spectral color. (*Radius-Bergmeyer Associates, Inc., architect. Photo: © Richard Mandelkorn.*)

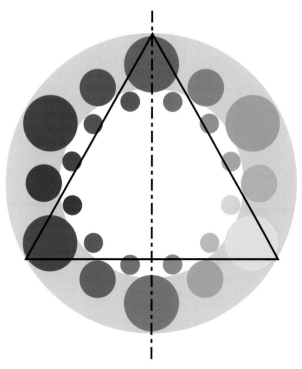

FIGURE 4.8 The diagram of a triad is an equilateral triangle. (*Illustration by author.*)

FIGURE 4.9 In this triad combination, primary colors appear at both full and reduced saturation levels. (*Design by Bryer Architects, LLP. Photo: © Thomas Lingner/The Able Lens.*)

Some designs that call for a combination of several hues do not depend on total harmony. A few colorists have proposed additional combinations of four, five, or six colors as spectrally balanced harmonies, which I include for reference. However, this group of combinations is not as effective harmonically as the classic forms discussed elsewhere in this chapter. Through classroom experiments, we've determined that such combinations are more harmonious than a selection of random hues. This is logical from a theory standpoint, since the polygon they create has a balanced centerline and includes the circle's center, and together the colors are likely to create a gray tone. However, the following combinations are *not as harmonious* as the others illustrated in this chapter and are offered in that context. This is a matter of degree. Because the positioning of the combinations delineates harmonic geometries, their placement is more balanced than an arbitrary collection of the same number of hues. However, some of the individual colors together establish new relationships that are not necessarily harmonious.

To explain, an argument can be made that any two pairs whose positions are mirrored along a center axis constitute a tetrad harmony as long as the trapezoid that they form includes the center of the circle. This is shown in the upper circle in Figure 4.14, which we'll call a *trapezoidal tetrad,* because of the geometry it forms. While the trapezoidal harmony is less taxing than some hue combinations, it does not have the immediacy of a complement or combination of complements, since relationships between some of the colors may be comparatively less symbiotic. In the ex-

ample shown, the true green and the blue-violet-blue are far enough apart to cause some effort for the viewer.

Similarly, a combination of hues could be developed using a combination of two split complements that either share a common anchor point or whose anchor points are complementary. The theory here is that if two split complements are truly balanced, then together they must form a balanced harmony as long as the split complements share a common centerline. The hue positions collectively form a five-sided polygon in one case (bottom left in Figure 4.14) or a six-sided polygon where the anchor points are complements. In either case, both diagrammatic triangles must include the circle center. In the absence of traditional terminology, we'll call these *double split complements* and present them in the same light as the trapezoidal tetrad. Such combinations may offer more balance than an arbitrary assortment of five or six hues, because their geometries are symmetric along one centerline. But the combinations are not always as easy on the eyes as harmonies that are derivative of complementary associations. Where a classic harmony is not required, the double split diagram is very helpful for resolving complex color conditions that don't quite mesh. By mapping the chosen colors as they occur, as suggested in Figure 4.14, we can uncover a *more balanced* solution that may involve adjustment in only one of the colors proposed. Again, the solution is a matter of degree. Harmonies derived from complementary color relationships will always be more effective than those that involve a little more work for the eyes to process them.

site instead of the complement itself. As a geometric form over the color circle, a split complement harmony forms an isosceles triangle that encompasses the center of the color circle (Figure 4.10). This means the anchor point and the flat of the triangle are on opposite sides of the circle's center, regardless of distance between the split pair. By

definition, a triad is a form of split complement, but all split complements are not triads.

This harmony offers a greater variety of color combinations than the preceding options. With this approach, more unique color combinations can be used in greater levels of saturation, adding the effects of simultaneous and hue contrasts without

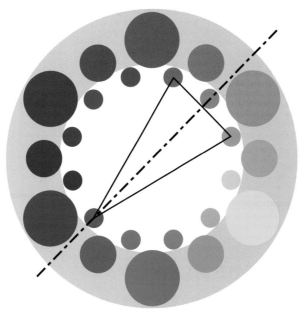

FIGURE 4.10 This diagram shows a split-complement composition, where two colors equally straddle the complement of the first. (*Illustration by author.*)

unpleasant discord. Sometimes one of the three colors will be used in low saturation with intense accents in the other two colors. In other situations, all three will be neutralized slightly, similar to a polychromatic harmony. In the example shown in Figure 4.11, one color is used in a very neutralized version on the vertical surfaces, while the more intense hues appear on the furniture.

▶ Tetrad Harmony

A tetrad harmony offers a tremendous range of options to facilitate four-color combinations. It's an increasingly complex form of color harmony, sometimes resulting in very active combinations and on other occasions forming very pleasing, sophisticated palettes. Because of its complexity, this harmony is best explained through its color circle geometries illustrated in Figure 4.12. The concept is that any two equally spaced hue pairs will offer a balanced harmony. It can be four equally spaced colors, which form a square, or any two pairs of complements, which form a rectangle. Either is a true tetrad harmony since it's based on a combination of comple-

ments. The result of a tetrad harmony is a more complex color scheme, which may be subdued in tone or quite bold in chroma, like the cafeteria in Figure 4.13. As we've noted with other spectral harmonies, unequal amounts of the representative colors result in more interesting combinations. In the example shown, a small amount of neon provides the fourth color as an accent.

▶ Hexad Harmony

To find a balanced combination of six colors, a hexagon may be imposed on a color circle in the same way that a square or rectangle is inscribed in the case of a tetrad (see Figure 4.15). The result is what's known as a *hexad harmony*. Geometrically, this is a combination of the three equally spaced pairs of color complements. The two most familiar hexads are (1) the combination of primary and secondary colors and (2) the combination of all six tertiary colors. Other less familiar hexad combinations exist between the colors just mentioned as the hexagon is rotated to less familiar hues around the circle. Due to the large number of hues, this har-

FIGURE 4.11 The formality and traditional appearance of this private club call for a balanced harmony, which was created using a split-complement combination. (*Design by Perry Dean Rogers/Partners Architects. Photo: © Richard Mandelkorn.*)

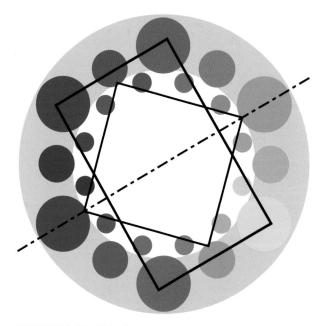

FIGURE 4.12 This diagram shows two possible tetrad combinations—one a diagrammatic square, the other a rectangle. (*Illustration by author.*)

FIGURE 4.13 The large scale and strong geometries of this cafeteria design are reinforced by colors of hue. Their appeal lies in the spectral balance they create in combination with each other. (*Design by Cubellis Associates, Inc. Photo: © Peter Vanderwarker.*)

mony is often appropriately used in conjunction with a polychromatic harmony for more sophisticated applications or in areas where high chroma is appropriate, such as children's activity areas, as in the example in Figure 4.16.

INTEGRATING CONTRAST AND HARMONY

The harmonies described on the previous pages are examples of color formulas that by nature result in harmonic color combinations. Of course,

not all color schemes need to be harmonic. The use of one particular harmony or none at all is a matter of choice, dictated by the overall design concept. Through these approaches there are an infinite number of combinations that can be described in the context of balanced harmonies, either through consistency or through spectral balance. When a color composition is not working well, a couple of options are available to make the combination visually pleasing.

- Try mapping the colors already selected on a color circle to highlight the one that needs adjustment to bring it more in balance.

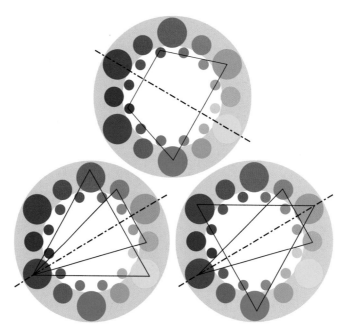

FIGURE 4.14 These color combinations are not traditional harmonies, but are based on theoretical harmonic geometries. The center top diagram shows a trapezoidal tetrad. The lower left shows a double split complement where both split complements share a common anchor point. The lower right is a double split complement where the anchor points are complementary. (*Illustration by author.*)

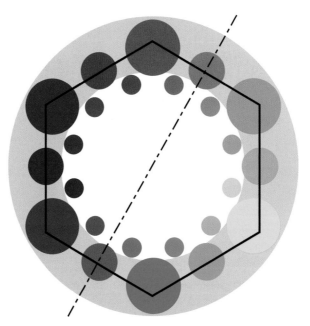

FIGURE 4.15 The uniform spacing of hues in a hexad harmony illustrates its strength as a balanced harmony based on the use of complements. (*Illustration by author.*)

FIGURE 4.16 The colorful combination used in this children's education center includes more saturated colors without visual discomfort. Balance is maintained by selecting hues that are equally spaced around the color circle. (*Design by ADD Inc. Photo: Tom Bonner, Tom Bonner Photography.*)

■ When any two specific colors within a scheme are not working well together, they can be separated by black or white for greater harmony. The interjection of a neutral at one end of the value scale distracts the eye by creating a strong value contrast. At the same time, it keeps the two colors of hue from influencing each other by allowing them to "read" independently.

▶ Compositional Balance

In working with both contrasts and harmonies, it's important to note that the amount of each color in the composition may be varied. **To create a balanced harmony, the amount of each representative color need not be consistent.** Harmony will be experienced with unequal amounts of each hue as long as the appropriate colors are present. Unlike harmonies of consistency, the colors in a harmony of balance may vary in terms of saturation or value—or both—without negating the harmonic effect. The diversity offered by this condition gives designers much room to create new and exciting color combinations. The decision to incorporate a color harmony is also flexible, since not all color combinations must be harmonic to be pleasing or appropriate.

What often does distinguish a successful color scheme is its sense of balance—or its conscious lack of one. Each design concept is interpreted as more than the sum of its parts. To understand a design, we look for its sense of order. Ideally, the eye is drawn to one point of focus and then continues assessing the space or object according to the way it's organized. We also look for emotional relief, for diversity rather than monotony. A successful color concept will offer the needed interest without exceeding the viewer's capacity for change. The goal is interest without confusion. This is a state of balance. To establish that balance, attention is given to three conditions: the degree of harmony, the frequency and degree of contrasts, and the tendency toward balance of extent. Balance is achieved when the level of harmony and contrast are consistent with the concept of the project and when extent is balanced above all. (For a refresher on balance of extent, refer to Chapter 3, "Color Contrast.")

Color and form together create the diversity and express some method of organization, which can either offer the viewer a logical approach and that sense of consistency or confuse the viewer, causing disorientation. Developing balance in color requires consideration for the users' visual interest, sensitivity to the form, and knowledge of the practical issues of function associated with the space. Decisions to incorporate greater contrast or to implement more harmony in a scheme are a matter of choice according to the overall intent. Without some sense of overall impression, neither set of tools is useful. But if intent is clear, decisions regarding each contrast or harmony can be made with well-balanced results.

▶ Unity and Complexity

Environmental designer and color consultant Frank Mahnke offers an articulate explanation of considerations for balance in *Color Environment & Human Response.* He describes it as a relationship between unity and complexity. To establish unity, all the components of the design collaborate simply and consistently to create a positive impression. Complexity is created through the amount of variation in the design, which was intentionally created to attract and arouse interest. These two attributes are mutually dependent in a state of balance.

From a design standpoint, either extreme unity or extreme complexity is distressing. A space of extreme unity is boring and can risk the sensations of monotony or sensory deprivation. On the other hand, an overabundance of complexity may overstimulate the occupant to the point of stress, evidenced by changes in pulse rate, blood pressure, or breathing. According to Mahnke, individuals' reactions to space, as monitored by electroencephalograms (EEGs) and electrocardiograms (EKGs), have demonstrated that the nervous system, the brain, and the heart are affected by spatial experience. The stronger the sense of balance, the longer a viewer's interest can be sustained. Imbalance invokes reaction of the viewer—which may be desirable, but in some cases is detrimental, depending on the purpose of the design. **The appropriate degree of unity and complexity is a judgment call to be made in each situation.** When greater unity is appropriate, conditions of harmony may be enhanced. If greater complexity is preferred, a state of greater contrast may be appropriate.

Principles of color aesthetics cannot be boiled down into simple formulas, but are a matter of judgment and taste. Mathematical comparisons, such as those offered by Goethe and Schopenhauer, to explain the concept of color strength can be helpful. Diagrammatic principles of harmony can be equally useful to understand and evaluate color work in process. However, when these guidelines are applied rigidly, the result is static, often trite. Successes rarely come from such literal combinations. Experienced designers seldom use color guidelines as a prescription, but rely on an intuitive sense of what will communicate an appropriate image. When the work in process does not present the desired results, then the logic of color harmony and contrast principles are used to make appropriate adjustments. The rules are not rigidly imposed but are regarded for potential application to work in progress. Decisions are made in the context of the overall design intent for each architectural work, each interior space, and each object of wearable art so its expression is unique rather than the result of a systematic formula.

COLOR PERCEPTION

Our perception of any single color depends not only on its relative characteristics, but also on how those characteristics are impacted by visual comparison to the colors around it. A medium-blue ball will look dark when resting in a field of yellow daffodils. The same blue ball will look relatively bright against the blackness of asphalt. Violet-colored grapes may appear quite cool in a bowl of oranges. But the same grapes placed in a blue bowl will appear warm by comparison. Each characteristic of color can be enhanced or reduced by placing certain other colors nearby. Figure 4.17 demonstrates how our impression of a particular shade of pale violet is adjusted when seen on a white ground, a blue ground, an orange ground, and a black one. On the black it looks slightly lighter than on the white. On the orange it seems somewhat cooler than on the blue. These are examples of *color influence.*

▶ Color Illusion

The tendency for the eye to make constant color comparisons generates great opportunity for those who understand subtle color distinctions. Color is used in combination to accentuate conditions of scale, depth, and form—and in some cases to create illusion. An illusion occurs when the eye perceives certain things that are not based in fact. They're created by carefully placing specific colors adjacent to each other so that they influence each other as the eye makes comparisons. One of the goals in mastering color in three-dimensional work is to capture this potential as a tool to enhance space and form. To this end, we briefly demonstrate how illusions work. In other chapters, the conditions that con-

FIGURE 4.17   Each change in background color causes an opposite change in how we see the object color relative to value and hue.

tribute to illusion are explored in greater detail for potential use with three-dimensional forms.

Framing Color

We've said that our perception of color is often influenced by the color around it. Framing is a simple expression of this. Consider the rows of boxes in Figure 4.18. Which row appears lighter at first glance? Which boxes are darker? As you look closer, it may become more apparent that the frame is what has changed color, not the boxes at all. Quickly comparing the boxes to their frame color leads us to the conclusion that they vary when they actually don't.

Colors of extreme variation have the strongest impact as framing color. In the illustration in Figure 4.19, the extremes of black and white are used to create an illusion of gray where it does not exist. This is sometimes referred to as the *Hermann grid.* Here the black spaces between the white squares are so intense that their intersections look gray by comparison, while the white bands between the black squares look so bright that the white intersections between them appear gray. In this case the frame color is consistent but the proportions of extreme color create the illusion.

Increasing and Decreasing Color

One way to give the effect of a more complex color scheme is to use colors of hue that influence each other so that a single color gives the impression of others. In *Interaction of Color*, artist and educator Josef Albers called this the "one color appears as two" illusion. Here, one color is made to look like two, through comparison of the background colors in terms of value, hue, and chromatic intensity, as shown in Figure 4.20. Two sets of colored circles appear to be different—the ones on the left seem close to the right-hand ground color. In fact, all the circles are the same. The shift occurs because the background imposes its influence on the inserted color. With color influence, the greater the distinctions between the two ground colors, the greater will be their impact on the color of the inserted object. (If you try this one, the temptation is to select the ground colors first when creating an increased color illusion. By experimenting, you'll find it's much easier to start with one ground and

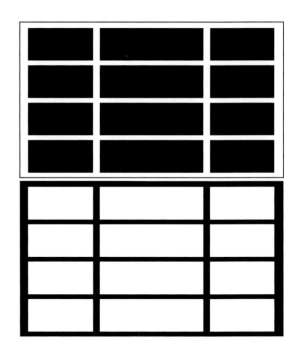

FIGURE 4.19　This pattern gives the illusion of grayness at the intersections of black and white bands.

the insert color, and then search for the second ground color.)

If one color can be influenced by the surrounding colors to look like two, then it's possible to impact two colors in the opposite manner to make them look more like each other—what Albers calls "subtraction of color." In Figure 4.21, circles are placed on backgrounds selected to make them look similar, even though they are two different colors. The illusion is made by first determining the differences in the inserted circles. If the difference is one of value, then the ground colors must have a greater difference in value. If the two colors are different in hue, then the grounds will require hues of different temperature or complement. If they vary in levels of saturation, the ground colors selected should be adjusted inversely. The more different the two initial colors, the stronger the background differences must be to exert sufficient influence over them.

Transparent Color

Another fascinating color illusion is that of implied transparency where opaque materials are

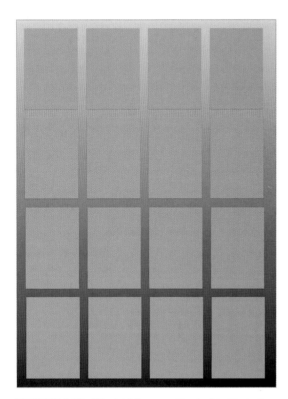

FIGURE 4.18　The initial assumption in this illustration is that the top rectangles are darker. Look again.

FIGURE 4.20 The circles in this diagram are the same color, but appear as different colors because of influence from background colors. (See Figure 4.23 for the proof of this illusion.)

used. After working with color firsthand, it's often possible to imagine what color might result from the mixture of two visible colors. If you could create this color effectively and then position it relative to the two original colors so that they appear to overlap, the mixed color will begin to read as if it's transparent. One of the original colors would look as if it's simply registering through the other. In the example in Figure 4.22, the circles on the left appear to overlap due to the selection of the particular violet where they collide. In truth, the circles on the right are truly overlapping using a 10 percent transparency of the upper (blue) circle. The illusion comes from our tendency to make assumptions about what the eyes really see.

The assumption often made with this illusion is that simply finding colors that would logically be mixed from two others—for example, yellow and red to make orange—can create the illusion of transparency. Effective solutions are more

Josef Albers

Bauhaus student and educator Josef Albers (1888–1976) was perhaps most well known for his ability to demonstrate effects of influence. His work, developed in paint and glass mediums, frequently involved abstract geometric forms. In the way that magicians use their knowledge of perception to convince audiences they have witnessed something other than reality, Albers used his knowledge of human color response to fool the viewer's perception and create color illusions. In 1933 when the Bauhaus closed, Albers immigrated to the United States. He initially taught at Black Mountain College in North Carolina, then at Yale University in Connecticut from 1950 to 1960, offering one of the first courses in color theory taught in the United States.

FIGURE 4.21   The two rows of circles in this illustration look very similar, but are quite different when seen on the same background. (For the proof of this illusion, refer to Figure 4.23.)

discriminating than that. There is a specific orange that is a believable mix between a given red and a specified yellow, which may or may not be a true pigmentary mix at all. Opaque colors are rarely equal in value or saturation, and disparity of these

two characteristics must be taken into account. To make this illusion more effective, the form of the color is often manipulated to give the appearance of an overlap, such as two strong geometries with an intersecting one, or one form that transitions

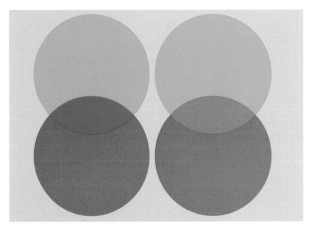

FIGURE 4.22   The purple color may look like the blue overlapping the red, but it's actually a mixed color. The circles on the right show a true transparency overlap.

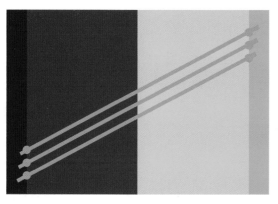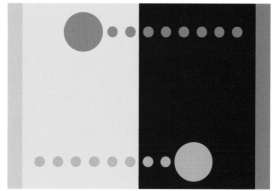

FIGURE 4.23 In this illustration, the compositions from Figures 4.20 and 4.21 are modified to show their true color relationships.

into another. When the area of one color is much larger than the area of the other two colors, the effect is more dramatic.

Conditions of contrast, harmony, and influence are the tools we have to manage colors used in combination. They can be applied to either two-dimensional or three-dimensional applications. Each choice is a means for creating an overall impression.

However, specific hues or hue combinations may have symbolic associations that are independent of their context within a design palette. Before we explore color and form integration in strictly three-dimensional terms, it may be worthwhile to look at cultural preconceptions we hold about colors of hue. Chapter 5, "Color Identity," is a walk through those associations.

5

Color Identity

Few would disagree with the notion that our response to color is subjective. It's because of this subjective aspect that we sometimes assume responses are therefore unpredictable. Not so. Our reaction to each individual color is the result of things that can be controlled, such as contrast and placement, saturation and value, or emphasis through proportion. It's also determined by responses we do not control but can anticipate, such as basic physiological response or association through long-standing tradition—the distinction between color psychology and color symbolism, where symbols serve as icons, thus establishing identity.

Strong color associations are sometimes consistent with color psychology, but they are not one and the same. Each basic color family provides its own unique impression when individual colors are viewed in isolation. Some emotional associations prevail when experiencing each color. Other connections are more subtle or are randomly experienced. These connections may be overtly inherent in the context of an overall three-dimensional color scheme or minimized through additional contrasts. The color of independent objects, however, frequently impacts the observer through these associations. Our most common uses form a collective symbology that is recognizable to a majority of the population.

This chapter is intended as a concise reference of the most prevalent color associations within North American culture—those we have learned through social interaction and those that are inherent in the nature of humanity. Responses that cannot be controlled through design are the result of associations that seem involuntary to the mind of the viewer. Each basic color family provides its own unique impression when individual colors are viewed in isolation, and certain emotional associations prevail when experiencing each color. These connections may be inherent in the context of an overall three-dimensional interior color scheme or minimized through contrast, but the color of independent objects frequently impacts the observer in ways that cannot be ignored. Our most consistent associations give us a cultural color context that is reliably recognized by a majority of the population.

CHARACTERISTICS OF HUE

Each hue family exhibits characteristics that differ from other hue families. Within each hue family, strong associations with specific hues of light or dark tendency also exist. If we compare saturated colors to each other in terms of strong associations, we find the following special qualities.

▶ Red

The color with the longest wavelength and shortest frequency of visible color is red. (See Figure 5.1.) This places it next to infrared on the scale of

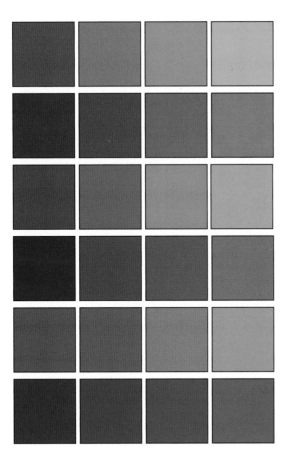

FIGURE 5.1   The red range includes tints of pink and shades of burgundy.

electromagnetic wavelength, which actually produces heat.

Red is often considered the most dominant hue, due in part to its ability to stimulate. In the right context, it vigorously grabs the observer's attention and can overpower the other hues. It has the ability to stimulate us into action, which may include emotional acts of aggression, courage, excitement, passion, hatred, and sometimes rage. Red is believed to sensitize the taste buds and sense of smell, increasing the appetite. It is warm, even hot, and in full intensities can exhibit a fierceness not experienced in other hues. All this occurs because the heart rate instinctively quickens, which causes a release of adrenaline into the bloodstream, raising blood pressure and stimulating the nerves. Some theorists, such as Faber Birren, have suggested that this is a physiological reaction to the color red, while others suggest that controlled tests tell us otherwise. Those in the second camp propose that it is a learned response due to common associations of our society. Whether the response is due to genetics or learned behavior, this color offers an ability to incite the viewer beyond what is expected from other colors of hue.

Social and Political Usage

The color red is often associated with a show of strength or intense activity. It has been used as the color of uniforms and flags for revolutionaries and has come to suggest the radical when used as a political reference. Red bandanas are worn when running with the bulls, and red attire is traditional when performing the flamenco. It's also a symbol of blood and the heart, which has resulted in the use of a red cross as a symbol of medical-aid.

Red is associated with fire and with danger, as evidenced by the contemporary use of red to identify fire safety apparatus. And it's the symbol of love, particularly when Valentine's Day approaches. In full saturation, red is sometimes considered a masculine color; but in reduced intensities of light value (pinks) it is considered distinctly feminine and delicate, lacking the forceful energy normally associated with red. The strength of red is used to establish the significance of an event. Red carpets have been used in recent years as a device to cater to executives who travel and as runways for weddings and promenades. Red is recommended in situations where the goal is to give its viewers energy and motivate them during physical activities. Statistically, red cars are involved in more accidents than any other color of car. Since red is also recognized as a sign of danger or warning in most countries of the world, it can be used for identification.

Reds are considered relaxing when used on large environmental surfaces in pale shades, such as conch-shell pink. (Owens-Corning used this to their advantage by trademarking pink as a comfort color for their insulation. No other manufacturers can market similar products in this color.) Some researchers also believe that pink can encourage one to fantasize, and most believe in the power of pink to generate a physiological response. When pink is in sight, the brain secretes a chemical (nor-epinephrine) that inhibits the production of epinephrine, the chemical that enables one to generate anger. In a predominantly pink room, the body is unable to generate a state of anger. This relaxed state lasts a short period of time—say 15 to 30 minutes. Some colorists believe that in the moments following a pink experience, a person may become even more agitated. For example, Dr. Kenneth Fehrman, an interior designer doing research in color psychology, describes studies with animals that show dramatic aftereffects of a pink environment, such as destruction and cannibalism. In the book he coauthored, *Color: The Secret Influence* (page 78), he points to this as an example of the potential physical impact of color.

Despite the temporary effect, attempts have been made to take advantage of this reaction, including application of pink in the visitor locker rooms at major sports events, as an experiment in weight-lifting areas, and for inmate behavioral management in prison. (See also Morton Walker, *The Power of Color,* page 43.)

▶ Orange

Working from longest to shortest wavelength, orange is the next visible color. (See Figure 5.2.) Orange shares some characteristics with red and holds others in common with yellow. Like red, orange in full saturation is a stimulating color, exciting and somewhat cheerful, warm and inviting, almost luminous. It also increases the appetite. This is the color of emotion, expression, and warmth. It inspires lively, energetic behavior in the viewer, but instead of anger, the energy is characteristically jovial and results in verbal expression rather than physical. One explanation is that orange raises the pulse rate but not the blood pressure. In fact, some analysts believe it actually slows the rate of blood flow. Because of its glowing strength, orange can seem intrusive in some situations.

Social and Political Usage

Orange is intuitively associated with fire and sunlight, particularly at sunset. It is considered a friendly color in that it appeals to a large portion of the population. It is particularly popular in autumn, especially on the Halloween and Thanksgiving holidays.

The use of orange in the United States suggests affordability and informality. It is rarely seen in full saturation in expensive hotels or restaurants. It is more often used in establishments designed to

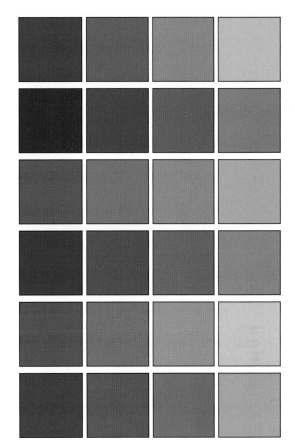

FIGURE 5.2 The orange family includes familiar forms in full saturation as well as spice tones. In three-dimensional space, orange is often used in its desaturated forms (the spice tones) for its warmth without overstimulation.

attract the majority of the population, such as inexpensive hotels, pancake houses, and retailers of do-it-yourself construction products. In full saturation, it's used for life rafts and vests because of its high visibility. As a pastel, orange enhances many skin tones when it's reflected on the skin. This occurs because medium to light complexions usually have either a pink (light red) or yellow undertone. Orange, of course, is a mixture of these.

▶ Yellow

Yellow is the lightest in value of the six primary and secondary hues. In fact, in darker values it is not recognizable as a yellow but appears to have a green tinge to it. It is the first color we recognize visually in terms of speed of response. And it holds its character in reduced saturation. (See Figure 5.3.)

Yellow maintains a reputation as the happy hue. It is an inspiring color, considered to be warm and joyful, radiant, cheerful, and approachable, generating a positive impact on its witness. People identify yellow as the color representing hope, wisdom, optimism, spiritual enlightenment, and mental well-being. It is a color of intellect and clarity. Yellow is also an attention-getting color. At best, it is inspiring; however, at its full intensity in the wrong context it can appear egocentric and glaring. In large amounts, yellow causes anxiety in people regardless of the saturation levels used. According to Carlton Wagner in *The Language of Color,* yellow rooms more than any other hue can cause tempers to flare, children to cry, and senior citizens to lose control of muscular movement, sometimes causing them to tremble. Yellow is also believed to

increase the incidence of allergy symptoms. This is not to suggest that a yellow room will automatically trigger such reactions. However, the added stimulation may be just enough to release the reaction if other conditions are contributing to the possibility. Color therapists also credit yellow for activating motor nerves and stimulating flow of bile, which may explain some of the observed responses.

Social and Political Usage

The strongest association to yellow is, of course, the sun and, by extension, sunlight. As a golden tone it connotes gold, wealth, and prosperity. Gold is also a sign of honor and loyalty. Yellow is usually associated with temporary or transitional concerns, such as the gold jacket of a successful real estate sales person, the yellow school bus, or the buds on flowers. It can also be festive when used for party decorations or to color Easter eggs.

Yellow is used verbally to suggest cowardice. The *yellow press* has been used to describe sensationalist newspapers. It is used successfully with black as a sign of caution—at the edge of the train platform, for example—and for some retailers, such as automobile rental agencies. One appropriate and highly recognizable use of yellow is seen in the famous golden arches of a certain fast-food establishment. A common use of yellow in the environment is in rooms intended to inspire. Yellow can make a room appear sunny even on a dark day. In spaces for senior citizens, yellow is less frequently used due to the tendency for older eyes to read colors with a yellow overcast. In these applications or in large areas, yellow is sometimes neutralized (e.g., using an ocher wall color). One's complexion may appear sallow if a light source is too yellow or if yellow is reflected from a large surface onto the skin, particularly if the hue leans toward green. This makes yellow unpopular in salons.

▶ Green

Green is believed to be the most relaxing hue to the eye. (See Figure 5.4.) It falls directly on the focal point, it does not advance or recede, but is in full focus exactly at the retina. It takes little physical effort to observe and focus on a field of green.

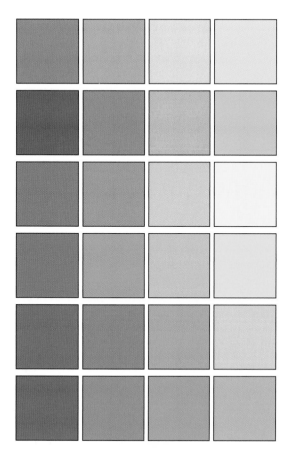

FIGURE 5.3 In this collection of yellows, notice how dark yellow leans toward green.

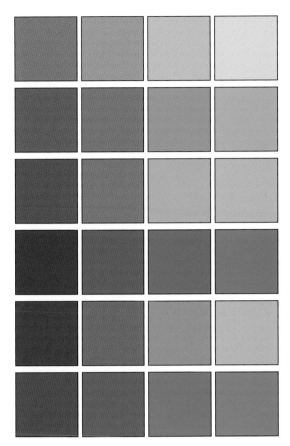

FIGURE 5.4 In a full range of greens, temperature shifts become more apparent than other colors of hue. In light values, warm green is often interpreted as yellow.

Reactions to the color green include tranquility, peace, quiet, relaxation, and even retirement. It can enforce a sense of balance and stability. It is refreshing and natural, suggestive of nature, growth, and a general sense of hope. Its appearance in nature signifies the coming of spring and life itself. Green is also a cool color, often associated with water or humidity, particularly in clear shades. Such attributes make it a color usually identified with emotional balance. Many believe that the presence of green has a positive physical effect on the body and may reduce allergic responses and negative reactions to food.

Social and Political Usage

In language, *green* represents envy and jealousy, followed by guilt. In politics, it is also associated with Irish culture, the Catholic majority of Ireland, the Irish Patriots, and Saint Patrick's Day. Being the color of foliage, green is synonymous with nature and good health. Most natural foods, health foods, and environmentally safe products are wrapped in green to make the point. By extension, green has come to symbolize fertility in Europe. In the United States, rustics from the country came to be known as *greenhorns,* and green has a strong association with money.

In environmental applications, green is used differently according to the type of space. In commercial space, light green is considered trite because of its frequent use in schools and institutions. Earlier in this century, the availability of green as an inexpensive pigment made it desirable for large surface areas to the point of overuse. In hospitality and residential applications, green is traditionally suggested as a welcoming color. It is often used for entry spaces and as a main color in rooms for people who have relocated. The backstage room where actors sit before and after a performance is known as the *greenroom.* In addition to its welcome factor, the color was chosen in an effort to give actors relief from the glare of stage lighting. The guidelines of fashion suggest that green is not a good color for business since it is not readily accepted by all—although it is considered a friendly color. Yellow-green is unattractive when reflected on the skin since it tends to make some skin tones sallow.

▶ Blue

The sight of the color blue causes the body to release tranquilizing hormones when it is surveyed, particularly a strong sky blue. (See Figure 5.5 for a full range.) This soothing effect is recognizable to anyone who has cast his or her eyes upon a large body of water or the open sky. *Cardiac blue* is often used in reference to this shade due to its use in hospital cardiac units to calm patients.

The most soothing of responsive behaviors are normally seen with blue. These include comfort, calmness, coolness, peace and tranquility, and spirituality. In the extreme it suggests quiet passivity and thoughtfulness. Many believe that it can lower blood pressure, slow the pulse rate, or decrease body temperature. On food it's believed to reduce the appetite. The connection of blue with water suggests wetness or cleanliness. The familiarity of

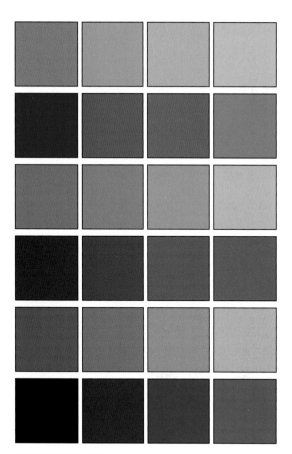

FIGURE 5.5 This image shows a range of value and saturation in blue hues.

blue can also bring on the sensations of security, orderliness, reliability, contemplation, solitude, and possibly isolation. In some tones and circumstances blue can be frighteningly sad, depressing, lonely, or cold. Its subduing effect can be experienced as melancholy or gloominess. In some cases it offers a sense of piety as well as trust.

Social and Political Usage

Blue is often discovered to be a good compromising color because so few people dislike it. It is used in terms of dignity such as *blue ribbons* in a competition or *blue blood* to describe someone who is well bred. The term *bluestocking* in the early twentieth century described a well-read, learned woman. And *blue chip* is considered to be of high quality or value. Alternatively, *feeling blue* describes a distinct

sadness. The *blues* describe music that offers relief for listeners who may be down on their luck. The *Blue Period* of Picasso's career signifies a time of great personal sadness when blue pigments dominated the artist's palette.

Light blue is a color that can also inspire fantasies. Its tranquilizing effect may be useful as an emergency waiting-room color, but it is not a good color for the exterior color of a home that is for sale—statistically speaking, blue houses don't sell well. The most popular color of blue seems to be the synthetic dye indigo commonly used in blue denim. Dark blue or navy is considered a very versatile neutral. It flatters everyone's skin tones and consequently is a common color for uniforms. (In many countries, it's the color of police uniforms.) In clothing it conveys authority and power, commanding respect.

▶ Violet

That visible color which has the shortest wavelength and highest rate of energy (frequency) is purple, or violet. (See Figure 5.6.) This is the color that borders on UV light and, subsequently, x-rays in the scale of electromagnetic energy.

Violet is a unique color. Often, color experts describe purple as a complex color in an effort to encompass its many meanings. It offers a depth of feeling not apparent in colors previously discussed, but is the direct result of the mix between stimulating red and calming blue. It is an exclusive color, regal and dignified, suggestive of royalty, nobility, or rank. It can appear magical, mystical, or nostalgic to many—pompous to some. In darker shades it can be lonely, melancholy, and mournful like the blues, even depressing, but in lighter shades it is highly spiritual, soft, and atmospheric. There is sensitivity in purple: it can be sensual or depressing, ostentatious or gloomy.

Social and Political Usage

In ancient times purple dye was expensive to produce, making it a symbol of wealth to the wearer. It is a color symbolic of the ecclesiastics, purple being the color historically worn by priests. In contemporary times it is considered nostalgic in light-

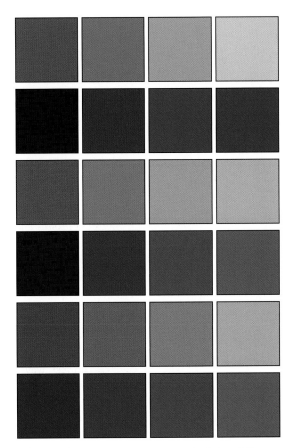

FIGURE 5.6 Because it is inherently dark at full saturation, violet can hold its hue while spanning a full range of light to dark values.

value tints and is associated with the Christian Easter season. Given its chameleonlike character, purple is not often used rhetorically, with one exception: the term *shrinking violet,* used to identify a person of low self-esteem.

Purple robes are still used for sacred activities, not just within organized religion. It is a color that works well in most wardrobes, but is particularly flattering to olive or deep brown skin tones since it's a complementary color to the yellow in the skin. In three-dimensional design, pale purple (lilac or light violet) is rarely used due to the conflict of violet's natural hue state as a dark color with the paleness of the color in view. In its fully saturated state, it is rarely seen as a room color, partly due to limitations of popularity and partly to its limitations in light reflectance.

CHARACTERISTICS OF NEUTRALS

We depend on neutral colors (colors with little or no chroma) in an ongoing way for their timeless character. In many areas of design they're considered classic colors. The implication is that emotional responses to neutral colors are less distinct or less consistent than their chromatic counterparts. However, the number of recorded associations in literary sources suggests just the opposite. Here are some of those findings.

▶ White

In light, white is the combination of all colors. In pigment, white is the absence of any hue and the lightest of all values. White is often used as the context for evaluating all other colors, but it has its greatest impact when surrounding another color. The image of white suggests cleanliness, goodness, and purity. Our heroes are *white knights* or cowboys with *white hats.* It is a truly spiritual color, full of zest and light in weight. It represents hope, innocence, and youth. In nature, it is associated with fallen snow.

Social and Political Usage

White has many symbolic connections. The *white flag* is a universal sign of submission, especially in war. The white dove represents peace. In some situations, white can suggest formality. White is the color of police uniforms in the Bahamas and worn by tennis players worldwide. In Asia, it is a color of mourning, but in the United States it's the color of Christian brides' dresses, and children taking their first communion are often attired in white. The residence of the president is referred to as the *White House.* In language, the use of white seems to defy its logical associations. A *white lie* is used to describe an indiscretion of innocence. A *white elephant* is a burdensome possession—one that cannot be given away.

White surfaces reflect the most light, enabling clear vision. Consequently, the eye is sensitive to tiny differences in whiteness when two materials are juxtaposed, making standards of whiteness important to control. This is evident in work with paper and textiles. No fiber is naturally pure white—most must be bleached. Since bleaching is a decomposing process, the trick is to take out all nonwhite color without damaging fiber.

White is by far the best-selling paint color in its many versions. In artificial environments, white is associated with cleanliness, as in medical applications or commercial kitchens. People become stressed when bored, and an overabundance of white can generate this state, so it's often used in space that people will move through but not linger in. Tinted whites are recommended when white is used as a wall color, since white offers a significant amount of light reflection, which causes the eye to constrict. White floors are rarely used, except for dramatic emphasis, as in a showroom, or in private residences, where less maintenance may be required.

Gray

The most neutral of all color is gray. It initially appears to have no definition and often takes on characteristics of one or more adjacent colors. Gray causes no afterimage, making it the simplest color for the eye to process. Gray is conservative, quiet, peaceful, and calm. Its value in design is its reliability and sense of respite. In its calmness, the color can also be passive to a point of lifelessness, tedious to a point of dreariness. Gray is often affiliated with the concept of old age. Issues of locality should be considered with the color gray. In areas prone to rainy seasons, gray may be considered an undesirable color.

Social and Political Usage

In language, *shades of gray* suggests a lack of distinction, something that is neither black nor white. The most common gray in politics is that of military vehicles, known as *battleship gray*. Clouds and shadows are presumed to be gray. Gray as a description of buildings implies concrete. To many city dwellers, this is the color of business and industry. It suggests intelligence, but not the strength of its darker cousin, black. In dark shades, gray shares some of the effects of black. For example, it can imply sadness or mourning, or it can signify power and authority.

It's generally believed that designers and artists are more creative in a gray environment than in any other. The assumption is that a creative person will feel compelled to fill the void it creates. In a practical sense, its neutrality easily permits distinction of all other colors. From a maintenance standpoint, gray helps to hide gathering particles. One architecture team developed a shade of gray believed to be the exact color of dust, dubbing it "dust gray," for use on exposed ductwork and equipment where routine dusting is unlikely to occur.

Brown

Any warm neutral color that falls somewhere between a full neutral and red to yellow-orange can be described as brown. The ground, soil, tree bark, and other forms of wood, canyons, and mountains are some of the many images in nature associated with the color brown. Because of this, brown offers a feeling of comfort, sincerity, and casualness not experienced in the presence of other colors. Brown is melancholy to some, but is believed by others to dispel mental depression and promote the synthesis of serotonin. It is a color rarely selected as a first choice in color preference tests. In fact, the most often rejected colors are the yellow-browns.

Social and Political Usage

Brown is known as the quintessential earth tone and often appears in color combinations during times of renewed focus on the environment. It is the color of many desirable objects, such as wood, coffee, and chocolate. As the earthiest of earth tones, it is often used to sell wholesome foods, such as brown rice or bread.

Given its natural association with familiar materials that make us comfortable, it's considered a friendly color. Brown is often used in various tones in hotels to make people feel relaxed and invited. It is not festive, however, so it is not effective in spaces intended to stimulate. Brown is recommended as a clothing color for people who gather information through interviews since it is informal and inviting. According to psychologist Carlton Wagner (*The Language of Color*), the wearer may be more liked in a job interview and may be told more in an informational interview. In fashion, this color is often recommended to people with warm skin tones, particularly brunettes; however, value contrast with the skin tone is needed. It continues to be a popular choice for leather goods despite our ability to produce leather in a wide range of hues. As a room color, brown appears heavy and consequently makes ceilings seem overwhelming, but establishes firmness and stability in a floor.

▶ Black

Black is considered the absence of light, as an additive color, and the darkest of all subtractive colors. Reactions to black are consistent and often negative. It has connotations of evil, darkness, night, and death. It is ominous and mysterious. Fear of the unknown is often accompanied by black imagery. Culturally, black has become synonymous with sorrow, grief, and, in North America, the end of life. It is symbolic of emptiness and spatial voids. It implies weight and solidity. Alternatively, black can suggest richness, dignity, elegance, and power. In metropolitan centers, it is considered quite stylish.

Social and Political Usage

Many associations of language incorporate the color black: *black list, black market, black sheep,* and those occasions of socioeconomic drama known as *Black Monday* or *Black Friday.* In the United States, superstition suggests that black cats are bad luck—just the opposite of European culture. Black and red in combination with each other are considered very strong colors, often to the point of dislike, but black and gold together can be a sign of luxury and sophistication.

There is the spatial concern for black. The *black hole* is that void where all things disappear into eternity. Any object covered in black will be perceived as heavier than if it were another color, making it impractical for objects that suggest lightness. For example, balloons are not colored black except to signify an over-the-hill birthday; neither are airplanes or moving boxes.

Black is reserved for formal occasions, including funerals in North America. It's a color of humility for traditional religions and has been worn by priests, monks, and nuns in many parts of the world, as well as by women in some Middle East countries. In general, it's more appealing to members of higher socioeconomic status. It is used as a power color for cars and business suits, hence the expression *power suit.* Black is overwhelming as a full wall color due to its visual weight. On a practical note, textural distinctions are more apparent in black than any other color because it absorbs all light waves. A coarse or matte black surface reflects very little light, but a glossy one can be highly reflective due to finish alone. This variation accounts for significant variations between blacks of differing material.

■ ASSOCIATIVE RESPONSE

In a practical sense, some reactions to color, primarily the unconscious ones, are universal to most people. In three-dimensional design, examples include the stimulation of warm spaces or the subdued feeling that comes from a lack of stimulation, such as in a dull, gray room. Use of color for behavior modification is apparent in many public spaces. Some combinations of color are intended to subdue or even intimidate a group of people. Other colors are chosen for their effects on the occupants' mood. Color is believed to impact our perception of room temperature, time, weight, and scale and to intensify other human sensations. Let's look at some examples.

▶ Temperature

It has long been believed that color temperature has a direct effect on the human body, that our visual and physiological processes are activated by warm colors and retarded by cool. Circulation is physically increased in response to warm-colored environments and subdued in cool-colored ones, causing people to feel physically different in rooms of the same ambient temperature. This reaction varies somewhat with age and condition of overall health of each individual. It is also measurably different in men and women—as room temperature is raised gradually, a man will complain 5 degrees before a woman. In the *Elements of Color,* Johannes Itten tells of an experiment in which two rooms of consistent form were painted red-orange and blue-green, respectively. In the blue-green room, the occupants felt that a temperature of 59 degrees was too cold. When the same occupants used the red-orange room, they were comfortable until the temperature was reduced to between 52 and 54 degrees. The conclusion is that this is the result of color temperature having its effect on us—blue-green slowing down the circulation and red-orange stimulating it.

Others who explore color response, such as Dr. Kenneth Fehrman and Cherie Fehrman, suggest color temperature response is more of a learned reaction caused by associations with certain colors than a physiological one. They believe that in some cases our acquired reactions to certain colors have existed long enough to automatically trigger a learned response, temperature being among them. Psychologist Carlton Wagner's findings were consistent with this conclusion. He suggests that strong associations play into our response to color, making the colors of a flame feel warm to us when we see them and making the starkness of achromatic white feel cool by association with snow. Regardless of whether temperature response is learned or felt, our responses in terms of environmental color are consistent and therefore reliable from a design standpoint.

▶ Time

Many tests have also been done to demonstrate a correlation between perception of time and colors of hue. The results have been dramatic, but not necessarily consistent. Most color analysts believe that differences in hue influence one's perception of time. Many, but not all, analysts, and most color psychologists, including Deborah Sharpe and Carlton Wagner, assert that we lose track of time and it therefore passes more quickly in warm-colored rooms, particularly red. Time is alleged to pass more slowly in blue rooms. In terms of saturation levels, the popular consensus is that time also passes more quickly in a brightly colored space than one of subtle coloration. This may account for the abundance of fully saturated red used in casinos and drinking establishments in recent generations.

Less recognized are the factors beyond hue that also impact our perception of time. An environment with some stimulation will hold one's interest longer than one without, unless it reaches the state of overstimulation. Once we are overstimulated, time passes slowly again as we look for the opportunity to leave. If the environment includes too many contrasts and if the majority of colors have strong saturation levels, an occupant can easily become tired from overstimulation, affecting the perception of time spent in the room. In the absence of contrast or any chromatic interest, we are equally motivated to leave since the space ceases to hold our interest—we're simply bored. The appeal of a design will also influence the perception of time spent in a space. An undesirable color combination will cause some discomfort, making time pass more slowly. If a room is generally pleasing to occupants, they are more likely to stay longer, although the same occupants may not tolerate a long waiting period in an unattractive room. Lack of acceptance in the latter case again makes time pass slowly. Comparatively speaking, rooms of high contrast, particularly dynamic contrasts, will be comfortable for shorter periods of time than their less stimulating counterparts. Often, a public space that depends on high customer turnover will rely on a high contrast of value or contrast of hue. Such a level of stimulation is pleasing to the patron for the short term, but he or she will not feel relaxed enough to linger. These factors suggest that color temperature alone is not enough of a factor to hold an audience for a long period of time.

▶ Weight and Scale

Value of a color can affect the apparent weight of the surface it's applied to. In the case of objects, darker colors appear physically heavier and paler colors appear lighter, or less dense. Bright colors are popular for handheld weights, and moving companies use tan or white boxes rather than dark gray for this reason. Color also changes our perception of scale. Dark color on objects makes them seem smaller or thinner—hence the popularity of the black dress and black suit.

In a room, dark colors make a wall or ceiling appear to be more dense, giving a sense of solidity and weight. A thin freestanding wall painted navy blue will have more visual weight than one in a lighter color. The brick wall that is painted white will have a perception of lightness that negates its true nature. Traditionally, designers have used darker colors on the floor to "hold them down" and lighter ones on the ceiling to make them seem higher. However, many successful spaces have been developed that break these traditions. In a room with a very high ceiling, a darker ceiling color can give the sensation of lower height, and indirect, nonuniform lighting will reduce the scale further.

▶ Synesthesia

Scientists have long been aware of a natural connection between response to color and the five senses. As the brain is stimulated by color, the senses are also stimulated. For example, Gestalt psychologists note that the eye becomes more sensitive to green and less so to red in the presence of loud noise and strong odor. Brightness and loudness are associated with warm colors, while cool colors reduce our sensitivity to these conditions. This type of association is known as *synesthesia,* which means a unity of the senses.

Sound

From his research into synesthesia (*Color Psychology and Color Therapy,* page 147), Faber Birren uncovered several scientists whose experiments confirmed its existence. He noted that in 1931, Karl Zietz exposed the eye briefly to color samples while sounding tones of varying pitch. The conclusion was that sounds of high pitch tend to shift the appearance of the color toward a lighter hue, while the occurrence of a low pitch shifted the same color toward a darker hue. During the experiment, red appeared more bluish to the viewer during low-pitched sounds and more yellowish or orange in cast during high-pitched sounds. Yellow became more brown or reddish when the person was exposed to low-pitched sounds and turned pale during high ones. In these same experiments, Zietz resolved that high-pitched sounds also sharpened the contours of afterimages, while low pitches tended to blur them.

The presence of sound in general has a distinct influence on color perception. When the ears receive constant vibration, the eyes are less able to accurately perceive colors of long wavelength. Generally speaking, the cones are more sensitive to green, and to a lesser degree blue, during sound, and less sensitive to warm colors, especially red.

Temperature-neutral colors such as yellow-green are unaffected by significant sound. The presence of some colors can also influence the perception of the sounds heard. Yellow will support high-pitched sounds, while olive green will tend to suppress them. To draw attention to the muffled sounds in an environment, dark colors should be used. Muffled sounds in a light-colored room become less distracting. Music has characteristics that are akin to those of color, leading to the occasional use of color analogies as a communication device among musicians. Fast music is normally associated with the intensity of red and slow music with blue. High notes are considered light in color and low notes dark. Many artists have used music to describe color. The artist Wassily Kandinsky often used musical analogies to describe his work—blue like a flute, dark blue a cello, and deeper blue a contrabass. Others use the word *noisy* to describe a color combination of harsh contrast and the word *quiet* to describe neutral, achromatic qualities.

Smell

The sense of smell is also affected by the presence of color and vice versa. Frank and Rudolf Mahnke

---

Frank Mahnke

One of the most articulate color practitioners of this day is Frank Mahnke (American, born 1947). He is an internationally recognized color consultant who has performed a significant amount of research on issues of color, the impact of artificial light, and conditions of human physiological response. He shares his results on the application of environmental color and artificial light through public speaking and written publications. Mr. Mahnke's rationalizations of lighting and its effect on color, as well as his explanations of the psychological aspects of spatial color applications, offer sound instruction to practicing environmental designers, architects, and interior designers. His professional affiliations include the International Association of Color Consultants (IACC), and the American Information Center for Color and Environment.

offer some useful findings in their conclusions on the use of color in industry (*Color and Light*, page 109). They note that sweet smells are enhanced by the presence of the color red, even in its light form, pink. But the effects of sweet smells are reduced in an environment of green or blue. Other researchers suggest that orange supports peppery, spicy scents and that perfume is enhanced by violet or lilac. By adjusting the color of an object with a scent, one can modify how it will be received. (For additional examples of this condition, refer to the discussion on industrial spaces in Chapter 14, "Commercial Applications.")

▶ CONCLUSIONS

The color associations described here are presented in an abstract sense. However, in three-dimensional work, we know that color effects are never absolute but are relative to the total situation. Each individual color has some associations that make it more or less appropriate for specific applications. Since color is considered most beneficial when the user finds it appealing, creating an object or space that will elicit a positive response has just as much to do with context as it does with individual hue characteristics. We can use knowledge about strong color associations to add a hint of something to an overall design without letting public expectations dictate full color solutions. The overall combination of colors, their relative proportions, the available contrasts, and the association of the colors with their form together establish impact and elicit the response from a user.

Associative data concerning human response to colors of hue are useful in establishing the comparative differences between them. While some reports do conflict, collective wisdom suggests some reliable insights. For instance, there exists a general consensus that red is comparatively stimulating and blue calming. The key word here is **comparative**—compared to each other, red is more stimulating to most people than blue. In this section, the characteristics that distinguish one hue from another were summarized as a comparison between equally saturated hues. To be clear, colors of full hue collectively elicit responses that are characteristic and distinct from colors of reduced saturation. They are almost always more stimulating than their neutralized counterparts. For exam-

ple, a fully saturated red may be stimulating and raise the heart rate and blood pressure, while a moderately saturated blue or green will pacify—comparatively speaking. Part of the effect depends on the fact that **colors of reduced saturation are more calming than those of full hue.** This means that a red of reduced saturation, such as pink, mauve, or mahogany, will be more calming than a fully saturated green. A true blue is more stimulating than an orange of reduced saturation, such as a spice tone or apricot.

The number of hues present will also impact perception. Generally speaking, **multiple hues in an environment increase arousal.** This initial stimulation will be maintained over time by nonsequential variations in hue and value. A blue-green space will never seem calming if the color composition includes several shades of intense cool hues and a range of value greater than 1 to 6 (white to black being 1 to 10). To put hue comparison information in its proper context, let's keep in mind that three major color conditions combine to impact human response as active or passive. In order of greatest impact to least they are as follows:

1. The amount of contrast in a color combination, where greater contrasts offer more stimulus
2. The level of hue saturation (degree of chroma), in that higher saturation spurs more active response
3. The particular hue used, with warmer hues offering more motivation to react

Another key point on this subject is that associative color information is useful in limited forms. The inferences made by particular hues or neutrals are reduced as variations are made in saturation, hue character, and value and as other colors are added in close proximity. No color should be eliminated from the designer's palette because of a potential association. The goal is to use available information to make the most effective solutions based on the overall goals and design concept of a project while managing proportions of each color to rule out any undesirable associations. Identification of a compromising association simply suggests that adjustments in color characteristic or the inclusion of additional colors are appropriate.

Color variety is psychologically beneficial for the greatest number of people, since it offers a variety of stimuli—calming or motivating, contemplative or mobilizing. Knowledge about each color's attributes may enable specific decisions for specific purposes, particularly in the case of marketable objects. But generally speaking, **our needs are best met by the combination of all colors in the visible spectrum.** Nature provides us the ability to see a full range of color. To deny access to any portion of that spectrum will reduce our visual experience. Instead, color research is recommended as a supplement to design experience. While an understanding of public association with a particular hue or neutral may suggest some appropriate uses, the most creative design solutions are often generated by unconventional use of color. Even respect for a color's historical context does not necessarily imply limitations in design use except in the case of regulated restorations and renovations.

Finally, the issue of color and public perception has some bearing on full-range coloration.

Given the individual associations and preferences of each person who uses a public space, the question often raised is whether colors of hue should be avoided to eliminate the potential for negative connotations. After all, the more people who will be using the space, the greater the opportunity for individual negative associations. More recent advice by colorists suggests that a mix of colors serves to reduce the possibilities of negative individual associations with any specific color while providing a spectral range more natural to human perception. This is frequently suggested as a healthy approach, since there are very few places in nature that are devoid of contrasting coloration. Yet the colorful environments of nature are considered most desirable for the majority of people. Such colors make sense to us within certain environmental contexts. In the next group of chapters, color assignments will be explored relative to successful human-constructed environments.

PART 2

Three-Dimensional Perception

Color Response

Color psychology is one of the most fascinating aspects of color work and probably the most challenging, since individual colors of hue are rarely seen in isolation. We respond to color in its context, meaning that our impression of space is based on the colors we see in combination with each other. Response to color is somewhat subjective, but our ability to anticipate that response improves based on our experience and our access to reliable data we find outside our own profession.

I wish I could spell out statistical evidence to support many of the conclusions about color psychology we tend to hold up as truths. Unfortunately, that's not where we are in the evolution of the field. While some rigorous scientific research has been done, much of what we have is anecdotal information accumulated over a period of about 50 years. Our collective wisdom is based on a combination of the two. During the 1950s and 1960s, Faber Birren was one of the few who accumulated data relative to color and evaluated its potential in design practice. In more recent years, several professionals have bravely offered their own conclusions relative to color in spatial application. They include psychologists Deborah T. Sharpe, Carlton Wagner, and Angela Wright, environmental designer Frank Mahnke, and writers Dr. Morton Walker, Dr. Kenneth R. Fehrman, and Cherie Fehrman. Some of their respective findings are mutually consistent, some are singularly unique, and others actually conflict. This means that in order to make good use of

their contributions in the context of design, we still need to exercise our own judgment.

The best information we have at this time is a summary of provisional facts derived from what many color specialists have been willing to put down on paper. Each aspect of color response is arguable, but the fact that they are debatable doesn't invalidate them. When such findings are consistent with our own experience we use the information to support our thesis. When they are inconsistent with experience, we hold out for collaborating evidence, like skeptics in the wake of a new paradigm. We must decide which new conclusions are reasonable, based on our own observations of people's response to space and its associated color characteristics, before we can apply those conclusions in practice. Some aspects of color response have already been noted in Chapter 5. In this chapter, we consider the conditions that influence people's reactions to color, the likely options that will appeal to individuals based on what we know about them, and the methods used to obtain such information. Each area of insight is offered for consideration of its relevance to design practice. Please take what is useful.

▮ THE SPHERE OF INFLUENCE

According to the *The Color Response Report* published by the Institute for Color Research, our first impression, a color impression, accounts for

60 percent of our acceptance of an object—a fact not lost to marketing professionals. Color is significant in leading a customer to a purchase. Designed space is also seen first as a color impression. Consequently, our ability to provide positive environments depends to a large degree on our ability to anticipate human response to the colors they contain.

In order to design spaces and objects that have the desired impact on humans, we make assumptions about which colors, or which combinations of color, will elicit that reaction. This reaction is known as *color response*. Color impresses each person according to a range of influences. Some color responses are involuntary, based on human instinct. Many are based on powerful influence, affecting a large group of individuals consistently. Still other color responses are unique to an individual or group of individuals. Some consistencies can be attributed to inherited response, and others are learned. Age, education, gender, income, and residential geographic location each impact a person's natural response to color.

No one color has universal appeal. But some colors are preferred by some groups of people and specific individuals idolize other colors. Acceptance of individual colors or colors in combination depends on personal experience. Some variations in color perception are purely physical or physiological in nature. For these we can assume that most people will respond similarly to the same visual impression. Others are psychological perceptions influenced by associations: personal memory, cultural influences, and other aspects of experience that make each of our views of the world unique. While the impact of these variations is more difficult to identify in a scientific sense, they are equally instrumental in framing our sense of the visual world. Responses to color can be anticipated. With group response we watch people for patterns of behavior. For individual preferences we need only to ask the questions. To find out what groups of people think about color, we often rely on test data or market surveys.

Human reactions to color, or color responses, can be comparatively described in three categories: *unconscious, semiconscious,* and *conscious.* Those who analyze color behavior usually focus on one level or another according to their professional goals. For example, the medical community depends on reliable consistencies in unconscious reactions to color as a supplement to recovery. Psychologists usually look for long-term patterns of color associations that may reflect semiconscious levels of thought. Colorists in the fashion and home furnishings industries track the more conscious preferences of the public in an effort to anticipate color trends. All modes of response have a bearing on how a design will be perceived by an individual.

▶ Unconscious Color Response

The most basic reactions to color are those based in the unconscious, the innate responses. Many of these reactions are primarily biological, inherited from prior generations, and as such are the most consistent from region to region, making them the easiest to anticipate. They occur instinctively, without formal thought. Characteristic responses that fall in this category are limited in number, but their impact is the most difficult to ignore. They come to us as naturally as the need to eat and sleep.

The survival-of-the-fittest theory of evolution suggests that animals who develop the behavior necessary to survive will continue to populate the earth, while those who do not develop such skills will die off. Behaviors associated with color that may have led to survival include the instinct to eat ripened (red or blue) berries rather than unripe (green) ones or the instinct to flee from the open mouth of poisonous reptiles (black and yellow). If we assume that these behaviors are rooted in the unconscious, then it follows that most humans will have some preference for the colors red and blue over green—a reality which has been confirmed by many color-preference tests. Similarly, the presence of the colors black and yellow together should cause an immediate physical reaction in humans, since human survival has depended on immediate flight from biting and stinging animals that display such colors. In fact, psychologists tell us that most people experience a brief shortness of breath when they initially view this color combination.

In addition to biology-based responses, unconscious responses include personal memories that are no longer a part of conscious thought. These are based on experiences that occurred so early in life we cannot recall the source, yet they remain strong enough to significantly influence our preferences and associations. The soothing

Biological consequences of color responses can be a valuable tool in health management. Presently, there is a growing interest in *color therapy* or *chromotherapy* as an alternative treatment for a variety of illnesses, injuries, growth problems, and other issues of health and well-being. For those who subscribe, it's a practice of applying selective color, usually (but not always) in the form of light, to elicit improvement through physiological color response. The concept is based on the knowledge that all color is electromagnetic energy received by the body in the form of vibrations. Each vibration frequency and duration supports one or more basic body systems. Just as the ultraviolet (UV) rays of sunlight pass through the outer layers of the skin to impact the body through more sensitive human tissue below the epidermis, other visible wavelengths are thought to affect human development through the body's surface. Some believe that colored light has a more powerful therapeutic effect, but others are also using colored pigment (surface color) to generate the desired frequency for patients, as well as food chosen for its inherent color. Since the body depends on all waves of the spectrum to function at its best, and since most contemporary humans are denied regular, continued access to full daylight, it's believed that some ailments can be attributed to a wavelength deficiency, or *malillumination*—like missing a vitamin in the diet. Recovery from such ailments or strengthening of a specific organ is treated by exposure to its corresponding visual color.

Individual claims have been made concerning health and recovery from injury or illness through color therapy. Examples cited recently by Dr. Morton Walker in *The Power of Color* include improvements in intellectual development of mentally impaired children and cancer victims. In the absence of any regulatory monitoring, some state medical boards show concern about chromotherapists' practice, as does the U.S. Food and Drug Administration (FDA), the agency that regulates medical equipment. What is conspicuously missing at this time is consistent, long-term evaluation of color therapy practice from a statistical standpoint to scientifically establish its validity as a healing influence—or its lack thereof.

The following is a very brief overview of the seven color ranges used in treatment and some of the associated body functions and dysfunctions treated through direct application. For a diagram of the seven major healing centers on the body, known as *chakras,* see Figure 6.1.

Red Activates the circulation system and benefits the five senses; used to treat colds, paralysis, anemia, ailments of the bloodstream, and ailments of the lungs

Orange Motivates the thyroid gland, expands the lungs, and increases the pulse rate; used to treat asthma, epilepsy, respiratory diseases, inflammation of the kidneys, and tumors

Yellow Used for muscle stimulation and motor coordination, helps to build nerves, and functions as a digestive aid; used to treat paralysis, arthritis, digestive problems, nervous exhaustion, and diabetes

Green Strengthens bones and muscles, disinfects bacteria and virus, and relieves tension; used to treat colic, malaria, back problems, cancer, nervous disorders, and ulcers, and to manage heart problems and blood pressure

Blue Raises metabolism; is used to stabilize the heart, muscles, and bloodstream; used to treat burns and skin diseases, glaucoma, measles and chicken pox, and throat problems

Indigo Purifies the blood, arrests bleeding, and influences vision, smell, and hearing; used to treat cataracts, deafness, and other diseases of the eyes, ears, and nose

Violet Subdues the lymphatics and motor nerves and maintains ionic balance (electronically charged atoms); used to treat cerebrospinal meningitis, mental disorders, nervous disorders, and rheumatism

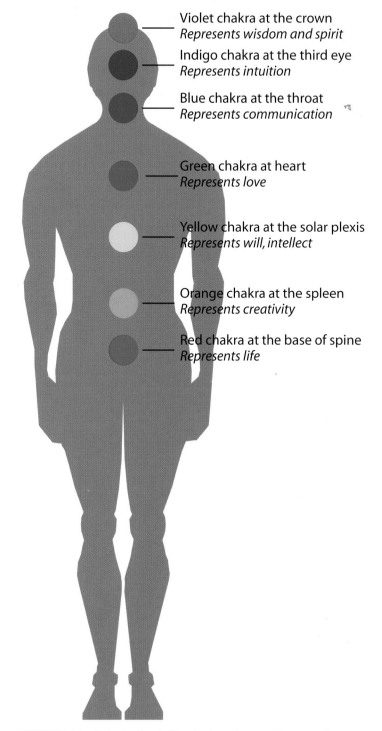

Violet chakra at the crown
Represents wisdom and spirit

Indigo chakra at the third eye
Represents intuition

Blue chakra at the throat
Represents communication

Green chakra at heart
Represents love

Yellow chakra at the solar plexis
Represents will, intellect

Orange chakra at the spleen
Represents creativity

Red chakra at the base of spine
Represents life

FIGURE 6.1   Color healers believe in the existence of an aura of electromagnetic energy outside the body that maintains our health through a balance of color. Chakras are the nonphysical channels of color force that exist within that aura. Each associates a position on the spinal cord with an area of color influence.

color of a grandmother's houserobe can elicit a positive response in an adult many years later. By the same token, a burn received in those early years may be long forgotten, while the color of the offending stove continues to have a negative connotation. Some adults have strong likes or dislikes for clothing color that derive from the clothes they wore as a child. Whether innate or relegated to the subconscious, unconscious color responses are the most difficult to change in people.

▶ Semiconscious Color Response

Another group of color responses are learned rather than instinctive. These are ingrained in our daily patterns of behavior, passed from parents to children, or grounded in social norms. Some responses to color in this category are personally unique, formed by associations, but many are cultural, and still others are associated with climate. The key difference between semiconscious and unconscious response as described here is the range of distribution. Most physiological unconscious responses are consistent across continents—that is, most humans share the experience. Semiconscious responses are acquired, meaning that not all humans will respond in the same way. Most reactions are tied to one or more geographic regions and are recognized by several generations. This makes them reliable within the appropriate context or geographic area.

Daylight quality can indicate some color response. Gray is usually least liked in areas of frequent fog or overcast skies. The things valued by a society also give positive connotations to their color. New Englanders prefer warm color while those native to India prefer cool color. People who spend time in Arizona often develop a liking for turquoise, due to its popularity as a local semiprecious stone. Cultural examples of semiconscious response include the association of green with products of nature in the United States. Green has become a frequently used color in packaging, particularly for food, due to the current societal concerns for health and the environment. To compare, green is rarely used in Islamic cultures due to its religious significance as the color of the cloak worn by the prophet Mohammed. This is evident in the lack of the color green in the oriental carpets imported from the Middle East. White is associated with death and mourning in many Asian cultures, yet remains the preferred color for bridal gowns in the United States as a sign of virtue. In contrast, the bride of India often wears red on her wedding day, and in Europe in centuries past, the bride wore green to symbolize fertility.

▶ Conscious Color Response

The third group of color responses that influence behavior are conscious. These are the preferences and associations made by each individual based on personal experience and are subject to the influence of fashion trends and current politics. Many of the associations and color symbols described in Chapter 5 can be identified as conscious color responses. Conscious responses vary with each generation. They are not consistent from region to region, but reflect the impact of society. Changes in the economy, social norms, the advent of war, and popular trends all have an impact here, as does personal experience.

Conscious color responses are a reflection of our personalities. They vary with income, education, sophistication, and personal exposure. This means that the more people grow, the more likely it is that their favorite color will change over time. The key distinction about conscious color responses is that they're current. They are reliable within a fixed time frame for a given audience. Conscious responses are also the easiest to influence. By

Faber Birren

One of the better-known twentieth-century color theorists was Faber Birren (1900–1988). Birren, who trained at the School of Art Institute in Chicago, practiced as a color consultant in New York City while focusing on issues of human perception of and response to color. In time he established himself as a scholar and a historian, exploring much of the writing done by previous scholars such as Harris, Chevreul, Rood, Munsell, Ostwald, and Itten. He redistributed translations of their works, along with his own contemporary explanations. Altogether, Birren wrote more than 20 books and over 200 articles.

nature they are less predictable, but they are often the responses that lead us to new ideas about color.

■ COLOR TESTING

Color-preference testing has long been a tool for psychologists and psychiatrists to understand the various thought processes used by clients. Its usefulness is based on statistical frequencies that illustrate patterns in humans over a large population. The results cannot be used as conclusions to predict choices for any one individual, although in areas of human behavior they are frequently indicators of personality traits. What they can offer us is a broad picture of how a group of individuals is likely to respond to the colors we apply. While not all tests have direct application in the practice of design, many of their findings do help us to understand more complex issues of human response to color. What follows is a brief discussion of color testing.

▶ Color versus Form

Color experience in any individual develops from an initial dominating adventure to one that is integrated with form. Traditionally, psychologists have tested children to determine influences of genetics, conditioning, physical development, and learned behavior. The distinction between color and form has been one tool for determining the degree of individual childhood development. According to Deborah Sharpe in *The Psychology of Color and Design,* children will respond first to color and then to form. In the earliest years, preferences for objects are based on the color applied to them. As the child matures to the ages of 4, 5, and 6 years, he or she becomes more aware of form, responding first to shapes. The common test for this stage of development for many years has been the *color-form test.* This test is a graphic of nine objects in three forms—three triangles, three circles, and three squares. One sample of each form is colored in red, one in blue, and one in green. The child (or adult) is asked to select the preferred object. Then a second object is selected, and finally a third. If the child is color-focused, three objects of the same color will be selected, such as a blue triangle, a blue circle, and a blue square. If form-focused, he or she will select three objects of the same shape but

FIGURE 6.2 Color-form tests often involve two sets of geometries—one that matches the test sample in color, the other in form.

different colors—for example, three circles, one each in red, blue, and green. Another way to test children for color-form focus is to give them a collection of red triangles and green disks, as shown in Figure 6.2. The child is asked which objects are the same as the red disk. Most 3- to 5-year-olds choose the red triangles, because at that age sameness means color, not form. A form-dominant child, or an adult for that matter, will choose the green disks.

In psychology, color-form preference tests are used to measure degree of maturity and other specific elements of development. A preference for form over color, or form dominance, is considered to be more mature than color dominance. The peak of color dominance occurs in children at an average of 4½ years of age, when only the most intellectually advanced (about 10 percent) of this age group will be form-dominant. Most children begin to make the shift to form dominance gradually, between 4 and 6 years of age, with the median age at 5 years. By the age of 9, the majority of children are form-dominant. Deaf children are an exception to this guideline, since they typically show a preference for color over form at all ages. In adults, form dominance is considered a genetically higher level of response than color, accounting for about 90 percent of the adult population. An adult predisposition toward color over form is highly unique. The 10 percent who are color-dominant are considered creative and flexible or impulsive and immature, depending on the evaluator's perspective. Those in the majority tend to have personalities that demonstrate greater stability or are socially controlled.

▶ Color-Preference Testing

While infants as young as four months of age have been able to express a preference for certain colors, adults are better able to communicate not only their preferences, but also the reasons that accompany such choices. Some correlations between color preferences and personality traits have been documented during the nineteenth and twentieth centuries. Psychologists, psychiatrists, and social workers who rely on color testing as a means of analysis do so with a basic assumption in mind—that a consistent preference for a particular color in individuals of one personality type implies that the next person who selects that color is likely to have the same personality trait. For example, if 100 intellectuals select yellow as their favorite color from a given group of samples, one might assume that the next random individual who prefers yellow is also an intellectual.

Much has been written regarding correlations between personality characteristics and color preference using the basic hues and a few standard neutrals. For example, one common generalization is that a person choosing orange is socially outgoing and one who chooses green is socially well adjusted and conventional. Such comparisons ignore the fact that orange and green come in many forms and that not all oranges will be preferred by the gregarious soul, just as not all greens are preferable to the socially conservative personality. The theory of personality matching also implies that if our basic personality does not change, neither will our color preferences. On the contrary, color preferences vary with each culture and with one's status in life. As our life experiences accumulate, personal color preferences change. From a design standpoint, preferences are useful when we are designing a private space for a specific individual, in which case the information is best gathered directly from that person rather than relying on general categorical guidelines.

Kinds of Tests

Color-preference testing is one resource for conclusions about color and its influence on people. Many color-preference tests are limited to colors of hue only and as such offer a limited perspective. Others are more complex, addressing the finer points of tint, tone, and shade and offering conclusions that have more meaning in design practice. Obviously the more complex the test objects, the more difficult it is to control the test situation and separate key issues that the administrator is trying to address. This is a challenge for all test adminis-

trators, regardless of their professional focus. Three major types of color-preference testing are currently in use, each serving a different purpose: market research, cultural psychology, and diagnostic tests for personality assessment.

The most common tests are those used to track short-term color trends or to evaluate proposed changes in them. Market research analysts often rely on this type of test data to determine effective product packaging or to ascertain the degree of acceptance of a new color. Color testing in this realm often involves a connection between color and a specific product or service and is focused on determining short-term changes in preference within specific markets. These tests are performed by manufacturing and retail professionals. Colors are usually shown in combination with each other rather than as individual samples. Results of these tests are useful to determine which new color trends are being embraced by the public, as well as which colors will make for a successful product or market strategy.

Psychologists looking for patterns in human behavior use a second type of testing. These are the long-term color-preference tests, whose results are often consistent within a geographic location and illustrate preferences that carry over from generation to generation. These results establish color preferences that are grounded in the culture of a group of people and offer a lasting reflection of society. For this type of testing, color is presented without association to objects to eliminate the influence of fashion trends and practical application. It's meant to be divorced from specific application and considered in a more conceptual realm.

Some psychiatrists and other mental health counselors evaluate personality traits using a third set of color-preference tests. These are based on patterns that emerge when psychologists or psychiatrists ask individuals to select preferred colors. Those taking the tests are asked to eliminate associations with fashions, products, or the environment. Test colors are specifically selected to reveal conditions of the mind and are considered reliable based on historic data. The theory is that individual preferences contribute to each person's color response because they are rooted in personality. These tests include those used by Swiss analysts Dr. Max Lüscher, author of *The Lüscher Color Test,* and Max Pfister. A short version of Lüscher's test involves eight cards in a range of colors: warm red, red-violet, green, dark blue, yellow, gray, black, and beige. The cards are selected in order of preference, twice. The administrator uses the order of selection to identify personality traits, psychic stresses, and glandular inbalances. The *Color Pyramid Test,* used by Max Pfister, is made up of 24 hue samples, which the participant arranges harmoniously and then nonharmoniously in a 15-space pyramid (with 5 spaces across the bottom row). In this case, the order of arrangement gives the administrator an indication of personality traits.

Administering Tests

The process of color testing offers some variables that are known to impact the actual results. As with any form of testing, the process must eliminate the administrator's apparent preferences from the participant's perception. An inconsistency in the presentation of the colors by the administrator can influence the results. In addition, consistent sampling for color testing is not always reliable. Until very recently, accurate reproduction of color samples was difficult to manage and very expensive. With color, slight variations can have an impact on the way that color is perceived and consequently received by the test taker. Coloration of dye is difficult to control, and photographic and reprographic processes leave much to be desired. Differences in surface texture and available lighting also change perception of sample color. (These are explained further in Chapter 9, "Color and Light," and Chapter 10, "Texture and Material.")

The context of the color sampling will have an impact on the test process. Color influence occurs as readily at a table of color samples as it does in any other context. The color of the room, the color of the table surface, and the color of the clothing the administrator wears when holding up a sample can all influence a person's perception of the color. This means that if several individuals who are not in uniform give the tests in separate locations, the results may vary significantly. When performing color comparisons, the best background is a medium-value, neutral gray. Both black and white may be hue-neutral, but they are extreme in value and will influence the process. In some cases, if gray is not available, a medium gray-violet or a neutral yellow-

green can be considered, since these backgrounds are temperature-neutral.

Test Results

Despite the potential for variations in color testing, conclusions documented over the past two generations have shown some consistent results. What we can rely on is the conclusion that most adults tend to choose colors of strong hue over neutralized and gray tones, and they choose light tones over dark. When given an abstract set of primary and secondary color samples to choose from, most people in the United States select blue, red, and green as preferred colors, usually in that order. The colors selected as the least liked are yellow, orange, and violet; violet, orange, and yellow; or violet, yellow, and orange, depending on the test.

In more developed color-selection tests, the more familiar colors are often chosen over less familiar colors. The least-favorite colors are typically those contrary to our expectations. For example, yellow, which is normally expected to be light, is undesirable when found in dark shades such as bronze, yellow-brown, or the greenish-yellow that occurs at high saturations in dark range. Positive reactions to orchid (pale violet) and lavender (pale purple) are equally limited, in part because one expects violet or purple to be dark in value. Orchid and greenish-yellow are among the least-favorite colors in the United States. Colors considered undesirable in test results tend not to be used in large areas. Instead, they are used more successfully in small areas to make adjacent colors appear more pleasing or to give some uniqueness to the overall color scheme.

Gender

Gender plays a part in color-preference test results. Blue is significantly preferred over the other five primaries and secondaries by adult men. However, women usually choose red or blue-green as their first selection, depending on the study. Men generally prefer orange over yellow, while their female counterparts select yellow over orange. Of the basic primary and secondary colors, red is consistently chosen by both men and women within the first three choices; however, women prefer blue-based reds, while men prefer yellow-based reds, as discovered by Carlton Wagner (*The Color Response Report,* page 16). Also, men prefer strong chromatic color, while women choose less saturated versions.

Age

Children have also shown some consistency in color-preference testing. Babies first see black-and-white contrasts. This is followed by red a few days after birth. They continue to focus on bright colors longer than on less saturated ones. Red and yellow or red and blue appear to be the favorites, depending on the test. At this age, eye tracking is used to determine the colors that attract the child's attention. Young, mobile children uniformly prefer brilliant colors—the brighter and more saturated the better. As they mature, their preferences shift to less intense colors. An appreciation for color harmony is evident in the artwork of children between 8 and 12 years of age. Mood associations become established in the 11- to 14-year-old bracket, such as the excitement associated with red and the calmness of blue. And between the ages of 6 and 17, tests show that girls prefer warm colors and boys prefer cool colors. (Conclusions by Deborah T. Sharpe, *The Psychology of Color and Design,* page 24.)

Color-discrimination capabilities change with age. A child's ability to match most colors increases from the age of 10 to 19. Discrimination peaks in the twenties, and our matching reliability decreases after that point, with the exception of yellow, which peaks in the forties. Educators have been able to use color-preference information to affect learning. Color used in combination with phonics and word recognition has been known to enhance the learning process. (For an example of this application in design, refer to Chapter 12, Figure 12.11.)

▶ Individual Preferences

Every hue has the potential to communicate positive or negative attributes based on its particular variation and its context. Rather than limit patterns of color preference to comparisons of hue, a few analysts have explored more complex variations of tertiary hues, ranges of value, and arrays of saturation. In past generations, correlations between color preference and extremes of personality were used to compensate for behavior patterns. For example, we presumed that if active, outwardly focused people and small children preferred bright colors, then more subdued colors would calm them down. The contrary proves to be more accurate. Environments with more active coloration are more comfortable to an active group, while passive coloration can be stifling for them. More contemplative individuals are not drawn out in an active environment, but instead become increasingly agitated.

The best environmental color seems to be that which matches the preferred coloration of the personalities who occupy the space. In this manner color is used to enhance individual experience. Mood changes in response to color are diverse, but some color groups tend to enhance moods in the way that music can. A more colorful room does not necessarily increase the heart rate—if it is balanced and of reduced saturation, it will actually slow the heart rate.

If we are designing for one person, preferences based on personality may be easy to discern. In fact, **the information gleaned from direct contact with the user is more valuable than any statistical data.** However, often we're called on to design space for a group, and access to the users is not possible. In the absence of direct contact, categorical information on color preference can be useful as a starting point. The most consistent range of behavior with a correlation to color is the comparison of introverted and extroverted personality types. All individuals exhibit varying levels of both introspective and outward-focused behavior. These tendencies have a direct correlation to color in terms of several color characteristics. To illustrate this range, the two ends of the scale will be considered as distinct, far-ranging personalities. Keep in mind that these are extreme comparisons. Most people fall somewhere in between the ends of the range in their overall personality and consequently in their color preferences.

Outward Stimulation

Color preferences change according to predominant personal orientation and fluctuating moods. People are most comfortable in spaces and with objects that support the overall behavior they display. In other words, outgoing personalities are most comfortable in spaces that stimulate them. The more outwardly integrated they are, the greater their inclination toward more intense stimulation. Generally speaking, extroverted individuals will show signs of rapid mental functions, a social pre-disposition, and a fondness for the visual world. If their environment does not offer the necessary stimulation, boredom will set in. A dull environment may not stimulate directly, but it will cause its occupants to turn inward, which produces anxiety in more active personalities, who will show signs of irritation and may have difficulty concentrating.

Color preferences for personalities have traditionally been addressed as issues of hue. Warmer hues have long been identified as the choice of outgoing individuals, especially orange. Cool colors, particularly blue, have been associated with more contemplative souls. However, other characteristics of color are equally divergent in their ability to stimulate or pacify when exposed to view. An increase in the number of contrasts or the degree of color contrast is very stimulating, while a sense of harmony will be more soothing within an environment. The degree of saturation has a tremendous impact on the intensity of a room. And lightness or darkness also impact color strength, adding to its overall impression. Given this, I propose the following correlations between personalities and appropriate color characteristics.

Spatial color for the extreme extrovert can be addressed according to three basic color characteristics. These are the use of **warmer colors,** the use of **lighter values,** and the inclusion of **greater levels of saturation.** The more outgoing people are, the more likely they are to prefer warm colors. This doesn't mean that all the colors in their home must be red, orange, or yellow. But it is probable that the inclusion of some warm color will make the palette most appealing to them. By the same token, the more outward-focused people are, the more likely they are to be attracted to colors light in value. They may also have a tendency to raise the light level in their space. In terms of saturation, these individuals will also enjoy more intense colors, which is more characteristic of active people. Higher levels of saturation offer greater stimulation regardless of the specific hue used.

When using colors in combination, issues of contrast and harmony, as well as pattern, can be used to manage the level of visual stimulation. For a more interactive space, **more dramatic contrasts** such as value, hue, and extent can be used, and more dramatic examples of lesser contrasts are suitable. Harmonic balance is not necessary in these spaces, particularly if the function is active. **Patterning** is also a positive attribute of the active environment. A sense of order and consistency are essential for the success of any design. But the extroverted client is more likely to appreciate the intensity and complexity of greater variation, as suggested by these characteristics. The illustration in Figure 6.3 identifies color strategies in very general, simple terms.

Inward Focus

Those who are more contemplative and introspective are more likely to be sensitive to color shifts in

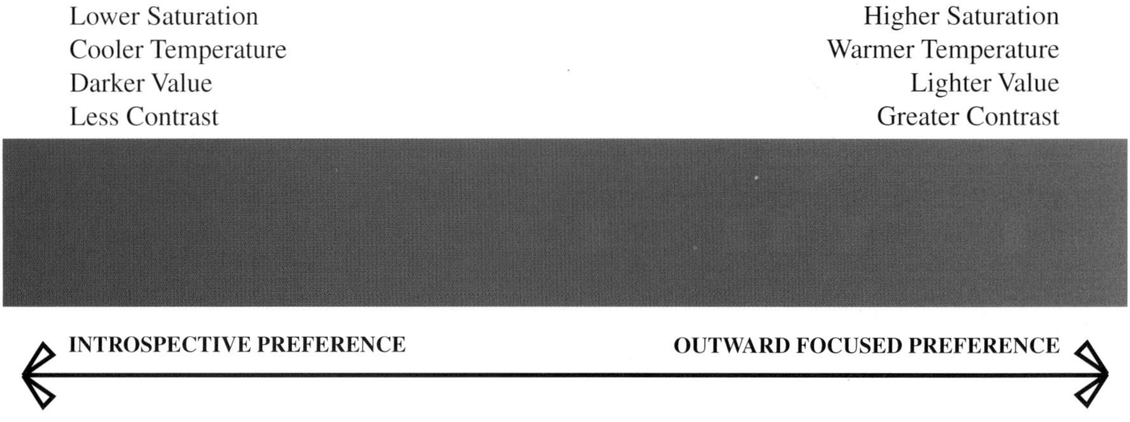

Lower Saturation	Higher Saturation
Cooler Temperature	Warmer Temperature
Darker Value	Lighter Value
Less Contrast	Greater Contrast

INTROSPECTIVE PREFERENCE   **OUTWARD FOCUSED PREFERENCE**

FIGURE 6.3   This diagram suggests comparative color characteristics that can be applied to polar personalities. Descriptions of selections are made comparatively speaking.

general and may prefer less stimulation in their environment or treasured objects. These people are comforted by the familiar, and they may use personal space for respite and privacy, to detach slightly from the outside world. Again, this is a generalization for the extreme personality, but the more introverted individuals are, the more likely they will be to prefer a calm, even subdued personal space. This type of client may be less than enthusiastic about any distinct color, especially those of strong hue.

Introspective people have a tendency to prefer **cool colors** (e.g., blue, blue-green, green, and purple) as well as cool neutrals (e.g., blue-gray rather than tan). They may also have a preference for a more subdued palette that is dominated by **less saturated color,** such as a spice tone accent rather than orange or an olive green rather than a bright kelly green. Blue is considered the more introspective of hues, but bright blue will be less appropriate for the quiet person's work space than a toned-down pink, such as mauve or a medium brown. The inward-focused person is often comfortable with **darker values** and may appreciate the richness of deeper tones, as well as the inclusion of shades rather than tints.

Color schemes for introverted people are also more effective when there are fewer physical forms articulated, thereby reducing stimulation, or visual clutter. A sophisticated combination using more **subtle contrasts,** such as saturation, with limitations to **one hue family,** may be very effective for this type of client. A **smaller range of values** or a very **balanced use of extension** is also appropriate for the introvert's surroundings. A contemplative person is more likely to appreciate the subtlety of saturation contrasts, small increments of value, or changes in surface texture. The point is to limit contrasts by working with a smaller range of individual colors. With an inward-focused person, less distracting color combinations are preferable. Establishing **harmony** becomes more important in this color scheme, whether through consistency, spectral balance, or both. Patterning is usually reduced, smaller in scale and proportion, and less contrasting.

To be clear, no individual color should be eliminated from a project palette on the basis of these associations. The point of this discussion is not to set limits on colors used for particular personal spaces

Carlton Wagner

Carlton Wagner (United States, twentieth century) was a practicing interior designer and clinical psychologist. He obtained a degree in psychology at California State University, Long Beach, and studied at the Carl Jung Institute in Zurich, Switzerland. Following this training, he taught psychology for 15 years and continued to communicate about color response through lectures and other media for many years. Wagner is best known as the former director of the Institute for Color Research in Santa Barbara, California, an organization he founded. The institute is dedicated to gathering and dispensing information about human response to color, providing consulting services, and offering color training.

but to offer a starting point. Some inward-focused people love orange, and some extroverts like achromatic environments. Again, direct feedback from the client or user regarding personal preference is more valuable than statistical or categorical information. When direct feedback is not available, then the categorical suggestions here may prove useful. The information that follows regarding socioeconomic class is offered in the same light.

Socioeconomic Class

Carlton Wagner offers some significant conclusions in the area of socioeconomic development in his video *The Language of Color.* He explained that while it's possible to age without growing, people who grow find that their color preferences change. As a person becomes more educated, is exposed to more culture, and has greater financial resources, his or her color preferences change. More colors become acceptable, and we appreciate a greater number of color combinations. We all identify with colors that allow us to fit in with our peers. When our peer group changes, so do familiar colors. The more limited one's circumstances, the smaller the range of hue that's considered appealing. This is because we prefer the familiar. With limited exposure, a smaller range of hue feels more comfortable. This means that an individual with less life experience or lower financial means may find fewer hues attractive than the individual with greater means, more education, higher intelligence, and broader life experience. While these generalities may not apply in every case, they do show tendencies based on individual background. Again, in the absence of direct feedback, such broad conclusions about color character may serve as a starting point for development of appropriate color combinations.

The more advantaged one is in terms of socioeconomic development, the more one is drawn to complex colors. Wagner explains that complex colors are those that have several hue characteristics and that are difficult to describe. A simple color can be described in one or two words: light orange, grayish blue, bright green. More complex colors require some narrative: a pale green with blue undertones, for example, or a very dark brown with a slight burgundy tint. Complex colors are rarely at full saturation, while simple colors are frequently clear and easier to describe in terms of hue. The less advantaged people are in socioeconomic terms, the more comfortable they are with simple colors. A jewelry box to be sold in a department store may be more appealing in bubble-gum pink, which is simple and familiar, but a Park Avenue boutique is more likely to render it in sable, a sophisticated and acquired preference.

Again, speaking in very general, comparative terms, the less advantaged people are socially and economically, the greater their preference for colors that are lighter in value. More successful individuals are more likely to choose darker values. More advantaged people tend to choose a smaller range of values when different hues occur in combination. To compensate for this, often a more complex color palette will include a range of saturation rather than value, which is more subtle and preferable to the person of means. Lower-income people are more comfortable with a greater range of value in a more complex color scheme. In Figure 6.4, color characteristics are keyed to personality tendencies in combination with socioeconomic influences.

Some colors are described as classifiers and declassifiers by Wagner. A *classifying color* is one that only a small percent of the population finds appealing, and these individuals are most frequently in higher socioeconomic classes. Forest green is a classifying color; so are burgundy and dove gray. A declassifying color is one that most people recognize with familiarity. Such colors communicate concepts of informality, low cost, and access for everyone. Orange and yellow in full saturation are declassifying colors. Orange, in particular, has been used successfully by Howard Johnson's and Home Depot to appeal to a wide customer base. Yellow brought the same success to McDonald's golden arches. The implication here is that if you want to attract a larger number of buyers, declassifying colors can help, but if your goal is to charge more per customer, classifying colors are more appropriate.

◾ CONCLUSIONS

Much light has been shed in recent generations on human behavior as a reaction to color. Fortunately, the conditions that impact our perception of spatial color, and form due to its color, are being identified with greater consistency. In time, new insights on color and behavior will most likely be shared with designers as behavior scientists recognize patterns and as access to information continues to increase through technology and cross-cultural communications. Although such information does not necessarily suggest the end results for creative designers, it does offer a starting point for color consideration. At the least, such facts offer a potential warning about less appropriate color or an explanation for unanticipated behavior that appears to have a color correlation. There are no wrong individual colors. Our perception of space and objects is determined by the combination of colors we see. Our understanding of color responses can help us make adjustments in the overall combination so that it is appealing to the target audience while making use of the colors we deem essential to the design.

This information is significant because it empowers designers to incorporate color with the same conviction demonstrated by fine artists. Color becomes a means to an end. Decisions about color and form are made simultaneously during the design process, resulting in a more cohesive, unique, and usually more effective design. Together, knowledge about color response and experience with color

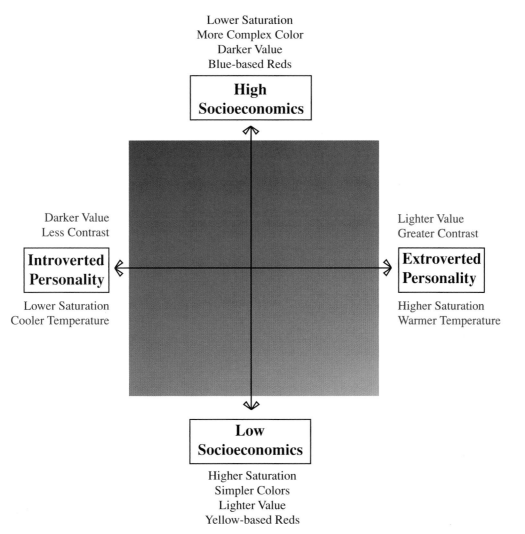

Lower Saturation
More Complex Color
Darker Value
Blue-based Reds

**High
Socioeconomics**

Darker Value
Less Contrast

Lighter Value
Greater Contrast

**Introverted
Personality**

**Extroverted
Personality**

Lower Saturation
Cooler Temperature

Higher Saturation
Warmer Temperature

**Low
Socioeconomics**

Higher Saturation
Simpler Colors
Lighter Value
Yellow-based Reds

FIGURE 6.4 In this diagram the likely preferences for outwardly focused personalities are combined with preferences based on socioeconomic status. Ideal choices for most people fall somewhere within the extremes.

contrasts and harmonies discussed previously are powerful tools for developing space that communicates our intent on a variety of levels.

So far, eight types of color contrast have been discussed. They are hue, value, extension, saturation, temperature, complement, simultaneity, and succession. We know that each may be used alone or in combination with one another depending on the amount of stimulation and complexity desired. Nine forms of harmony have also been identified—achromatic, monochromatic, adjacent, polychro-

matic, dyad, triad, split complement, tetrad, and hexad—with a few variations thereof. Each color harmony provides a formula for selecting colors that are more likely to be compatible or pleasing to the human eye. We know that it is possible to combine a spectral harmony with a harmony of consistency for the most balanced of color combinations and that it's common to combine contrast effects within an overall harmony to express a design more fully.

In Chapters 5 and 6, we identified the human factors that impact desirable response and general acceptance of specific color selections. In Chapter 7, we look at how the tools of color management and information about color response are used to establish strong design concepts. Because we can anticipate many of the color associations people make and the connections they will draw from color during their first impressions, we enhance designed forms by anticipating user reaction. The examples presented in the following pages illustrate ways that color and form are integrated more effectively as color is understood more fully and managed more proactively in design.

Three-Dimensional Concepts

Color and form are the fundamental components to any design or work of art. Together they make a statement, which may be physical, emotional, or spiritual in nature. Its essence is known as the *design concept*. While each individual color can establish an association that supports the design statement, the colors seen in combination tell the whole story. A color grouping can enhance, neutralize, or negate the three-dimensional form to which it's applied, depending on placement and the use of contrasts. Each color choice either reinforces or diminishes the original design concept to some degree because of its influence over form. When color integration is at its best, it enhances the form and supports the overall concept. Individual color relationships establish clues about the spatial relationships of the project.

In this chapter we look at concepts employed in design projects and discuss the role of color in the context of three-dimensional form.

▓ DESIGN CONCEPTS

Design encompasses a tremendous range of creative disciplines that are distinguished from the fine arts by one common element. It involves the resolution of functional needs in association with aesthetic ones. The object of design becomes a mission in satisfying the creator's aesthetic goals while at the same time serving one or more practical purposes.

Within each area of design, the function gives context to creative solutions. Clothing fashions enhance the spirit and visual appearance of the wearer. An industrial design addresses some human need, from transportation to dental floss, often incorporating electronic or mechanical means. Interior design addresses functional issues of human scale, orientation, and social context. Pottery is usually intended to hold something, and jewelry is meant to be worn. Architecture must provide shelter and sustain human beings who breathe, move, vocalize, eat, and do a whole host of other things for which they depend on their environment.

Color decisions are made in this context. Each problem has many solutions, but experience tells us that designs are much more successful if the creator can point to one concept or big idea as the basis of decision making. Design solutions that lack a clear concept may solve the problem, and they may even meet all the practical criteria established for the project, but they may lack the clarity and strength evident in more successful projects. The existence of a strong concept during design serves as the framework for decisions about form, texture, lighting, and, to a large degree, color. If the design begins with an expression of color, consideration of the form, which expresses it, ideally follows close behind. If form is the initiator, then color will follow its lead. The design solution is integrated by working both form and color simultaneously. Some favorite approaches to integrated concepts are offered here.

▶ Concepts of Emotion

Ideas for color often are inspired by a particular emotion or spiritual sensation, which the designer hopes to draw upon. Many spaces for religious assembly are articulated in colors selected to be consistent with the organization's approach to religion. For example, contemporary Unitarian Universalist churches, known for a philosophy of inclusion for all, use very little chroma. Compare this to the many contrasting hues used in Byzantine churches, whose interiors included gold leaf, glossy tile, and various metals and gems designed to awe patrons. The Byzantine church image reflects a hierarchical religious structure where few could proclaim spiritual enlightenment.

The personalities of individuals in a residential project can also be a powerful resource for ideas. Concepts for spaces used by children often display colors intended to meet the emotional needs of the users. For an adult, if the memory of a grandmother's kitchen evokes a feeling of security, using the colors associated with that space might connote protective feelings. The desire for romantic space can suggest soothing hues of beach rocks in moderate saturation.

In concepts of emotion, it's not necessarily a replication of colors seen, but more an expression of the spirit in color that sets the concept. Some combinations of color illustrate moods more abstractly. Colors may be selected to suggest the movement of the ocean, the brilliance of a sunny day, or the festivity of a tropical beach without limiting selection to light tan and baby blue. The excitement of a big win at the baccarat table in Atlantic City can be expressed through vivid color contrasts, especially value contrasts, which may or may not have any relationship to the color evident at the table itself. The subtle shifts of color in a Scottish landscape may inspire a very sophisticated palette of earth tones without the slightest hint of grass green.

Hard and Soft Color

Individual colors are recognizable as having subtlety or great strength by virtue of their saturation and value levels. Some colors in combination can also appear to be exceptionally strong, or *hard,* and comparatively passive, or *soft.* These are opposing

FIGURE 7.1   An example of soft colors.

effects that can be developed starting with virtually any color. The premise is that a color group makes a stronger statement than a single color. A soft color combination is often made up of a small range of values, with little contrast between colors that touch each other, as shown in Figure 7.1. Each color is reduced in saturation and most are fairly light in value. No one color dominates. Soft colors are often used in contemplative or passive concepts.

A hard color combination is the result of stronger contrasts and more abrupt color transitions. These often include at least one highly saturated color and a greater range of contrasts, especially value. (See Figure 7.2.) The increase in contrasts causes greater eye movement and increased user response. In a hard color scheme one color often dominates, such as the lipstick red shown here. Hard color schemes are often used to stimulate the observer and establish outward interaction.

▶ Concepts of Association

It's been popular in many design situations to incorporate impressions of vernacular architecture. Sometimes the goal is for a new design to fit into an existing environment. Alternatively, theme restaurants use imagery of a remote part of the country, or another country altogether, to uniquely establish themselves. The Disney people have a long-standing collection of spatial concepts that use new localities,

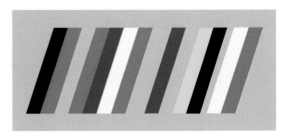

FIGURE 7.2   An example of hard colors.

including some places that exist only in our imaginations. In each case, colors that adorn these environments are used in combinations and proportions associated with the place Disney identifies. For an environmental agency's office, a nature photograph by Eliot Porter may inspire a color concept by suggesting outdoor colors for interior use.

Some places are recognizable by consistent use of specific colors. In cities that developed over long periods of time, architectural colors may have a strong correlation to particular periods in their history. Neutral shades of gray and white are reminiscent of key buildings in Paris. Hong Kong is familiar to most people for its bold red. For the U.S. embassy in Jordan, shown in Figure 7.3, architects used colors indigenous to the host country. By mirroring the colors they observed in local religious and government buildings, the new structures were integrated into the fabric of the local architecture.

Concepts of association are not limited to geographic places. One designer tells of a successful color association concept his team developed for a new headquarters space. The corporation it housed had acquired several smaller companies, each of which had an identifiable corporate color. The color concept proposed for the new facility incorporated those of all subsidiaries—with minor adjustments to balance the hues according to a spectral harmony. Employees of each subsidiary company recognized their touchstone color in the new collective palette of the parent company. In some projects this idea has been taken further, using the subsidiary colors as accents in departmental areas, while the main lobby, building atrium, and cafeteria incorporate all the colors in combination.

▶ Organizational Concepts

Color can be used as a device to support organizational functions. In environmental design, it can assist in way finding by identifying landmarks, routes, and intersections. It can subtly establish zones of public and private interior space. In an industrial product, color may be selected to conceal joints or to draw attention to a mechanical feature such as a dial or switch. Three organizational concepts appear frequently in spatial design: hierarchy, identity, and focus.

Hierarchy

A sense of orientation is a valuable thing in architectural contexts. In a large, complex building interior, users look for a logical transition between major building sections and a distinction between main walkways and secondary routes. When these cues are communicated visually, it's known as *establishing hierarchy,* which is accomplished by varying color intensities, by changing color values, or by increasing and decreasing the complexity of color combinations uniformly. Either way, color is assigned systematically, enabling others to understand spatial organization by a quick visual comparison. Hierarchical color can imply a sense of priority, such as the use of a strong red to highlight the emergency entrance at a hospital, or it can be used to signify main circulation routes, such as a

FIGURE 7.3 Bold colors familiar to local residents were used to delineate this six-building embassy complex in Amman, Jordan. (*Design by Perry Dean Rogers/ Partners Architects. Photo: © Richard Mandelkorn.*)

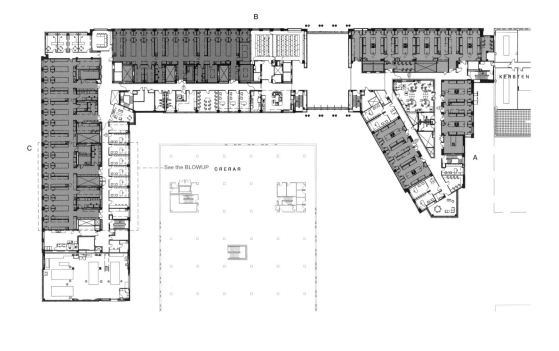

FIGURE 7.4 This floor plan has been rendered to identify the buildings by color—figuratively and literally. Each major area is identified by a single color of hue. (*Design by Ellenzweig Associates, Inc., Architects.*)

yellow brick road for the promenade or blue wain-scoting that leads to the Blue Room for dining.

In larger projects, dramatic changes in colors of hue can signal distinctions in the organization of space, while smaller shifts delineate detail. For the University of Chicago project shown in Figure 7.4,

the design team proposes using color to articulate distinct building sections. This complex facility will be organized in three sections, each with a strong color of hue that students and visitors will be able to identify. Each section's assigned color will appear both in accentuated floor patterns (bottom left) and in accents at key vertical planes (right). The position and proportion of the accents are consistent, regardless of their assigned color.

Identity

Color is also used as an identifier in environmental design by combining key colors in consistent proportions, such as the facade of a retail chain store. Sometimes color patterns are used to visually group independent structures together. Consider a cluster of private residences that includes smaller structures such as garages and garden sheds. The color of smaller structures often identifies which homeowners they belong to, such as the Jones's yellow house with the yellow garage. In the large-scale project developed for the public school shown in Figures 7.5 and 7.6, existing and new structures were combined. Identity was established by using a checkerboard tile pattern in a variety of scales appropriate to both interior and exterior applications.

Focus

Color is often used to emphasize a key element. In this concept, known as *focus,* the most important element is given the most dramatically distinct color. The greater a color contrasts with its context, the more useful it is as concept of focus. In most cases, the brightest color is the strongest focus, but this is not always the case. Context colors define the focus color. If all surrounding colors are light, the single dark object will be a focal point. In a sea of chromatic color, the white object holds our attention. Objects of focus can be entrances, information centers, or display areas. Outlining is a technique often used to establish focus. A recessed niche in a gallery might be alternately colored or outlined in a contrasting color to draw the eye to an object inside. The openings to classrooms at the school shown in Figure 7.7 are outlined in a dark frame color to distinguish them from the other visual activity on the surface of

FIGURE 7.5 The exterior patterning uniquely identifies this building as well as other city structures it's connected to. (*Design by Flansburgh Associates, Inc. Photo: © Steve Rosenthal.*)

FIGURE 7.6 When traveling through the interior of the building shown in Figure 7.5 and its connecting links, the same color relationships appear, reinforcing its identity. (*Design by Flansburgh Associates, Inc. Photo: © Steve Rosenthal.*)

FIGURE 7.7   The contrasting frames in this interior give focus to classrooms by outlining them. (*Design by Flansburgh Associates, Inc. Photo: © Steve Rosenthal.*)

corridor walls. Each framed opening is read as a portal to the classroom.

The amount of a single color used also determines it effectiveness as a focal point. When a color is limited to one component, it gives that component greater emphasis. As the color appears more frequently in the vicinity of that component, its strength is diminished. Case in point, clothing that is designed to show off body shape may incorporate limited contrasts. But if the goal is to draw attention to one aspect, such as the neckline or waist, a small amount of contrasting color will do it most effectively. This is the concept illustrated in Figures 7.8 and 7.9. Figure 7.8 shows an elevation with five openings, or panels, which will be used to illustrate several points in this chapter and Chapter 8. In Figure 7.9, one opening is presumed to be more important because of the applied focal color.

Some areas of design rely on emphasis to a greater degree. Advertisements, public service establishments, and information centers must use emphasis to seize our attention and guide us toward a product, service, or solution, respectively. Just as a design may call attention to itself by contrast with its surroundings, too many dominant elements cause a lack of emphasis and read as a pattern at best or as clutter at worst.

FIGURE 7.8   This simple elevation is shown as a baseline reference for other illustrations that follow.

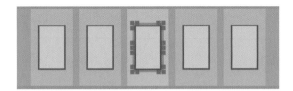

FIGURE 7.9 Here the same elevation as the one shown in 7.8 has applied color to establish focus.

FIGURE 7.10 Points and lines can establish the form of a two-dimensional plane through contrast with the background color.

▶ Expressions of Form

If color and form work together to generate the big idea, which drives the other? Many projects manage a healthy mix of expression on both levels for spatial interest. Some designs focus on more highly developed three-dimensional forms, which are enhanced by more restrained use of color contrasts. Others rely on fairly simple forms with very sophisticated coloration to express the concept. Let's consider how form can drive color selection.

Basics of Form

Form is traditionally described in four levels of expression: point, line, plane, and volume. The theory is that a point is one-dimensional and the line is two-dimensional. The plane is also two-dimensional, and its limits are established by the difference between its color and the surrounding color, which form an edge. A volume is any three-dimensional form with an inside and an outside. Our ability to understand the form of the three-dimensional volume is determined by the color we perceive on and around it as well as distinctions within the volume's surface color. Elements that are very small in scale are usually read as points. When several points are grouped together and colored similar to each other but different from their background, they are read collectively as a larger two-dimensional form. The same happens with a series of lines. Several lines colored together create a pattern, the form of which is read as a solid. Both are illustrated in Figure 7.10.

Color is essentially contained by the form on which it resides. Exceptions are limited to the ocean, smog, and the evening sky, which appear to be limitless volumes of color. Although we instinctively react to hue first in an environment, this reaction is immediately followed by a search for form, making the two fundamentally connected. We rely on color as the critical device to communicate form with clarity. Apparent variations in color are read as shading, implying a change of form. To distinguish a flat plane on the surface of a building from a three-dimensional building, we look for distinctions of tone and shade.

Implications of Form

Some colors elicit certain reactions, as do some forms. It's quite common to use forms and colors together that generate similar reactions or impressions to ensure the strength of that concept. Training at the Bauhaus school in Germany during the early twentieth century involved analysis of geometric forms and colors of hue for inherent characteristics that paralleled each other. Many theorists of the time accepted relationships for the primary colors similar to those shown in Figure 7.11 on the left. The artist and instructor Wassily Kandinsky proposed that the deep tone of blue is enhanced by the smooth form of the circle, while the sharpness of yellow suggested the triangle to him as a corresponding form. (Kandinsky's concepts are illustrated in Clark Poling's book,

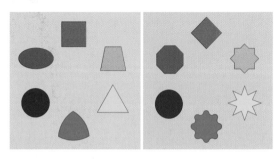

FIGURE 7.11 Here an example of form and color integration using the Bauhaus philosophy on the left is compared to Karl Gerstner's color and form pairings shown on the right.

Kandinsky's Teaching at the Bauhaus: Color Theory and Analytical Drawing.) Some of Kandinsky's contemporaries went further to suggest other color-form relationships, such as an ellipse for the color violet.

The more contemporary Swiss artist, Karl Gerstner, makes a very convincing case for his association of specific geometric forms with each of the primary and secondary subtractive colors. These are shown on the warmer background to the right in Figure 7.11. He suggests that the dynamic nature of the star makes it a match for the power of yellow, while the soothing nature of blue suggests a compatible form, such as the circle. Gerstner established a characteristic match between each color of hue and a geometric form such that the shape of each form transitions from one to another logically, just as their colors transition. These preferred unions of color and form are used extensively in his work, along with an infinite number of intermediate color-forms that can be generated between each pair. They establish a philosophical approach to his graphic designs of integrated color and form (illustrated in *The Forms of Color*). Both the Kandinsky and the Gerstner approach are valid, in that there is a logical connection between the selected forms and their associated colors. **Selected forms and colors enhance each other when they are characteristically similar. However, these examples demonstrate that such associations are not mutually exclusive.** This is a basic principal of many color-form design concepts.

Contrast Applied to Form

Changes in surface brightness and hue interacting with a form can maintain its visual proportions or change our perception of it as the eye compares each individual color to those that are adjacent. If we anticipate the way colors will influence each other, we can use color to modify the viewer's impression.

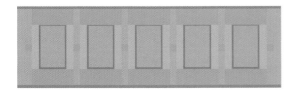

FIGURE 7.12 Here the scale and relative importance of the openings in the elevation are maintained through consistent coloration.

FIGURE 7.13 In this elevation, color is applied inconsistently using a hierarchy approach and emphasizing some window enclosures over others.

Within one plane, the spacing of a series of colored objects can be made to look uniform by consistent application of color, as shown in Figure 7.12. Or they can appear unequal in size and spacing by changing the level of color contrasts, as suggested by the same elevation shown in Figures 7.13 and 7.14.

The greater the color contrasts and variation, the more complex an assembly of volumes becomes. To simplify a form, color variation is often reduced or eliminated. White is a color that is often used—and sometimes overused—to allow the form of an architectural space to be clearly understood. When a light, neutral color, such as white, is used on a well-defined architectural surface and the details are properly lit, that surface can be quite elegant. However, if the surface is somewhat simple, subtle shifts in the surface color can yield the same effect. **Greater contrasts will draw attention toward or away from specific features of the form.** The stronger the greatest condition of contrast, the more it will minimize the other details within view. In the example in Figures 7.15 and 7.16, strong color was used in a large university library to articulate key building forms and to draw visitors up the stair to one side. The position of each color helps to orient users as they move from place to place. Red adds to the monumental sense of the thick curved wall that contains

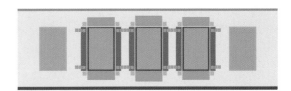

FIGURE 7.14 In this elevation, the applied pattern suggests there is a functional relationship between three of the openings. Because of the pattern, they are read together as one element, establishing focus.

FIGURE 7.15 The scale of this atrium is celebrated through colorful articulation. Red on the curved form helps to draw visitors toward the circulation desk at one end or up the monumental staircase to technology areas at the other. (*Design by Perry Dean Rogers/ Partners, Architects. Photo: Anne Gummerson Photography.*)

FIGURE 7.16 The strength of architectural forms in this lobby is enhanced by dramatic color contrast. (*Design by Perry Dean Rogers/Partners Architects. Photo: Anne Gummerson Photography.*)

vertical ductwork. Each member of the triad harmony of red, yellow, and blue identifies a key functional area it encloses.

Integrity, Enhancement, and Manipulation

In some cases, color placement communicates something distinctive about the materials that make up the form. On other occasions we may find it advantageous to manipulate our impression of an object or space through color to make it preferable. If human perception of form is first established based on the contrasts that present themselves, what happens if these contrasts occur in places other than the edges of the subforms? What if the color breaks along diagonal lines rather than where the wall meets the floor? Does a ceiling always have to be a different color from the wall? Must doors be a different color from the wall? The less consistent color is in meeting our expectations, the more difficult it is to distinguish between true form and perceived reality. Therefore, a key color decision we make in establishing color concept is what we intend to communicate about the designed form. Do we consciously deny the form and its context, subtly reinforce the form, or enhance the form as dramatically as possible? A few methods are currently in use.

Intrinsic Color

One approach to color selection and placement is that of matching the substrate to an identifying color so that the essential nature of the material is communicated through its surface. By maintaining consistency of color with its underlying fabrication material, a consistent concept of form is presented, with each material expressing color and texture as an integral component. In many cases, the colors are *inherent in* the materials chosen as opposed to colors being *applied* onto the materials. This is the concept of *intrinsic color*. **The color of an object is considered intrinsic if it reflects the very nature of that object.**

By a strict application of intrinsic method, each change in substrate, and consequently in surface material, is expressed by the change in color appropriate to the materials used. For example, concrete may be highly textured and rectilinear, but its color in intrinsic applications is limited to shades of gray. Metal framing is typically alu-

minum or anodized; wood may be stained slightly, but would not have homogenous color applied. Clay would have undertones of earth colors, while porcelain would remain light in coloration, true to its nature. Manufactured products such as textiles may have a strong color, but in a strict intrinsic color approach, they would not have colors overprinted onto the material. A popular theme of intrinsic philosophy is that of natural materials. America's best-known architect, Frank Lloyd Wright, was famous for his intrinsic approach to color. His work displayed a commitment to using natural materials in combination with each other, each expressed in its natural coloration. Where synthetic materials were combined with organic ones, he gave them solid colors of high saturation.

In the more contemporary example shown in Figure 7.17, designers used intrinsic and applied colors and texture of materials in combination to give the impression of flowing water in a large interior space. Cool colors in a combination of smooth and irregular surfaces, several tones in close range, and highlighting through reflective surfaces together create the intended atmosphere without any water being present.

Applied Color

An alternative approach to the integration of color intrinsically is the use of *applied color*. Here color is added to the surface of assembled materials in a relatively consistent manner. For instance, metal surfaces might be painted a teal green rather than the cool gray we usually associate with steel. Selections are assigned conceptually, even arbitrarily, regardless of the materials used.

Applied color is often used with some philosophic intent. In some cases, the relationship between the project and its context is important, suggesting that application colors be derived from the context, such as the colors of materials found elsewhere on the site or on neighboring structures. This approach is illustrated in Figure 7.18 using a method well established by Jean-Philippe Lenclos, a French colorist and designer who specializes in applied color derived from context. His team of designers gathers samples of soil, paint chips, old brick, organic matter, and other found materials in and around the site of a proposed project. The samples are ground into a powdered pigment and organized in a grid similar to the arrangement

FIGURE 7.17   The color selection in this project reflects a combination of intrinsic and applied color methods to express the concept. (*Design by ADD Inc. Photo: © Warren Jagger Photography, Inc.*)

shown at the top of the illustration. Proposed color combinations for the new architectural form are derived from this reference collection. Not all schemes incorporate all the contextual colors, as shown in the sample palettes below the reference grid. And no color appears in any scheme that was not first observed at the site.

Enhancing Form with Color

In design, form is frequently enhanced through color application. One fairly common trick of the trade to make a room feel less boxy is to significantly change the color of one wall. A low ceiling, windows with odd proportions, or an irregularly shaped room may be improved simply by using collective color wisdom to deliberately impact its

apparent form. Value contrast has the most dramatic effect as a tool for enhancement, followed by equally incremental changes in saturation and hue. When contrasts are used in combination, the effect is cumulative. Objects may be colored to "disappear" into the wall; or the poor proportions of architectural elements may be modified through applied color to give them more appealing proportions. In the example in Figures 7.19 and 7.20, color selection and placement are used to make the same row of windows blend into the wall or become more pronounced and elongated.

Enhancement is a method for reinforcing or improving form by using response to color relationships to draw attention to its positive characteristics. Depth can be added to a relatively shallow

FIGURE 7.18 The box-grid method for evaluating colors of context has gained popularity in recent years due in part to the work of Jean-Philippe Lenclos.

space by adjustments in value, saturation, and temperature; cramped spaces can be modified to appear more moderate in proportion; or an over-scaled room may be minimized through color application. Horizontal lines at a chair-rail height or other repetitive coloration would lengthen the same physical space. The long, narrow passage is a form frequently improved by the application of color. Changes in color that are irregular and inconsistent with expectations shift the line of sight away from an otherwise linear viewpoint. In the model in Figure 7.21, the depth of a colonnaded room is reduced by an abrupt change in color value and temperature. The result is a change in our perception of the room's shape without a change in form. Compare this to the same model in alternative col-

FIGURE 7.19 The windows in this illustration are meant to be a subtle protrusion in the wall that contains them, allowing the wall plane to read continuously.

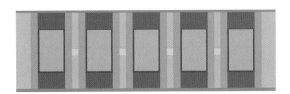

FIGURE 7.20 Here the same windows shown in Figure 7.19 are rendered to seem proportionately taller and more pronounced.

FIGURE 7.21   In this model the designer has reduced the apparent depth of the space through color manipulation. (*Design by Melissa Weiss.*)

ors shown in Chapter 8, "Color Enhances Form" (Figures 8.5, 8.6, 8.18, 8.19, 8.20, 8.21, and 8.22).

Less common but equally appropriate is the practice of adjusting the general room color on one wall slightly from its adjacent wall to bring about a subtle shift in room planes. For instance, a rectangular room that is slightly long can appear more square if the two end walls use advancing colors. The fact that two colors are used may be imperceptible, since color varies slightly due to shadow casting and one expects to see slight changes where two planes collide. Most observers will assume they are the same color. A ceiling does not have to be white to look higher. The effect is achieved as long as the ceiling is lighter in value than the color of the walls. In a room with dark walls this allows for experimentation. To give the impression of a lower ceiling, it would be slightly darker than the walls. If the ceiling is low and the walls are light to begin with, it may be beneficial to use the wall color on the ceiling, thereby eliminating contrast between the planes and minimizing the edge where they meet. To make small windows appear larger, more elaborate window treatment is often used. If they are

particularly short or narrow, added pattern can reduce the effect by drawing the eye's attention. High contrast around the window will draw attention to its relative scale. (These conditions are explored further in Chapter 8.) Contrast can also be used to enhance an object. In the elevation in Figure 7.22, the diamond object is visible as a dark object in front of a light wall. As the value of the wall gets closer to the object, the object loses its presence. To make it stand out, the color of the

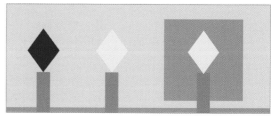

FIGURE 7.22   In this elevation, the relationship between object and background determines which objects are more noticeable. If the color of the object is lighter than the background it will come forward. If it is darker than the ground, it will recede, or read like a hole when viewed face front.

area immediately behind can be modified to increase contrast.

Illusionary Color

The opposite approach to the integration of color intrinsically is considered to be *illusionary*. **Illusionary color is applied color in an extreme application, where surface color predetermines our perception of form.** It can mean covering a blank concrete surface with another geometric color composition or upholstering an otherwise flat surface in a bold textile to give depth and color intricacy. The most extreme form of illusionary color is the practice of trompe l'oeil, which means, "to fool the eye." In the atrium space shown in Figure 7.23 it's difficult to determine the edge of the mural painting from the painted framing of the adjacent interior window

FIGURE 7.23 This enclosed city atrium makes good use of illusionary color to make the most of its volume. (*Design by Howard F. Elkus, FAIA principal-in-charge while at The Architects Collaborative. Trompe l'oeil by Richard Haas. Photo: © Bill Horsman.*)

FIGURE 7.24   Color and pattern in this model were developed to reduce the depth of the space. The change in pattern scale has the same effect as adjusting the scale of furniture to distort our sense of perspective. (*Design by Susan Allison Bomzer.*)

wall. The clever play on scale causes the small water feature in the foreground to appear larger than it is because it is indistinguishable from the applied image behind it. By using colors of the adjacent building materials in the mural, the line between reality and illusion is lost—everything appears to be three-dimensional.

There are many ways to create color illusion in design practice. Faux finishes come in and out of fashion periodically as an illusionary source. Patterning is also frequently called upon to reduce apparent scale, such as using handwoven area rugs to incorporate color composition over a large, flat plane. In the model in Figure 7.24, the designer reduced the apparent depth by using an alternative approach to the one in Figure 7.21. She applied patterning to the columns and changed the scale in the reverse of what we normally expect from patterned

surfaces in perspective—the larger pattern is the farthest away. This in combination with strong horizontal lines on the floor and an advancing color on the rear wall give the sense of shorter distance.

In this chapter, we've stressed the strength of color as a component of the design concept through built and unbuilt examples. Approaches range from expressive to symbolic and, finally, to integrated methods where color enhances form. In earlier chapters, we observed how colors are used in two-dimensional combination to impact each other either by influence or contrast. Color relationships have a bearing on the way we perceive each individual color as well as the way we see shape, distance, and relative scale. In the next chapter, we revisit the color conditions that serve as tools for enhancement of form and consider their potential in three-dimensional design practice.

Color Enhances Form

The two basic essentials common to all areas of design are color and form. Form is the two-dimensional or three-dimensional nature of a designed object. It's the rectangular page of a magazine, the circular shape of a Frisbee, or the slope of a gable roof. Color is the surface media that enables us to see the form for what it is. A rubber ball is round by necessity. But it is the redness of the ball against the green of the grass that enables us to recognize its roundness.

Color is inextricably linked to form. Without form, there is no color. Even the artist's canvas is dependent on the relative flatness of its gessoed surface and the proportion of the frame to provide a form for the colored pigment to be applied. Without color, there is no form. Consider the experience of walking through a dark room at night. Without the benefit of a lamp to cast shadows and illuminate colored surfaces, it's impossible to determine the shape of the rooms or the placement of objects within it. Even an all-white room is without recognizable form unless the light is uneven enough to cast shadows, changing the color of the white and exposing the corners of the room.

The way we apply color to each form determines the clarity of its shape and the definition of its character. Our intentions to reinforce, delineate, modify, or enhance through color application establish the criteria for color-form integration. Let's explore those opportunities.

■ COLOR AND SCALE

There's an old expression, "You can't change the shape of a barn by giving it a coat of paint." This may be true, but the apparent scale of the barn is another case altogether. A barn will be more imposing if its color is strong and if the contrast between it and the color of its surrounding environment is great. The strength of the contrast gives the effect of a barn with slightly larger scale. If color is integrated with the components of a designed form, it serves to unify the overall design. Inconsistent color assignments serve to diffuse the clarity of an otherwise uniform design. When objects of consistent form are colored consistently, the relationship is reinforced. When rendered inconsistently, they lose their conspicuous likeness. (This was illustrated in Figures 7.12 through 7.14.) The relationship of the colors used dictates the perception of relative change in scale. Details are enhanced through color contrast—the more an object's color contrasts with the color of its background, the more pronounced it becomes. Subforms with hard, rectilinear edges can be strengthened by a dramatic value contrast or softened by adjacent tones that are very similar.

When color is observed in space, it is seen relative to the boundaries that frame the view. In other words, the deep, cool green of a garden seen through a picture window might be made more dramatic by a window frame in a light, warm tone. The rich, warm color of a piece of wood cabinetry will appear more dramatic if the color of the wall behind it is cool or of a complementary tone. The amount of each contrast between a shape and its surroundings determines how much visual interest it will attract. If there is little contrast between shapes within an interior space, the viewer might be easily distracted by something in the space beyond. Alternatively, if the contrast between an object and its background is measurable, the viewer's ability to distinguish subtle color shifts within shapes may be reduced. If there is contrast within the object, the eye will be quickly drawn to its detail.

Stronger contrasts can impact perception of scale. **Context is the key for the influence of color over scale.** Each individual color is recognized in relationship to surrounding colors. Color combinations can be experienced as an overall neighborhood, a particular street, a single building, or the details of the building. The more contrast is used to draw attention to a detail, the greater its apparent significance. For example, an all-white house may blend into its surroundings on a street of modern-style ranch houses. The same home might establish a consistent elegance in a neighborhood of classic constructions. But it's likely to visually stand out in its sterility when positioned in nature's landscape or alongside a row of Victorian "painted ladies" in San Francisco. Perception of each color combination is made in the context of its neighborhood. In a different scale, we may choose to blend the house with its landscape while drawing attention to the front door by painting it red. The red door will have the desired effect provided the rest of the house is noticeably lighter or darker than the red and less saturated. The red-door effect will be even greater if all the houses on the street are similar in tone to the house being rendered. If the neighbor's entire house is maroon, it diminishes the singular effect of the red door. Within nature's landscape, several colors may be used in combination to camouflage a residence within its surroundings, or uniform color may be employed to give the home a sense of grand scale.

▶ Scale and Value

The scale of any form can be influenced by the value characteristics of its assigned color. Darker colors, whether they have strong chroma or not,

will give the impression of reduced scale when viewed at a distance. This is most apparent when the surrounding color is very light. In this case, the dark object will appear decreased, while its lighter counterpart, the wall, will seem larger. Comparatively light color on an object seems to increase its visual scale in many circumstances. (See the upper boxes in Figure 8.1.) The greater the value contrast between a single element and its surroundings, the stronger the influence. Simply put, the rule of thumb to impact the appearance of scale using color value is this:

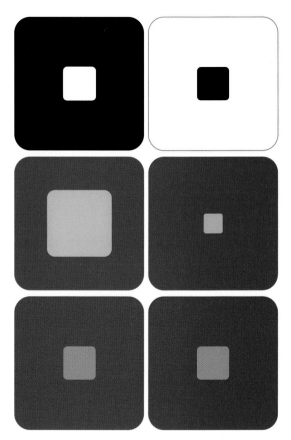

FIGURE 8.1 Which of the two boxes at the top is larger? To most eyes, the black object appears smaller than the white one of equal size. In the center boxes, the larger area of goldenrod color on the left allows it to read as a more saturated version than the same color in a smaller scale on the right. In the bottom comparison, the more saturated color of the box on the right gives this impression that it's larger than its equivalent on the left, in part because of the contrast with a neutral background.

- Darker color against a light background reduces scale.
- Lighter color against a dark background increases scale.

▶ Scale and Saturation

Scale can both impact saturation and be influenced by it. Nonchromatic characteristics of form can change our perception of saturation, specifically the proportion and location. A small amount of a saturated color exhibits its inherent intensity. As the area of a color is increased, its apparent saturation also increases, up to a point. (Refer to the center boxes in Figure 8.1.) Beyond that point—usually about 20 degrees horizontal range of visual field—the purity or intensity of that color seems to decrease. The reason is that the color ceases to be read as an object color but becomes the context itself, influencing the other colors in view. This means that the intensity of a saturated color will look as if it is increased as its scale is increased, as long as the color occurs only within some portion of the view plane. The effect becomes void when the color moves around us. Unfortunately, the condition is overlooked if decisions are made using small handheld samples. An accent in this situation may appear to be more intense than it will in the final analysis.

In terms of its influence on scale, saturation is probably not reliable. Saturation appears to reduce as full room color. Several colorists have noted conditions where higher saturation level increases apparent scale, while reduced saturation decreases it. However, this is the case only when the colored object resides on a neutral background. To be specific, a color-scale effect is possible when the background offers a visible contrast of saturation with the object. In some cases, the highly saturated object on a low-saturation background looks larger than the same object in low saturation on a background of similar saturation level. But the reverse is not true. **Objects on a high-saturation background do not necessarily exhibit scale differences.** To capture a saturation-scale effect for design purposes, a test model is suggested to be certain. Under conditions of **neutral background,** the rule of thumb on scale influence over saturation is this:

- Larger scale of a color of hue increases its saturation (up to a point).
- Smaller scale of a saturated color decreases its saturation.

■ COLOR AND DEPTH PERCEPTION

Several conditions combine in our mind's eye to create a perception of three-dimensional form. When one object overlaps another, we assume that the overlapping figure is closer to us. When an object appears to be smaller than its known size, we presume that it is far away. Our sense of space depends on our comparison of objects that share a linear perspective. This comparison helps us to determine each object's relative position in space. Brightness and the relation of light and shade are clues in our assessment. We assume that a less bright version of the same object is farther away. If one plane is slightly darker than a similarly hued adjacent plane, we suspect it is attached but facing away from the light source. If it is darker than a larger adjacent object, we assume it is positioned in the shadow of the larger object. When the edges of

---

Lois Swirnoff

Lois Swirnoff (American, contemporary) is a colorist whose experiments address the abstract, three-dimensional realm. She initially established herself as a painter and photographer after earning B.F.A. and M.F.A. degrees at Yale University, where she studied with Josef Albers. Swirnoff is well known for her work in illusionary color using three-dimensional form, including color influence and depth perception. Her teaching positions have included Harvard University, Skidmore, Wellesley College, the University of Southern California, the University of California at Los Angeles, and Cooper Union Art School in New York City. She has published several books and articles, including *Dimensional Color,* which addresses issues of depth perception.

these objects become less clear, the loss of detail suggests greater distance. Our conclusions are not based solely on what we see, but also on what we know from experience and therefore assume to be so. It's because of this experiential dependency that color can be used to modify our perception of three-dimensional depth.

▶ Visual Distance

Color behaves in a unique manner when it is viewed at a great distance. If a colored object is clearly visible as a form, its color will be tied to the specific object. Although this seems like common sense, there are two conditions where color seen at great distance behaves more independently of its surface. These conditions are known as *film color* and *volume color.*

Volume color has some depth and translucency to it. It's the fluidic color that exists in conditions of fog, smoke, some atmospheric conditions, and in fluids that contain some particulate matter (e.g., gases in air or solid particles in water). If we look at the landscape through a glass of ginger ale, the colors seen are adjusted according to the density of the ginger ale. The environment can impact perception in the same manner. Water vapor in the air or smog will cause some adjustment in the colors available. This adjustment depends on the severity of the translucent fluid and the distance of the observation. Consider the colors of green in the landscape in Figure 8.2. Planting in the foreground is darker and more saturated than that of the same plants seen at a distance.

Film color is another condition associated with extended view range. It occurs when a large area of a single colored surface acts as though it is independent of the object it's attached to. In this case, the color will appear to fill the frame through which it is viewed. The frame can be a window frame, the view between two trees, or an opening between buildings. Film color is most likely to occur with colors of strong contrast or extremes in value or saturation (as depicted in Figure 8.3). It looks as though its limits are imperceptible, allowing the color to influence the observer's understanding of where it exists in reality according to its inherent color characteristics rather than its form. When images are perceived as film color, they usually appear enhanced in their brightness.

This can be exaggerated by a contrasting color in the view frame.

When we experience film color, each distinct color assumes a position of distance from the viewer that is only partly determined by its true location. Visual perception, especially depth perception of each color, is distorted slightly according to its chromacity. Due to conditions of film color, a series of planes at a distance will advance or recede when the eye compares the planes to each other, regardless of their actual positioning. The condition of film color is what we re-create when using color for its potential to modify depth perception.

▶ Chromacity

Chromacity, as previously mentioned, involves the characteristics of a color according to its relative hue, value, and saturation level. Each of these three scales has an impact on the depth at which we perceive the color to exist. When a color of medium value, average saturation, and moderate temperature is observed, the observer's sense of its distance should be reasonably accurate. Our impression of this distance can be influenced as hue, value, and saturation shift, because we adjust our assumptions about distances accordingly. This condition is a human phenomenon, comparable to the influence one color imparts on another during contrast of simultaneity or extent.

Distance and Objects

Chromatic attributes of color impact the perceived distance of the objects according to two sets of rules, which we'll distinguish as objects/landscape and contextual environment. The most common conditions include viewing forms at a distance, as in landscape views, exterior work, graphic design, and three-dimensional objects. Color influence on depth perception behaves similarly in these conditions since our perception in each case is relative to some color context. As we discuss here, the rules change slightly when the color in question is the context, such as within a closed room.

In all conditions, the degree of contrast between individual colors determines the effectiveness of the color influence. In distance viewing, where color is sometimes without apparent form, the eye compares colors to each other and adjusts

FIGURE 8.2 This landscape image demonstrates the effect of volume color in three-dimensional space. (*Photo: Janice Kopacz.*)

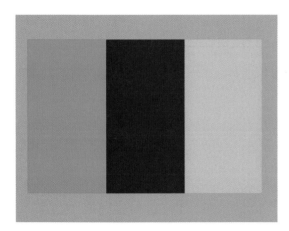

FIGURE 8.3 The position of the three color samples shown here would not appear to be at the same distance if they were seen from afar. If seen through a handheld view frame, they may appear to move slightly, behaving as film color, even though we know they are on the same flat surface of the page.

their positioning according to the accelerative or recessive reaction in the eye caused by their chromacity. Generally speaking, if two colors are similar in value and temperature but are of different, equally saturated hues, they will assume the same plane within a given view frame—unless other cues suggest that their distances vary.

To test conditions of color and depth perception, try creating a neutral window frame through which to view color samples by cutting a square opening in a piece of matte board. Ideally, the board should be a true gray, without hue, in a medium value. Then look through the neutral window frame at the sample colors in Figures 8.3, 8.4, 8.7, and 8.11, masking out the gray borders as much as possible by moving the frame closer or farther away from the eye. Intellectually, we know that the colored shapes are sitting in the same plane, that is, the face of the printed page. However, if you relax and look at the colors long enough, they may behave more like film color, allowing you to see the depth characteristics of the colors.

Distance and Value

If two or more adjacent colors are unequal in value, only the lighter color will appear closer while the darker color will recede. For example, a pale yellow will advance before a reddish-brown.

White will move forward in comparison to a dark gray. In the example in Figure 8.4, the light green advances before the dark blue. The greater the difference in value of the two colors, the stronger is their tendency to separate according to depth perception—as long as the view frame is a medium-value neutral. (If the view frame is very light, its contrast with the darkest colors may give them greater strength, causing different depth-perception results.)

The tendency for color to advance or recede is based on relative value changes when color is applied within contained rooms. As color surrounds the viewer, the comparative nature becomes the reverse of object color—that is, lighter values recede and darker ones advance. The tendency for colors to behave differently in the mind's eye offers us opportunity to use color in constructive ways. In the model in Figure 8.5, the designer uses knowledge of advancing and receding color to give her designed form reduced depth. Compare this to the same model in Figure 8.6, which was rendered to increase visual depth of the same scale model by reversing values within a contained space.

Distance and Temperature

Color temperature also affects visual depth perception because of variation in the way different wave-

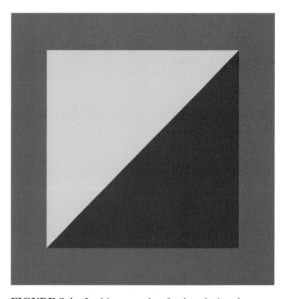

FIGURE 8.4 In this example of colored triangles, the light section may seem to move slightly closer due to conditions of advancing and receding in human perception.

FIGURE 8.5   In this spatial model, value contrasts are assigned to decrease perceived distance. (*Design by Tammy Couture, Seaside Spaces.*)

FIGURE 8.6   In this spatial model, value contrasts maximize the depth of the same space. (*Design by Sofia Willis.*)

lengths are refracted in the eye. **Typically, a color of warmer hue will appear closer than a color of similar saturation in a cool hue.** The warmer the color, relatively speaking, the more it will advance. A yellow-orange object will advance before a green one of equal saturation and value. Red tends to dominate blue when it comes to film color, as suggested in Figure 8.7. The cooler the color, the greater is its tendency to recede. Again, this condition assumes a neutral view frame. If the view frame or background is very warm, then cool colors may advance more than warm due to the effects of contrast.

Positioning of colors in space can influence our understanding of planar relationships. In the elevations in Figure 8.8, the color of one building section is evaluated in a warm color, positioning it closer to the forward columns, then in a cool color, which gives it a more recessed appearance. In the cool version, the distance between the front columns and the blue wall looks greater, placing the blue wall closer to the rest of the building facade. Depth-perception color attributes can be used to enhance depth of physically smaller increments. In the atrium in Figure 8.9, the dark, cool tone of the recesses allows the geometric forms of the architecture greater prominence within the

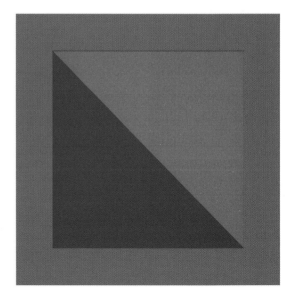

FIGURE 8.7 Here the conditions of depth perception relative to temperature may influence our impression of the position of the color on the page.

three-dimensional space without adding significant physical dimension.

The reasons for changes in depth perception are open to debate among theorists. Faber Birren is among the colorists who identified the effects of

FIGURE 8.8 This elevation study was performed using layers of colored board, so that one layer could be replaced for evaluation of color options of that plane. (*Design by Sarah Krieger.*)

FIGURE 8.9 The depth of the key elevation here is enhanced by a combination of light color and comparatively cooler, darker recesses. (*Design by Flansburgh Associates, Inc. Photo: © Steve Rosenthal.*)

color on depth perception as a condition of where the eye sees each color. He suggests in some of his books that humans focus on red at a point behind the retina, causing the lens of the eye to be convex and visually drawing the color closer. Blue is normally focused in front of the retina, which makes the lens flatten out, giving us a subtle sense of the color moving away. Theoretically speaking, it's the movement happening within the mechanisms of the eye that causes apparent movement between various colors. The movement is uniform from front to back rather than side to side, in accordance with the way the lens functions.

Other researchers suggest that the theory of red advancing and blue receding is a concept we have become conditioned to accept as a part of our culture. In their attempt to separate fact from myth concerning color, the writing team of Kenneth Fehrman and Cherie Fehrman propose that contrast with background color has more of an impact on color movement (*Color: The Secret Influence*). The greater the contrast of a color with its background, the more it will stand out, or appear to advance, regardless of relative temperature. This suggests that our assumptions need to be tested, or mocked up with contextual color, before final application to ensure reliable results.

In either case, colors of hue do have a tendency to cluster according to color temperature. When observing a spatial field of many hues, the individual colors have a tendency to organize themselves so that warm tones are visually connected to each

Since most architectural design is first seen at a distance, color is critical to establishing the overall scale. If the color is very uniform, the building will appear monolithic, making it more difficult to ascertain its scale—a desirable thing in some situations. If individual elements (openings, changes in plane, alternative surfaces) have some color contrast, the scale will be easier to read. Color strength seems to parallel characteristics of color in depth perception. It's difficult to test depth tendencies of one characteristic completely without one of the other two conditions impacting comparisons. In such cases, the stronger of two colors, as a combined comparison of value, temperature, and saturation, will be the advancing color. In general, for **exterior environmental design, external form color, and two-dimensional applications,** one or more of the following conditions will cause a color to influence form:

- Darker values recede, lighter values advance.
- Cooler hues recede, warmer values advance.
- Lower saturations recede, higher saturations advance.

This suggests some considerations in architectural work to support the uniqueness of architectural compositions:

- Sometimes a building form of limited depth will be generously enhanced by using advancing or receding color to give it greater apparent depth—a darker color at a recess or a lighter one along a protrusion, serving as highlight. Color can be used to simplify the form of the building, to modulate it, or to give it greater complexity.

- Architectural forms intended to link other forms can also make use of color to reinforce the concept. To connect two colors that are distant from each other, intermediaries may be used. When the intermediates are placed between the original two colors, the eye draws them closer together.

- Value contrasts are more easily registered in extreme lighting conditions. This implies that when subtle variations of hue are used in exterior work, they should be accompanied by a change in value: Otherwise, the change in color will be lost under most exterior lighting situations. Direct sunlight will cause the colors to wash out a bit, obscuring subtle differences in hue. At night, the comparison of bright light under floodlamps to darkness of shadow will also reduce one's ability to perceive slight variations in hue.

other and cool ones likewise appear connected. The overall view will then be read first as an image of warm colors as opposed to cool colors. Consider this when looking at the collection of irregular squares in Figure 8.10. The grid reads more like a cool solid over a warm one where they share a diagonal edge.

Distance and Saturation

Saturation is the third attribute that affects depth perception at great distances or in two-dimensional composition. Colors that are highly saturated tend to capture attention before their counterparts because of their greater strength. This leads the viewer to conclude that a more saturated color advances, while neutral colors tend to recede, comparatively speaking. More chroma increases the

tendency for a colored plane to seem closer to view. As saturation decreases, distance from the viewer correspondingly seems to increase. Gray has a tendency to disappear into the background, while cobalt blue can be very eye-catching. In Figure 8.11, the high-chroma violet has the greater strength, giving the sense of advancement, over a more subdued violet.

Contrast is the key factor used to establish a change in depth of form. If the color of an object has a high contrast with its background, it will have greater strength, causing it to advance slightly within one's view. This effect is used frequently to accentuate portions of overall design. A highly saturated accent color may be used on a wall to make it seem closer than it is. The same color on a ceiling will make the ceiling seem lower. In Figure 8.12,

FIGURE 8.10 The squares in this composition seem to separate along an irregular form due to our eye's tendency to group warm and cool colors together. (*Design by Sheila R. Selby, 2002.*)

higher saturation along key planes in the red scheme on the right brings them forward, minimizing depth between the columns, while the beige scheme allows the ceiling and walls to read more clearly as a continuous volume.

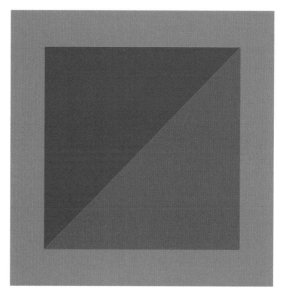

FIGURE 8.11 This illustration shows colors of different saturation levels. If they are observed as film color through a frame, the triangle of higher saturation will appear to inch forward.

What is interesting about the saturation-depth phenomenon is that it is difficult to determine with certainty if these conditions are physiological or learned reactions. While some reactions to color are logically associated with reflexes of the cones, it is

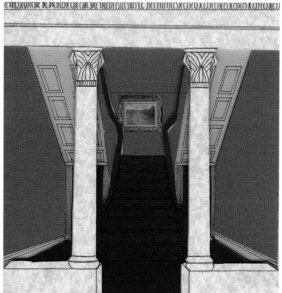

FIGURE 8.12 Using a layered board technique, the designer of this entry stair tests the impact of different saturation levels. (*Designed by Jane Toland.*)

possible that personal experience tells us that grays in the distance are due to atmospheric conditions—the sense of volume color due to particles in the air. Depth perception in the case of saturation may be based purely on experience.

Context Depth

For most humans with binocular vision (two eyes), color contributes to our perception of distance by combining with observations of shape and form as well as general depth perception. A note of concern is in order when working with variations of value within enclosed spaces. Peripheral brightness is very undesirable in most applications. This means that the area of focus will almost always be the brightest view in the room, allowing the eye a central field of lightness and relative darkness, or equal value, at the perimeter. Placement of a focal point in opposition to this general preference will result in some discomfort to the viewer.

As color becomes the context, comparative effects for color-based depth adjustments are reduced, and the conditions for value shift. This occurs because in controlled environments, applied color becomes the context. **When color surrounds the viewer, dark colors tend to advance or close in and light ones to recede or enlarge the space**—the reverse of observations of objects or landscapes.

Within a room, the influence of the color on overall scale takes effect, and the influence of other environmental color is lost. In the absence of comparative color, room color behaves more like object color. Within closed rooms, the depth effect of the other two chromatic characteristics—saturation and temperature—are constant, but their impact is reduced as other effects become more influential.

The condition of value influence on depth is related to the field of vision, or viewpoint. Once a colored surface expands into peripheral vision, its tendency to advance and recede changes. In this case, it is no longer relating to the context of other colors but becomes the context itself. For designers who work within architecturally contained space, the following comparative colors will advance, and when used as a major room color, these changes will make the room seem smaller: darker value, greater saturation, and warmer hue. As surrounding color in interior space, the following adjustments in color will cause surface to recede, making the room appear larger: lighter value, lesser saturation, and cooler hue. These conditions are less pronounced than under the conditions previously discussed, unless seen from another environment that offers context. Given these particular conditions for interior work, several guidelines are suggested to adjust color selections for their desired effect on scale and distance.

Design Goal	Hue (Yellow-Red-Blue)	Value (Light-Dark)	Saturation (Chroma)
Ceiling to appear higher	Cooler hue	Lighter value	Lower saturation
Ceiling to appear lower	Warmer hue	Darker value	Higher saturation
Room to appear larger	Reduce contrasts Fewer hues	Lighter value Higher value	Fewer contrasts
Room to appear smaller	Increase contrasts Greater range of hue	More contrasts Darker value	More contrasts Higher saturation
Bring a wall closer	Warmer hue	Increase contrast	Higher saturation
Make a wall more distant	Cooler hue	Decrease contrast	Lower saturation
Draw attention to detail	Contrast temperature or extent	Increase contrast	Higher saturation than background
Obscure a condition	Consistent hue	Consistent value with background	Consistent saturation with background

Interior Design Tips

While the conditions described here will not be present in every case, together they do provide a traditional formula one might use in the absence of experience. The conclusions for **interior applications, or any self-contained environment,** suggest that one or more of the following conditions will influence interior form:

- In the case of room color: lighter values recede, darker values advance.
- As accents: light values advance, darker values recede.
- As room color and accents: cooler hues recede, warmer hues advance.
- As room color and accents: lower saturations recede, higher saturations advance.

A few notes are offered relative to conditions of interior color applications:

- Consider the transitions from room to room in terms of successive contrasts, as each room sets up the context for the next one. At the entry point, the plane of the outer wall will be seen in the same view as that of the inner wall. If the orientation of color assignments is determined according to the direction one normally approaches, undesirable combinations might be avoided. Such decisions become more complex if the room has many entry points.
- If a little more contrast serves to maintain contrast on the outside during bright or harsh light, subtle color contrasts are more effective in interior applications. The primary reasons are the close proximity of observation and the greater degree of control we have over light sources.

The Small Room

Color for the small room is a concern for many projects, and successful approaches to this room type vary. Conventional wisdom suggests that we keep things light to give an appearance of greater scale. However, this approach ignores several conditions of equal importance. One is context—the color of the room from which the small room is entered. If the preceding room is much larger and darker in value, a white room can appear as a hole by contrast. A small room that is light in color can also appear very cluttered, reducing the overall scale, if the objects contained in the room are much darker in value than the room itself. Another concern is that the lightness of white allows the edges of the room to be read clearly from a great distance, serving to reduce its scale with clarity of form. If the edges are in shadow, the condition with a medium value, the corners may appear softer, less defined. Therefore, small rooms can be made to appear larger, or at least not smaller, through several approaches:

- Avoid large areas of highly saturated color. These tend to fill the space visually, and when seen from the adjacent room they advance, making the surface or object to which they are applied seem larger.
- Limit the number of contrasts or use less dynamic ones. Contrasts break the space visually, as we can see in Figure 8.13. Subtle contrasts such as saturation or use of texture add interest without scale reduction.
- Soften the transition from the large room into the small room through minimal value shift in the major room color. To draw someone into the room, keep the focus at the far end with a small amount of a highly saturated color or pattern.
- Avoid dark value, warm hue, or high saturation on a ceiling if the goal is to increase height. Darker values give the impression of reduced height. Try to avoid colors on the floor and ceiling that are similar in value yet different from the wall. The eye will connect these planes, effectively reducing the distance between them.

▶ Layering

Layering is an effective way to use color to reinforce a three-dimensional design. When colored surfaces are seen as spatially separated—that is, one in front of the other—their positioning is readily apparent if the colors are sequential. An incremental change in value or hue will enable the view to be established more clearly as a receding series

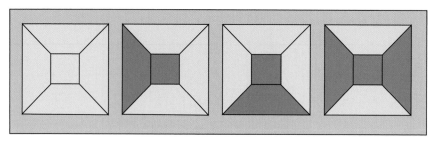

FIGURE 8.13 This simple diagram illustrates how contrasting colors break the continuous flow of a cube-shaped room, reducing its volume.

of planes. If the colors vary from each other in a nonsequential way, they are more likely to be read as if all are coplanar, effectively flattening the observer's impression of the space.

Transition from one space into another can be articulated at a distance in order to draw people into—or to give a preview of—spaces they are about to experience. This is most effective when the layers are distinct and clearly associated with specific forms. Architects of the Arts and Crafts era used layering techniques in many interior spaces, creating stimulating wood-framed views by integrating colors with their forms. In the contemporary headquarters space shown in Figure 8.14, a

FIGURE 8.14 This executive office area uses color shifts to signal a change of plane, where the view extends from one space to another. (*Interior Design by GHK. Photo: Marco Lorenzetti © Hedrich Blessing.*)

Albert Halse

Albert Halse, AIA, ASID, was an American contemporary of Faber Birren. He established a practice in the field of color consulting in association with his work as an architect and interior designer. An associate professor at Columbia University, he wrote extensively on the use of color in architecture and interior design practice, including the analytical text, *The Use of Color in Interiors.* Halse considered the lighting an integral component of a color palette. He also demonstrated the effective use of general color-reference tools, such as those developed by Munsell and Ostwald, as a part of design practice.

change in color with each wall plane allows us to understand the complexity of the interior.

Simple models are often used to test the effect of colors on a layered design. A series of flat boards with successively smaller windows are mounted one behind the other so that the color of all the planes can be seen from one end. Working with an abstract model like this allows the color to be liberated from the materials. Comparisons between two or more colors are about the color only, not their position or form. When the color sample has no structure to establish its limits, it tends to float as in film color. If viewed through a frame, the color will appear to attach itself to the frame, similar to the way fluid behaves in a container. This allows us to test the effects of a color in a layered space at small scale.

■ ARTICULATING FORM

The way that we integrate color with elements of form determines how readily we understand the form itself. Some of the most expressive architectural forms are those that allow us to read each of the edges of each shape with clear color definition. This means that the colors used to express those forms are visible regardless of conditions of light and shadow and have tendencies of film color behavior. Often, such expression communi-

cates the essence of a building structure, such as the university setting in Figure 8.15. In this example, each change in building material is accompanied by a dramatic change in color. The red identifies the elevator enclosure, the beige stucco wall extends through the glass curtain wall to the exterior, and the large pale blue plane makes a conceptual connection with the skylights above. Together they create a dynamic story of color and form integration.

Clarity of form adds to our sense of environmental design not only for aesthetic purpose, but also for ease of use. The example in Figure 8.16 shows an outdoor stair that might be considered unsafe by some code standards. However, the contrast of color created by the natural reddish debris against the light granite steps makes the edges of the form very easy to see. Visitors are comfortable exploring the area below without safety rails in part because of clarity of the steps' form.

FIGURE 8.15 This project illustrates strong use of color and form integration as a design methodology to articulate building elements. (*Design by Perry Dean Rogers/Partners Architects. Photo: © Richard Mandelkorn.*)

FIGURE 8.16   Notice how safe this walkway appears due to the visibility of the edges of each step. (*Photo: R. Lerch Gallery, Rockport, Massachusetts*)

▶ Shadow

The relationship of light and shade contributes to a sense of dimension and allows the observer to understand greater complexity of form. When a three-dimensional art object is displayed, light orientation becomes critical in allowing the viewer to see the subtle changes in form and texture on the object. If the lighting is too uniform, it has a tendency to flatten out the object in the mind's eye because there's not enough variation in color as a result of the casting of shadows. In architecture, this condition is of particular concern, since our perception of spatial form is directly tied to the shadows that articulate it.

The case is illustrated in Figure 8.17. If a cube appears to be uniformly colored with one light surface, one medium, and one dark, its shape as a box can be clearly understood (top left). However, if all the planes of the cube appear uniform in value, it will tend to flatten as a form (top right). If a portion of one surface is distinctly dark, it may register as a hole (bottom left). If the square surfaces are broken into smaller forms of different value, the flat surface can appear to have a different shape altogether (bottom right). The key point about applying color

to form that depends on shadow casting is this—if color selection counteracts the effect of the shadow casting, the form will not be clearly understood. If perception of the form depends on a lighter top and darker side, the surface color should not be darker

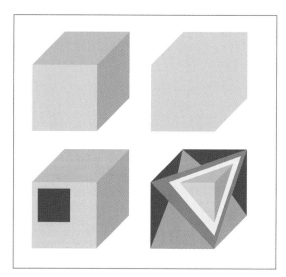

FIGURE 8.17   This illustration shows how our understanding of the cube's shape changes according to its applied color.

on the top than the side. Otherwise, it may cancel necessary shadow effects.

▶ Definition

When there are functional concerns to be addressed, color can be used to articulate these in a positive way. One of the most common detail elements of color is that of attention getting. In fashion, the most important details are given prominence through selective use of contrasts. The same is true in several forms of architecture. Contrasts are used to draw attention to some elements of spatial form over others. In the examples shown in Figures 8.18 and 8.19, color is used to make the columns more or less pronounced by either blending or contrasting them with the wall beyond. The columns in Figure 8.18 are much stronger elements.

Proportion

Sometimes an architectural element is not in ideal proportion with the rest of the space or its function. In such cases, color can be applied inconsistently to visually adjust those proportions. A molding at an undesirable height might be engaged with a color

band to raise or lower it proportionately. Window treatments offer the same opportunities. Vertical planes that are too tall may be reduced through horizontal lines of color, either through pattern or edges of contrasting color. In the study models shown in Figures 8.20 and 8.21, one designer placed color to make the columns appear shorter, while the other worked to make the columns look taller. In both cases, room and columns have the same physical proportions. In Figure 8.20, columns are made to look short by breaking color along horizontal lines to draw the eye across the width of the forms, allowing them to read as a series of stacked elements. In Figure 8.21, columns are consistent from floor to cornice and distinct from the background color.

In another exploration of this columned room, shown in Figure 8.22, the designer changes our perception of the space in another way. Here the consistently symmetric room is colored to distort the overall shape through variations in column color and uneven floor patterning.

Periodic color demarcations in a wall surface can minimize the monotony of a long corridor by helping it to read as a series of planes. Surface pattern has the same effect to a lesser degree. Patterning with some scale variation offers greater impact,

FIGURE 8.18 The designer of this model used strong color contrast to give the columns more strength as a spatial feature. (*Design by M. Beth Hanssens.*)

FIGURE 8.19 In this model, which has the same proportions as the one in Figure 8.18, the designer consciously minimized the columns by applying color and texture similar to that of the wall behind. (*Design by Brenda Reishus.*)

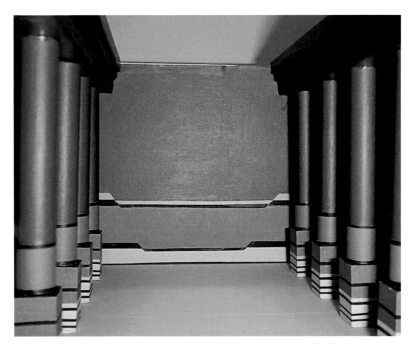

FIGURE 8.20 Here the color study model is rendered to make columns read shorter and wider. Compare this to the solution in Figure 8.21. (*Design by Georgianne Healy.*)

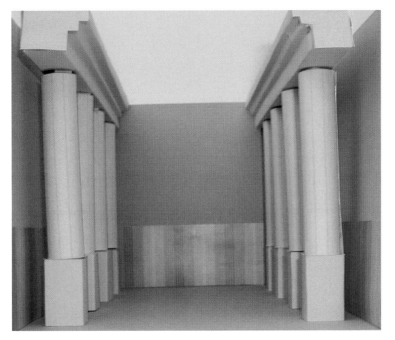

FIGURE 8.21 In comparison to Figure 8.20, this study model was developed to reinforce the column height. (*Design by Claire R. Bassham.*)

FIGURE 8.22 Here the same space shown in Figures 8.19 and 8.20 is made to appear asymmetric through a variation in color assignments and a shift in floor pattern. (*Design by Lisa Smith.*)

FIGURE 8.23   The architects who developed this educational facility took advantage of color as a device to give the main corridor interest and break up its visible length. (*Design by Flansburgh Associates, Inc. Photo: © Robert Benson.*)

particularly if the various scales can be seen at a distance. In the example in Figure 8.23, people comfortably relate to the large volume of space because its scale is managed through planes of color along the floor and the canopy-framing system.

Repetition

Some of the interest that is established in design is through the repetitive use of color in rhythm and pattern. The changing scale of a pattern in perspective is one of the cues that enable the viewer to gauge distance. A repetitive device can also conceal something or it can be used to tie unre-

lated things together. Some conditions of color in the context of patterning make this a useful tool for creating form. Here are examples of patterning in spatial applications.

- The presence of pattern can draw attention to larger expressions of form, as suggested in Figure 8.24. The slight shift of an angled wall becomes more evident when a uniform floor pattern is interrupted by the shift. The same effect can be used in vertical planes and curvilinear forms.
- Pattern helps to camouflage some elements just as it highlights others. In the five-panel

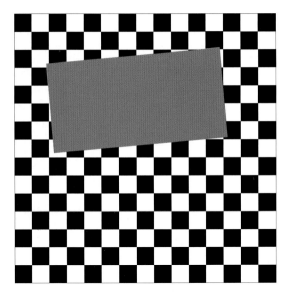

FIGURE 8.24 Juxtaposition of pattern with unrelated forms can maximize the effect of the forms themselves. (*Sheila R. Selby, 2002.*)

elevation in Figure 8.25, color and pattern are managed to do both.

- Color can be applied in the form of pattern to refine the scale of something, adding a layer of detail as shown in the example in Figure 8.26.

Pattern Emphasis

When working in two-color patterns, the rules of depth perception for distance/object viewing apply. Most two-color patterns are read as figures and ground, where the figure is the shape that is more readily distinguishable as an object. The ground is the space that remains between each pair of figures. The greater the contrast between figure and ground, the stronger the figure will appear. If neither shape is recognizable, the viewer will assume that the larger shape or the one placed higher in the pattern is the object. If information relative to form is unclear, the advancing color is presumed to be the figure and the receding color the background.

In patterns with more than two colors, emphasis and proportion are determined by the position of the greatest contrasts. The pattern in Figure 8.28 is rendered in three different color combinations. The comparison shows how the geometries seem to change depending on the position of colors with the greatest emphasis.

Pattern Depth

Compare the two border patterns shown in Figure 8.29. The form of a two-color pattern with significant contrast will be clearly read, even at a distance; however, it is more likely to cause some afterimaging. More than two colors can soften the edges of the forms and give an illusion of depth. This is known as *tonal patterning*. According to recent tests performed by Patricia Rodemann and documented in *Patterns in Interior Environments,* tonal patterning is preferred in many pattern types such as stripes and flowers over strong geometries and hard-edged (high-contrast) organic patterns.

Stripes

Stripes are often used as a source of pattern and may be either even or uneven in proportion. If sequential colors are used in a stripe pattern, an illusion of *fluting* will occur. (This is demonstrated in Figure 8.30.) Fluting is due to the simultaneous

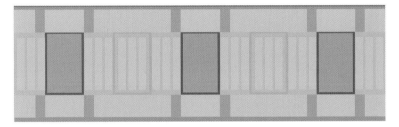

FIGURE 8.25 Five paneled openings exist in this elevation—three are intended to be opened as needed, while two others are intended for access by security personnel. The latter are concealed through color and pattern.

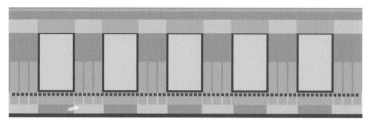

FIGURE 8.26 Here pattern determines the proportions of the elevation more than the form of the wall itself. A common method of patterning involves continuous rows and columns of single-hue geometry with narrow lines or spaces between. Examples are tile and brick patterns and the use of painted grilles. Color selection within such patterns can change the overall tone of the surface without replacing key elements, as we see in Figure 8.27. By adjusting the space color (grout lines, reveals, or framing) the overall tone is impacted while the object color (tiles or panels) remains intact. This effect is known as the *Bezold effect,* named after the scientist and colorist Wilhelm von Bezold (German, 1837–1907) and appears in oriental rugs, carpet patterns, and fabric constructions.

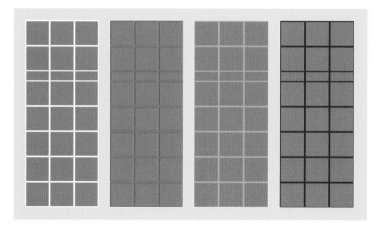

FIGURE 8.27 Notice how the overall value and tone of this tile pattern is increased or decreased according to the grout color.

FIGURE 8.28 This series of illustrations shows how pattern emphasis is managed through a change in color contrasts. (*Sheila R. Selby, 2002.*)

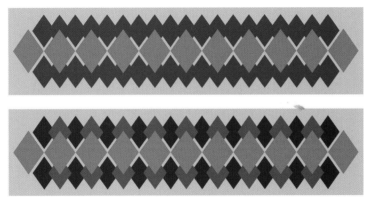

FIGURE 8.29   In this illustration the same pattern is given greater depth through the addition of a third color and an increase in range of light to dark overprinting.

contrast occurring at the edge where the two colors meet. It causes the color being influenced to visually curve slightly. If they are changing in value, the edge next to the darker color will appear lighter and the edge next to the lighter color will appear darker. The same will occur with shifts in hue or saturation level. By sequential placement of the color variant over the length of the object, followed by a reverse placement, a physically flat rectangle can appear convex or concave. Another technique used more frequently to prevent patterned surfaces from appearing flat is to vary the line weight and color of

objects. In the stripe shown in Figure 8.31, the pattern uses both for more undulation.

In this chapter, common methods of color and form integration or manipulation have been explored for their potential to support a design concept. Many can be demonstrated in two-dimensional compositions as a way of testing combinations before their appearance in three-dimensional form. This is particularly helpful when regarding the impact of color on proportion and when considering issues of emotion, organization, and balance relative to color associations. Concepts such as depth perception,

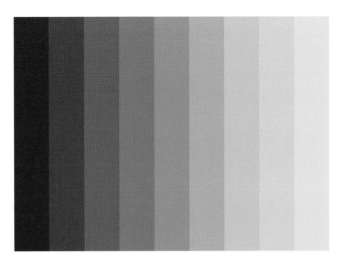

FIGURE 8.30   If a rhythmic variation of color occurs in a striped pattern, it will give the appearance of fluting, as though each band has a slight curve.

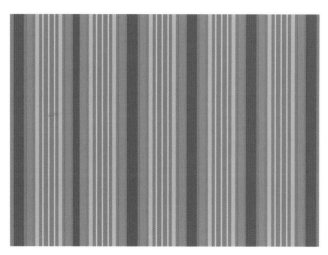

FIGURE 8.31 This stripe uses variation in scale and value of the bands to provide more depth.

Object Tips

Based on the discussion of color-form integration in terms of scale and depth perception in this chapter, a few thoughts are offered relative to the proportions of the freestanding object:

- The lighter the value, the larger the object will appear. To reduce scale, consider dark, solid colors.
- If there is little or no contrast in the composition, the linear dimension will be emphasized due to contrast at the edges. To reduce volume scale, patterning can be used.
- The proportions of an object are often influenced along the line of high contrast, regardless of the type of contrast. Bright orange knobs on a small cabinet say "pull me." Strong color contrast in the relief sculpture of a pediment will draw attention above the door. A white shirt with dark jeans draws attention to the waist.
- It may be undesirable to incorporate warm and cool colors in the same piece with freestanding objects. Because the eye tends to separate colors according to temperature, a warm-cool contrast may detract from the physical form of the object.

shadows, and illusion are best tested by working three-dimensionally. The quick and simple approach is to use handheld samples and view frames. Where time permits, the study model or computer-generated model enables us to anticipate a space more realistically and remains the best way to explore the physical realm of color use.

At this point, we've explored issues of color theory and application relative to subtractive color management. Needless to say, the impact of lighting on these design solutions cannot be underesti-mated. In order to fully recognize each color in a subtractive composition, the light available in the space or on the object must include them all. If the available lighting has limitations in its quantity, quality, or both, a proper rendition is not possible. In other words, if the light source does not include goldenrod in its spectrum, we will never see the goldenrod object it illuminates in its proper coloration. The next chapter offers a brief comparison of the most common types of lighting currently in use.

Color and Light

The success of any design depends to some degree on the designer's technical expertise. Just as there are general conditions and limitations inherent in each of the materials used, each selected light source adds impact according to its characteristics. The quantity and placement of fixtures, the way the light drops off, and the inherent spectral strengths and weaknesses affect the aesthetics of the physical design. Successful integration of these additive color characteristics with the subtractive ones already discussed makes for a strong design statement.

In this chapter, technical issues of lighting are explored in the context of their impact on color in design. These include the conditions of lighting that impact human appreciation of design, the implications of each manufacturing process on the quality of light output, and the characteristics of lighting that have a direct impact on color solutions. Taken together, this information is meant as a comparative assessment for consideration of alternative lighting options relative to color decisions.

LIGHT ENABLES COLOR

The color of any exposed surface is visible only if available light permits it. In other words, our ability to see a specific color is established if the light that shines on it includes the hue contained in that color. Under full-spectrum light, the apple is clearly red. If we shine only a green light on a red apple, the apple will appear gray. Since red is not available, it cannot be seen, and the form of the apple is seen simply as a gray shape. Each light source, natural or artificial, offers a range of spectral color that enables color vision. The depth and extent of that spectral range varies with each source. Our challenge is to use knowledge about those sources to anticipate how each selected pigmentary color will be rendered in the final analysis. When we have control over selection of artificial lights or can establish access to daylight, decisions regarding additive (light) and subtractive (pigment) color can be made simultaneously. In other cases, our choices are limited and the effects of predetermined light sources on color can be taken into consideration during the development of design solutions.

▶ Natural Conditions

Nature has a way of adding delightful surprises with the same frequency as disappointment. Conditions of the environment can either help or hurt a cause. To consider the effects of light on color perception, let's first consider the natural conditions of color influence relative to lighting and follow with a look at daylight as a resource.

Metamerism

A common condition of color relative to lighting is *metamerism.* This phenomenon occurs when the color of an object appears to change due to a change in light source. Metamerism specifically refers to the condition of light variation that causes two objects to appear the same in one situation and different in another. Two objects with surface color of the same wavelength will appear to be identical under any light. When two objects whose color is of slightly different wavelength seem to be the same under specific light conditions, they form a metameric pair. Under another source, their differences become apparent.

Metamers are the light sources that render sample colors differently due to a difference in spectral distribution, even though the sources may appear similar. As an example, compare the spectral power distribution data shown in Figures 9.8 and 9.10. An orange object of about 685 nm is likely to read as highly saturated under the metal halide lamp (Figure 9.10). As the spectral composition of a light source is modified, the physical colors observed under it change accordingly. The same orange object seen under the 4100-K fluorescent (Figure 9.8) would be less saturated by comparison due to the difference in spectral distribution.

Differences in texture also cause metameric conditions, sometimes called *geometric metamerism.* Any solid color on a printed piece of paper will seem adjusted slightly when the paper changes to a heavily textured matte or glossy finish. (This is illustrated in more detail in Chapter 10, "Texture and Material.") Similarly, changing the position of a textured color surface relative to the light source will modify its color, since any change in refraction of light will result in a corresponding change of color. In these cases, the apparent adjustment is one of value or saturation, since the spectrum of the light source has not changed. The perceived adjustment in coloration is considered metameric because it's light-dependent.

Day and Night Vision

In higher light levels the eye receives visual information via cones. This is known as *photopic* vision. Most photometric analysis for lighting is measured based on photopic vision. *Scotopic* vision occurs in darkness, when rod cells are relied upon, as explained in Chapter 1. Under scotopic vision we do not perceive chroma and our ability to discern detail is diminished. The eye shifts between photopic and scotopic vision in response to environ-

mental changes, resulting in dynamic adjustments in visual acuity. *Mesopic* vision is that in-between state when both rod and cone photoreceptors are stimulated. Spectral clarity is then possible, but not ideal, and details are inconsistently recognizable.

In the nineteenth century, the Czechoslavakian physiologist, Johannes Purkinje (1787–1869) identified variation in diminishing color strength under scotopic vision. He noted that in more intense light levels, such as daylight, the eye sees yellow as having greater strength or brightness, which we now attribute to the combination of warmth and lightness. In low light levels, he proposed that blue actually appears brighter than other colors of the same saturation level and brightness. His reasoning was that rods are more sensitive to shorter wavelengths of light and cones have a greater sensitivity to long wavelengths, the warmer colors in the spectrum. This perception, which is currently debated, is known as the *Purkinje effect.*

▶ Daylight

Direct sunlight offers the most complete form of additive color, which we perceive as white light. Colors developed and experienced in full-spectrum daylight offer the truest vision; however, even the whitest of daylight has color tendencies that can alter human perception. Our impression of color under sunlight varies considerably due to atmospheric conditions. The most active rooms of a residence are often positioned to take advantage of direct daylight because they offer the most stimulation and variation over the course of the day.

Sunrises illuminate the sky in colors other than blue because longer spectral wavelengths (reds and oranges) appear first. During the day, the light that reaches the earth is a bright white, but our sky appears blue. This is because the small water particles in our atmosphere reflect the short-wave light rays most effectively, scattering them, which we recognize as light blue color. Large bodies of water in turn reflect the color of the sky with an equally blue appearance. As the size of particles in the air increase, such as water vapor in a fog or in clouds, more wavelengths are scattered equally, giving a white appearance. At sunset, daylight has a very warm cast to it, due in part to the reflection of the light off of dry dust particles in the air. When viewed at a great distance, the

FIGURE 9.1 Blue skies give way to warmly colored skies at sunset. (*Photo: Jillian Stone.*)

concentration of reflected warm light causes the orange sensation visible in the setting sky on clear days. (See Figure 9.1.)

As light is reflected through a more humid atmosphere, its color appears cooler, more bluish. A subtle form of the shift from warm to cool daylight occurs daily as the sun is positioned higher in the sky, passing through a greater concentration of water droplets high in the atmosphere. In an overcast sky, the temperature of daylight is slightly cooler in tone as light of shorter wavelengths more easily reaches the earth. Generally speaking, on overcast days contrasts of hue are minimized. Under these conditions, contrasts of value tend to be more effective if they are slightly exaggerated.

As the sun makes its 24-hour pass across a facade, more subtle variations in color are most visible for some period of time in the morning and late day. However, they are often completely lost at noon, due to the intensity of the sun, and in the evening and early morning, due to reduced illumination. This means that the only color variation that will be realized consistently on many exterior surfaces is that of value. When subtle shifts in hue are desired on an architectural form, it's recommended that they be accompanied by a slight shift in value. Otherwise,

the distinction between the two colors will be lost. They will appear to be the same color to most eyes.

Climate and Weather

Direction of the source of daylight also influences color perception. Consider a building in the Northern Hemisphere of the earth. Each of its surfaces will be seen under a different amount of light according to its relative position to the sun. Shadows are intensified by strong contrasts of direct sunlight. The effect on the building is one in which each plane appears to have a different color, negating any subtle pigmentary distinctions that may have existed.

Direct light that comes from the south will make any saturated surface intensify. This increase in intensity makes contrasts of hue effective in areas of bright sunlight. Direct sunlight will also make the building surface appear lighter in value, if the building surface is light to begin with, because of greater reflectivity. In extreme conditions of direct daylight, the color receptors may be overstimulated, causing color discrimination to diminish. This is what causes colors to appear faded in full daylight, sometimes reducing hue contrasts.

147

Alternatively, the light from the north is indirect, implicitly less intense, and subject to atmospheric changes. It causes less dramatic shadow casting and will yield reduced reflectivity. This is traditionally the preferred light for artists' studios because spectral shifts are reduced, allowing for more consistent color clarity.

Other conditions have an impact on daylight and the way it renders color. In the Northern Hemisphere, daylight is strongest in the summer and the least intense during the winter. Countries in the earth's far north and south have cooler (bluish) daylight. In these areas the sun is low in the sky and the surrounding atmosphere contains more water vapor, which diffuses the light, cooling and softening visible color. Countries closest to the equator receive sunlight from directly overhead through a clearer atmosphere, rendering stronger colors with clarity. The seasons and weather conditions also change our perception of light. Water droplets, dust, and pollen cause light to be distorted. The more water vapor there is in the air due to mist or rain, the more it refracts direct rays from the sun, giving a bluish cast to the light that lands on surfaces and causing warmer colors such as orange to be slightly reduced.

Daylighting Interiors

Two considerations occur when interiors rely on daylight as a primary source. One is the quantity and coloration of the light that actually enters the interior. This is determined by the size of the window openings and the color of the glass in them, if color is used. When the glass has a tint, it will act as a subtle light filter, reducing some of the light rays that are complementary to the tint. To be specific, a green pane of glass in some conditions will cause a slight accentuation in green surface color and minimize red surface color somewhat. This tendency is very subtle. The visible tint of the glass itself is far more apparent than its impact on interior colors.

A second condition is the position of light as it enters the room. The angle of entering daylight determines which surfaces will be intensified. The perceived saturation level of each colored surface will be modified as the light source (the sun) moves. Since the position of the sun varies over the course of the day, so does its angle of illumination and the consequent intensity of color on interior

surfaces. In the example shown in Figure 9.2, daylight is used to highlight value contrast and add texture to the large wall surface.

■ ARTIFICIAL LIGHT

Two key attributes of artificial light—quality and quantity—make its use more restrictive than daylight. Lighting quality is usually regarded as a combination of both its ability to render color and the degree to which the light is diffused. The greater the ability to render individual colors, the better the quality of light. The more diffuse the light, the greater its quality. To increase the level of diffusion, the number of individual light sources may be increased or an indirect light source may be used. The location of the artificial light sources determines the direction of light and its intensity as it reaches room surfaces.

By necessity, artificial light is significantly reduced in quantity from its natural counterpart. As the amount of light is reduced, the apparent value of any color darkens slightly and, at the same time, its degree of hue is reduced, effectively neutralizing it. As light level is increased, color becomes lighter in value and greater in saturation, up to a point—in extreme light levels, the intensity will be reduced again due to overlighting, giving a washed-out appearance. These variations are subtle and relative, meaning that lightness and darkness are relative to the overall visual context, since our eyes adjust to compensate for changes in surrounding light level.

▶ Color Criteria

As decisions are made about lighting in the context of color, two criteria become key—the overall temperature of the source and its ability to properly render the full spectral range. Both *color temperature* and color ranges, usually called *color rendition,* can be measured scientifically. Such comparative statistics gives us a little insight into the consequences of our choices. The following offers an explanation of these two conditions and a summary of the most readily available artificial light sources, followed by the statistics that identify the temperature and color clarity of each.

FIGURE 9.2 The movement of daylight across the interior provides changing coloration for this lobby. (*Design by ADD Inc. Photo: © Richard Barnes.*)

Color Temperature

A key indication of how a light source will illuminate color on an object or within a room is its *color temperature.* This is based on the overall appearance of the light itself, indicating a tendency toward a warm, moderate, or cool tone. Color temperature is based on the theory that any object will emit light if it is heated to a high enough temperature. As the temperature is increased, its color shifts in increments that can be measured numerically. The device used to establish relative temperature is a *blackbody*—a surface that reflects virtually no radiant light. As the blackbody is heated from a cold black to a hot state, its color shifts to red, orange, yellow, white, and blue-white, in that order. These shifts are measured in degrees *kelvin* (K), as illustrated in the comparative chart in Figure 9.3. The overall tone of a light source at 3500 K (degrees kelvin) would match the color of the blackbody exactly at the 3500-K point (information provided by Osram Sylvania through its publication, *Lightpoints: Understanding the Science and Technology of Light*). We should note that an ideal blackbody that absorbs and discharges all wavelengths of energy indiscriminately does not exist, but artificial materials get us close.

Two conditions of color temperature in lighting can cause some confusion. First, the Kelvin scale is organized in the reverse of what is intuitive to most people—the higher the number, the cooler the light, unlike Fahrenheit or Celsius scales. Second, an overall warm or cool tendency of light does not guarantee a specific warm or cool color will be fully rendered by that light. Each source emits a different level of energy at each wavelength of visible light. This can be charted using a *spectral power distribution* (SPD) curve, as shown in Figure 9.4. The more even the distribution of power (energy level) across the spectrum, the more consistent the color rendition of objects illuminated by the source. Irregular power distribution, evident on the SPD curve by formation of spikes, indicates that some specific colors will appear much more intense and others will appear much more subdued than they would under a true white light. In the example used to explain metamerism, the two lamps are relatively close in temperature. Differences in their spectral power distribution is what causes the change in color perception.

Color Rendition

Artificial light is ideally selected according to its intended use to minimize major differences in color rendering and to ensure the visibility of all subtractive colors present. The degree to which a light source renders the full range of color is called its *color rendition,* and this is measured according to the *Color Rendering Index* (CRI). The CRI is a system of visual evaluation, one that takes both color temperature and color acceptability into account. First the color temperature of the source is established. Then eight standard colors are used to meas-

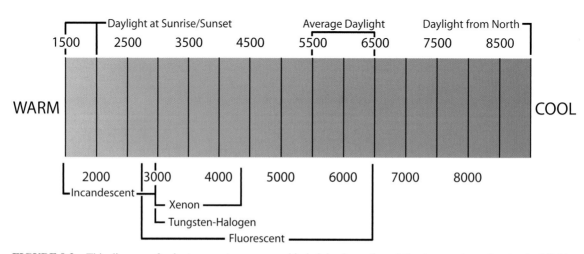

FIGURE 9.3 This diagram of color temperature measured in kelvin shows the relative temperatures for standard light sources.

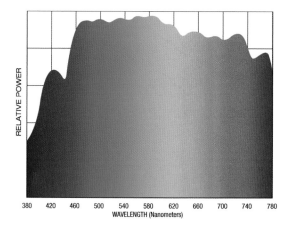

FIGURE 9.4 This spectral power distribution for noontime sunlight shows that the colors of the spectrum are fairly equal in their rendition, with some drop-off in the purple-violet range. (*Courtesy of OSRAM SYLVANIA.*)

ure the CRI. These colors are lit by the light source and then by a blackbody that has the same color temperature. If none of the samples appear to change in color, the light source is rated 100, as in 100 percent rendition. Apparent changes in color reduce the rating. In the United States, a CRI of 80 or more is considered high, indicating a light source with good color properties. Lighting engineers in Europe, where lighting is more heavily regulated, recommend a minimum of 85 CRI, and in some countries lighting with less than a minimum of 80 CRI is outlawed by code for certain applications.

CRI alone does not indicate how every individual color will be rendered. As noted, the index is calculated based on an average of eight specific colors. A high rating simply suggests that, given a broad range of colors, a higher percentage of them will be illuminated properly. **To be sure a specific color will be accurately rendered, it must be tested under the proposed light source.** To illustrate how differences in color temperature and CRI affect color in design, let's compare some of the most commonly used lamp types.

▶ Artificial Lamp Types

Scientists have determined that there is a connection between the light energy received by the eye and the functions of the nervous system. They have also concluded that the production of hormones in many organisms, humans included, depends on visible light energy. This is what leads us to assume that elimination of some wavelengths over a prolonged period will impact health in some way. Obviously, each artificial light source in use today has some bearing on human functionality in this context.

Coupled with this is a concern for the amount of energy we consume in the act of lighting space. Energy efficiency continues to be a motivator in the design of lamps, especially since the implementation of comprehensive federal legislation, such as the Energy Policy Act of 1992. The balance between these two areas of responsibility, as well as our concern for the aesthetics of visual space, increases our needs for greater discrimination in our light sources. One consequence of this struggle has been an increase in the combination of lamp types found in many facilities. Another is the increased accessibility of useful information. Keep in mind that statistical information does vary between lamp manufacturers.

Incandescent

The lighting traditionally preferred for interior residential space is incandescent. This is the conventional glass bulb, which contains a filament that is heated to emit light. It includes ER, PAR, and R-shaped lamps, as well as tungsten-halogen, which will be discussed separately. For the purposes of color discussion, incandescent light sources also include candles, torches, any kind of electric filament, and luminous gas lamps. It's difficult to get very even light distribution with incandescent light, since it is a point source and most of the lamps are comparatively small in size. This makes them impractical for areas where large surfaces of color must be seen uniformly. Incandescents are used primarily for focused applications and are easily dimmed.

Categorically, incandescent lights are much warmer in overall temperature than most other types of artificial light and most forms of daylight. Although they offer a less balanced rendition of the full spectrum, they are preferred in moderate climates for the psychological advantage offered by their overall warmth. The greatest strength is in long (red) wavelengths, with progressively less for orange, yellow, and green, in that order. Blue and

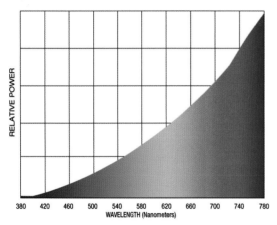

FIGURE 9.5 This shows the SPD curve for an incandescent lamp. (*Courtesy of OSRAM SYLVANIA.*)

cool purple are not rendered well by this light source, and cool greens tend to have somewhat less clarity. Because of their warm bias, incandescent lights are not recommended for applications where a clear distinction of color is required. The spectral power distribution (SPD) for an incandescent lamp is shown in Figure 9.5.

- Color temperature in kelvin: 1000 to 3000 K
- Color rendition: 95 CRI

Halogen

Halogen lamps, which include tungsten-halogen, quartz and quartz-iodine products, are smaller point-source lights with some of the same advantages as incandescent lamps. They are easily dimmable and offer excellent color rendition capability. The advantage over larger incandescent lamps is longer life. Recent innovations have led to low-voltage incandescent lamps, such as the MR 16 EXT lamps, a multimirror reflector spot. These offer very controlled beam spread from a small-scale lamp. In terms of color tone, this is a whiter light than most lamp types. It is cooler than larger incandescents and warmer than discharge lamps. They tend to generate a significant amount of heat for such a small lamp, causing concern as a fire risk in some applications.

- Color temperature in kelvin: 3000 K
- Color rendition: 95 CRI

Fluorescent

The most commonly used lamp types, fluorescents, are popular due to their low cost and very efficient nature. They also provide more diffuse light than the types mentioned thus far. And thanks to the progress of technology, they can be dimmed without causing a variation in the color of the light. One disadvantage is that they require ballasts, which, until recent years, generated an audible hum and caused flickering at low light levels. Newer, solid-state dimming ballasts offer a greater range of control without either audible sound or flicker at a fraction of the scale required in early models. Increasingly smaller lamp types offer us greater flexibility in their use—linear or point source, direct or indirect.

Fluorescents are made by mixing phosphors in different concentrations to produce lights that are slightly tinted as opposed to a true white. This allows manufacturers to offer a broader temperature range than most other light sources. Generally speaking, light from fluorescent lamps appears more blue, offering comparatively fewer red and yellow rays than incandescent lamps. Each engineered lamp type has a slightly different effect on the color of the surfaces illuminated by them. Over time, lamps with a warmer overall tone have been developed. These are specified as 3000 or 3500-K lamps and have become the most frequently used fluorescents. To illustrate some of the distinctions in color rendition, Figures 9.6 to 9.8

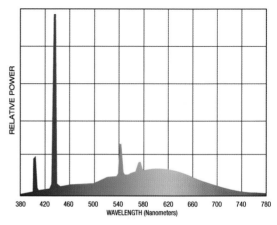

FIGURE 9.6 This SPD shows a cool-white fluorescent lamp. Note the spike that occurs at blues in 430 to 440 nm wavelengths. (*Courtesy of OSRAM SYLVANIA.*)

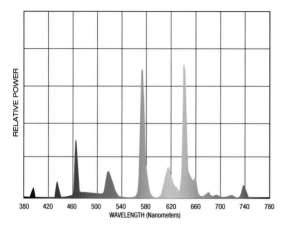

FIGURE 9.7 This SPD represents the Octron®
835XP 3500-K fluorescent lamp, which was developed
for higher efficiency and offers better CRI than the
standard cool white. (*Courtesy of OSRAM SYLVANIA.*)

show the SPD data for three different lamps from
the same manufacturer.

The CRI of standard fluorescent lamps is lower
than incandescent and halogen point sources,
although 95 CRI lamps are now available. As a
phosphorous product, it tends to peak in some areas
of color and show a deficiency in others. This
makes it more challenging for the colorist to anticipate how specific colors will be rendered under it.
The differences in color characteristics change with

variations in overall temperature, and they vary
from manufacturer to manufacturer even using the
same-temperature lamps. Fluorescent lighting of
higher CRI offers the greatest accuracy in color
rendition across a wide range. This lamp type can
cost as much as two to three times more than
common warm-white or cool-white lamps, but is
preferred where color rendition is important (photographic studios, art display, some labs).

- Color temperature in kelvin: 2700 to 6500 K
- Color rendition: 60 to 95 CRI

High-Pressure Sodium

Sodium is similar to metal halide, neon, and other
xenon gas lamps in that it uses an electric arc to
power a gaseous discharge lamp. High-pressure
sodium lamps produce a very intense yellow, yellow-
orange, or yellow-green light that is powerful enough
to illuminate a large area, even in conditions of fog or
other forms of water vapor. (See Figure 9.9.) Although they are extremely efficient, the range of
color rendition in sodium lamps is very limited. This
limitation makes it difficult to discern color contrasts
and to some degree disables proper depth perception.
For this reason, metal halide is quickly replacing
these lamps as a preferred source. The most common
remaining uses for high-pressure sodium lamps are
streetlights, industrial applications, and large building surfaces.

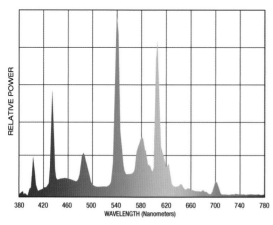

FIGURE 9.8 This SPD is for the Octron® 4100-K
fluorescent lamp, which was engineered for improved
color rendering, as evident in the more pronounced
energy bands at the primary colors. (*Courtesy of
OSRAM SYLVANIA.*)

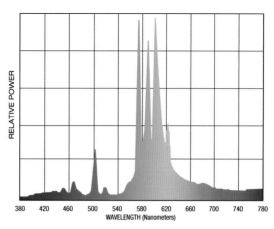

FIGURE 9.9 This SPD for a Lumalux® high-pressure
sodium lamp shows an intense concentration of spectral
energy in the yellows. (*Courtesy of OSRAM SYLVANIA.*)

- Color temperature in kelvin: 2100 to 2300 K
- Color rendition: 22 to 65 CRI

Metal Halide

Metal halide is the most accepted high-intensity discharge source. It's fabricated by adding an arc tube of metallic vapors to improve color rendition. (See Figure 9.10.) The lamp is still considered highly efficient and offers a long life, but a ballast is required. It's not as diffuse as fluorescent light, but it does offer increased output, which can mean glare problems if not properly positioned. Currently available lamps have much better color rendition than past generations and give us the added benefit of a smaller scale. One disadvantage of these lamps is a long start-up and restrike period. To make them more practical in interior applications of periodic use, they're often combined with other light sources. Metal halides are most frequently used in hotel lobbies, airports, large retail spaces, and in outdoor applications.

- Color temperature in kelvin: 2900, 3000, and 4200 K
- Color rendition: 65 to 82 CRI

Xenon

For more specialized applications, light sources using xenon gas are available in either compact or linear form. Xenon light produces an especially white light, which is considered the best suited for accurate color reproduction. It is most similar to daylight except that it has slightly more purple because of greater emissions at the two ends of the spectrum. It's often used to replace natural light without being perceived by the occupants. Because of its excellent color-rendition capabilities, xenon light is used in commercial film projectors, floodlights, flash photography, and colorimetry (the science of measurement and analysis of color).

- Color temperature in kelvin: 3000 to 4300 K
- Color rendition: 99 CRI

Lamp manufacturers lead the charge, bringing improvements in the quality of lamp sources. As improved lamp types become available, light-fixture manufacturers are quick to develop new fixture designs that take advantage of new lamps. In years to come, we can expect to see increases in CRI of available fixtures, smaller lamps in many forms, and ever more efficient sources for general illumination.

▶ Practical Issues

There are some practical issues relevant to individual color perception in controlled environments. For example, as a group, *high-intensity-discharge* (HID) lamps can shift in color about halfway through their life expectancy. Fluorescents can reduce their total output at about the same point. There are also conditions for which a specific color tendency in the light source is desirable. For these applications, *cold cathode* lamps are available in sizes similar to fluorescent tubes, and *neon* can be fabricated in much smaller sources. Cold cathode coloration can be adjusted to a controlled tint, and the lamps can be bent to take curved forms. Neon is used for more distinct colors of hue and can be bent back on itself to form very complex shapes.

Placement and Distribution

Just as the color attributes of a light source can modify the apparent surface color, so can improper placement of the light source. Here are some examples of lighting details that can impact color perception.

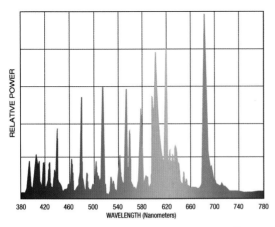

FIGURE 9.10 The SPD curve for the Metalarc® metal halide lamp shows relatively even spectral energy distribution; however, gaps do exist. (*Courtesy of OSRAM SYLVANIA.*)

- **Cast shadows** can cause a value contrast stronger than any contrast otherwise present in a palette. When a large amount of light is focused in one place, it can wash out the surface it is directed to and cause stronger shadows on adjacent surfaces.
- **Additive color** has a very different impact on the viewer than subtractive color. For example, in a salon, the surface color green can suggest organic products, natural cosmetics, or other healthful images. The same green as a chromatic light source will have a negative effect in the same space. Cool light on the face turns the lips dark and reduces any warmth in skin tone, which most people find undesirable.
- The **color tendency of a light source** that enhances one surface color may negate another. This condition is most apparent in food service facilities: a cool light source illuminating a green salad can improve its visual appeal, but the same light source will make red meat appear old.
- Proper color rendition cannot come at the expense of **practical issues** of technology. Consider a clothing boutique specializing in jewel-toned silks. While an incandescent or halogen light may be considered, given their superior color rendition, the heat output from these sources can burn the silk material if placed too close, or at least cause it to fade quickly.

▶ Reflected and Projected Color

There are essentially three ways to create a color effect: surface color, light color, and reflected color. If a box is painted orange and illuminated by white light, it will be recognized as an orange box. If the box is white and an orange light illuminates it, it will also be seen as an orange box. Without other cues, we cannot discern a difference between the orange-pigmented box and the orange-lit box. A third option is to reflect orange onto the surface of the box by shining a bright white light onto an adjacent surface of orange pigment. The surface is then positioned to reflect the colored light onto the white box. Again, the result is a box with apparently orange coloration. The subtractive color of a surface determines how much light will be reflected. The lighter in value it is, the higher the percent of light that will be returned. An off-white will yield a

90 percent incidence of white light reflected. A light blue will reflect about 50 percent of the same light. The use of these three methods of color interaction is very popular in architectural applications. I am reminded of a colleague who described with delight the paint colors in his recently renovated bedroom. Each morning, strong sunlight shines at an angle on the blue house next door, which in turn reflects blue light directly into the bedroom. By late morning, the sun is overhead and a brilliant white light shines through the skylight into the room, exposing all the subtleties of the colors inside. In the afternoon, the angle of the sun is more oblique, causing dramatic value contrasts by the shadow casting that occurs on the more complex surfaces. In the late afternoon and evening, the warm spotlighting of the incandescent lamps offers a completely different range of tones from the ones brought on by morning. Each day the sequential color display repeats itself.

Reflected Color

Figure 9.11 shows an example of architecture using reflected color. In this installation, light is reflected from very bright, high-gloss surfaces onto other planes of concrete and acrylic, adding to the drama and complexity of the space. The only applied color of hue that appears within the area of this photograph is the yellow paint on the object suspended in the enclosure.

Projected Color

Use of projected light is another option gaining popularity in retail and public areas. This is handled in several ways. In some cases, light projectors are used with a rotating disc that contains different color lenses. As the disc moves through its rotation, the glowing color of a large surface nearby changes. One full rotation offers the full range for that system's spatial color. Sometimes the lens color is varied seasonally, or signage is created through a silhouette embedded in the disc surface. This is particularly effective in urban locations where the surrounding surfaces can be used for enhancement, such as a concrete wall or a sidewalk. In the case of the retail store shown in Figure 9.12, colored imagery is projected onto a relatively flat surface for a very theatrical effect. When appropriate, the image

FIGURE 9.11 Color was incorporated in several unique ways for this university project. Here it's reflected into a larger area both inside and outside of the building that contains it. (*Design by Perry Dean Rogers / Partners Architects. Photo: © Peter Mauss / ESTO.*)

can change as selling seasons change. In the case of the Fine Arts Center shown in Figures 9.13 through 9.17, several colors emanate from the building in sequence. The timing is established to run a complete cycle in the time it normally takes a pedestrian to approach the building.

Colored Light Sources

Light of a single color will distort all the other colors in the room but will enhance its own. For example, orange light will neutralize green-, blue-, and violet-colored surfaces, making them comparatively grayish or brownish. The same light intensifies warm-colored objects, particularly anything that is a true orange. There are occasions when it's

advantageous to modify or limit the color tendencies of a light source. In theatrical stage sets, color-filtered light plays an important role in establishing mood as well as symbolism during a performance. Some color testing is done using colored light rather than colored objects. This eliminates the influence of environmental colors. Retail and entertainment environments also benefit from the use of colored light, either as a stimulus or as a way of modifying images temporarily. (For an example of this, see Chapter 13, Figure 13.3.)

When colored light is used in the overall color composition, it can be challenging. As Chevreul discovered many years ago, **colored lights combine to form hues inconsistent with our expectations.** Most designers have experience mixing subtractive color, but filtered lights are a form of additive color. If a yellow light and blue light are combined, they will appear close to white on a white surface—a surprise to those expecting green. Colored light may be used in a three-dimensional composition to either enhance the overall environment or modify the impression of specific objects. We know that if a blue light is focused on a white object, the object will appear to be blue. However, if the same blue light is diffused over the full environment, the object will appear to be white compared to other surfaces within view. This occurs because the eye continues to make color judgments by comparing colors adjacent to each other. One fascinating color phenomenon associated with shadows is that of complementary casting. Each shadow contains the complement of the color of the

light cast. Red-colored light will cause shadows of the objects it lights to appear slightly green. This is why shadows at the end of the day, caused by a setting sun, which is very warm in color, cause the shaded surfaces to appear quite cool in tone. The stronger the light source, the more pale the tone of the shadow. Paler light sources will result in more dramatically colored shadows.

Generally speaking, **it is not recommended that designed environments offer single-color light except in controlled medicinal circumstances.** Each colored light has a unique physiological effect on the viewer, which may be therapeutic when applied by trained professionals, but can be equally disturbing in other situations. In moderation, warm light is flattering to skin tones. Conversely, green light is detrimental to the skin

FIGURE 9.12 The colorful images on the upper wall surfaces shown here are projected from light using colored filters. (*The Levi's Store—Checkland Kindleysides. Design by Bergmeyer Associates, Inc., architect. Photo:* © *Robert Canfield Photography.*)

FIGURE 9.13–9.17 The light projected from this building through its enclosure effectively draws and holds viewer attention. (*Design by Perry Dean Rogers / Partners Architects. Photo: © Peter Mauss / ESTO.*)

while enhancing to foliage. In large quantities, many believe that the presence of red light will increase blood pressure and respiration, while green has a more calming effect. Some also suggest that the presence of green light improves complex motor coordination. Yellow light serves as a stimulant. Blue light is believed to lower blood pressure, offering relief from headaches. Violet-blue light is also considered calming and is believed to increase concentration. While these effects may have some benefit in short-term applications, continuous or repetitive use is not recommended because it is counter to normal human experience. In medicine, a form of blue light has been specifically developed to treat premature babies who suffer from jaundice; however, these lamps differ from cool fluorescents in that they include ultraviolet rays not visible to the eye.

Ultraviolet light is used to treat psoriasis. And some medical practitioners have been able to use single-hue lighting to stimulate the brain, the circulatory system, and the involuntary nervous system, speeding recovery of specific conditions.

Fortunately for colorists working in the field, information on lighting performance and various lamp characteristics is readily available from many lamp manufacturers. Successful integration of light and its rendering capabilities with the colors we choose allows us a level of color control that was not available to prior generations. We now have more choices between adjusting color from the surface by using subtractive techniques or, additively, using illumination. To add to our level of color control, we might also consider texture and its implications. This will be the subject of Chapter 10, "Texture and Material."

10

Texture and Material

Every surface has some textural characteristic, which affects our perception of its color. We've already noted that a light source can modify our perception of the hue characteristics of a colored surface. Subtle adjustments in value and saturation levels of the color exhibited can also occur through changes in surface texture. This means that the quality of the color the eye sees is really determined by three conditions in combination:

- The chromatic characteristics of the subtractive color
- The color quality of the lighting applied to it
- The surface texture of the material containing the color

Surface texture impacts subtractive color by changing the angle of reflected light. This in turn causes a variation in the amount of light that reaches our eyes. As colors transition from one medium to another, their appeal may increase or decrease depending on the surface characteristics of individual choices. For example, a clear coral color developed on paper may work equally well in plastic, glazed ceramics, or fine wool. The same color may lose its appeal on a wood surface or on a metal substrate.

In this chapter we look at how material choices impact potential color selection and how visual perception changes according to textural differences. This involves analyzing materials commonly used in design applications for their chromatic limitations

and surface character. The point, of course, is to increase our control over design results by anticipating the implications of the materials we use.

TEXTURAL IMPACT

To make textural comparisons, we need a baseline. Let's assume that a smooth, flat, nonspecular surface offers the least distortion to any given color. The light reaching this surface is fairly diffuse, reflected in many directions simultaneously in a reasonably uniform manner. Relative adjustments to this texture will cause a redirecting of reflected light rays, changing the quality of light reaching the eye from the surface. Each change in direction of light reflectance determines how the color will be perceived. Keep in mind that these changes are subtle, worth the extra effort in situations where textural variation is key, but lost in the context of other more dramatic conditions that compete for attention.

▶ Coarse Texture

Course textures offer an irregular surface from which light will reflect color. When the texture of a surface is increased, direct light will be unable to reach a small portion of the exposed surfaces, causing shadows. The original color in shadow can appear darker and less saturated in those unexposed pockets. As the eye visually blends the original

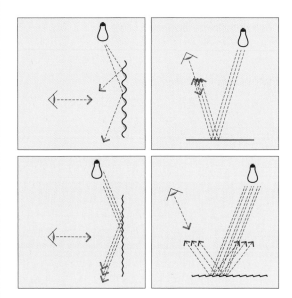

FIGURE 10.1 Slight changes in surface color can be attributed to the consistency and direction of light reflecting back to the eye as a result of its texture and its relative position.

color and its shadowed subset, the overall tone may differ from the original. Orientation is the key, since a coarse plane that reflects the light directly into the eye will always seem lighter.

Porous materials such as concrete and brick have surfaces coarse enough to cause surface shading. A heavy textile on the wall that is lit from above will look slightly darker than the same color in a smooth textile. When light is cast in such a direction as to accentuate the surface characteristics, the color shift is more evident, as suggested in the upper left diagram in Figure 10.1. However if the same materials are placed horizontally under the same overhead light, fewer pockets of shadow can occur, and variations in color are less likely.

▶ Moderate Texture

Even a true matte finish has some impact on color tone. A moderate surface texture changes the angle of reflection of the light into the viewer's eye. Most noncoarse surface textures are uniform and directional. The orientation of the grain is what changes its color perception. When a textured sample is held vertically in one direction, and another is rotated 180 degrees next to it, they often look like slightly different colors. This occurs because the incremen-

tal effects of shadow and reflected light impact value, saturation, or both. This is what causes many oriental rugs to look lighter or darker depending on their orientation within the room. Changes in orientation of the texture to the light source can change the visual results, as suggested in the lower illustrations in Figure 10.1.

Textiles with a pile, such as corduroy, velvet, or mohair, are an exaggerated form of moderate surface texture. The pile usually leans to one side or the other. Our perception of the yarn color changes depending on whether the light is reflected off the side or the end of the yarn. Upholstery fabrics with a pile, such as chenille, are desirable because of the multitoned effect that results from their texture. Plastic laminates with matte or textured surfaces fall in this category as well. Acrylic panels, such as Plexiglas and Lexan, usually have a textured surface and impact the tone of the images seen through them, as evidenced in the mock-ups displayed at a photographer or framer studio. The graphic image is softened or becomes more crisp according to the texture of the surface that covers it.

▶ Gloss Texture

A high-gloss finish is accomplished in a number of ways. In dense materials, such as stone or metal, it's produced by honing the surface until it has a hard polish. In more porous surfaces, such as wood or fabric, a coating is used to fill the open pores and create a smooth, more reflective surface. The chemical composition of paint determines its textural quality, including opportunities for very hard, glossy finishes. In each of these applications the result is a more light-reflective, durable surface as expressed in the upper right illustration in Figure 10.1. When the texture of a colored material is made harder and finer, as with a glossy surface, most of the light's rays are reflected off the surface in a fairly uniform direction. When enough light reflects directly to the eye, it causes a brightness known to artists as a *highlight* and to lighting designers as a *veiling reflection*. In most cases, this increase in white light within view of the surface can make the color of the surface lighter in value overall and may increase the intensity, or saturation, of the surface color.

This characteristic is apparent in wood refinishing. Often the application of a varnish to a piece of wood furniture makes the wood tone richer in appearance. The approach is effective up to a point. When the amount of reflection caused by the finish is extreme, this is known as a *specular surface.* Specular surfaces are very difficult to light in a way that shows off the finish without causing undesirable veiling reflections, where the color of the surface is virtually lost. When the light is concentrated in one spot, the color of the light is what's reflected, as in the hot spot under a downlight with a polished stone table directly below.

Not all applications of glossy surface treatments will offer predictable results. Most often, a gloss finish will brighten the surface. However, an increase in saturation is not inevitable with every method used to create a glossy surface. If the glossiness is applied to the surface color, as in an acrylic coating or a chintz glaze, the intensity is reduced because the color is seen through another material. In general, colors that are inherently dark will often appear darker in a glossy finish due to the increased intensity of the color.

▶ Visual Color Mixing

Unique colors can be created by techniques other than homogenous mixing of media, such as paint or dye. Some are the result of visual mixing, which is another form of texture very much like the Pointillism technique used by the French Impressionist, Georges Seurat (1859–1891). In this case, small dots, lines, yarns, or blotches of different colors are placed close to one another so that the eye will blend them as an overall tone. As we get closer, the characteristics of the individual colors become apparent. As we move away or increase the angle of view, the colors blend together, creating a mix of the originals. This condition is known as *optical mixing,* or *visual color mixing,* and is shown in the example in Figures 10.2 and 10.3.

Visual mixing occurs most readily with colors close in value. A popular application is the use of two colors that are similar in value but opposite in temperature. The result is a very soft, neutral color at a distance, but a very textural surface with a temperature contrast up close. When any two noncomplementary colors with some hue character are mixed optically, they will blend to form a new hue. For example, magenta and blue will combine to form a purplish hue. As with pigment, if the two colors are complements, they will visually blend to form gray at a distance. A mix of colors of different value results in a value between the two colors.

Applications

Examples of visual color mixing can be seen in a number of places. We understand the way printed dots are combined, usually in three or four colors, to create a full-color photograph. An enlarged version is the Sunday comics, where the dots are far enough apart to be seen. Textile weavings often incorporate subtle color blends by placing individual yarns close together. Weaving two or three yarns together may create a solid-color textile with some visual depth. *Interference colors* are a popular use of pigments with fibers in them to give a metallic or luminous look. The result is a surface that looks like one color from one angle, but a different tone or hue from another perspective.

Undertones are often used in visual mixing to give added depth to a surface color. Many paint and glaze techniques incorporate this tool. An undertone is created either by incorporating a color into a visual mix or by placing the color across the full surface underneath all the other applied colors to create a subtle shift. Undertones are usually marked by temperature shifts. Similar to the behavior of solid colors in three-dimensional use, an optical mix with a warm undertone will cause the overall color to advance; a cool undertone will cause it to recede.

Patricia Lambert, Barbara Staepelaere, and Mary Fry explain how visual mixing occurs in textiles just as it does in paint and other finish materials in *Color and Fiber* (page 152). The smaller the scale of the mix, the more easily the eye blends the colors. In textiles, this occurs primarily through two methods. The finest scale is the combining of different-colored yarns to create a new color of yarn through the visual mixing of the originals. Blending occurs when the individual yarns are thoroughly carded and blended together into one yarn. A more expressive blend involves two yarns of differing colors combined into a two-ply yarn, which Chevreul called "mixture by threads."

Another approach, which can yield a more tactile effect, is the combination of different *warp* and *weft* yarns. The warp yarns are the ones that run lengthwise through the loom. Weft yarns run across the loom from selvage to selvage. The interweaving

FIGURE 10.2 In this example of a layered paint technique, four colors are combined to suggest texture. *(Original color design for installation of painted wall finish by Barbara Jacobs, Color and Design.)*

FIGURE 10.3 At a distance, the colors shown in Figure 10.2 soften and neutralize as the eye blends them together. *(Original color design and installation of painted finish by Barbara Jacobs, Color and Design. Interior design: Cynthia L. Brumm. Architect: Dan B. Goodenow, Cape Ann Design Group.)*

of these two sets of yarns results in fabric. When two or more different-colored yarns are used, the overall tone of the fabric changes according to the angle at which it is viewed. This causes a slight shimmering effect, which Chevreul called "mixture by hatchings." As the fabric folds, the flat-faced areas reveal the distinct yarns; but when viewed at an angle the yarns blend into one color.

■ LIMITS OF MATERIALS

The textural characteristics of each material suggest variations in their successful application. A fine silk fiber dyed in the same color as a coarse wool fiber will result in dissimilar coloration. The natural color of a porcelain tile offers a surface visually different from a glazed ceramic tile using the same form of pigmentation. Glazes, coatings, and many paints sit on the surface of a material, while dyes, stains, and a few paint products penetrate the finish surface. Each color selection will

have greater long-term success if it is done with respect to the inherent capabilities of that material, the manufacturing abilities available at the time of selection, and the specified surface texture. Consider the case study in Figure 10.4. The occupant of this private office enjoys very strong sunlight and dislikes window treatments. Ultraviolet rays significantly impact each surface material. In this solution, a species of light wood that is known to darken over time was combined with dark textiles. Through this combination the wood is expected to darken and the textiles will naturally fade to a softer patina, ensuring an ongoing contrast of value.

Every human-made material has some limitations in terms of the colors it can inherit due to the process used in its development. Materials such as concrete and glass are limited to inherent color use, not to mention what we will accept aesthetically. As color-duplication technologies improve and become more cost-effective, and as effective primers and

FIGURE 10.4 Materials for this office were selected with attention to the impact of ultraviolet light on the proposed color and material. *(Interior Design by GHK. Photo: Greg Premru.)*

other bonding agents are developed for each surface we come into contact with, the number of available options increases. The manufactured materials discussed here are among the most commonly used in design practice. The intent is to identify specific color issues inherent in each material and to offer words of warning that have been provided by practitioners.

▶ Paint

Paint is one finish material that offers an infinite range in color selection and at the same time a fair number of options for texture. In order of most reflective to most diffuse light reflectance, paint is normally specified in the following finishes: high gloss, lacquer, gloss, semigloss, low-luster semigloss, satin, pearl, eggshell, low-luster eggshell, matte, and flat. A high gloss is a very hard, durable

surface. Water will bead on anything from satin through high gloss, making maintenance easier. The more reflective or glossy a paint, the easier it is to enhance its color with direct light. At the same time, its surface will show imperfections more readily, which translates into more time to prepare the surface properly.

One concern with painted material is its ability to sustain its color over a long period of time. Artists struggle with this issue frequently, since many of the natural materials used to produce pigments are innately *fugitive*. That is, they fade over time, particularly when exposed to sunlight or any form of ultraviolet light. Designers who are involved in restorations come face-to-face with fugitive color issues as well, since the goal is often to restore original color. Accuracy is restricted if the available color of an original work of architecture has faded due to fugitive pigments, weathering, or both. For new applications where fading is of concern, the permanence rating for paint materials can be obtained from the paint manufacturer.

Selecting Paint Colors

When the majority of the color expression in a design will come from the paints chosen, it is worth taking some extra precautions during selection. The transition from small paint chips to planes of color in the form of walls is often a leap of faith, but some conditions that impact such a transition are predictable. Our perception of paint colors changes as the scale changes in the transition from paint chip to wall plane. When a color covers a single full wall, it generally looks lighter in value and more saturated than its diminutive sample.

The color of the unfinished surface can change the finish paint color by creating an undertone. One way to counteract this is to apply several coats of a white primer. This will keep the color clean by reflecting more of the white light that hits the surface. If two adjacent materials, such as a steel panel next to drywall, are to receive the same final color of paint, the lighter of the two surfaces can be given a dark shade of primer to eliminate any variation due to undertones. Of course, some selections call for testing in the actual space for which they are intended. On large commercial building projects, a full-scale mock-up of key wall details may be produced during construction, offering an excellent method to test color relationships while resolving techniques of fabrication.

Working with Manufacturers

Paint manufacturers usually keep technical data on the color standards they use, including the amount of light reflectance, which is measured as *light reflectance value* (LRV). Some go so far as to publish them on the fan decks. This is useful information when developing the lighting concept. When indirect lighting is being used, reflectance of the lit surfaces needs to be high—say, 85 percent reflectance or greater. In theory, total reflectance is 100 percent and total absorption is 0 percent, which gives us a scale for evaluating the total amount of light reflected by each color. In reality, the absolutes of 100 percent and 0 percent reflectivity cannot be produced, even by scientific methods. So

our available range is something slightly smaller. Another condition affecting the amount of light reflected is the quality of the painted surface. Needless to say, a smooth, clean, polished surface will reflect more light than one that is rough, coarse, or covered with dust.

Some projects call for an investment in specialty paints. In such applications, we rely on the specialist who prepares the paint for information on long-term physical attributes of each treatment being considered. For example, the pigment verdigris tends to darken with age, which may be desirable in some color schemes and undesirable in others. Artist's powder colors can be used to tint some mediums for more vivid color choices; however, they are more difficult to use because of the particles suspended within them and may require a sealer.

Softening Color

There are several ways to soften the visual impact of a given paint color, making it appear less flat. Each technique makes the surface color decidedly inconsistent. Sometimes this is accomplished by a change in quality of the pigment, such as using natural pigments from clay to produce softer, better-quality earth tones. Examples include yellow ochre, the umbers, the siennas, and green and red oxides. After-painting surface treatments can also be done to soften the painted look, and this is usually recommended for large surfaces. A *glaze* is a translucent layer of paint, slightly tinted, that is applied over a ground of a different color. It causes subtleties in the surface color by varying the refraction of light reflected off the painted surface. The smaller the amount of color used in the glaze, the greater its transparency will be. Each combination of glaze and undercoat offers a different nuance. A *wash* is a powdered pigment suspended in a clear liquid with high surface tension, such as water or thinned latex, and applied over a painted surface. *Antiquing* is a process used on many surfaces to give the impression of aging or cracking. It's performed on surfaces of all scales using layers of paint materials specifically designed for this purpose. Each specialist who uses layered paint processes has his or her own methods for creating unique textural color. One of the more interesting examples I've heard described is John Saladino's use of instant coffee to tint his scratch-coat plaster walls so they would "appear lichen-covered and ancient" as expressed by John Esten and Rose Bennett Gilbert in *Manhattan Style.*

Other painting techniques include overpainting a surface using various tools. *Check rolling* uses a tool created for wood-grain techniques and offers an uneven linear pattern; *combing, dragging,* and *flogging* involve dragging a comb, paintbrush, or flogger respectively over a wet glaze. *Stenciling* is popular for regular repeated designs at a larger scale. *Spattering, sponging, ragging,* or *stippling* paint offer very uneven paint textures. Faux finishes, such as tortoiseshelling, wood-graining, and marbling are other ways to incorporate soft color on a finish surface.

A few rules of thumb will ensure greater success when using complex paint finishes. The smaller the range of contrast in the colors combined within a surface, the more sophisticated the look. Washes or ragging with a greater amount of value or hue contrast tends to appear stylized, reading more like a positive negative print than a texture with depth. When using variegated vinyl paint materials, the greater the number of colors, the more depth can be created. Four colors in combination will offer more of a sense of texture than two; six offers more than four. The distance of normal view is also worth considering. If you want the texture to be discernible from across the room, greater contrast of value or saturation will ensure it. If the goal is to maintain some contrast of hue at any distance, complementary colors and those very close in tone should not be used.

Even in installations where flat paint will be used, variations in the tone of complex planes can be established by varying the color of the primer. Donald Kaufman, who is known for his work with painted surfaces, suggests using an undercoat that is lighter and warmer to create a luminous effect, with dark undertones for more formal settings (*Color and Light: Luminous Atmospheres for Painted Rooms*). This is effective in conditions of large amounts of light, usually daylight. As strong daylight washes the surface, the color of the primer acts as an undertone and changes the surface color to appear more like the primer. As the light level decreases, the topcoat takes over. This paint technique allows a daylit space to vary over a 24-hour period without the use of expensive materials. It can

be demonstrated by finding a space where two adjacent walls are lit, one primarily with direct daylight, the other primarily with fluorescent lighting. If they are painted first with peach, then with a layer of beige overpaint, the wall lit by the artificial light will look more beige, but the one with daylight will look peach by comparison.

▶ Textiles

There are three techniques for manipulating color in textile fabrication: visual mixing through weaving as described earlier in this chapter, color management through the dyeing process, and manipulation of yarn orientation. Our understanding of these processes dates back to the writing of M. E. Chevreul in the early to mid-1800s. His work included the areas of visual mixing, the effects of simultaneous contrast, the logic of harmonies, and the chemical aspects of dyeing processes at a time when the shift from natural to synthetic dyes was occurring. The conclusions based on his experience in the Gobelins tapestry works established many of the basic guidelines for the manufacture of fabrics and carpet.

Dye Methods

Dyes are developed specifically for individual substrates. The colorant that produces a particular blue in cotton will not yield the same blue in a wool fiber. Color is either woven into textiles in the form of dyed yarn or applied to the surface of the textile in the form of pigment. The principles of applied color are similar to those of paint and other pigmentary media just discussed. With surface color in fabrics, the pigment is applied to the surface using a bonding agent. This pigment lasts essentially until the bonding agent wears away due to abrasion. Methods of applying surface pigment to fabrics include silk screening and block printing.

Color manipulation through dyed material offers a tremendous range of options that result from the combination of yarn materials and dye methods. Experienced designers know that the dyeing process can result in minor variations with the same products. Any subtle variations in dye color will be obvious in a large installation. To guard against undesirable edge matching, fabric or carpet to be used within one area is specified from only a single dye lot. When this is not practical, samples from a series of proposed dye lots are reviewed for approval. Similarly, some streaking is possible if a dye is not processing consistently. A visual inspection of the product as it completes fabrication will uncover these conditions.

One concern we often have for dyed goods is the long-term stability of the color. The lightfastness of each fiber in combination with the dye method used will determine color stability, particularly for products installed in direct sunlight. Wash fastness can also affect textile color, especially in situations that call for significant maintenance, such as in medical, food service, and child-care facilities.

Fabrics

Dye is essentially a colorant that is dissolved in a fluid and specified to chemically attach itself to the fiber being treated. For fabrics, this is done as a vat process for natural fibers such as cotton, wool, and silk. With synthetic fibers, such as nylon, the dye is introduced either after the yarn is spun or chemically, while it is in a liquid state, which is known as *solution dyeing*. All colors fade to some degree, particularly those created through the dye process. However, generally speaking, the earlier in the manufacturing process the dyeing occurs, the closest to the raw material that the dye is applied, the more colorfast the fiber will be. This makes solution-dyed nylon advantageous where the colorfast fiber is desirable. The disadvantage with solution-dyed nylon, though, is that it is so uniform in color, it can look flat. If this is undesirable, optical mixing of solution-dyed yarns offers a good alternative color solution.

There is a science to textile dyes just as there is for any other color manufacturing process. Some types of dye are better suited for bright colors; some fibers take certain dye colors more readily. Some freshly dyed materials can appear a little brash, or strong, similar to the effect of an artist's raw paint used directly from the tube. When this happens, the color can be toned down by second immersion of shorter duration into either black or dark brown dye. Black is used to give a cool undertone and brown for a warm one. The density of constructed material also affects the color of a finished piece. The more tightly woven the fiber, the darker or more intense the color may appear, since a dense or compact structure offers more individual fibers for the dye to adhere to.

Carpets

The majority of carpet today is produced in synthetic fibers, such as nylon, olefin, acrylic, and polyester. Of these, nylon and polyester are known to have the strongest reputations for color clarity and colorfastness. Natural fibers are less color secure due to the difference in dyeing methods and tend to be chosen more for their luxurious feel. They are available in wool and cotton for large installations. Jute, hemp, and sisal carpet fibers are also available for specialty items such as area rugs. Tufted carpet may be dyed in the fiber or yarn before tufting (predyeing), or the undyed tufted fabric (greige goods) may be dyed before the backing is applied. Woven carpets are predyed and in some cases overprinted.

Synthetic fibers are produced through the process of heating raw material to a liquid, then extruding it through tiny holes into a filament, and finally cooling the filament as it's drawn into yarn. The extrusion process is what determines the cross-sectional shape of the fiber and consequently its luster and texture. During extrusion, additives are mixed with the molten polymer fiber to modify its appearance. These can include color pigments, in which case the fiber is solution dyed. Solution-dyed carpet, whose fibers are only synthetic by definition, is becoming increasingly popular. With such products, any crimping or application of other textures occurs after the extrusion process.

Multicolored effects in carpet are created by treating fibers so that they take dyestuffs differently. *Stock dyeing* involves coloration of staple fibers before the yarn is spun. This method is used for nylon and wool. To produce a multicolored product, stock-dyed fibers of different colors are spun together into yarn. Berbers and heather blends are examples. Spun yarn is colored by *skein dyeing*. This method is used in smaller-volume production such as custom color work for most yarn types, except olefin. *Space dyeing,* primarily used for nylons, is a technique of printing color in segments along the length of continuous yarn, either evenly or unevenly. Undyed carpet woven with a primary backing is called *greige goods.* It can be dyed in a vat, a method known as *piece dyeing.* Printing onto woven carpet is traditionally done with flatbed or rotary screen printers. The more expensive *jet printing* is done with rows of computer-controlled color jets positioned across the width of the carpet.

Yarn Orientation

Subtle color variation results from the changes in scale and orientation of the yarns themselves. Some of the most sophisticated textiles are those created in a subtle range of values, often described as a *tone on tone,* using just one yarn color. By changing the position of the yarn or its physical character, it will appear slightly different due to the corresponding change in light reflection on the fiber. Several techniques produce this effect according to the Lambert, Staepelaere, and Fry team.

The most common method of a tone-on-tone textile is accomplished by changing the orientation of the spun fiber, or yarns. Again, basic fabric construction involves a series of warp yarns, running lengthwise through the loom. These are interwoven by weft yarns, which run back and forth across the full width of the fabric, from selvage to selvage. As the weft yarn moves under and over every other warp yarn, cloth is formed. The combination of a light color image floating over a slightly darker ground, or the reverse combination, is accomplished by changing the orientation of the fiber through variations in the surface exposure of warp and weft yarns. This is illustrated in Figure 10.5. The lightness or darkness of the fiber is realized according to the amount of light reflected directly back to the eye. The traditional *damask* is a well-known example of fabric assembled using this method.

In woven carpet, subtle adjustments in tone are accomplished in a number of ways. These include twisting as in a *frieze,* uneven height of loops in a loop pile, or the combination of cut-and-loop pile. In each case, the direction the yarn is reoriented to give a more textural effect through the appearance of subtle color variation. In the example of cut-and-loop carpet, the loops appear darker, since one is looking at the side of the yarn, which reflects less direct light than the ends of the cut yarn in the same dye color. Such tone-on-tone carpets are also created by *tip shearing,* where the longest loops of an uneven-loop carpet are sheared across the surface. If done precisely, tip shearing results in a very soft, elegant texture. (If done improperly, it can give the appearance of a variation in dye lot because of the unevenness that is apparent under direct light.)

Oriental rugs readily demonstrate the way color appears to change due to orientation of the fibers. Most oriental rugs are woven in a uniform direction, causing the yarns to be trimmed as if they lean slightly. This causes the pattern to be directional even if the graphic pattern is symmetric. The effect can be seen by standing at one end of the rug and then the other—one view will always be darker.

Another type of construction that takes advantage of the ability of longer yarns to reflect more light is the use of piles. A *pile* on a fabric occurs when the fibers are cut to expose the end, such as *mohairs* and *chenilles.* By comparison, *linen* is

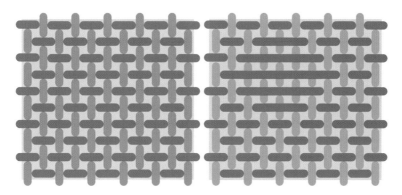

FIGURE 10.5 In this illustration different colors of hue are used for clarity of the technique. The left diagram shows a uniform construction technique called a *plain weave.* On the right, several weft yarns skip over the warp to create a block of tonal color. These are called *float* yarns.

almost always woven because of its short staple yarns, resulting in a less luminous surface. The first generation of cut-pile nylon carpets were highly reflective in comparison to then popular wools, which were highly mottled in color due to their staple yarns. Over time, synthetic fibers were engineered to reduce reflectance, then known as *sheen,* and appear more wool-like to make them seem more expensive. Eventually, nylon fibers suitable for carpet could be created with virtually no sheen at all.

Fiber and Color

We should note that the characteristics of the raw fiber, before surface treatment, have an effect on the characteristics of lightness in the finished material. Wool and cotton fibers are inherently grainier due to the use of shorter staple yarns. On the opposite hand, many extruded synthetic fibers can be created using more continuous filaments to make them shine. As the angle of reflectance shifts, finished materials in these fibers appear to change in intensity.

Another condition that can affect the perceived color value of a textile is its fiber profile. A finished yarn that is made up of many finer fibers will have more reflective surfaces and therefore appear lighter than a similar-weight yarn made of fewer, more coarse fibers. The cross section of the yarn will also affect its light reflectance. A very flat cross section of fiber, similar to the pasta linguini, can be used to create an interesting visual texture. As the fiber is twisted during construction, the areas of flat surface will reflect more light than the narrow edges. *Crimping, straightening, spiraling,* and *twisting* are some of the ways fibers are modified to enhance surface characteristics to positively affect textural color. The more highly twisted a finished yarn, the darker it will appear in comparison to a slightly twisted yarn as light is absorbed into the texture of the yarn.

When textiles are created using this knowledge of fiber and color, the value of the colors appear to change as the fabric puckers in an upholstered piece or floats in a hung drapery. At those points where the most reflected light is directed toward the eye, the material will appear lightest. Surrounding material will appear slightly darker, as if in shadow. In fact, any change of direction on a textile product will cause a change in the appearance of surface color. For this reason, fine furniture is always upholstered with the fabric oriented in a uniform direction. Carpet as well must be installed in a uni-

form direction. Otherwise, abutting sections will not match.

Surface Treatment

The last textile process to be addressed here as it relates to color is that of surface treatments. To increase light reflectance of rougher fibers, surface treatments can be applied. The most common is the shiny look of *chintz* on printed cotton. This glazed treatment is created by running the woven fabric through rollers and heat-setting an applied glaze or an impregnated resin. The ribbed look of a *moiré* is created similarly using rollers. To create *flocking,* yarns are applied to the surface of a woven textile to create a nap, which has the effect of shifting the overall color value slightly by exposing short fibers and therefore more ends. Many other surface treatments are available in textiles, but those discussed here have the greatest impact on color.

Complex Color

Nowhere are the conditions of the Bezold effect (described in Chapter 8, "Color Enhances Form") more dramatic than in the selection of color for textiles. Creative selection of the colored yarns can make woven construction appear more complex or less so. The combination of yarns in different hue, value, and saturation characteristics creates more complex fabric color overall. While the scale of these patterns can vary widely according to the method of construction used by each manufacturer, the final pattern will appear different to the viewer depending on what color combination is used. Changes in contrasts between yarns draw attention to different characteristics of the constructed material and give the impression of more than one product. The examples of a single textile in Figure 10.6 demonstrate this.

As with paint treatments, a larger number of colors within a small range can give the surface greater depth. Selections can make the material seem finer or coarser. This characteristic of color allows us to create textiles with a wide range of applications and appearance out of one basic textile design. The textile shown in Figure 10.7 exhibits a tremendous range of complexity through variation in contrast of the yarns rather than changes in its construction.

When developing a custom color carpet, it's common to start out with three or four yarn colors that appear to work well together at close viewing

FIGURE 10.6 The samples shown here are the same construction with different combinations of yarn color. Notice how the eye is drawn to each aspect of the pattern depending on the color variation. *(Nile designed by Hazel Siegel, President Textus.)*

range. One suggestion is to view these colors at a distance as well so the graying effect that inevitably results when the carpet is on the floor can be visualized. If the dominant tone of the colors in combination is not as intended, often a shift in proportion or an adjustment to one color will impact the whole composition. Also, when customizing carpets with only two yarn colors, a small range of value is recommended. Otherwise, the pattern may read like a positive-negative graphic image and give the sense of something very flat, regardless of the type of construction.

Wallcoverings

Wallcoverings are available in several forms. They can be created from woven textiles with a paper or sprayed acrylic backing. They are also made from completely synthetic materials such as vinyl and, more recently, fiberglass. A key advantage to wallcovering rather than painting surfaces is its effect on scale. Because wall coverings are often patterned rather than solid in color, they can be used to affect one's impression of the overall proportions. Stripes can make the room look taller; larger, nondirectional patterns can give the impression of coziness by breaking down a large plane into smaller sections.

The color concerns regarding these materials are indicated by both their material characteristics and the method of color application. Because wallcoverings have a surface texture, they are directional. This means that they need to be applied in a consistent orientation or there will be a visible difference in

FIGURE 10.7 The complexity of this construction demonstrates the designer's skill in contrast and harmony. *(Patricia Palson Handweaver.)*

surface color. (Each vertical section of wallcovering is known as a *drop*. If one drop is oriented upside down in comparison to the rest of the wall material, it will look lighter or darker in color than all the drops that are right side up.) If the material has any pattern, this variation also needs to be taken into account during installation. Some wallcoverings, such as traditional grass cloth, have significant variations in the pattern that make matching at the seams impractical. The greater the range of color in the overall pattern, the more evident this variation will be after installation, making the seams more evident.

Several printing methods are currently in use for wallcoverings. *Surface printing* produces patterns that appear textural, almost hand-painted, while *rotary-screened* prints offer a flat matte look. *Hand-screened* patterns are silk-screened by hand and also produce a flat matte appearance. This process is used for custom designs, murals, and in other situations that call for an unlimited number of colors. For tonal patterns, which can look like watercolors, *gravure* printing, or a less expensive alternative known as *flexo,* is used. With any four-color printing process in wallcovering production the goal is to use the fewest number of individual pigments possible to reduce the risk of metamerism. If similar colors are produced through a different combination of pigments, they may appear less similar under certain lighting situations. To reduce the possibility of metamerism, some manufacturers of high-end screened products use three-color primary pigments exclusively. For variations in value, a pattern may include some variation in the amount of background color showing through, as in Figure 10.8.

FIGURE 10.8 The designer of this wallcovering uses her knowledge of pattern preferences for softer edges and increased color variation to create a marketable product. *(Diane Richmond, designer. Web site: www.dianerichmond@earthlink.net.)*

▶ Formed Materials

Each material available to designers offers its own inherent characteristics that influence our color choices. Paint and textiles currently offer the greatest range of options relative to color integration, in part because of the manufacturing technologies available. For cast and formed materials, color is best maintained when the surface is similar to the substrate color. Brick tends to be medium to dark in value and warm in tone, with a few exceptions— some yellow, green, and gray products are produced. Wood tones render best on wood, but the same colors are very unpopular in paint. Every material offers some limitations or concerns, each of which may affect the successful integration of color.

A great range of color is available in synthetic materials, particularly those produced for finishing architectural interiors. Resilient tile, which was developed as a derivative of polyvinyl chloride, is one such product. The combination of certain resins, stabilizers, plasticizers, fillers, and pigments combined to produce a homogenous, durable floor material about 0.08 inch thick whose color is maintained throughout its thickness. Inexpensive and durable, it is manufactured in a large number of colors to increase its appeal. Other synthetic products offer choices for functional and aesthetic forms of design, such as the example in Figure 10.9.

FIGURE 10.9   Here, a vinyl tile is made to have characteristics of slate through the use of photographic imaging and texture in the surface of the tile. *(Courtesy of Armstrong Commercial Flooring.)*

FIGURE 10.10 The artist who created this piece is well known for the multi-color layering technique shown here. *(Courtesy of Bill Campbell Pottery. Photo: Jerry Anthony.)*

Ceramics

Ceramic products, such as pottery, sculpted art, and manufactured tile, come in many sizes, thicknesses, and forms. They can be made unglazed, in which case the natural earth tones of the material are displayed, or colored glazes can be applied. These glazes are fired, which hardens the surface, making the tile waterproof. Like paints, ceramic glazes are manipulated to offer a range of textures, from a highly textured matte to a highly reflective gloss. Some are available in transparent or translucent form to allow the natural color of the clay to permeate. In strict color terms, ceramic glazes offer a tremendous range of hues, values, and chromatic intensities.

Ceramic artists are well aware that some color uncertainties exist in working with glazes. The applied material is not an indication of what the color will look like after firing. The final color of each glaze varies according to the composition of the clay to which it is applied, firing temperatures, and the length of firing time. Ceramicists often cre-

ate test chips to monitor variables in the glazing process, adjusting one variable at a time until the desired result is established. The formula may then be guarded, similar to a secret family recipe, so that others cannot duplicate it. Additional colors are created through layering of glazes so that they mix on the surface during firing, like those in Figure 10.10. These factors indicate two guidelines for the practicing colorist: (1) specific custom color is highly unlikely with manufactured glazed products, and (2) the sample provided by a manufacturer generally occurs within a range of the final product. For glazes with greater variation, it makes good sense to see several samples of a product to assess diversity. Those who work with ceramic tile find that many manufacturers offer more extensive ranges of blue or green tile, but tiles in the orange range are limited, as this glazed product is more difficult to fabricate consistently.

For architects whose work incorporates dramatic color combinations, ceramic glazed brick is available. This is regaining popularity as a building material due to its durability as a surface material, its reasonable initial cost, and the wide variety of colors available.

Laminates and Solid Surfaces

Plastic laminate is another synthetic building material made in a large range of colors and in several textures. Color in a high-gloss sample and a matte sample will exhibit some variation in surface tone. As with any other material, the textured finishes cause slight shifts in color due to direction. This makes laminates a poor choice for color matching with other material samples. If a painted finish matches a laminate sample held upside down, it may not match the same sample right side up.

Most plastic laminates are made by bonding sheets of clear or translucent vinyl to printed paper and a backing material through compression. The result is a product that can easily take pattern but whose color does not transfer through its thickness. This opens the door for highly visible scratches on darker samples. On light-colored products, the edges may stand out if the substrate is a dark neutral color. Solid surfacing materials, which have integral color throughout, were developed to offer a solid-edge alternative; however, they, too, show scratches in the darkest choices.

Glass

Glass is the last synthetic material to be addressed for its color concerns. Although it is most often used in a clear state, glass can be produced in a variety of transparencies and colors by introducing metallic oxides into the raw material before fabrication. Glass artists have further demonstrated the properties of visual mixing by combining glass in various colors into one sculpted element or by overlapping portions of colored glass. Glass has also become a source for three-dimensional ornamentation through unique applications of color and texture, by changes in positioning of textured surfaces, or by casting into nonplanar forms, as shown in Figure 10.11.

Glass is usually a high gloss, except when texturing processes such as etching are applied. The luminosity of glass traditionally made it popular as a mosaic tile material, as seen in Greek, Roman, and Byzantine architecture. When a color was viewed through these glass tiles, they became brighter and richer. This was particularly true of glass tiles with gold leafing.

Plaster and Stucco

Many textures are available in plaster, including very fine, smooth surfaces, slightly pebbly or scratched surfaces, and even thickly troweled surfaces. Plaster can also be manipulated to resemble the surface form of stone, tile, brick, or wood. This material is usually specified to be light in value, most often white, but can be colored during the skim and finish coats. The advantage of a pigmented plaster is that the color permeates the surface of the wall or other feature. In a very coarse application, the color will be consistent, except for the variations posed by changing light reflectance. If the surface is damaged, it will be less apparent since the substrate is consistent in tone. When color of hue is applied to plaster, the same subtle variations of value inherent in the texture are able to show themselves—provided the selected color is medium to light in value. Plaster can handle the full range of saturation.

Stucco is a form of exterior-grade plaster with integral color that is usually light in value and low in saturation. It's marketed as an exterior insulated finish system (EIFS), under trade names such as Dryvit, in a range of standard colors. It can be shaped and carved as a decorative element. *Fresco* is a traditional form of wall painting that is done while the plaster is wet. A lime-compatible pigment in powder form is combined with water and applied onto fresh plaster. It's usually used on a plaster surface with a very fine texture. Other synthetic and lime-based decorative plasters are currently available in a variety of surface finishes. With fresco and colored plaster applications, one should be aware that the material looks much darker when wet. Unlike paint, it is difficult to gauge the true lightness of the finished product on the basis of a wet field sample.

Concrete

One very popular traditional building material is concrete. For many years, this material has been used in relatively intrinsic colors—shades of gray,

FIGURE 10.11 These contemporary tiles appear luminous due to the application of color in the formation of the glass. *(Courtesy of Architectural Glass.)*

both warm and cool, or off-white, depending on the cement and aggregate mix used. In recent years, concrete staining has become popular, increasing the options to colors of subtle hue. Variations in form, such as overhangs and insets, add color as a range of values through shadowing. The material is ideal for the expression of large-scale architectural design and clean, simple geometries, such as the transportation center shown in Figure 10.12. Surface texture has been added through the use of added aggregates, or by textured formations, such as

corduroy concrete, which is created during forming and may be jackhammered for maximum texture.

Today, more colorful work is being performed with concrete through an increase in integral color and the technological possibilities of more complex patterning. At the same time, the sophistication of casting methods in this material makes it ideal for expression of complex form. Despite its neutral traditions, this is one material with the potential to change our expectations for color in future works of architecture.

FIGURE 10.12 The subtle nuances of concrete materials leave room for color variation through lighting, as suggested in this daylight image. *(Design by Ellenzweig Associates, Inc., Architects. Photo: Greg Premru.)*

The warm-tone metals, often called the *yellow metals,* include gold, brass, bronze, and copper. Cool metals, or *white metals,* include steel, aluminum, chrome, and pewter. Each offers a silvery look of one kind or another. Figure 10.13 shows warm and cool metals used in combination.

The degree of reflectance on metal depends on its texture. From most light-reflective to least, common finishes are polished, matte (usually referred to as *brushed* or *satin*), textured, or embossed. A *patina* can be created in some metals through natural aging, rubbing, oxidizing, or antiquing by synthetic means. The most popular patina is the green coloration that copper exhibits when left untreated and exposed to the elements. Without treatment, pewter darkens over time. Bronze, a combination of brass and copper, is often rubbed with oil to darken it.

The more decorative metals are available in either a metallic powder or in sheets, called *leaves,* which are similar to very thin tissue paper. *Gold leaf,* the most popular of these, is available in either material and is commonly found in traditional decorative arts, particularly government buildings and historic furniture. *Silver leaf* is also available in leaves and powder, but must be varnished as it tarnishes. Both gold and silver leaves are used sparingly in most applications due to their significant cost. Aluminum leaf is available in large leaves and is more economical than silver. It is installed more quickly, but is slightly grayer in color than silver. *Dutch leaf* is another option as a metallic colorant. An alloy of copper and zinc, it is available in shades of gold and is less expensive than the gold leaf it mimics; however, it needs to be varnished to prevent tarnishing. Bronze, available in powder form, ranges from a gold tone to a dark bronze color.

Paint manufacturers have found ways to incorporate metal fibers into the mix to create very metallic-looking applied finishes. These are significantly less expensive than gold and silver leaf and come in a much larger color range. In comparison to flat paint, they are often more difficult to use and are more expensive. However, they may be appropriate in situations where the true metal leaf products are not.

▶ Organic Materials

Organic materials are inherently rich in color by virtue of their inconsistency. Stone in its many

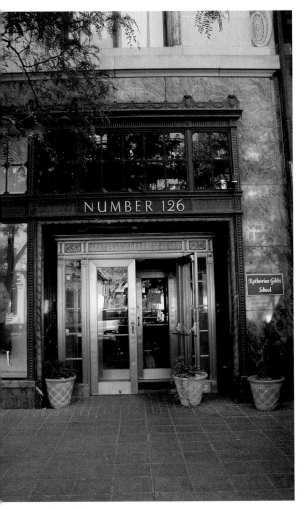

FIGURE 10.13 This entry shows brass used in combination with a darker steel finish, accentuating the richness of the yellow metal through contrast.

Metal

The natural colors of metal offer a reasonable range of lightness to darkness and warmth to coolness. One of the few metals that are frequently finished in unnatural colors is steel. This is obvious in buildings where steel remains exposed or where hollow metal framing is used at doors and windows. Very often, this metal is not sufficiently pleasing in its natural state and must be painted or enameled for practical use. Other metal materials are available in a more natural-colored state and are used in three-dimensional art forms, building construction, interior surfaces, and industrial products.

forms offers a traditional building material. Marbles, granites, limestones, and slate provide a rich range of color and pattern for exterior and interior work. Sandstone is available in a smaller range of color, in red, reddish-brown, white, earth yellow, or gray, depending on the cementing material within (see Figure 10.14). The basic philosophy of many who incorporate natural materials in their work is to take advantage of the color inherent in the material in its natural state. If we apply surface color, maintenance becomes more challenging. Over time, the color of natural materials often changes more than that of synthetic counterparts. This is part of their appeal. The rule of thumb is that the more deeply an applied color permeates the surface, the more consistent its color will be in the long term. Leather, one of the most popular natural materials, was traditionally dyed only in the tan to brown range, or black, due to limitations in dyeing processes. In recent years leather manufacturers have produced dyed products in which the color

penetrates the surface more completely, opening up the options to a range of colors previously associated with synthetic vinyls.

Wood

Wood materials have intrinsic color tendencies. As an organic material, wood has natural color variations. (See Figure 10.15.) Most wood tones are essentially yellow, orange, or red in nature. The exceptions are the very exotic woods, such as ebony, which has charcoal graining, and purpleheart, which, as the name implies, is purple. The natural color tendency of any wood is apparent if a transparent or translucent finish is used. If a red stain is applied to wood that is inherently yellow, its yellow undertone will counteract the stain to some degree. The result may be more orange than is desirable. If a purple stain is applied to a wood with red undertones, the result is likely to be magenta in hue. The same color stain applied to a wood with

FIGURE 10.14   The rich stone colors of this Richardsonian building have survived many changes of use.

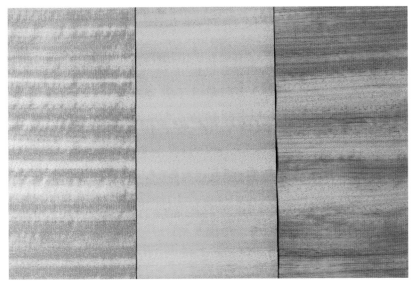

FIGURE 10.15   Three flitches of wood are shown in their raw state (unfinished). Together, they show overall tones of yellow, orange, and red inherent in their respective species.

yellow undertones will result in a softer shade of purple as the yellow undertone neutralizes it. Bleaching, or color impregnating, in addition to staining, can be used to alter wood color. If the texture of the wood competes with its intended surface color, this can be reduced by applying a filler before adding surface color.

Time has some impact on wood coloration, which can be used to a design advantage. Many woods, such as cedar, will turn gray in outdoor applications or change their value during indoor use when exposed to direct sunlight. Oak and cherry are woods that darken over time in direct light, yet walnut gets lighter and grayer. Also, some wood stains are known to fade over time if exposed to direct sunlight.

Many fabrication materials are available other than those discussed here, each with its own color characteristics. To some degree, fabrication plays a part in successful color solutions. While some materials are logically restricted in potential color ranges, others present overwhelming opportunities for the creative display of color.

In Part 1, we discussed the process of color selection from the perspective of color theory and color associations. In Part 2, we considered aspects of color in design that are primarily three-dimensional: human response, color and form concepts, and the technical issues that impact color use. The next step is to explore how this information is used in professional practice. In the remaining chapters, color criteria for each area of specialization are offered based on the knowledge accumulated thus far and the insights shared by designers in each field.

Three-Dimensional Applications

11

Inspirations, Precedents, and Trends

The context of any three-dimensional project establishes some criteria for its success. Context implies not only a sense of location and intended use, but also an understanding of the place in time for a developing project. This is particularly evident when dealing with environments of historic significance. The nature of the historic period and the type of project tell us the degree to which historic character will direct, inform, or inspire the color solution. *Direct* in this case means using very definitive criteria; *inform* implies the use of guidelines or recognizable distinctions; *inspiration* suggests a range of acceptable solutions with common aesthetic characteristics.

Even contemporary designs establish the context of a here and now or attempt to connect us to our future. Criteria in this case are derived from contemporary color preferences or from social and economic indicators to ensure acceptance. In some cases, a need to be on the "bleeding edge" of consumerism or technology is communicated through logical color application. The point here is that the context of time offers criteria for color selection.

In this chapter, we explore the methods used to establish criteria for successful color selection relative to a time context—those in the past or here and now.

■ APPROACHING HISTORIC SPACE

The colors Americans have chosen, and continue to choose, reflect the state of a culture. Each case is a sign of individual or collective experience at a point in time, expressing our mood, our stylistic preference, our degree of economic concern, and the things we value. Uncovering such expressions in layers of paint and other applied material is in some ways an archeological excavation of history. Very often, designers are involved in the preservation, restoration, renovation, or alteration of a property with historic significance. Some are examples of impressive architectural detail; some are registered landmarks. Examples of historic applications cover the full range of use groups—commercial and residential, public and private, interior spaces, freestanding buildings, clusters of structures, and large plots of land. Conceptually, the issues we consider for each are consistent from project to project, regardless of use group. Final choices, on the other hand, are quite varied.

A project with historic character deserves some consideration before color selection can be made. The most basic decision is that of historic authenticity. Is the intent to replicate original coloration with technical accuracy? Is the purpose of

Six approaches to the use of old structures are described here. Four of these—preservation, restoration, rehabilitation, and reconstruction—are government regulated, whereas renovation and adaptive reuse are not. The secretary of the interior sets the standards for preservation and protection of cultural resources. These regulations apply to any project assisted by the National Historic Preservation Fund, those projects seeking certification for federal tax benefits, and properties that are listed in or are eligible for the National Register of Historic Places. (For information on the regulations, which were established in 1995, contact the preservation or historic society local to the project site, or obtain a copy of *The Secretary of the Interior's Standards for the Treatment of Historic Properties* from the secretary of the interior, web site www2.cr.nps.gov. To find out if a property is listed, you can access the National Register Information System database at www.nr.nps.gov).

- **Preservation.** Involves retention of a property, including each stage of its evolution. The focus is on retaining and repairing as much existing material as possible, including an entire building, parts of a building or site, and various architectural components. This is an attitude in design work often taken on behalf of museums and preservation societies or for owners of significant landmark properties. Preservation may include details from more than one historic period, demonstrating the character transitions experienced by the property over time. New paint material is usually mixed to match existing remaining surfaces, but it's applied using the chemical composition of contemporary paint. Existing paint material is saved as much as possible by cleaning and, in some cases, by coating its surface.

- **Restoration.** An approach taken to depict an estate or structure in a single, specific period of time. Often, restoration occurs in areas where several historic structures coexist. Improvements are made to display history, architectural value, and cultural significance possessed by the building during its period of greatest significance. In this case, original forms are uncovered or replicated, with a focus on accuracy. Details of other periods are removed. Surface color is professionally re-created to reflect the property at the designated point in time as accurately as possible.

- **Reconstruction.** Done to re-create a previously existing home or structure. It involves new construction made to look like the original, matching forms and features from the restoration period. Reconstruction is often undertaken when no significant property has survived from a historically significant era and the new structure has interpretive value. In reconstruction, new methods and materials may be used.

- **Rehabilitation.** Undertaken when an existing property must be altered or expanded because of changing needs or a change to another compatible use. In this context, evidence of the building's historic, cultural, and architectural character is retained, but repairs, alterations, and additions that enable more contemporary use are allowed. Period-typical paint color and placement is used, but proportions may be adjusted slightly to accommodate improvements such as a new elevator or concealed ductwork.

- **Renovation.** This process involves improvement of an existing property. Usually, renovation is undertaken when there is a problem to solve, such as a change in use or some undesirable conditions. Renovation may or may not incorporate details inconsistent with the historic details of the domain as well as new materials. Upgrades of an existing structure generally fall in this category of work. *This approach is not classified as historic by governing agencies.*

- **Adaptive Reuse.** As the term implies, a method of changing the overall function of a building or site. This means conversion of the structure to something other than its originally intended use, often because the original function makes the structure obsolete. Such examples include conversion of a factory to office space, a boxcar to a diner, or a fire station to a private residence. *This approach is not classified as historic by governing agencies.*

the design to restore the character of the original period style while incorporating colors appropriate to the historic period—not necessarily those that appeared on the specific property? Is the owner asking to see color that is inspired by the period of the architectural elements, using similar contrasts and levels of complexity, but in hues more consistent with the owner's and designer's personal taste? Or are colors being selected for their ability to enhance historic detail in an aesthetically pleasing way while making a connection to the time of the improvements? One of the first steps to addressing issues of form and color in historic work is to establish the overall approach.

The issue for the colorist is a fundamental determination of design approach. Historical significance, intended use, and physical condition of the existing building all contribute to determination of the method. In preservation, the owner's personal tastes have no bearing on color selection, while a reconstruction project may incorporate a range of color from the historic period, allowing the owner some room for personal taste. Once a basic philosophy is established, a methodology for color selection in association with the historic context can be adopted.

▶ Historic Restoration and Preservation

Some historic restoration and preservation projects are intended to serve as museum pieces, replicating as accurately as possible the context of original designs. In other situations, restoration is tied to a particular date or family who may have owned the property at its most significant point in history. For projects using these approaches, data must be gathered to support, among other things, the color condition as of that date or period. Often in these cases, preservation of original material is key for its authenticity. If the original material was protected, its color may be relatively consistent with the color of origin. Otherwise, it will have faded or suffered weathering or chemical reaction.

When the design significance of the architecture exceeds the value of remaining materials and features, new materials are fabricated with an eye toward the explicit re-creation of identical form, color, and pattern of the date of origin. Success depends substantially on the evidence of available

physical material and documentation. Projects that call for this level of accuracy rely on an architectural finishes specialist and the samples of finish material with original color gathered from the site. These samples are evaluated under a microscope and by chemical processes to ascertain the impact of the aging process. Once the technician has determined as closely as possible what the original material probably looked like, an alphanumeric reference standard is assigned. The designer then uses the reference standards to match new finish treatments.

By working within the guidelines established by a historic period and documented by precedents, the requirements of most local historic-district ordinances can be met. Where a historic property or area has been registered, it's important to find out what limitations are binding to the owner in terms of color application, including those restrictions added where tax credits for rehabilitation are offered. On the national level there is a National Register of Historic Places (www.cr.nps.gov/nr/research) as well as one for Historic Landmarks (www.cr.nps.gov/nhl). In addition, there are local and state historic registers, which often have individual guidelines, including limitations for color selection. Inclusion in a register solidifies the historic value of a property, but it also attaches some restrictions for improvements. Exterior colors in historic neighborhoods are often regulated by local authorities due to the impact they have on the overall context of and influence on properties in close proximity, such as the South End Historic District in Boston, Massachusetts, shown in Figure 11.1.

Data Gathering

In the absence of a trained specialist, it's difficult to generate authentic color matches, but general criteria can be determined by a visual inspection. Indications of color placement and lines of contrast can be found by physical exploration or from available photography. We can establish whether a house was outlined, whether the moldings matched the windows, and whether the porch was treated as an extension of the house or the fence. Determination of overall tone and whether the structure matched others in the area can be quickly ascertained if some original surface material remains.

FIGURE 11.1 The close proximity of each private residence to its neighbor in this historic area demonstrates why color limitations are imposed. Contextual color for the historic structure depends on reasonable consistency and cooperation as individual units are restored.

In the absence of existing surface material at the site, other resources can shed light on the color of a historic property. Supply lists, specifications, or recipes prepared by the original painters are sometimes uncovered at the property, as are owner's ledgers or journals or the paint manufacturer's archives. Some historic photographs kept in personal archives may include a home being restored. Even if black and white or sepia in tone, photos demonstrate a range of values and their relative placement as they would have existed originally. If the property was passed from generation to generation in a single family, old photographs depicting key events may shed some light. Often, these images were taken either on the front porch and steps or in the main living room of the family home. Sometimes prints or paintings are available. If the property had social significance at the time it was built, a written architectural critique may have been published and preserved by the local library. The city hall may have information in old tax records, records of purchases or building permits. The local or state historical soci-

ety may also be a good source of design information. Sometimes written narratives are documented for a home about to be destroyed, as in the case of the John Hancock House, which was demolished in 1863. Less direct, but equally valuable descriptions are the words contained in letters from family members to friends. In the days of letter writing, a developing home or one being improved made an exciting story to tell relatives traveling abroad or distant friends. Such written accounts offer a visual picture of the household as it would have existed at the time in question. All of this suggests that a historic search may be time-consuming, but the results can be invaluable for the accurate depiction of a historic residence. The mansion shown in Figure 11.2, is one example of a project completed using a preservation approach where new color was restored to the original context of the property.

Case Studies

When information is not available pertinent to a specific residential property, the next source is docu-

FIGURE 11.2   This museum-quality example of a restored Rococo Revival bedroom at Marble House is among several historic mansions opened to the public in Newport, Rhode Island, by The Preservation Society of Newport County. *(Photo © Richard Cheek for The Preservation Society of Newport County.)*

mentation of similar houses built in the same time period and in the same architectural style, preferably in the same region. Case studies of historic residences usually describe the vernacular—the most common characteristics and the most prominent residences in a particular district. Many contemporary books are available with color representation for the more popular historic styles; and anthropologists and historians have prepared more detailed research summaries that may be available through the local preservation society, the library, or museums offering architectural and decorative arts programs.

Findings relative to properties that are geographically close to the one in question are most pertinent, since color during period styles varied significantly with each region. For example, the

hues found in Victorian residences of the western United States included more muted yellow and orange tones than those found on the New England Coast, which relied more heavily on burgundy and dark green. Southern residences have frequently incorporated lighter values of the same hues than Northern contemporaries, regardless of the period style. This means that research of a historic period by a California society may be quite accurate for indigenous work, but somewhat misleading if applied to a Virginia residence of the same period. Also, color trends often shifted during periods that spanned long stretches of time. Specific selections used early in a period were not always the norm late in its development. Knowing specific dates may help to resolve details of original owner selections.

Color Matching

When removal of superficial elements exposes original surfaces with applied color intact, an accurate historic palette can be extracted at the site. This is the fortunate experience in the case of a house whose interior surfaces have long been sheltered by subsequent "improvements." Wall areas that have been protected from weathering are the most accurate sources of original color. An experienced technician can investigate using simple tools: a small sharp knife, a magnifying glass, lubricating oil, sandpaper, and a portable light. A section of paint less than an inch wide is cut away from the substrate at an angle. Then the surface is lubricated and sanded slightly to expose layered rings of color similar to the grain patterning of decorative wood veneers. The layers tell us the order of colors as they were applied to the structure chronologically from the one closest to the substrate to the top layer. General color matching can be done at the site using a reference standard such as Munsell's System of Color Notation or that of the Commission Internationale d'Eclairage (CIE).

Onsite matching is best done under consistent light conditions, using natural daylight from a north-facing window. The best time of day is usually midmorning, when the effect of the changing sun is minimal. In the absence of such ideal conditions, the closest approximation through a combination of natural and artificial sources can be attempted. Keep in mind that direct sunlight is more intense in the yellow range and will accentuate the highlights of surface material, suggesting perhaps that moving around the property to less directly lit locations may make matching yellows easier. Because it's generally impossible to get an exact match for each color onsite, the goal is to get as close an approximation as possible, taking into account the natural fluctuation of the color over the area of exposed surface. The best place for this is the area of highest saturation, particularly where glazing has abraded. Locations of greater reflectivity due to a glossy surface or applied glazing will appear lighter than the inherent color.

Once onsite colors have been replicated, a reference set should be arranged in combinations as the colors appeared at the site. The goal is to reestablish the original mood of the historic color palette rather than to organize by hue or complements. Usually, warm and cool colors are combined in historic contexts, as are lights and darks. Samples arranged in order of hue family lose their juxtaposition of temperature. Where strong colors were evidently used as small accents, a chip of reduced size can be used.

Processing Paint Samples

Actual paint samples enable a technician to ascertain the physical composition of the pigment used. From them we can extrapolate the method most likely used to apply the historic material and the type of raw pigmentation available at the time of the application, ensuring a correct time line for the color visible at the site. In *Paint in America: The Colors of Historic Buildings,* the Preservation Press offers an explanation of the sample-gathering process (page 72). Viable samples are removed by scalpel or microdrill and range in size from one-sixteenth to three-quarters of an inch.

Frequently, architectural conservators seek to expose a critical paint layer by scraping subsequent layers of material for examination onsite. If the material can be removed intact, a paint sample is taken with a scalpel and mounted for examination under a microscope. Samples taken from a flat, exposed surface will have experienced the greatest adjustment from abrasion and exposure to light. More true to its integrity is the sample taken in the cracks or along joints, where the paint is thicker and somewhat protected. Drips on the interior surface of window trims or along an applied mantel may be good sources for sampling. This means that when exploring painted surfaces, it's useful to note variations in the profile of woodwork and trims or irregularities in plaster planes that may indicate alterations to the original work. Even a little surface variation can suggest a hidden treasure, such as underlying decorative painting.

The conservation laboratories of major fine arts establishments typically perform pigment analysis. To determine the pigmentary composition of old paint, fluorescent staining or other chemical testing may be used. The accumulated layers of paint taken from architectural elements are sometimes used to date the elements by comparing them to adjacent forms. This is an expensive process and requires significant commitment to authenticity. As such, it's normally reserved for projects whose success depends on conservation treatment, such as museum restoration. If a room will be replicated with contemporary media and the intent is to simply match period coloration, technical analysis of the material is not nearly as meaningful.

Once historic paint color is identified in a lab, an assignment is made using either reference cards developed for historic applications, a commercial paint color reference, or an alphanumeric color reference system. (An example of a color-reference system is the one produced by The Society for the Preservation of New England Antiquities, called *Historic Colors of America,* available online at www.spnea.org. Martin Senour Paints distributes commercial paint color recommendations such as *The Williamsburg Collection,* available online at www.martinsenour.com or by phone at 1-800-MSP-5270.)

Commercial paint colors are frequently used for speed and reduced cost, but the owner runs the risk that material will not be available in the future, as the manufacturers' standards change. Reference standards that are maintained consistently over the long term are a trade-off, since they require a knowledgeable painter experienced in color mixing to accurately match them.

▶ Historic Renovation and Inspiration

Historic renovation is a category of work where historic context is desired without the need for museum-quality authenticity. In such cases, decisions about color are less scientific and more subjective. Projects in this category can include reconstruction or rehabilitation, provided the work is in conformance to applicable local regulations. Nonregulated renovation and adaptive reuse projects also benefit from the historic approach, or at least a historic inspiration approach, as appropriate to the overall project goals. For these cases there's often a desire to incorporate aesthetically pleasing surface colors of original decorative elements with newer, compatible colors in more durable surface materials. The degree to which one adheres to the rules of order for the historic period is a question of judgment, predetermined by the overall design intent. In projects involving renovation and inspiration, the first step is to assess existing materials for their potential in the new context. Surfaces age over time, often resulting in dramatic changes in their surface characteristics. The result may be more desirable in the new context than replication of the original material, in some cases offering new textural sensations. In other cases, new material that is available can give the impression of historic context by creating the appearance of an aged surface. Alternatively, new material can be used to re-create the appearance of the material in its original state.

Exterior elements suffer *abrasion* from exposure to wind (and consequently to airborne particles), rain, and bleaching from the sun. The result in painted surfaces may be display of knots in the grain, cracking patterns in layered paint, or the roughness of circular sawmarks. Metal finishes change in color as well—aluminum corrodes, steel dulls, and copper oxidizes. *Adhesion* is the effect of nature that is opposite of abrasion. In this case, surface depth is added, not removed. The most common incidence is accumulation of lichen or moss on exterior surfaces. The combination of plant spores, sunlight, and moisture enables life to take form in a way that results in soft, organic coloration. Some designers go to great lengths to create the impression of surface softness that looks old and is organic in nature.

Interior surfaces are less exposed, but offer evidence of age just as well. *Patina* is the word used to describe the surface impact of any natural aging process. The softness and inconsistency resulting from such processes is often desirable and frequently mimicked through artificial processes. Donald Kaufman, a designer known for his color work in painted finishes, points out that patinas are acquired, not bought (*Color and Light: Luminous Atmospheres for Painted Rooms,* page 249). They are the result of a process that takes years. This kind of expression readily establishes historic context. The accumulation of layers of paint on a wall also gives visual texture and depth to a large plane. Sometimes this is more desirable aesthetically than to establish a sense of place in history by restoring the original flat coloration of the past era or applying wallpaper. Sometimes the pigments of yesteryears are fugitive, meaning that they fade quickly from exposure to light or moisture. In other cases, the layers have delaminated unevenly, exposing a range of surface color. When finishes like these are

FIGURE 11.3 This palette shows a combination appropriate to an East Coast Victorian renovation project. *(Design by Ann Aranibar.)*

fashionable, faux finishers often re-create the effect artistically in renovated space or new construction.

Precedents

Like the restoration approach, for the designer developing color for a historic renovation project, precedent studies are a valuable resource for decision making. Unlike a restorative approach, renovation allows the designer and owner to make appropriate selections more consistent with personal preference, as long as they are consistent with the period or style. Historic properties physically near the project in process and built at the same time are the most valuable precedents to analyze for historic surface color and for developing a reference palette. The intent is to select colors appropriate to the style, type, and date of the residence or building at the time it was designed and built. Certain hues tend to dominate several historic periods, but their respective proportions, as well as shifts in value and saturation, are what make each historic palette unique. In the examples of historic palettes in Figures 11.3, 11.4, and 11.5, the use of red, green, and a warm neutral color dominate. Distinctions in the particular red, green, and neutrals establish the unique character of each period style color—in this case the Victorian, Colonial Revival, and Arts and Crafts movements.

To give a general overview of historic color in residential use, American home exteriors were minimally painted in the seventeenth and eighteenth centuries. More often, paint was used in combination with natural finishes. Generally speaking, those built throughout the nineteenth century were painted in pigments, but they had very simple color schemes. One color was used for the body of the house. In the late *Federal and Neoclassical* periods (1820–1840) the most popular color combination was a white house with dark shutters, most often a dark green. As it became more fashionable to blend with nature rather than to stand out as classical architecture, home colors shifted. Initially whites were tinted, creating the pale earth tones of the *Early Victorian* period (1840–1870) such as fawn and gray.

By the *Late Victorian* period (1870–1890), darker earth tones, particularly shades of brown, were in vogue. Trim colors were darker: greens and browns, or to a lesser degree, maroon. During this time, bolder pigment combinations appeared on many homes, particularly those done in the *Queen Anne* style, using multicolor schemes to enhance architectural details. When a multicolor scheme was used, the main house was done in one hue range, with a light value at the third floor, a medium at the second floor, and the darkest shade at the ground-floor level. Even the most colorful combinations were kept low in saturation, to blend with the environment and to hold down the cost of producing the paint. Finally the *Colonial Revival* (1890–1920) brought with it a return to white and very light pastel homes. Clapboards and trim were painted a lighter

FIGURE 11.4 Here a palette has been developed for a Colonial Revival renovation using hues similar to those in Figure 11.3. *(Design by Linda Taylor.)*

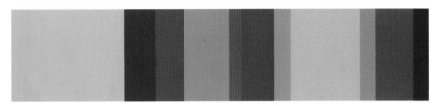

FIGURE 11.5 This example uses some of the same hues as the two color combinations previously shown, yet the character is quite different. In this case, the palette was proposed for an Arts and Crafts project. *(Design by Claire R. Bassham.)*

color than the body of the house, often cream or white. Bold Victorian combinations and the traditional white-with-green combination disappeared after the turn of the century.

▶ Enhancing Historic Form

Surface color has been used since the times of ancient Greece to enhance complex forms of architecture. We know this because in the middle of the eighteenth century archaeologists discovered fragments on the temples and statues confirming that either stain or pigments were applied to their surfaces. The Parthenon had a frieze that was painted and to which gilding had been applied. Through color contrast, the depth of the carved frieze could be recognized at a greater distance by travelers as they approached the city.

The use of color to enhance residences and commercial buildings with significant architectural detail continues today. In some situations, choices are dictated by the documented requirements of the historic register, as previously noted. In other projects, the choice of color is without limitations, leading to experimentation and on occasion to a collection of period styles in new colors. One of the best-known trends in reapplied color is that of the so-called painted ladies of San Francisco, California. An example is shown in Figure 11.6. In the 1960s, a movement of self-expression led to the introduction of more saturated color in complex combinations on old Victorian homes. The trend progressed to varying degrees in selected historic neighborhoods across the continental United States. The unique, complicated, and often-conflicting color combinations often had very little to do with historic context. Nevertheless, they were very successful in drawing attention to finely detailed forms of historic architecture.

This type of treatment is sometimes called a *boutique color* approach. It's most effective when color decisions are sensitively made with an understanding of contrasts and harmonies coupled with a respect for the architectural form underneath. Contrasts are used to draw attention to key details, and more subtle distinctions of form are articulated through less dramatic contrast. Characteristics of color weight are taken into account, and the overall scheme is developed in a harmonic balance to ensure a strong sense of overall form. In less successful attempts, where color is more randomly applied, the results risk effectively destroying the historic character of a form by negating its depth and detail.

Basic Color Placement

In the case where a conscious decision is made to transform the original palette, placement of each color is key. Ideally, the new color palette should enhance the design by communicating an impression consistent with its earliest occurrence. The original designer presumably had some preferences regarding what should appear dominant and distinguished these details from those that should recede or be minimized. In other words, more contrast is needed in areas of focus using relative positioning of lights and darks consistent with the original architecture.

Architectural historian Roger W. Moss offers general guidelines for historic coloration in residential applications (see Bibliography). He tells us that most nineteenth- and early-twentieth-century homes were painted in a combination of three colors. One color was applied to the main body, one was used to define all the decorative woodwork on the surface of the house, and a third was applied to the movable components such as doors and window sash. In

FIGURE 11.6   This example of a painted lady of San Francisco, California, demonstrates how color placement using contemporary selections can enhance historic architectural detail. *(Photo: Janice Kopacz.)*

many cases, adherence to this system will bring a color scheme closer to historic context. The simpler the house, the fewer the colors needed for a successful scheme. More complex structures can successfully support a greater complexity of applied color.

In the traditional three-color method, body color belongs on the main sheathing material, such as the shingles or clapboards. Other woodwork adjacent to the sheathing is considered trim. Usually the trim can be identified as a framing system that consistently connects to other trim pieces. This includes corner boards, cornices, and a belt course if one exists. The color used here was normally applied to the molding along the fascia under the eaves of the roof, including secondary rooflines on porches and bays. Sometimes a large house was made to appear smaller by making the trim color significantly darker than the body color. In the nineteenth century, sash and doors were often recessed further into the face of the house by making them darker than the trim (*Century of Color: Exterior Decoration for American Buildings,* page 13).

Ceilings are traditionally white or very light in color, except in very large public spaces where elaborate ceiling detail adds a level of richness. For the lobby of the private banking establishment shown in Figure 11.7, one designer proposed drawing attention to the old white plaster coffer details by adding rich surface colors, comparatively darker than the white. As a mock-up, a single coffer was painted. Unfortunately, in the context of an otherwise white ceiling, the sample appeared as a hole to observing clients. The work was allowed to proceed in spite of some reservation, with very positive results.

▶ Technical Issues

A few common color terms are specifically associated with historic applications and are summarized here. *Antiquing* is the word used to describe any process that causes a surface to appear significantly aged. This can include the cracking or scraping of surface paint, abrasion on leather or fabric, or yellowing of wallpaper.

As we've said, *patina* is used in similar contexts to identify the resulting finish. The *oxidized* look of copper, the smoothness of old leather, and the softened look of old paint are often referred to as a patina. When a surface color is dulled from

fading, it's called *muted,* but when the pigment disappears almost completely, it's said to be *fugitive.* And when the surface finish of an upholstered piece has been rubbed off, this is called *crocking.*

Some terms are specifically associated with painting processes. When a color has a hint of another hue in it, this is called a *cast. Gilding* involves painted surfaces in which a semiprecious metal, such as gold or silver, has been applied. And *trompe l'oeil* is the illusionary imagery, painted on the surface of walls or furniture, that appears to be three-dimensional.

Paint

The chemical nature of paint itself has changed dramatically over the past 300 years. The availability of certain materials has had an impact on the colors considered stylistic with each generation of building. Most pigments change with age. For example, surface paint that has linseed oil usually yellows. Some historic pigments of blue and green hue have been known to fade easily. In terms of chemical composition, exterior architectural paint is usually categorized by two eras—hand-mixed recipes created before the Civil War and factory-made products produced after 1875. Trim pigments tended to identify a period style prior to World War I. For example, ochre ground in oil was most popular for all exterior woodwork. Unfortunately, over several decades the oil dried completely from the primer, leaving a layer of clay dust between the wood and the paint film.

Wall surfaces of the seventeenth and eighteenth centuries, which were mostly plaster, were frequently covered with water-based paint called *whiting,* or *whitening.* Its application is known as *whitewashing,* and the pigment used was a powdered chalk or lime suspended in a mixture of water and salt. This solution tended not to yellow but had a tendency to rub off onto clothing. Later, an animal-glue sizing was used as a binder to eliminate this tendency. In the eighteenth century, oil paints were also fabricated from linseed oil, pigments, and ground white lead. This solution was expensive and produced the very flat finish preferred in England during the mid-1700s.

Until the late nineteenth century, when factory-made paints became available, most American pigments were coarsely and unevenly ground by hand.

FIGURE 11.7 The use of traditional colors in a new orientation enhanced this private banking establishment, which has experienced several renovations. *(Design by Glenn Mead. Photo: © Edward Jacoby.)*

There are many regional historic societies in the United States that can offer historic data, insights, and specific resources for those involved in refurbishment of historic properties. Many historic districts, particularly in major cities, have preservation organizations. In addition, two well-known agencies offer a broader regional outreach.

The **National Trust for Historic Preservation** is a nonprofit organization based in Washington, D.C. The trust was chartered by Congress to encourage preservation of significant historic and cultural sites, buildings, and objects in America. Its publishing arm, the Preservation Press, is responsible for many significant documents on issues of preservation and restoration. Funding for the trust is derived from membership dues, contributions, and federal grants.

The **Society for the Preservation of New England Antiquities** (SPNEA) is located in Boston, Massachusetts, and fosters the preservation of New England's cultural heritage. The society is a museum made up of 35 properties in five states, as well as a collection of furniture and other decorative art objects, some of which can be seen in its Boston gallery. Representatives of SPNEA provide walking tours, courses, literature, research, and advice on conservation. Membership dues, the Institute of Museum Services, and the Massachusetts Cultural Council fund this organization.

The grainy pigments in combination with the coarse boar bristles used for application produced subtle unevenness in the surface color of original structures. In the nineteenth century, gloss in painted surfaces was less desirable, and painters' recipes were developed to eliminate any sheen. Sand was often mixed into the paint or blown onto the wet painted surface of frames, cornices, and porch details to give the impression of stone. Historically, homeowners depended on the expertise of local painters, who worked with lead and oil to prepare paint for each application. For decorative interior plaster, *distemper paints,* also known as *calcimine,* were used. These were thin pigments made up of water, glues, and whiting with tinting pigments that could be removed with hot water.

In the twentieth century titanium dioxide replaced lead as the hiding pigment that gave paint its opacity. Stenciling, gilding, and faux finishes were first used with frequency at this time. From 1930 through the 1950s simpler coloration became popular, driven by Art Deco, Art Moderne, and Bauhaus aesthetics and the range of enamel available to produce satin, semigloss, or eggshell surfaces. In the middle of the century, cool green was used on painted surfaces of large public spaces because the pigment could be produced inexpensively. As the oil embargo in the mid-1970s took effect, materials made from petroleum products became more expensive, and preferred colors shifted from highly saturated ones to earth tones and neutralized shades of blue and green.

■ COLOR FORECASTING

Nothing in design is static. As we explore alternatives of insight and as new technology is developed, our expectations of the three-dimensional world we live in change by necessity. Consequently, the colors we use change, too. Contemporary changes in color preferences—known as *trends*—can lead consumers to acquire new material goods. In this case, color is the initiator, not the consequence of change, as the function of color is to generate a need rather than respond to one.

Several organizations and individuals make it their business to stay ahead of changes in our color associations, trends, and preferences. These professional color analysts or color forecasters monitor public moods and reactions to anticipate the impact of social change on color response. They use their findings to inform clients and the community at large about what color movements to expect. The basic assumption in color forecasting is that there will always be a need for change. However, new color choices are not successful merely by virtue of the change they bring. Color forecasters use analytical methods to anticipate new color preferences both as individual colors and as color combinations. They offer us suggestions about what is possible. Designers are often the first to see the potential in new color opportunities and to use them effectively. As new color trends are made available, consumers decide, via their pocketbooks, which trends will be successful. If customers do not like the new colors presented, they don't buy the products. The majority of consumers don't lead color trends—they simply authenticate them as they occur.

▶ The Role of Analysts

Professionals who provide us with color forecasts are analysts. Their work is research-based, fairly complex, and their identification methods are proactive. The results may incorporate decision making or advising those who actually make product and image decisions. Often the analyst will work with clients on specific products, through the dissemination of information, group collaborations, or one-on-one work sessions with product designers. To predict trends, analysts anticipate logical movements in color preference and to some degree enable the transition to new key colors, often through collaborative efforts with the manufacturer's design team.

Color analysts watch simultaneous activity in a variety of areas. They identify contemporary images in terms of new products, new or enhanced environments, and consumer preferences. Information is gathered on contemporary culture from periodicals, fashion and lifestyle magazines, newspapers, billboards, industry trade shows, retail marketing, and television broadcasts. Media attention and day-to-day language are a source of trends and fads, and prerelease films offer indications of what is gaining in popularity. Restaurants and other sources of new cuisine, sources of ethnic distinction, and local retail shops and print media also offer a sense of these details.

Social context and political climate have an impact on acceptance of new colors, as does a positive or negative economic outlook. Case in point, a renewed concern for environmental issues of the 1990s is credited for sparking an interest in earth tones. National pride, or lack thereof, is particularly influential when it comes to the trendiness of one's national colors. Red, white, and blue are never as popular as when America is at war. There's also a tendency for a single generation to dominate the appearance of trends for short periods of time and to consequently predetermine the fields that will most impact overall trends. Baby boomers are well known for their attachment to nostalgia and its associated colors; members of Generation X are

Leatrice Eiseman

Leatrice Eiseman is a contemporary color specialist who advises both commercial and residential clients. She analyzes color for its application in product identification, brand imaging, and the enhancement of commercial and personal space. Eiseman contributes to the collective knowledge of color by sharing her findings through books, articles, and public appearances, including collaborative efforts with the Pantone Color Institute. She has been involved in the Industrial Designers Society of America, the Fashion Group, the American Society of Interior Designers, and the Color Marketing Group.

known for their optimistic grip on technology and a shift to harder color combinations.

Research

Color analysis is a long, involved process, some of which is done intuitively by observation and projection. We see the first wave of acceptance by the fashion-conscious in high-visibility establishments of major cities. Forecasters also watch current events, attend art exhibitions, view theatrical events, and travel. They monitor key activities in the design realm, such as the opening of furniture showrooms, automobile shows, boat shows, and fashion shows. Some indications of what is to come may be found in the clothing celebrities wear to award presentations, in feature films, in music videos, or to important theatrical events. Success in forecasting comes from attentive observation of visual stimuli relative to identifiable groups of people and the ability to recognize patterns in recent acceptance and contemporary change.

Other research is done by qualitative measure. Potential consumers are asked to evaluate new products in specific colors or color ranges. Sometimes color analysts may participate in focus groups to comment on color application before products are shown to customers. In either case, evaluations are made in the context of contemporary market color as well as conventional imagery. The value in this process is to eliminate selections of least-probable success. Such findings are often shared with the product manufacturers. At the same time, research is being done to ascertain people's likes and dislikes of particular images and how this relates to individual lifestyle and taste. Ultimately, findings for specific products are analyzed in the context of overall trends. Through this, decision makers reach consensus on identifiable imagery that is expressed through specific colors or color combinations.

▶ Trends

The life cycles of trends for both color and style often follow historically consistent patterns. Not all aspects of society are affected by each trend at the same time, but the point at which each area will embrace a trend is predictable to some degree based on an understanding of trend history. A key factor is that the catalysts that drive changes in color direction are self-propelling. Changes in color preference are the result, not the cause, of other movements. The area of greatest influence shifts over time—architecture, politics, fashion, fine art, communications, or performing arts, to name a few. Overall acceptance of a trend is more rapid when it feels familiar, suggesting that the generating source may determine where the trend is first embraced.

Harold Linton

Harold Linton, a contemporary designer and colorist, is also a university instructor and an accomplished author. An expert in architectural color theory, he is a strong proponent of color training in design education. His written contributions include publications about the state of color consulting and color research, often using the case study method. Linton is a graduate of Yale and Syracuse Universities. He has held distinguished positions with Bradley University in Peoria, Illinois, Lawrence Technological University in Southfield, Michigan, and the University of Art and Design in Helsinki, Finland. In addition to teaching, Linton does technical research on color performance and materials and serves as a color and design consultant.

Manufacturers are very attentive to color trend cycles due to the serious investment they must make to develop and market new product lines. Their goal is usually to generate an average sales life of three to five years on each new line. Since most trends do not change every year, this is a reasonable expectation, as long as the manufacturer does not mistime the market by delaying production or misjudge public acceptance of the trend. Color selections by fiber and textile designers precede those of the fashion industry. However, most colorists recognize the significance of designer runway walks in Paris, Milan, London, and New York as new tints, tones, and shades of color are forecast for women's fashions. When these are presented to the public, they often become the first indicators of trend colors for both fashion and nonfashion industries. This is true in part because women tend to wear the greatest range of color seen on any one product and to accept trends first as consumers. Trend colors are subsequently presented within other industries as appropriate, including package design, home furnishings, automotives, and other forms of environmental and industrial design. Color for a specific product is often chosen about 18 to 20 months in advance of its buying season. It is presented as a series of palettes, organized by type, which may include categories of neutrals, shades, tints, tones, highly saturated colors, and/or pastels, such as the example shown in Figure 11.8. Each palette often addresses a specific need within the range of predictions and illustrates colors that are likely to be accepted by consumers.

Order of Color Acceptance

It's generally believed that manufacturers of nongarment products originally adopted the color forecasts of the women's fashion industry for two reasons. Primarily, the obvious success of the industry in dictating fashionable taste through advertisement lent credibility to the specific selections. Those offering other products took advantage of that credibility, hoping to ensure their own success. Second, manufacturers assumed that if women make the majority of color decisions, especially with regard to house paint and interior furnishings, using the colors they consider fashionable would increase market share. Preference tests have demonstrated some consistencies between the most popu-

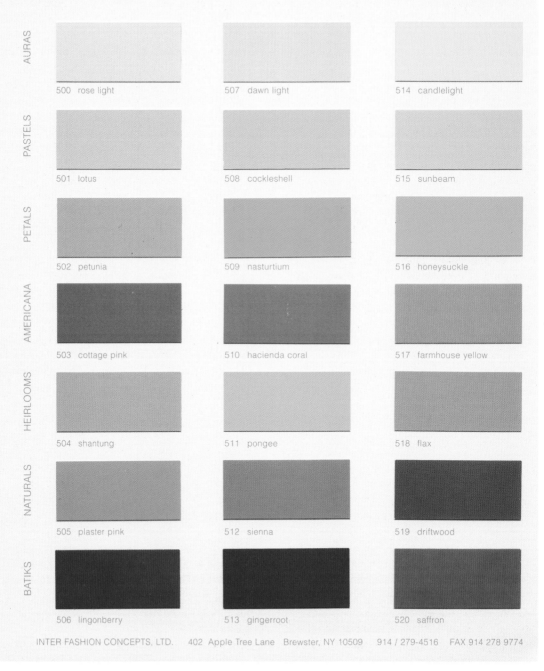

Cheerful Hues *2001/2002*

AURAS
- 500 rose light
- 507 dawn light
- 514 candlelight

PASTELS
- 501 lotus
- 508 cockleshell
- 515 sunbeam

PETALS
- 502 petunia
- 509 nasturtium
- 516 honeysuckle

AMERICANA
- 503 cottage pink
- 510 hacienda coral
- 517 farmhouse yellow

HEIRLOOMS
- 504 shantung
- 511 pongee
- 518 flax

NATURALS
- 505 plaster pink
- 512 sienna
- 519 driftwood

BATIKS
- 506 lingonberry
- 513 gingerroot
- 520 saffron

INTER FASHION CONCEPTS, LTD.   402 Apple Tree Lane   Brewster, NY 10509   914 / 279-4516   FAX 914 278 9774

FIGURE 11.8   Example of a color palette used by product designers, manufacturers, and retailers of interior products as a guide to incoming hues. *(Inter Fashion Concepts, Ltd.)*

lar colors of both clothing and nonwearable products. We have a tendency as consumers to apply in-fashion colors to everything around us.

Manufactured Products

Naturally, acceptance of a color in women's fashion does not necessarily translate into its acceptance in all other applications. The range in color for women's wear is typically greater than what's considered appropriate for some other products. Short-term uses, such as cosmetics, often include the full range of new colors. For other products, such as men's and children's wear, a portion of the trend range is used. Men's clothing usually incorporates the darker and more neutral colors of contemporary trends, while brighter and more pastel colors of the group are accepted for children's products.

Some industries are more dependent than others on market trends—graphic design and product packaging are among those fields where cutting-edge color appeal is critical to success. And each industry does influence the others, in part because of the collaborative nature of colorists in various fields through their professional organizations. Sportswear tends to impact equipment colors. Home furnishings lead standards for ready-mixed paint. Other product lines, particularly items that involve significant cost, are less likely to be replaced quickly. Building products constitute a market in which product life spans are longer and color serves as a background. The use of white or beige plumbing fixtures in rental apartments has sustained many generations. Linen white has been the single best-selling color for one paint manufacturer for over 25 years. Long-lived products in wood and leather continue to be sold primarily in neutral tones despite manufacturers' abilities to produce a myriad of other colors.

Automobile manufacturers are known as the last holdout on color trends for a couple of reasons. Auto manufacturers must predict colors for newly designed models three to four years before they will be sold due to the length of the design and production cycle. It also takes time to chemically formulate and test a paint coating (two years) so that it will withstand the most corrosive exposure situations. In addition, the cost to an auto manufacturer to prepare each new hue is significant, estimated at $500,000 in 1998 (*USA Today,* October 26, 1998). In addition to the car's exterior paint, new colors need to be implemented in a variety of ancillary materials, such as molded dashboards, trim, seat upholstery, and floor carpet.

Bridge Colors and Display Colors

The selling cycle for each industry's color trend has a different time frame as a consequence of business cycles and pure economics. Women's fashions and cosmetics change about every two years. Home furnishings tend to run in 5-year cycles, automotives in 7-year cycles, and architectural interior design in the 7- to 12-year range. In other words, from the time the trend first generates sales in women's fashions until we stop buying appliances in that color is about 12 years. New palettes are established that take current color in a new direction while incorporating key references to past success. New accent colors are then added to introduce a subsequent direction, in some cases serving as an extension of that approach.

As each industry makes a transition from one trend to another, the consumer is prepared for acceptance by visually bridging the most recently accepted colors with new ones. Rarely are we prepared to replace all of our home furnishings or wardrobe to stay fashionable. Instead, new colors are often incorporated gradually, replacing the most outdated product in the shortest time frame. *Bridge colors* are those that connect last year's colors to this year's colors by making them compatible in an overall scheme. The best bridge colors are often intermediate steps between two disparate trend colors. For instance, in 1997 forecasters were proposing more clear colors, such as magenta, coral, and periwinkle blue. Such strong colors require greater sensitivity to be used effectively. When presenting these colors with their predecessors, more neutralized versions were often included, such as pale pink, flesh tone, and muted blue.

Some colors are included in a trend not because of buying potential but because of their effect on other products. They are included to make the total collection more enticing even though the odd colors are not likely to be purchased. We call these *display colors.* For example, a sock manufacturer may include a trendy version of yellow-orange in its men's sock collection because it makes the whole range more appealing. The manufacturer does not expect to sell many yellow-orange socks (men tend to prefer darker tones), but may expect to sell a large number of its blue and purple ones because the presence of yellow-orange in the display makes the blue and purple socks visually more appealing.

Cultural Influence

Color is the design concept that ignites an immediate public response. Since many of our responses to fashion and trend colors are impacted by the conscious and semiconscious realm, our respective cultures have a strong influence on acceptance. The influence of multicultural resources through satellite communications has given us exposure to the colors of many ethnic groups around the world. This is advantageous, since a mix of cultural expression offers creativity and originality of expression in design. Some cultural barriers, however, limit acceptance of key products, which is noteworthy for products intended for export. Such biases cannot be uncovered in the design studio by experimentation the way that other color issues are resolved. Cultural reaction is anticipated only through cultural experience.

A few general observations have been offered by the experts. In comparing European color forecasters to their American counterparts, Diane Calvert notes that the latter tend to make more basic choices. In *Color Forecasting: A Survey of International Color Marketing,* she states that Europeans tend toward subtle, sophisticated color ideas. Trend-conscious clientele, such as New Yorkers, tend to seek a more European flavor of color, while retailers who must produce for a larger group of buyers lean more toward American ideas, using more approachable, recognizable colors. Calvert points out that Europeans tend to highlight brown in forecasts more than Americans, who are less likely to wear the color. In general, Europe is recognized as the traditional source of fashion, resulting in a long-standing influence on our market. Classic American color trends include the use of the traditional palette: camel, navy, burgundy, forest green.

The nonprofit umbrella organization for color research in the United States is *The Inter-Society Color Council* (www.iscc.org). Members include professionals from the fields of art, science, and industry. The society was founded to promote practical application of color work in the respective fields mentioned for public benefit. Most participants are technical specialists in their field. Their accumulated data is distributed to artists, designers, and educators. The Inter-Society Color Council includes 19 member bodies. Among them are the Color Association of the United States, Inc., and the Color Marketing Group.

Manufacturers of American domestic architectural products of the late 1910s first prepared and sold color forecast swatch books using the philosophy similar to that of the Inter-Society Color Council. In 1915 they founded The Textile Color Card, which later emerged as *The Color Association of the United States* and was subsequently incorporated. The association's primary function continues to be color forecasting. Forecasting is performed by committees of about 12 individuals, selected from among color authorities in their field. Each committee has an area of focus, such as interiors or fashion. Conclusions are issued as color swatches in booklet form to subscribing members each year in September and March. The swatches are between 12 by 22 inches and 12 by 29 inches in size. Timing of their release is intended to be 22 months in advance of the buying season. Membership in the Color Association currently exceeds 1000 (www.colorassociation.com).

Professional Organizations

Most professionals whose work is knowledge-based form associations through which they share information. Color consultants are no exception. At least three established organizations support ongoing accomplishments in advanced color research, industry concerns, and the formation of new solutions. These groups are noncompetitive, functioning under the assumption that free education to the public can only add value to the service provided by individual members. Collaborative efforts by color marketing associations regularly produced forecasting cards with swatches and printed color samples for distribution to organization members. Because of the need for color accuracy and small quantity, these are expensive to produce, which makes them a valuable resource in expert hands.

The *Color Marketing Group* (CMG) is a non-profit association formed in 1963. At this writing it has about 2000 members, from which about 550 forecasters meet twice a year to produce color swatches by committee using a workshop method. Each committee, headed by a chairperson, focuses on a section of industry. Participating industries include fashion, hospitality, health care, industrial design (e.g., toys and household products), recreational products, residential design, entertainment, transportation, and architecture. Each group constructs color boards by consensus, and the results are later published in modified form as a collection of forecast palettes. CMG holds two annual international conferences on color forecasting to address the needs of its consumer-focused membership (www.colormarketing.org).

In past years the delay from color acceptance in women's fashion to its appearance in home furnishings and industrial products was about two to three years. Recently, the speed of communications has accelerated color trend cycles much as it has impacted a variety of other life experiences. The result for color acquiescence is a reduction in real time as manufacturers embrace new colors in their products and these gain acceptance from the public.

Late in the cycle, a color may be so successful that it becomes overexposed. The public becomes tired of it, and consequently it takes much longer for the color to make a comeback. Such examples include avocado of the 1960s and mauve of the 1970s. Avocado regained popularity around the turn of the century with many consumers, but it's packaged as olive, yellow-green, or chartreuse. Mauve was popular in the Victorian era and resurged in the 1970s.

Inspirations derived from historic context or current trend are quite complex by nature. The criteria introduced by either situation add to the challenges of a given project. Historic projects can be developed for virtually any use—a residence, a public space, a hotel, or an educational facility. Projects that focus on current color trends can also appear within any use group, but are more often found in the retail sector and in projects with a focus on communications. Whether rooted in a historic context or a newly launched trend, every project has functional criteria that impact effective color choice. These range from the practical to the logistical. Now that we've addressed one layer of criteria, let's look at the functional issues for the major use groups in design practice. We begin with the private residence.

12

Residential Applications

Residential design offers us the unique opportunity to explore spatial solutions for specific individuals. The projects are personal, as unique as their inhabitants—we know the individual users by name. Residential practice focuses on understanding how our clients live and what they hope to accomplish. We inquire about their handicaps and physical needs in the hope of maximizing comfort. It's our privilege to explore the users' ideal world by developing the optimal space that supports it.

Given this rare opportunity to enhance people's moods, stimulate individual motivation, or calm their personal experience, color can be a tremendous tool. Obviously, personality characteristics are key in the selection process for any private space. We also consider the impact of color on the human condition, particularly in terms of the aging eye, and the needs of developing children. In this chapter, we look at color criteria in terms of individual perception and influence as it relates to residential practice.

■ PRIVATE RESIDENCES

Ideally, color selection in residential work focuses on the specific needs and preferences of the individuals who will live there. This is a truly collaborative process. It requires familiarity with the occupants in order to recognize their character and, in some cases, their personal limitations. It means exploring solutions in both form and color that are unique to the

people involved. Residences may include areas for a variety of leisure pursuits, may incorporate workspaces, or may require space for entertainment in addition to meeting the basic functional concerns of daily life. The results often demand greater variation than any other type of designed space.

The home is recognized for its ability to offer emotional security to its inhabitants. In its most balanced state, a private residence would offer each person a sense of comfort and nurturing, as well as the inspiration to fulfill personal desires. The complexity of these requirements often results in an expression of the personality of the individual or group of individuals who live there. Color is key in this expression.

▶ Programming Color

In order to develop a design that reflects the individual inhabitants, it helps to have a very clear sense of who the users are, how they spend their time, and how family members best relate to each other. A walk through the client's current residence can suggest certain things. The way people communicate about their existing space can offer clues about which areas are more important to them, especially in terms of the need for improvement. At the prospect of an addition or relocation, people often focus on the things that most need change. In the process, they may take for granted successful details that are already in place. The words they use to describe existing color are also revealing. One person's bold color is another's calm neutral. Since taste comes in all forms, even descriptive words such as *sophisticated, colorful,* or *soothing* can mean very different things to different people. Being able to observe the colors a client associates with descriptive words ensures a better translation of their words into meaningful color combinations.

Every designer has key questions that enable him or her to uncover the real program needs for their client. The following checklist is meant to address program items that explicitly affect color recommendations in residential work.

- *Who will live in the house? Who will visit frequently?* Ideally, colors chosen for personal spaces would be appropriate to the personalities of each resident, not just one representative.

- *What are any strong personal likes and dislikes relative to color?* A strong aversion to green by one individual suggests that it might be used sparingly in common rooms or not at all in his or her personal space.

- *Try to identify those rooms that will be used primarily by one person and those that will be occupied by many.* Most people have a space they go to frequently that feels comfortable. It can be a kitchen, a workshop, a bedroom, or a reading area. Color selection for each person's favorite space will ideally reflect his or her personality.

- *Which areas will be transition points, falling between rooms with different needs or those customized for individuals with diverse preferences?* Some family areas comfortably reflect the group rather than one individual. When one tires of the group space, he or she can retreat to a private one.

- *Where will guests be entertained and which spaces need a level of privacy?* Some families recognize very distinct boundaries of privacy, just as certain individuals do. Color can be a subtle way to communicate these distinctions.

- *In which areas will the greatest amount of activity occur?* This implies color of greater stimulation, such as more color contrast or the use of higher saturation and value.

- *Are there any areas where color should serve as a backdrop?* If the client has an extensive collection, whether it be high-quality art or bottle caps, those objects depend on environmental color to enhance them.

- *In the case of an existing home, what features will be retained, and what are the colors of those key elements that cannot be modified? Are there family heirlooms that fall into the must-keep category?* Since these will need to be included in the overall composition, color combinations may be more effective in a harmony that includes them.

Obviously what is pleasing and exciting to one family unit may be monotonous for another. When the overall palette is in tune with the collective members, a series of color transitions will result. Extreme differences are less likely to occur in a household where members have been together for a very long period of time, since the same things will feel familiar to each member. Greater differences are more likely to surface when members of the household span significant age ranges or come from different socioeconomic backgrounds.

Personal Preference

Since residential design is about creating a safe haven, when it comes to color selection, familiarity does lead to acceptance. This explains to some degree why the popular colors in home furnishings often follow fashion trends. Colors that have already been deemed fashionable for a few years start to feel familiar in a positive way. One interior designer tells of her desire to convince a friend to paint her cathedral-ceiling living room a particular color of hue. Prior to introducing the suggestion, she cleverly gave the friend a sweater in a matching hue. Her hope was to establish some familiarity so that the friend would embrace her bold idea when the time came to present it.

To uncover the tendencies of particular individuals, it may help to have them identify objects or spaces they enjoy. Another approach used by many residential interior designers is to look at the clothing in a client's closet for insight into their personalities. Personal color for the client who owns several red-sequined dresses is likely to be quite different than for the client with an extensive wardrobe of primarily beige cottons and linens. In the concept boards shown in Figures 12.1 and 12.2, designers demonstrate how personality im-

Color Palette for Ray Romano

Ray is...
* Comedic
* Down-to-earth
* Extroverted
* Masculine
* Casual

Ray's colors are...
* Simple
* Highly saturated
* Contrasting in hue

Claire R. Bassham • Color for Interiors • Instructor: J. Kopacz • Suffolk University • 11.07.02

FIGURE 12.1 This concept board illustrates a logical connection between simple, familiar colors and the personality of comedian Ray Romano. *(Design by Claire Bassham.)*

FIGURE 12.2 Sharon Stone's presumed personality is expressed here through an alternative color concept of more complex colors. *(Design by Dave Pirro.)*

pacts color preference using some assumptions about two individual personalities as expressed in their public personas. One suggests the familiar range of red, green, and blue colors in simple form that might be comfortable to the character played by comedian Ray Romano due to his casual style. The other suggests more complex and dramatic color that is likely to be appropriate for the movie star image of Sharon Stone. (For a review of color preference and personality, refer to Chapter 6, "Color Response.")

Most people can point out the color they prefer most and the color they like least more readily than they can describe it. Sometimes it's easier to discuss color, at least initially, on an individual basis using real samples and observing reactions. Strong reactions usually imply a long-standing bias, even if it cannot be articulated. If a color reaction is positive, there may be underlying associations worth exploring in the new environment. If the reaction

is negative, it's sometimes worth uncovering the source of that reaction to establish whether it is still valid. On reflection, a client may realize that the reason for having rejected a color no longer exists. By uncovering the negative connection, he or she may freely accept the color for its own merits in the context of a new color composition.

▶ Color Sequence

Ideally, residential work will involve a series of spaces whose tone varies somewhat through the space. We know from the discussion in Chapter 6 that an introverted individual is more likely to be satisfied with color combinations that exhibit subtle nuances of color shift. This person may prefer more structure in color placement or greater consistency in its use. The more outwardly focused a person is, the more desirable it is not only to increase the degree of overall stimulation, but also to vary color composition from space to space. The broader the range of tastes in the adventurous soul, of course, the more exploratory the color resolution. When making these relative assessments, keep in mind that even in extremes, the inward-focused person does require stimulation at times and the extrovert needs to find opportunity for contemplation.

Color sequence in a residence is in some ways a series of successive contrasts. Dark or neutral frames, such as doorways, interior windows, and portals, will give the bright color greater intensity, even at a great distance, drawing the eye toward it. Framed openings in a medium value actually soften the transition between adjacent spaces. The entry is where the initial impression is formed. Even if the form of the entrance is fairly simple, color selection can be used to establish the image of a home. The colors of each space beyond the entry will be experienced in the context of the room that precedes it. In a deep, cavernous home, this may mean placing the brightest color at the farthest wall plane. In the example in Figure 12.3, compatible colors are used in both the kitchen and dining rooms. However, the increased saturation and strong geometries suggest more activity in the foreground room (the kitchen) compared to the sophisticated combination for respite in the dining area beyond.

Mood

Part of the mission in getting a resident to communicate his or her intentions for each room is to help them describe the mood or feeling they desire in the space. This is different from discussing how the room will be used. The purpose here is to visualize an image that embodies the mood desired. By focusing on this image, colors can be identified that establish the appropriate mood for that particular client.

Leatrice Eiseman, a professional color consultant, shares the methods she uses to enable her clients to address this aspect of residential space in her book, *Colors for Your Every Mood.* Examples of possible room moods suggested by Eiseman include whimsical, tranquil, nurturing, traditional, contemplative, dynamic, romantic, and sensuous. Other color combinations she's developed, which appear in *Pantone Guide to Communicating with Color,* communicate feelings characterized as energetic, delicate, robust, capricious, and so on. The options

are limitless. By showing her clients images that capture each feeling, she helps them understand how color assignment can provide the same sensation. Once a mood is identified, several palettes can be explored that exemplify its spirit in the context of a designated room. Such methods are not meant to imply a finite number of mood options. The idea is to help the user recognize his or her desire and find ways to communicate the feeling.

Colors have the power to maintain strong associations in the mind that are emotional in nature and very personal based on experience. If an identified place offers the kind of respite being sought, it can usually be described. By visualizing a favorite place or situation (e.g., rock colors at the beach), it's possible to reconnect with the colors prevalent in that setting and to reestablish the positive feeling in a new space. For some, a temperate preference has psychological benefit, suggesting the use of either all warm or all cool colors, as in the living room in Figure 12.4. If the residential client can articulate positive color associations, these may be used to enhance space in a way that is unique to personal experience.

Shigenobu Kobayashi, a contemporary Japanese color psychologist, writes about color and mood associations in *Color Image Scale.* He organizes color along a matrix of two scales—one in a range of hard to soft and the other warm to cool. By organizing color combinations along these two scales, he establishes a basic grid of color reference palettes in which each palette is categorized according to its sentiment. Color categories include, but are not limited to, casual, elegant, chic, romantic, and natural. References such as this are often beneficial as a starting point. However, since the experience of color is so individual, specific selections for residences should reflect this individuality and depend on confirmation from the client personally. Just as language may at times be subjective, so it is with color.

Placement

The position of each color or color combination in the residence often will involve other considerations in addition to mood. The relationship of the rooms to each other may suggest temperature decisions. In some cases, cool colors are more appropriate for rooms with a southern exposure (in the Northern

FIGURE 12.3   The transition between these functionally diverse rooms is softened through thoughtful color placement and consideration of framed views. *(Glenn Pacheco, architect. Bill Philbrook, designer.)*

Hemisphere), while warm tones can enhance the apparent coolness of a north-facing room. Color can suggest context for a room within the complete residence. One warm room in a cluster of cool ones or one bright room among several that are understated will draw attention to itself. To engage two or more rooms as a suite, their colors might relate to each other, particularly if they can be seen from one to the next. If the goal is to create a different color impression in each room, a central room can serve as the neutral transition space between them. Or a central space may have the strongest color combination to establish its focal function. In this case, the more subdued rooms that surround will offer respite. A dark corridor can be quite dramatic if it leads to a lighted space at the end. Consider how each space sets up an expectation of the next through the use of successive contrast.

In residential work, avoidance of the traditional white ceiling is the easiest way to change the overall feeling of a room. The degree of intensity of color on the ceiling plane will have a direct effect on the apparent room temperature. I'm reminded of a handsome New York City condominium that had a red ceiling in the living room. To the Hispanic resident, her ceiling was a neutral color. Combined with some uplighting, it gave tremendous warmth to the room. However, it attracted much attention from the street level as people passing by took notice. To local traditionalists, the lack of white evident in the ceiling was cause for concern.

Contrasts

Specific details are often enhanced by contrast. Strong contrast draws attention to edges, and complementary contrast enhances hues. In the renovation in Figure 12.5, the architect used a subtle shade of violet as a complement on the porch ceiling to enhance the yellow clapboards and offer value con-

FIGURE 12.4   The combination of colors in this room gives it a distinctly cool feeling. *(Design by Koo de Kir. Photo: Greg Premru.)*

FIGURE 12.5 The colors in this residence are positioned to take advantage of contrast effects and highlight architectural detail. *(Glenn Pacheco, architect. Bill Philbrook, designer.)*

trast with the adjacent turned woodwork that's been painted white.

The color of trim often serves a key role in residential work. Trim that is consistent in color from room to room serves to unify the different moods experienced in each, creating a smooth transition as people move from one to another. White is a popular trim color for this purpose when walls are painted in colors of moderate to strong hue. Natural woodwork is often used with earth tones. If windows are highly recessed, attention can be drawn to them by painting the inside face of the recess a contrasting color. Outlining is another technique for drawing attention to the geometry of a space. Whether or not trim exists, a border pattern in paper or stencil can accentuate the edge of any element.

The key to using contrasting colors in combination is to maintain them in unequal amounts. A scheme in which colors have equal proportions loses interest quickly. It's read as a large-scale pattern—not a fulfilling composition. Uneven color is more interesting to view and provides a sense of hierarchy in terms of what to look at first. Typically, one color family will be given greater importance to set the tone. This dominant overall impression is then supplemented by contrasting colors. By using the rules of extent, the scale of each color can be adjusted to draw the eye to one color and then another, engaging the viewer with the space. Such attention to detail is noticeable in residential space since it is likely to be occupied for long periods of time by people who are not necessarily focused on performing tasks.

When the client has access to a residence that's being renovated, the transition period can be trying. Elements of the old design are removed and pieces of the new color palette appear while work is in progress. Often there is a strong temptation to change the new color that's seen out of context. For the client, this experience can be overwhelming. He or she feels the loss of the old space, for which there is some emotional attachment. Only some of the new colors are being seen, and these are in the company of either the old color scheme or the unfinished combination of raw drywall and plaster, exposed metal studs and concrete, and untreated wood. The first *new* color applied is out of context and appears to be "too much" *something*—too dark, too blue, too saturated, to name a few. Successful residential designers are often very good at managing the situation to minimize this risk by convincing the client to wait until all the new colors are in place, when adjustments can be made properly.

SENIOR CITIZENS

Living spaces designed for more experienced residents offer a special set of challenges to the designer, whether they're community settings or private properties. The human eye changes to a greater or lesser degree sometime after the age of 40, beginning with a reduction in acuity, followed by losses in spectral perception after the age of 60. The cumulative effect of those changes can have a tremendous impact on one's view of the world, including sensory loss in terms of color perception. In addition, the proliferation of Alzheimer's patients among our senior population and their associated visual difficulties complicates matters regarding color management. The potential for disorientation and other symptoms of this disease add to the challenges of properly designing residential space for an aging population.

Generally speaking, designers serve their clients well when the consequences of aging are minimized through sensitive decision making regarding color, light levels, and the use of patterning. Experts do not recommend simplifying color through the use or overuse of white walls, ceilings, and floors. On the contrary, senior citizens tend to spend a large percent of time at their place of residence. Being exposed continually to a colorless environment can cause vision to degenerate due to a lack of stimulation.

Staring at blank walls has a tendency to make one lethargic; surfaces seem to fade and the mind is understimulated. The way to test a color palette for its appropriateness in a senior residence is to consider the known changes in vision experienced by the occupant(s) and to be attentive to the contrasts and patterns selected in terms of their positioning within one line of sight.

▶ Vision

Several changes occur in experienced eyes according to the *IESNA Lighting Handbook* (page 3-13). Adjustments to the shape of the convex lens and a decrease in its flexibility result in a reduced ability to focus, particularly at close range. This is known as *presbyopia*. As a consequence of this condition, we lose accuracy in depth perception. At the same time, the pupils get smaller, increasing the depth of field and reducing the amount of light reaching the retina. More of the light that's received by the retina is scattered, and its spectrum is altered as more of the short wavelengths are absorbed. The neurological components also deteriorate, resulting in reduced visual acuity and a reduction in color discrimination and contrast sensitivity. Sensitivity to glare is increased, and the time it takes the eyes to adjust to changes in illumination are significantly increased.

The occurrence of cataracts, glaucoma, and macular degeneration also adds to the difficulties in visual experience for older residents. *Cataracts* involve an increased opacity that develops in the lens, causing more of the light passing through to be absorbed and scattered, further reducing contrast sensitivity and visual acuity as the contrast of the retinal image is degraded. *Glaucoma* causes narrowing of the field of vision due to damage to the retina and the optic nerve, which means a decrease in the ability to see at night, an increase in difficulties due to glare, and slower adjustments to changes in light levels. *Macular degeneration* also contributes to potential difficulties, as bleeding and atrophy cause neurons and photoreceptors to become inoperative. This, too, causes a reduction in visual acuity, decreased ability to discriminate color, and reduced sensitivity to contrasts. In this case, reading is more affected than peripheral vision, and increased lighting can help, at least in the early stages.

▶ Range of Hue

Color combinations are seen very differently between older and younger observers. Increased reduction in visual acuity and reduced contrast sensitivity are normal for aging eyes. As we've said, our ability to discriminate color diminishes, particularly in certain hue families. The lens of the eye is the major contributor here, growing harder and thicker and gradually becoming more yellow. **The yellow filters out some short wavelengths of light from reaching the retina.** Consequently, the viewer becomes less sensitive to those short-wavelength colors—violet, blue-violet, blue, and blue-green. Instead of recognizing these hues with clarity, they appear darker and less saturated (more gray). Colors that are visible are seen as if through a yellow-tinted window, as suggested in Figure 12.6. White becomes indistinguishable from yellow, and blue (the additive complement to yellow) is neutralized. As a result, the intensity is lost in some hues, and colors of reduced saturation are less distinguishable from each other.

To anticipate this shift in perception, color consultant Jill Pilaroscia (Solour Studio Inc., San Francisco, California) fashioned a pair of glasses for herself with yellow mylar lenses. It was her responsibility to develop a stained-glass color palette for a large rotunda skylight in a senior community center. As each color mock-up was developed, she put on her yellow mylar glasses to observe the palette as the residents would see it.

Another potential limitation in hue perception for the aging is called *luminosity loss.* Generally speaking, this is the loss of recognition for colors at the extreme ends of the spectrum. Any senior individual may have luminosity loss at long-wave color, short-wave color, or both ends of the spectrum. Some eye disorders also have an effect on long-wavelength light, which includes red-violet, red, and brown (neutralized red) colors, making them look dark by comparison. Although this condition is less prevalent across the aging population as a whole, the possibility is best considered when designing for a specific individual. Many individuals also experience a loss in contrast sensitivity; for others there's a loss in the ability to discriminate saturation. Most realize some overall wavelength (hue) discrimination loss. A smaller number of people are affected only by luminosity loss (at one or both ends of the spectrum). When designing for a

FIGURE 12.6   To illustrate the effects of aging eyes, cover the lower palette and look at the upper one. Then cover the upper and look at the lower. The upper color palette represents one seen with youthful eyes, while the lower band shows the same color palette adjusted to show how it is likely to read to a pair of older eyes.

Elizabeth Brawley

Elizabeth C. Brawley is an environmental designer known for her experience with facilities for long-term care and special care for Alzheimer's patients. In her quest for positive solutions for senior residences, she addresses issues of design criteria, spatial organization, and therapeutic practice, including practical advice on color and lighting. She speaks publicly on local and national public policy and environmental design for the aging population and publishes books and articles on this subject. Her articles appear regularly on the Center of Health Design web site at www.healthdesign.org. Brawley maintains membership in the International Interior Design Association (IIDA), the American Society of Interior Design (ASID), and the National Board of Directors of the Alzheimer's Association.

specific individual, knowing his or her visual acuity can suggest appropriate solutions. Understanding the potential for visual limits across the population may help us offer more effective solutions for community living. While the senior's circumstance does not eliminate the use of any color in the designer's palette, it does suggest that contrasts be stronger and that hues be slightly more saturated for the user's benefit.

Form Perception

The aging eye offers additional concerns that have a direct impact on a person's perception of the environment. Typically, we rely on subtle variations in the value of vertical and horizontal planes to tell us when they are closer or farther away. As the size of the human pupil is reduced, value becomes more difficult to discern. At the same time, it becomes more difficult to recognize variations in distance due to the hardening of the lens. As we lose the ability to recognize subtle distinctions, we lose the sense of changing planes and thus the dimensional form of our environmental space and objects within the room.

The aging process also causes a reduction in visual memory, particularly among Alzheimer's patients and other victims of dementia. This decreases the ability to recognize colors and to associate some significance to them. When traveling through familiar territory, one typically trusts memory as a means of orientation. As this tool is diminished, we must rely more completely on color recognition and depth perception skills, which, as we have said, have been compromised. The cumulative effect of these conditions makes it more difficult to negotiate movement through space.

Increases in value contrast will enhance a resident's visual functioning since hue and saturation distinctions are minimized to some degree. The example in Figure 12.7 demonstrates this point. By making conscious color choices to articulate the edges of planes and to identify objects, the daily activity of the senior resident will be improved. This means developing the palette according to a range of values that offer variation. Light doors with medium frames, furniture that contrasts with its background, or medium-light countertops against dark floors can make it easier to avoid bumping into things. Changing the value of the floor covering at the point of the rise can reduce the hazard of a change in floor level. If the edge of the bed is distinct from the floor, it's easier to locate in peripheral vision. An all-white toilet room may look more sanitary, but it is easier to identify the edge of the fixtures if they have some contrast with the white tile walls and floor.

Preferences

Some trends in color preferences are unique to the aging population. In public settings, warm tones are usually preferable because most elderly individuals are able to discriminate them more easily. Warm colors offer the added sense of stimulation. Of course, discriminating selection is in order here, since the colors will tend to be seen with a yellow undertone, and highly saturated warm colors can quickly become imposing. A yellow wall seen through a yellow lens will appear too strong for most tastes. An orange or green wall will shift slightly to the yellow side, which is pleasant in some combinations, less desirable in others. Cool tones are appreciated for their calming influence, but the variation between them is less apparent, suggesting that larger shifts between hues or higher saturation levels may make the cool palette more successful.

FIGURE 12.7 Contrasts are used effectively to articulate changes in plane and distinctions between rooms in this senior residence. *(CBT/Childs Bertman Tseckares Inc., architects. Interior design by Wellesley Design Consultants. Photo: © Edward Jacoby.)*

For many seniors, colors of reduced saturation, such as light pastels, are difficult to distinguish from each other, especially the cooler ones (those of shorter wavelength). **Clear colors**—those that fall somewhere between full saturation and slightly neutralized tones—are those most easily distinguished and, consequently, the most preferred by older audiences. One study published by the Interior Design Educators Council (IDEC) showed blue to be the preferred color of hue by 100 Alzheimer's patients, followed by red. **Highly saturated colors** were also preferred, and **medium values** were preferred over the very light or very dark.

When using more complex color combinations, one point is worth noting. While a greater range of hue may be more rewarding to ensure visual relief from monotony, residents who suffer from cognitive impairments find it difficult to process a large number of stimuli at one time. Several very different colors may be confusing to them.

► Pattern

Pattern has a way of defining spatial form for an aging resident. This was demonstrated beautifully in the movie *Awakenings*, which starred actors Robert De Niro and Robin Williams. The movie depicted several patients in a mental health institution, including a severely withdrawn, aging woman. This woman would stare toward the window and walk only as far as a specific point in the middle of the room. Day after day she would stop at the same point. Eventually, the staff determined that she could not continue because the large checkerboard pattern of the floor stopped at that point. To enable her to read the floor as a continuous plane and continue her walk to the window, they painted the floor pattern across the remainder of the room.

Integrating pattern and texture in design can create more interesting rooms. However, if used inappropriately, they can make life more difficult for a person who suffers from dementia. Visual and auditory cues are experienced with less clarity in the aging adult. When coupled with dementia, a person can easily be overstimulated by too many patterns within one line of sight. For example, if the bedspread pattern matches or is similar in scale to that of the carpet, the edge of the bed will not be easy to distinguish. To minimize this possibility, patterns can contrast with solids, or small-scale patterns can be used with a lower-contrast, large-scale pattern. A sharp, contrasting edge such as a trim or welt can also define the limits of a patterned surface. Value contrast should be less dramatic when used in large-sale patterns on the floor. A sharply contrasting border in the floor pattern might appear as a step or trench; a random circle might stand out as a visual hole in the floor, particularly if it's very dark. The example of the floor pattern shown in Figure 12.11 may be highly appropriate for the children's space it was designed to enhance, but in an elder-care facility, some residents would perceive the dark squares as holes in the floor. Glare from a shiny floor finish is equally disturbing to a person who has some visual impairment. The distrust that ensues due to color influence in these circumstances obviously hinders reasonable movement through the space.

Preferences

Many senior citizens enjoy large-scale patterning in bold coloration. According to the same IDEC report mentioned earlier, **large-scale patterns** were preferred over smaller ones; **organic patterns** were preferred over geometric. The community residence shown in Figure 12.8 makes use of a very colorful rug, which is popular with many of the local residents in the over-70 age bracket. (Some of their younger neighbors think it's a bit bold.) This pattern works in part because of its complexity. Patricia Rodemann, who does design and product research,

has found that age has an influence on pattern stimuli, which she explains in *Patterns in Interior Environments.* Specifically, older viewers are more concerned about the context, or familiarity, of a pattern, and they prefer organic forms over geometric ones. This may be due to an increase in afterimaging that results from the harder edges of geometric patterns when compared to irregular forms.

Some patterning may call for moderate contrasts, particularly because of their location. Some institutional patients may become disoriented or experience slight vertigo in the presence of over-scaled, highly contrasted geometric patterning. Large stripes in high contrast can be stressful to some residents as well. In fact, some patterns that undulate or incorporate strong geometries can give a sense of movement, making the viewer uneasy or slightly nauseated. Alternatively, small-scale patterns in high contrast are not appropriate for early-stage Alzheimer's patients, as they will try to pick the pattern off the wall, a tendency shared with two-year-old children.

Texture

There's something therapeutic about tactile surfaces, especially in the place one calls home. The sense of touch can be a great healer. Unfortunately, beneficial texture may be lost to someone with slight visual impairment. By pairing contrasts with each change in material, users are more likely to notice. The lightest or the darkest tones in the room may be on the surfaces covered in chenille or mohair. The grass-cloth wall might have a warm tone in comparison to the coolness of the other three walls. Or the fine silk pillows may be the ones with the highest level of saturated color.

▶ Lighting

Designer Elizabeth Brawley offers much insight into the design improvements that support the aging population (*Designing for Alzheimer's Disease: Strategies for Creating Better Care Environments*). She points out that while some changes in vision can be managed with prescription lenses (either glasses or contacts), visual impairments (i.e., conditions that cannot be corrected through lens management or medical intervention) impact our perception of the world around us. Impairments include gradual changes, such as an increase in farsightedness and a decline in depth perception, as well as the need for higher light levels and increased time to adapt to dramatic changes in illumination. There's an increased sensitivity to glare, which adds to the amount of time needed to recover from the afterimage of bright lights. Consequences can include temporary blindness when ˉmoving into a room of dramatically reduced light, a loss in the ability to focus, reduction in depth perception, shifts in color perception, loss of central vision, and/or loss of peripheral vision.

The need for light increases as the visual field narrows, as the pupil size decreases, and as the lens of the eye thickens, causing less light to reach an already less-sensitive retina. The older we become,

the greater the level of illumination we need for reasonable sight. As depth perception and the ability to distinguish details diminish, reduction in the level of available light becomes disruptive to proper vision. By comparison, a 20-year-old may need only one-third the amount of light required by a 75-year-old. These increased levels of light are readily available from the sun. However, as more and more time is spent in controlled environments, the senior citizen's ability to function safely and independently is reduced. Higher light levels overall are needed to ease eyesight, and transition light levels are needed between the areas of high-level and low-level lighting. An increase in the quality of lighting is also beneficial to avoid veiling reflections.

FIGURE 12.8 The pattern in this area rug is characteristic of many of the preferences stated by active seniors: saturated hues that are distinct from each other and inclusion of organic forms. *(CBT/Childs Bertman Tseckares Inc., architects. Photo: © Peter Vanderwarker.)*

Artificial Lighting

Changes in vision can be managed somewhat through effective lighting. One concern is *glare,* which is caused by light scattering instead of focusing on the retina. It's experienced as a bright flood of light. This experience, or any significant change in light level, causes an afterimage. As an elderly person changes view, the afterimage remains for some time, rendering that person unable to judge depth. Shadows are also of concern. A shadow on the floor or on a wall recess can be misinterpreted as a change in distance, disrupting the path of travel. In more extreme cases, they may be frightening. Both glare and strong shadow casting can contribute to the hallucinating images of an Alzheimer's patient.

Higher light levels and uniform lighting help to minimize the potential problems described here. In addition, color temperature and color rendition may warrant adjustment in the residence of a senior citizen. A color temperature of 3000 to 3500 degrees kelvin (K) is recommended for general lighting. A color rendition index (CRI) of 80 or above is recommended, since the aged eye does have a reduced sensitivity to short wavelengths. Together, these improvements offer the resident an improved quality of life.

Conclusions

Elizabeth Brawley offers hopeful observations concerning designed community living environments (*Elizabeth Brawley on Alzheimer's*). She sees the trend in long-term-care facilities moving toward higher-quality cluster concepts—settings that are small in scale and more residential in nature. Several bedrooms are clustered closer to the shared living and dining activity spaces. In these settings, color selection may serve well to help distinguish shared community space from personal space, such as the bedroom and bath. Selections can also be made to keep more stimulating colors and color combinations in the areas that are intended to promote physical activity.

Given the conditions we understand at this time, several recommendations are offered by Brawley and others for color management in spaces frequented by senior citizens.

- Do not remove any colors from the overall palette, but consider adjusting some hues to be farther apart so they are distinguishable from each other. Do not contrast hues from adjacent parts of the color wheel unless they also contrast in lightness.

- Exaggerate the value differences between foreground and background colors. Visual accessibility will be improved as light colors are lightened and dark ones are darkened.

- Consider a greater use of clear colors so that their hues may be appreciated. These are less than fully saturated but higher in saturation than the midpoint of most neutral-to-full-hue scales.

- When using cool tones, try to incorporate a greater range of hue than might normally be attempted so that the differences between colors are recognizable. Or, if using a small range of hue, try adjusting value and saturation to help signal a color change.

- Avoid contrasting light versions of blue, violet, purple, and red (extreme wavelengths) against dark versions of blue-green, green, yellow, and orange. Do not place hues of similar saturation and value side by side, since their distinctions may be lost.

- Consider dark red, red-orange, or red-violet in key areas for community space since these colors are most easily recognized by many seniors.

- Consider the impact of a yellow undertone on the developing palette to anticipate the perspective of an elder viewer.

- Avoid colors of low saturation in combination with neutrals, since the two will be indistinguishable. This includes combinations of pastels or light colors against white or light gray.

- Try to limit high contrasts in large-scale patterns so that the resident does not perceive the darkest forms as a change in plane.

- Avoid potential confusion by limiting the number of patterns that are similar in scale. For optimum results, be selective about the use of textures and small-scale patterns.

- Provide as much access to daylight as possible through proper planning, the use of glazing, and integration of interior and exterior forms.

- Increase the overall level of lighting throughout the space frequented by the aging resident, naturally or artificially.

- Eliminate distracting shadows by providing an even distribution of light within each room.
- Use transition areas to establish gradual changes in light levels and reduce afterimaging.
- Reduce the effects of glare by minimizing hot spots and limiting the use of specular (reflective) surfaces.
- Select lamp types that provide at least 80 percent color rendition (80 CRI) to help signal a color change.

In addition, color may be used as a tool for way finding in a community center (e.g., finding the "blue cabinet" or the "orange door"). If so, consider combining it with other features to increase its effectiveness for the visually impaired—as in finding the "bulging blue cabinet" or a "large orange door." Objects that are bright and distinct become targets for orientation. This is particularly useful to mentally impaired older people who tend to focus on shapes and tactile cues to orient themselves. Other features can also be enhanced through color. By dramatically contrasting the handrail color with that of the wall, it's seen more readily. Staff can then direct residents to "follow the yellow handrail to the end of the hall." Color can also be used to identify resident's rooms within a facility. Variations in the doors distinguish them easily from one another. If each resident chooses his or her own door color, it will be quickly identifiable to him or her personally.

CHILDREN

One of the most exciting color opportunities for a designer involves objects and environments intended for children. Highly saturated color and intense contrasts of hue and extent are successfully used in this application more frequently than any other. Reactions by children to color and texture are much more immediate than those of an adult. Their environmental experience tends to be more visceral, and their perceptions are more instinctive and closer to the surface of behavior response.

Designers who demonstrate success with children's products and spaces often take their cues from parents and educators and solicit active participation of the child in the development of his or her own space. Color used actively in children's spaces can exhilarate the child's spirit. By investigating what stage of development the child is in, his or her physiological growth can be enhanced through selective color application. Alternatively, when parents impose their own color preferences, it eliminates the opportunity to explore the child's emotional connection with color.

▶ Color Selection

Parents, teachers, and therapists often encourage children to express themselves in a variety of ways. Expressions are realized in the form of dance, music making, model building, puppeteering, finger painting, story writing, and science experiments. Each form of self-expression enables the child to develop another aspect of his or her skills and intellect.

Physical aspects that touch the senses have a tremendous impact on children, such as the sound of music, the tactile sense of surface variation, and, of course, the vision of spectral color. Each engages the child in some way, serving as a tool of self-expression. Color in particular can encourage creative response in a child. As each new color is discovered, it stimulates possibilities in the active imagination of youth.

Age-Related Issues

Response to color for the majority of young children follows a predictable pattern. The consensus is that babies are first drawn to black and white in the early weeks of life. This is attributed to an ability to perceive value coupled with limitations in their ability to distinguish colors of hue. As babies' eyes develop in the first few weeks, they respond more readily to bright colors, beginning with the first color we believe they recognize—red. Since newborns are unable to appreciate form, color is their primary stimulus. And because they are naturally shortsighted, bright colors need to exist within their short range of focus in order to be recognized.

Based on this, two things are recommended for children during the first 18 months. First, **the periodic presence of strong colors is desirable to encourage brain activity**—bright colors for toys, clothing, and other objects of activity. Second, a baby's personal space is best rendered in soothing, subtle color combinations, such as flesh tones. Otherwise, the child may experience sensory overload and become confused by a continuous experience of strong color sensations. A simple background makes it easier to visually establish the form of the object presented. Depth perception and sensitivity to movement occur at about 4 to 5 months. Shortly thereafter, the child develops perception of hue contrasts, making combinations of several hues appropriate stimulation for toddlers.

By the age of 3 or 4 years, children form a clear sense of color preference. Most choose clear, bright colors like those shown in Figure 12.9, especially orange, and frequently pink, purple, or blue-green. Personal choices about toys, clothing, and other objects are usually made based on color before all other characteristics.

In interior design, hues are rarely used in their fully saturated forms unless to serve as accents. **Babies and small children, however, tend to prefer the most saturated hues.** For them, expressions of temperature shift, combinations of hard and soft color, and contrasts of loud and subtle color have positive impact. There's a strong sensory effect to color for children in residential design that can result in emotional resonance. This suggests that greater saturation is appropriate for play areas. It does not mean that random dramatic color placement is best; rather, a sensitive placement of color in various forms of expression will be most appreciated. Most knowledgeable designers have stopped using primaries as the quintessential color combination for children, since too much intensity can

scare some children—the primary triad being the strongest color combination possible at full saturation. Instead, balanced harmonies of several colors in medium to high saturation work best. In fact, according to color analysts Fehrman and Fehrman, recent tests show that when given a greater range of color to select from, many children make fairly sophisticated choices. They suggest that the old assumption that primary and secondary combinations work best was based on traditional test data that included only those colors.

More positive use of color sensation is handled through selective color choice. According to Barbara Aria *(Nursery Design: Creating a Perfect Environment for Your Child),* the Montessori schools (started by early childhood education expert Maria Montessori) incorporate color exercises into the daily activities of toddlers. The children are given bricks in contrasting hues, such as red and blue, or in closely analogous hues, such as shades of blue. The goal is to enable the child to recognize subtle variations of color through training just as she or he is trained to recognize tonal variation of a musical scale on the piano.

Spatial Understanding

The early years of a child's development are primarily tied to the senses, not to material evidence. Because of limitations in depth perception and a heightened status of the senses, color response clearly takes precedence over form. Babies experience three-dimensional space as a psychological experience. The fact that lines converge to a point in

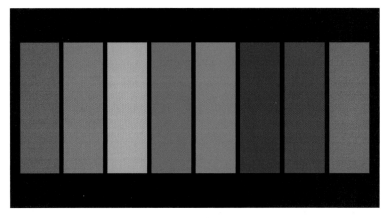

FIGURE 12.9 Clear colors such as these are more stimulating to young children, with individual preferences developing at 3 to 4 years of age.

the distance does not imply that the room has depth until children accumulate an experiential history to tell them so. Instead, space is determined by how each plane is broken down and filled with color.

Older children, however, learn to think in terms of form and depth. Shapes become identifiable icons, and there's a growing sense of the hierarchy of physical things, which occurs as a learned response. As children develop, the eyes' ability to focus at greater distances increases. The patterns of what constitutes three-dimensional form can be recognized based on this increased power of observation and acquired knowledge. Experience shows a child, for instance, that when the lines of the wall converge, it means the wall is moving away. When the bottom of the box turns the corner, it's square. Environments where form and color are truly integrated can ease the transition from sensation to perception. If color is applied to form in a way that allows normal shadow casting and clarity of edges, physical experience can be trusted. If perception of form in the child's environment is purposefully distorted, it denies the child the opportunity to trust what he or she sees. An illusion may be desirable in places like Disneyland, where it serves as a source of entertainment, but that condition is less desirable in an educational or recovery environment.

▶ Color and Development

Professionals sometimes use art therapy to evaluate a child's state of mind. For example, the way a parent is drawn may suggest something about the parent-child relationship. The use of a particular color can also indicate something that is unfamiliar to that child. Similarly, a child's space can serve as a form of artistic self-expression if the child is encouraged to participate in its development. By soliciting the child's involvement, we can establish which colors will have the greatest positive effect on him or her at that point in time. This might be overt, as in the question-and-answer method, or by observation of children at play. The first crayon color used is often the one most preferred, as is the first color chosen in a group of plastic cups. If children compete for a colored object, this can indicate group preference.

Children are emotionally drawn to images around them as they grow and mature. Characters from movies, television, the educational sector, or the retail market may have a strong impact and offer a tempting source for color in the form of a theme. For example, a room design based on *Star Wars* (the movie) or filled with insignia emblematic of a sports hero can appear to be the ideal respite at a given point in time. Unfortunately, the child is likely to outgrow this preoccupation just as quickly as he or she discovered it. Objects that can be replaced easily are more practical as theme identifiers. Colors that will offer a long-term benefit are more effectively used on permanent surfaces to sustain the child through a range of daydreams. Another approach to theme color is the focal wall, where one surface is treated to display removable theme paraphernalia with pins, magnets, or tape.

In children's day schools, where the average age remains constant but the individual users change, color is more easily integrated into the architecture for functional purposes. In the example in Figure 12.10, the designer uses colored letters in the tile patterns within the child's viewing range. The letters are placed on complementary backgrounds to offer effective contrast with balance—

Antonio Torrice

Antonio Torrice (American) was a twentieth-century child development counselor and environmental designer who specialized in children's spaces. Trained in early childhood education, human development, and theater arts at Villanova University and in the Montessori methods for child learning at Ravenhill Academy in Germantown, Pennsylvania, he worked with emotionally troubled residents at the Devereux Foundation in Devon, Pennsylvania, and with severely retarded and physically disabled children at a state hospital in the same state. Torrice followed this experience with visual merchandising and display for the retailer, Design Research, before starting his own design service, Just Between Friends, which was dedicated to the design of living and learning environments for children. A recipient of the Human Environment Award, he was a professional member of the American Society of Interior Design (ASID) until his passing in 1992.

FIGURE 12.10 Color is an effective tool to draw attention to the environment in educational ways. *(Design by Flansburgh Associates, Inc.)*

and perhaps to give teachers another tool for color discussion. Additive color can also be incorporated into a child's environment. Colored mylar on the windows or a prism hanging strategically to capture daylight each offer a change of spectral color within the room as daylight shifts. Track lights with gels can be stimulating, particularly when positioned to bathe a play area or to facilitate shadow puppets. Color that depends on daylight has the added feature of shifting during the day, making it a more interactive solution.

A Room of One's Own

Antonio Torrice dedicated many of his professional efforts in psychology and interior design to the subject of children's space. He recommends against the imposition of adult tastes on the child's personal environment and instead proposes proactive partici-

pation of the child. There are several advantages to this approach, as explained in the reference *In My Room,* which he cowrote with Ro Logrippo. The most obvious, of course, is the opportunity for personal expression, which fosters a positive self-image. The more invested the child feels in the establishment of personal space, the more he or she will be drawn to it, looking for opportunities for play, for learning, or for simple enjoyment. It's also believed that children will invest time and energy in the upkeep of a space for which they feel ownership. Who owns the maintenance of that space may be less of a debate for some, since a child clearly sees his or her space as distinct from the rest of the home.

To establish the color palette for the child's room, color preference needs to be established. This choice is made much as any color-preference test is given—without association to the room or any object or space. The child is simply shown a range of saturated colors and asked to choose a favorite. Torrice used six cards showing the primary and secondary colors and offered them on more than one occasion to establish either strong hue indication or a combination of preferred colors. On another occasion, the child was asked to color a design sketch of his or her room using these colors. Ideally, the sketch incorporates elements that designer and child have determined belong in the space. In this exercise, the things children color first with their preferred colors are the elements most important to them.

The next step in color selection for the child is to gather paint samples in a range of value for the key color or colors chosen from the cards. The child is asked to choose which of those colors will be used on the surfaces he or she colored correspondingly in the sketch. These selections may be reduced slightly in saturation or value since they will intensify on a large plane, as long as the child recognizes that the final colors in the space are those he or she selected. Frequently, if the client (usually the parent of the child) is uncomfortable with the strength of final color selections, some adjustments are made. The saturation of a highly chromatic color can be reduced while maintaining its specific hue, or the area of greatest color intensity might be reduced. For example, one wall might be painted in the strongest color rather than four walls. Alternatively, the fully saturated color can be applied to elements in the room that are easily changed, such as a quilt or drapes. Instead of painting built-in woodwork, a large frame with stretched fabric in the favorite color may be used. Since a child's desire for certain colors will change as he or she ages, it's easier to manage the change if less permanent surfaces in the room have the strongest colors.

Behavioral Observations

A significant observation of Antonio Torrice concerns individual color selection. He observed that children are not drawn to personal color preferences in the way that adults are. Children tend to select color according to needs, the more aggressive children choosing blue, the more passive seeking orange. He further noted that children with speech impediments preferred green, those with learning disabilities migrated to purple, and others with motor skill limitations chose red. By experimentation, he found that children reacted positively when they were illuminated in light corresponding to their color

preference. To determine if childhood preferences have some correlation with health and physical development, Torrice established an environment of six colored zones at a pediatric hospital. Children in recovery for various treatments or dealing with various disabilities could choose the space for their activity. By observing children's preferences as well their developmental and recovery progress, Torrice identified a correlation between specific colors and their association with developmental stages in growing children or the recovery of body functions. His associations are paraphrased here (*In My Room: Designing for and with Children,* page 49).

- **Red**—motor skill activities
- **Orange**—nervous and circulation systems
- **Yellow**—chest, heart, and lungs (asthma)
- **Green**—throat and vocal chords (speech skills, language)
- **Blue**—eyes, ears, and nose (sight, sound, smell)
- **Violet**—head and cerebral activity (concern, confusion)

Whether or not these findings suggest specific solutions for developing children, they do identify an explicit value in the use of spectral color to establish a positive holistic environment for their growth and well-being. The more interactive the process used to solicit input and to evaluate appropriate color selections, the more likely the solution will parallel a genuine need in the child. When children pick a certain color, this is not necessarily a signal that its corresponding body function is undeveloped or damaged. Color preference can also suggest the occurrence of natural growth in an area or an inspirational association with one color, either of which has value as a positive outward stimulus. For instance, a child learning a new language may be drawn to blue, if the association supports his or her current activity.

Color and Form

Form integration offers many opportunities for the children's environment. Developing children look for anything that will inspire a full body experience. In the presence of an open manhole, an active child doesn't stand back and peer from a distance, but is more likely to lie down, stomach to pavement, and stick his or her head fully into the opening. Large-scale patterns adjacent to the child's body can help identify specific zones of activity. A primary circle on the floor can signal a sitting area for a group sing-along. By linking a key color with a recognizable repetitive form, children are encouraged to incorporate the environment into their own imaginative play. Some examples of this include white floating clouds along the wall, rust-colored bricks, green trees, or a yellow-orange sun. In the absence of elements of play in the design, a key color can be used in the building architecture, such as bright pink to articulate exposed piping or sponged white with blue on a large form of ductwork to simulate the sky. In the public school shown in figure 12.11, designers used strong value contrast to accentuate large-scale forms. The combination of the spools, a concept derived from the local textile industry, with squares in the floor offer children a source for full body experience as they walk through the open area.

Another way to use color to facilitate interaction between children and their environment is to use color to coordinate cleanup. Ro Logrippo, a contemporary of Torrice who continues to write about the design of children's spaces, suggests that color coding can be used to identify what items are to be stored where (*In My World: Designing Living & Learning Environments for the Young*). Drawers or their pulls can be assigned different colors. A colorful knob can be mounted on each door of a cabinet. Shelves in a wall unit can be lined with different-colored shelf paper. By coloring storage modules consistent with the items to be stored, a visual connection is possible.

FIGURE 12.11   Strong contrast is used here to accentuate large-scale pattern and form for the benefit of growing children. (*Design by Flansburgh Associates, Inc.*)

Pattern

Pattern is often incorporated in the design of children's space, especially in bedrooms or playrooms. However, the scale of patterning tends to vary according to its function, either as a decorative element or as a functional or educational device. As noted in the prior section, two-year-old children have difficulty with small-scale surface prints. They have a tendency to try to peel the shapes off the wall, particularly if the contrast is strong, forming a positive-negative effect. This suggests that large-scale patterning may be more beneficial to the younger age group or that more colors can be included to soften the edges and give it a little depth.

The location of color as a pattern or design device is critical in a child's space. Younger children experience the world completely in terms of their own bodies. In order for a child to relate to a colorful element, it must exist within the realm of his or her own height. Otherwise it cannot be experienced. If a bold-patterned dado is applied at a height the child can touch without reaching upward, he or she will be consumed with its intricacies. However, if it's outside the field of vision, say, above the eye, and is seen obliquely as in a cornice, the child will not consider its potential as form to be touched. By measuring the height of the child's eye line and positioning the pattern accordingly, the child can appreciate it more fully. Border patterns in paper or stencil are particularly effective at drawing visual attention when well placed. About 24 inches above the finish floor is appropriate to the eye level of a toddler.

Conclusions

A few key recommendations may be drawn from the recent research noted here.

- Involve the individual child in the development of his or her own color palette as completely as possible.
- High saturation in young children's living space is a good thing, except when they are babies.
- When designing for a group of children, be attentive to the preferences based on age and the optimum locations for color detail based on age.
- Keep combinations of color and form appropriate to the size of the child and in areas clearly definable.
- Consider theme concepts only if the client's budget will allow for redesign when the child's interests move on to another theme, which is a relatively short time period.

As we've noted in this discussion, personal needs relative to age, development, personality, and group function each can have an impact on successful color assignment. As with senior residents, none of the criteria suggest elimination of any individual color. However, each situation offers the possibility for greater inspiration and comfort in the personal environment through individual selection.

If residential design is about uncovering characteristics and preferences unique to the individuals who use a space, then design for public space suggests the antithesis. Now that we've considered the most individual of spaces—the residence—let's look at color for the spaces we use for work, growth, health, and play. In the final chapters, we explore criteria appropriate to public spaces, areas for work processes, educational environments, and places for healing and recovery. For these projects, color has its effect on the largest numbers of people.

Public Space Applications

Every day, members of our society are impacted by color in its many variations. Some of those expressions serve as visual cues: they lead us in or deter access, or they persuade us to participate in some activity, such as dining, shopping, or entertainment. Still others simply remind us of the familiar and offer identity. For those who design public environments—landscape, environment, architecture, and interior design—color selection is driven by the overriding purpose of that environment. Ideally, environmental color relates directly to its form, which is derived from function. Color may also communicate primary and secondary purposes of the space with practical as well as cultural applications. In addition, color selection at its best reflects sensitivity to the physiological and psychological well-being of those who occupy the space.

In the final two chapters, color is discussed in terms of spatial public service, with emphasis in Chapter 14 on color relative to our health and well-being, particularly in the workplace. The current chapter focuses on color in the public arena as it's used to influence behavior—getting groups of people to do what we want them to do, whether it's spending money, consuming refreshments, relaxing, learning, or praying. While each spatial function has its own set of criteria for successful color application, retail, hospitality, and assembly spaces share one common concern. The proprietors of these facilities must compete with each other for the consumer's attention. Unlike the goal in personal space, which is to address the uniqueness of the inhabitants, the goal in the design of public space is to appeal to a large number of individuals. Users may come from different socioeconomic backgrounds, and they may be using the space for very different purposes. What remains consistent is the need to make the experience of the gathering meaningful through a spectral expression of form.

■ RETAIL

One of the strongest applications for testing color effectiveness is in retail space, where the primary function is to promote the consumption of products in the form of objects, services, or both. Products are sold through images. Each manufacturer establishes an image believed to be inspirational and irresistible to the target customers. The built environment establishes that image through physiological response and association. Each decision of space, scale, form, and color is made in support of the image presentation, with color contributing the strongest visual and emotional impact.

Product lines sold on the retail market are developed to reach an identifiable section of the general population, known as the *target customers*. Target customers are selected according to a variety of characteristics: age, socioeconomics, level of education, level of mobility or athleticism, proportion of disposable income, gender, and regional demographics, to name a few. As the target customers are identified, concepts are developed using imagery deemed most likely to attract them and convert them to consumers. They are analyzed categorically, not individually, for the purpose of reaching holistic, and to some degree less precise, conclusions. Often, interviews are held with individuals from the target group to establish a sense of preferences. Taste, of course, comes in all levels and varies both regionally and socially, suggesting that consistent customer sampling may or may not lead to the volume of purchasing anticipated. This lack of scientific reliability results in some highly successful retail campaigns and also in some that lack commercial success.

▶ Tuning in to Customers

Once target customer groups are identified, goals are set and the imagery is fleshed out. Physical space is developed to support the retail image, and colors are identified to support desired visual associations. The color of the current product line is rarely considered when establishing spatial color. Only the common characteristics of the products have influence, not specific products themselves. Product designs must change frequently, and they can often lag a trend. Because of the time necessary for their development, some products become available just as the peak of a trend is over. Other products simply change coloration due to seasonal conditions or the addition of other designs to the collection. Only specialty stores, such as jewelers, are likely to show product in the same colors year after year.

Retail merchants rely on a high degree of visual focus to attract consumers and enhance their products. Because the color of the storefront or display area is key in securing the customer's attention and getting him or her to approach, it must communicate image quickly. Statistical information from color-preference tests may be consulted. The specifics of colors in combination depend on geographic location of the store, current trends in color, and social issues of the time, such as the occurrence of war, a strong economy, or a shift to environmental concerns. As a case in point, if color and material designed to draw consumers appear to be pricey, and the economy is in a downswing, buyers may immediately assume the products themselves are too expensive—regardless of the price.

It's already been established that some aspects of color combination serve as attention getters. These include higher levels of dynamic contrast and the use of more saturated colors. **The key in retail is to draw attention with colors that depict the appropriate image while ensuring that they also support the specific products shown.** This means offering enough stimulation to inspire consumers to make purchases without overwhelming them. It requires some sense of what mood will prod the target consumers to buy. Color selection becomes a device to help establish that mood in the presence of the products for sale. For example, lower levels of saturation and contrast will attract the eye of a bonsai shopper, whereas the athlete looking to purchase a kayak might respond positively to more intense coloration. The Pavo Real storefront shown in Figure 13.1 is an example of a strong image for products with an ethnic flair. The solution is eye-catching and gets the message across. It's interesting to look at, but does not compete with the very colorful clothing inside.

Socioeconomic class has the most apparent impact on color selection in retail applications. Statistically speaking, low-income groups prefer stronger, more saturated colors, while high-income groups migrate more readily to very neutral combinations. (This was discussed in more detail in Chapter 6, "Color Response.") Establishments that offer low-cost products or high-turnover products usually do best with bright colors—the classic impulse purchase. In locations where leisure shopping is possible and the products have a higher price tag, more muted and sophisticated coloration has been shown to attract the appropriate consumer. Other aspects of the customer personality profile may suggest warm colors over cool or a varied level of color saturation. Although jewel tones are a source of strong, eye-catching colors that draw the customer, when viewed close up in a large quantity they may be overpowering. A transition to more muted counterparts may be more effective in display areas.

▶ Color in the Store

Retail designers stress the need for products rather than space to tell the big story. Space becomes the backdrop to show off product and support its sale. The greater the number and scale of products dis-

FIGURE 13.1 The earthy coloration in this retail facade communicates an image suitable for a specific target market.
(Pavo Real—Bergmeyer Associates, Inc., architect. Photo: © Lucy Chen.)

played, the smaller the area of backdrop that remains visible. Shelving, cabinets, and rod systems for hanging garments are a part of the backdrop. None of these should attract interest to the detriment of the product. Some refer to the process as building the envelope, where the product is the "action." By keeping color clean and simple, it more clearly enhances the store's image without competing with products. A good example of this is the Rockport store shown in Figure 13.2, which uses accents in a warm-cool contrast.

Context of color also has implications in selection. The bright orange of an adjacent tool shop may influence a shoe storefront in a retail district. In this case, an abrupt change in overall color helps to distinguish the shoe store from its neighbor. However, in a large department store, which has several distinguishable areas, too many abrupt changes in unrelated adjacent colors can be distracting. Here it's preferable to nudge the shopper from one department to the next using subtle color shifts or colors coordinated so that they have a visual relationship with each other. Supermarket designers do this by using specific colors symbolically to establish product identity. The store name maintains its integrity through color identity using a very limited number of colors.

Knowledgeable manufacturers use color in packaging to affect consumer perception. The package delivers the promise of satisfaction. A pink box visually ensures that its contents will be sweet. The ice-blue paper cup promises to slake thirst. Color symbology will effectively communicate the fulfillment of desire as long as the expectations are known up front. This is the value in cultural color associations such as those noted in Chapter 5, "Color Identity." Since not all associations can be anticipated, market research is often performed to test the packaging of new products before they are advertised. Fehrman and Fehrman tell of a market research survey performed for a package of laundry detergent. The women participating in the test determined that the detergent they tested in the yellow package was too strong, the one in the blue package was too weak, and the one in the blue-and-yellow package was just right. This was remarkable given that the same detergent was used in all three packages (*Color: The Secret Influence*, page 145).

Products

Some specific color tendencies have demonstrated reliability over the years, as outlined in *Designing to Sell,* by Vilma Barr and Charles E. Broudy. Clothing for mature men is generally displayed successfully in neutral spaces, while younger men are attracted to much brighter colors. Wall colors for women's clothing probably vary the most, since the products colors change most frequently. The concern here is that the wall color may negatively impact the clothing colors being displayed. If colors of hue are appropriate to a particular retailer's image, use of a couple of wall tones will allow the retailer to display more product around the store and prevent negative color influence. Color can also enhance the evaluation process. For example, warm colors such as light oranges are suggested in dressing areas to make skin tones more appealing when viewed in the mirror.

Some products are very colorful in and of themselves, suggesting a limited amount of environmental color for their display. (For one such example, refer to the accessories shop shown in Chapter 3, Figure 3.6.) This includes housewares, such as sheets and towels, music, books, and crafts. Products that are more limited in hue, such as appliances and shoes, may be displayed more prominently by using a contrasting background where it's appropriate to image. In the example in Figure 13.3, colored lighting in the ceiling and colorful mobiles catch the eye at a distance and establish the impression of being in an aquarium. Once inside the store, the toys and clothing draw attention through their strong coloration, while the white display modules serve as a backdrop. Only the back wall of the display areas has a color of hue to draw one all the way through the space to those products.

Fine arts are best displayed on neutral or low-saturation surfaces of medium value unless there is a commitment to one specific artist whose colors can be complemented. White is not necessarily the best background for the display of fine art. As an extreme value, it does not read as a neutral against a colorful painting. The eye is distracted by the contrast of white against the dominant color of the canvas, and the more subtle nuances of the piece become less apparent. If the piece has dark overall tones, it may read as a hole in the wall, and the nuances of the

FIGURE 13.2 The use of a light, neutral background and natural materials with intrinsic color work together to create a handsome display for this manufacturer's collection of fine leather products. *(Rockport—Bergmeyer Associates, Inc., architect Photo: © 2003 Chun Y. Lai. All rights reserved.)*

FIGURE 13.3   The color in this aquarium gift shop supports a strong image while allowing the products to communicate the promise of fun. *(The Tennessee Aquarium Shop—Bergmeyer Associates, Inc., architect. Photo: Richard T. Bryant.)*

darker layers are lost as the eye keeps adjusting to take in the adjacent wall. Light to medium grays are suggested where white is not appropriate; in the case of landscape work, a neutralized olive green is gaining popularity as background color.

Seasonal Color

Many retail establishments depend on the changing seasons to signal the need for additional purchasing. For these environments, the designer may want to create a system in which the seasonal color "drops in." In this case, supplemental decoration is needed to ensure that the space looks complete during less definitive seasons. In Figure 13.4, the museum store includes a large wall that is painted with an image from the current special

exhibit. This painted image reinforces the mood and style of the show and tells consumers what products to expect. Colors in the rest of the store are maintained in an ongoing way—only the seasonal wall changes color.

■ HOSPITALITY

Color is a valuable tool in spaces that provide temporary respite, entertainment, or social interaction for relatively infrequent guests. For the purpose of this discussion, these will be grouped as hospitality and specifically include hotel and restaurant spaces. Like their retail counterparts, hospitality providers make every effort to appeal to a specific

FIGURE 13.4 The designated image wall on the right of the entrance to this gift shop is intended to change frequently, as special exhibits change. *(Museum of Fine Arts, Boston Shop—Bergmeyer Associates, Inc., architect. Photo: © Warren Jagger Photography, Inc.)*

audience through effective imagery. This means that knowledge of color associations or analysis of color preferences through test data may be useful for some projects. For others, such as historic renovation or international work, consideration of cultural, architectural, or historic context may be more meaningful. Sometimes a conceptual association with another function, such as a conference center, museum, or library, is essential to the design. Key colors identifying those functions can enable one to make an appropriate visual connection.

In hospitality, the image is established at the front door and a promise to meet a certain set of expectations is made. The fulfillment of promise in this application takes the form of nourishment, relaxation, or respite, depending on the space. Often these are combined in one facility, in which case color is a primary tool used to communicate those distinctions. The area for quiet reading often has different coloration than the check-in desk or the nightclub. In some hospitality spaces, areas of public reception are combined with other functions, such as a cocktail lounge in the hotel lobby or a restaurant in the transportation center. In these cases, color contrasts offer an effective way to distinguish the public from the semiprivate while allowing visibility into both.

▶ Restaurants

The criteria for color in eating and drinking establishments covers a broad range of functional space. Restaurants are the most apparent application, followed by cafeterias, cafés, and fast-food establishments; ballrooms, bars, and cocktail lounges; and nightclubs and discotheques. Although these spaces incorporate significant functional differences, the criterion for color development is reasonably consistent. Solutions are drawn with attention to three key issues: establishing image, supporting function, and the colors' relationship to the food and beverages served.

Image

If a retail image is about setting an expectation that sells the product, restaurant images are about selling the image itself. A bottle of Budweiser or a glass of Chateau Haut-Brion tastes the same no matter where we drink it. What we're buying from

the proprietor of a food-service establishment is the right to participate in its image, even temporarily. In this respect, color has a big job to do. It combines with form to project a positive impression that is a departure from daily life. In doing so, it reaches out to the target customer and makes her or him feel comfortable, stimulated, or relaxed for the duration of use.

Like retailers, restaurateurs have identified a group of target consumers and established a range of refreshments that will ideally be enhanced by the overall image. Unlike the retail space, color in this application is much more controlled. The product may change seasonally, but the color concept in a restaurant image is static, defined almost entirely by the environment. While the napery, flowering plants, or other decorative elements may have strong coloration, these, too, are usually chosen along with knowledge of the permanent room colors. People are the action, and spatial image establishes some level of that interaction. Consider the Radius restaurant, shown in Figure 13.5. A rich red appears in key places both inside the space and on the building's exterior, but its impact is balanced by the presence of a color complement in the form of gray-green. Forms, particularly those along the radii, are easy to read due to use of solid color (no pattern) and the strength of value contrasts along the radius's form. The result is an understated elegance consistent with the restaurant's sophisticated cuisine.

Lighting

Since food-service facilities often center on the concept of seeing others and being seen, lighting has a role in supporting that function. If the overall color temperature of the lamp types is warm, it will render skin tones positively, since most skin colors have an undertone of either yellow or red (pink). This enhancement is subtle but effective. The warmth of gels used in more theatrical situations may offer too much of a color enhancement to be comfortable in most food-service settings and can negatively impact the visual appeal of some foods. We know that incandescent lighting is often preferred in key locations due to its positive impact on both skin tones and food. In the absence of incandescent lighting for a dining space, the color of lamps can be specified in a high CRI to enhance skin tones and food appearance.

FIGURE 13.5 This elegant restaurant design uses complementary color harmony and strong contrasts of value and saturation to establish its image. *(Radius—Bergmeyer Associates, Inc., architect. Photo: © Richard Mandelkorn.)*

Low light levels are preferred in more intimate settings. However, even in a private dining atmosphere, lighting needs to be high enough to read the menu and make eye contact. In a serving area, the light level is often higher than in the dining area. Since we rely on a visual impression of food to establish an impression of taste, the color of the food needs to be clear to the eye, especially at the point of purchase.

Function

In terms of function, color has been used to impact the amount of time the patron is expected to stay in the establishment, provide a differentiation in acoustic levels, and support distinction of staff areas from patron areas. Some restaurants encourage leisure dining, while others depend on frequent turnover of patrons. **Color influences the length of stay along the lines of contrast, particularly value: the higher the contrast, the shorter the average length of stay.** Soft contrasts are easier on the eyes and allow for long-term viewing as the patron uncovers the subtlety of a color scheme. In comparison, the more eye-catching color scheme that has dramatic shifts in value will attract diners' attention more readily, but will lose the diners' interest after a short period of time. Because higher value contrasts are harder on the eyes and become tiresome more quickly, the use of high value contrasts in the color scheme encourages guests to move on, similar to the effect of providing a slightly less comfortable chair. Other contrasts can impact this condition to some degree. A strong hue or saturation contrast in combination with a value contrast can move things along, while the use of patterning or intermediate values will make the space more comfortable for an extended stay. The example in Figure 13.6 shows a café offering prepared foods to a downtown business community. Its success depends on a higher volume of clientele, making higher contrasts appropriate. The busy color-form combination is pleasing to the eye, in part because of the spectral balance (dyad).

Acoustics

Environmental stimulation has an impact on noise level as a human response to the environment. The higher the level of stimulation in a space, the greater the noise generated by the patrons. This stimulation can occur through the addition of sound (as in music systems), through the reverberation of sound (by using hard surfaces), or through the addition of strong color, which causes a subconscious reaction to a visceral condition. Color stimulation, as we have learned, is caused by increasing the amount of contrasts, by raising the saturation levels of color, or by combining hues that result in unbalanced harmonies. The relative choices of colors may reflect the distinctions between a quiet room for dining and reading versus a high-visibility espresso café or piano bar. **The simple rule of thumb here is that higher stimulation through color translates to a greater noise level in response.** (See Figure 13.7.)

Spatial Differentiation

Color is sometimes used to distinguish dining areas from service areas. Wall colors in the food-preparation area are often kept light and neutral, with a higher light level than that of the dining room. A quick shift in color when passing through the kitchen door reminds the server that he or she is back in the public eye. Obviously the success of such color distinction depends on the position of doors, since a direct line of sight from the soft coloration at the dining table into the bright white kitchen would be quite distracting. If a restaurant facility is quite large, key colors may be used in way finding. For instance, one might follow the blue checkerboard tiles to get to the Blue Room. The rest rooms might be behind the coral wall. Sometimes a room for private functions is given a different color aesthetic from the main space to make it special. Usually, the lounge area has some variation from main dining areas. In a cafeteria, the servery often has different finish materials from the actual eating areas to support higher traffic and more aggressive maintenance. Figure 13.8 shows a cafeteria space that is a focal area to a larger corporate facility. Here color is used to offer relief from the workspaces while reinforcing a positive professional image of a company that supports its employees.

Food

Color in food-service areas can support consumption through symbolic associations. (Examples of these were described in Chapter 5, "Color Identity.") Colors that remind us of the food itself are most effective, such as yellow for corn or beiges for breads. Red that is slightly orange suggests toma-

FIGURE 13.6 The use of value and hue contrasts at the edges where juxtaposed forms meet suggests a higher turnover rate of patrons. Compare this to the lunchtime eatery shown in Figure 13.8. *(Caffe Briacco—Bergmeyer, Associates, Inc. architect. Photo: © Lucy Chen.)*

Public Space Applications

toes, whereas red on the violet side implies wine. Coffee and espresso will always be seen as derivative of brown. The idea here is that consistent coloration enhances the desire for the particular food. Other positive associations involve the historic context of color. Green continues to be the color of choice for the health conscious and consequently adds value to healthy imagery. Brown implies an association with natural foods, as in whole grains. And red continues to be associated with the richness of red sauces used in pasta and pizza, reinforcing the concept of southern Italian cuisine.

Appetite

In addition to making symbolic connections, color has a bearing on the presentation of food on two other levels. It can impact the diner's current appetite, and it can influence the appearance of the food being presented. A correlation between specific colors and increased appetite has been observed in recent years, appetite being a condition distinct from hunger itself. Just as unpleasant sounds, a sense of uncleanness, or poor lighting will make food less appetizing, color can enhance or diminish dining experience. A fellow designer discovered this in a banking facility where she recolored the cafeteria walls in lieu of a more expensive renovation. The patrons, not recognizing what had really changed, commented readily on how much better the food tasted during the period of time following the color alterations.

Dr. Morton Walker tells us that food is more aromatic and **people will eat more in the pres-**

FIGURE 13.7 Lively colors and strong value contrasts are used in this jazz pub to create a strong, stimulating image, appropriately suggesting more interaction and movement. Compare this to the luncheon space within a corporate setting that's shown in Figure 13.8. *Brooklyn Jazz Bar—Bergmeyer Associates, Inc., architect. Photo: © 2003 Chun Y. Lai. All rights reserved.)*

ence of red. Carlton Wagner's findings concur. He notes that people will not only eat more and eat longer, but they are willing to pay more for food under the influence of red (*The Color Response Report,* page 7). Additional colors of hue that enhance a person's appetite are red-orange and orange, as suggested by the diagram in Figure 13.9. Hues that appear to reduce or minimize the sensation of hunger include yellow-greens, yellow, orange-yellow, violet-purple, and violet-red. Blues and greens as environmental colors seem to have little synesthesia with appetite. (Note that blue is considered a definite appetite suppressor when it appears on food. In this context we're dis-

cussing *room* color rather than *food* color.) **More saturated colors tend to increase satiety over neutralized colors simply because they are more stimulating.** Black and gray, particularly cool grays, are considered a deterrent to dining. They give a sense of emotional coldness, whereas psychological warmth stimulates satiety. This does not imply that all dining space should be dominated by red or red-orange. On the contrary, many dining events are not about increasing food quantity at all. Some restaurants are about atmosphere and qualitative dining experience over consumption. Obviously, the goal of the dining establishment will influence some of the color decisions.

FIGURE 13.8 Compare the image of this corporate dining facility to the more formal dining space shown in Figure 13.5 and the livelier lounge in Figure 13.7 developed by the same design team. *(Intex Solutions—Bergmeyer, Associates, Inc., architect. Photo: © Lucy Chen.)*

Appearance

The color of food has a tremendous influence on how appetizing it is to the diner. Professionals in food-testing facilities are well aware of this and carefully control the color of lighting on the food being tested so that only taste affects decision making. This is accomplished by specification of the lamps, by the adjustment of light quantity, and by surrounding the food-test area with neutral colors to eliminate any color influence. Ideal lighting, including reflected light and shadow casting, does not minimize food coloration. Generally, warm lighting is preferred, since cool lamps render red meats and vegetables unappealing, pushing them toward gray. To enhance the colors of food, display areas and serving items are sometimes adjusted in color. The space shown in Figure 13.10 is an example of space designed to enhance the appearance of food.

Complementary and simultaneous contrasts are helpful in food display. A slightly pink plate will make lettuce appear greener compared to a blue plate. White servingware enhances dark food colors, as in plums or currants, while a dark dish accentuates lighter colors, as in sherbet. White is the color of many processed foods, such as bread, rice, and pasta, as well as seafood. These foods are enhanced by stronger colors and appear flat when served alone on white porcelain. Since blue is undesirable to most people as a food color, it's often the color of choice for dishes that are white or strong in hue because it offers contrast.

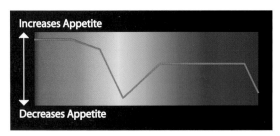

FIGURE 13.9 Recommendations vary according to specifics of color use as an appetite enhancement, but generally speaking, colors of hues offer enhancement along these relative ranges.

▶ Hotels

Hotels are commercial buildings that want to be residential. By that, we mean that for people who travel they are a home away from home. The question is, whose home should they emulate? Each hotelier tries to provide a refuge so comfortable in every sense of the word that the guest returns again and again, choosing the familiar while ignoring competing facilities. The challenge is to determine what will make the space feel most familiar and inviting so each guest will choose only your hotel. The more people who choose a given establishment, commonly referred to as "heads in beds," the greater the hotel's success.

The location of a hotel often drives color selection in one direction, unless the hotel is a chain, in which case the chain image presides. Boutique hotels are expected to communicate local color so that guests aren't disappointed. This vernacular might be expressed through visual access to the area's nature or architecture if the available views are dramatic, in which case color is played down to support the exterior vision. Alternatively, colors consistent with local culture can be integrated into the hotel design, responding to the positive aspects of the region. Guesthouses near natural wonders of the world often incorporate the colors of nature, while extensive use of rich, dark colors, particularly black, might be associated with the culture of a metropolitan city like New York.

FIGURE 13.10 In this self-serve restaurant, lighting with good color rendition highlights the food itself. (*Marché— Moncur Design Associates, Inc., design; Bergmeyer Associates, Inc., architect. Photo: © Lucy Chen.*)

Image

One goal in hotel coloration is to establish a strong impression that's consistent within the facility, even though functions may vary significantly. Spaces include places to rest, socialize, and dine, room for business meetings or for performing research, and areas in which to be entertained or simply relax. Color throughout the facility is developed to accommodate this range while reinforcing one conceptual theme that guests will remember in the hope that familiarity of that theme will bring them back.

Hotel designers communicate a sense of security through the familiar. Of course, what's familiar will vary with each audience. The American guest of substantial personal worth who is grounded in tradition and family will feel at ease with the colors of traditional American culture. A guest who is less advantaged in a socioeconomic sense will more likely relax in a hotel of declassifying colors. The European guest may prefer the welcoming colors of greens, browns, and beiges. A trendsetter will look for the unique sophistication of a contemporary boutique hotel. **Image analysis then becomes a process of identifying the target audience and the hotel place in the mind of those customers.** If all the colors in combination are to tell one story, the key is to establish what story will be told. The hotel in Figure 13.11 shows a very distinct facility in a historic neighborhood of a small, established city. The guests who feel at home here are buying an image quite different from those who prefer the bold clarity of the contemporary hotel in a major international city (Dubai) shown in Figure 13.12. This contemporary hotel structure expresses a nautical form inside and out. Because it stands in a warm climate, cool, saturated colors are inviting to guests.

Since hotels can be very complex spaces, color is often used to give focus or punch to key elements of the space. Unlike some of the other use groups covered in this text, color is rarely used in hotels to distinguish public and private space. The whole facility is for guests. So the hierarchy of space has more to do with orientation than with separation of space.

In terms of guest-room colors, some hotel philosophies assume that guests who return frequently will tire of rooms that all look the same.

FIGURE 13.11 The image of this hotel suggests old-world elegance, historic context, and attention to detail.

In such cases, the approach is to vary colors from room to room, using palettes that allow furniture, linens, and other accessories to be interchanged. Historically, the focus of the hotel room has changed, making the placement of color or pattern a moving target. For instance, over the years the desk went from a small writing stand to a multifunctional hardwired work surface with plenty of plugs for the laptop and printer and a connection for high-speed Internet access. Its woodframe chair was replaced with an ergonomic one. Society's current emphasis on cocooning has brought attention to the bed as a focal point, including the use of large-scale headboards and more decorative bedding. Over time, the trends shift toward more simplicity on one end of the spectrum and more sumptuousness on the other. As the priorities shift, they impact color selection, its placement, and the use, nonuse, or overuse of patterning.

FIGURE 13.12   In this view, looking from the main lobby up to the interior atrium, the form is expressed by applying strong hues to the undersides of balconies. *(Photo: Robert Polidori.)*

Practical Issues

The hotel offers some unique challenges that have a bearing on color selection. On the one hand, the spaces strive to offer a residential feeling. On the other hand, they suffer abuse as some of the most highly trafficked commercial spaces available. In addition, the hotel is designed to accommodate a large range of functions within a comparatively small space. These characteristics in combination make it particularly challenging to coordinate color effectively and ensure a successful installation that performs well over time. That said, here are a few pointers offered by hotel designers to ensure success in this use group.

- ▪ **Floor surfaces** in major spaces in the hotel are high-traffic areas. They're used 24 hours a day by a large number of people. The forgiveness of patterned flooring and the use of medium values will make maintenance in these spaces more manageable.

- ▪ Larger hotels have **long corridors** to deal with on the guest-room floors. Clever solutions that break these walls intermittently or incorporate strong colors of hue at the ends improve their visual aesthetic. Like the large restaurant facility, color can be used to aid way finding. Examples are selective patterning to guide guests to the main ballroom and alternating colors at elevator lobbies to distinguish floors.

- ▪ Hotels undergo **frequent renovation**—on average every six years. However, the building cannot be closed while renovations are progressing, as this gives the guests an opportunity to find another hotel in the region. This means that work tends to be sequenced, one area at a time, and the time frame for disruption must be as short as possible. **Image transitions** happen over long periods of time, and transition colors must be used to connect the old and new images into one cohesive look. Transitions also respond to changes in functional needs. For example, as more businesswomen have taken to travel, the average light level has been raised to make them feel more secure, and lighter surface colors have been employed.

- ▪ Changes in **manufacturing technology** also impact color selection in hotel work. Solution-dyed fibers are preferred in fabrics and carpets for reasons of durability. In the past this has set some limitations on color selection since it eliminated the option of custom color in many applications. The gap has been reduced in recent years as new synthetic fibers provide colorfastness in a broad range of colors and manufacturers move to just-in-time production rather than stocked product.

In hospitality spaces, lighting plays a more dynamic role in the overall composition than in many other applications. First, variations of light level are highly desirable, which can result in more complex shadow casting. For most social situations, it is important to properly light people's faces. This means positioning lights to enhance the experience by making everyone look their best. Exclusive use of lights that cast shadows on the face, such as those positioned directly above the head, will detract from the success of the space itself, regardless of other color/form conditions.

Many rooms in the hotel are used for a variety of functions over a 24-hour period. The same room can be used for a family breakfast, a client lunch, a group meeting, and/or an educational presentation. To accommodate those needs, several light sources are used intermittently, possibly including daylight. This means that each set of room colors will be seen under a variety of lighting and by a variety of users, adding to the challenge of selection.

▪ ASSEMBLY SPACES

Large-scale spaces warrant special consideration when it comes to applying color. This includes assembly spaces, such as theaters, transportation facilities, and any other functional areas in which hundreds of people gather for any purpose. Unlike residential spaces and smaller commercial spaces where color is often used to break large planes into elements of personal scale, color takes on a grander scale in the public eye. The exteriors of some government buildings often benefit from uniform, neutral coloration to reinforce a sense of monumental scale. In other cases, color is used to make human connections. Inside the large-scale space, the color function changes as people attempt to orient themselves. We facilitate the orientation process by making the edges of the room immediately apparent and by establishing greater clarity through fewer colors. The following suggestions are offered regarding large meeting spaces.

- Provide easy **orientation** by changing the color of the area of focus (e.g., making the front of the lecture hall different from the sides or the stage different from the orchestra seating, as in Figure 13.13).
- Use large planes of solid color to **reduce the visual clutter** that results from a mix of signage, doorways, windows, ceiling devices, and other small-scale elements. As these planes become more readable, the volume of the room becomes clearer.
- Consider **breaking down the major elements** of overscaled volumes without compromising the simplicity of the overall form by positioning color contrasts consistently with architectural elements. This can be a series of ribs in an airport terminal or panels in presentation room, as shown in Figure 13.14.
- Use color that can be seen in peripheral vision to **cue visitors.** This means contrast between seating and the surrounding surfaces and between handrails and the balcony itself. Both examples are evident in the performance hall shown in Figure 13.13.

▶ Religious

Color is often used as a communications device in religious institutions. This is done both symbolically, as in assembly spaces, and in subtle ways to establish the philosophy of the organization. White is a symbolic sign of purity in some religions. Purple is reserved for clergy in some Christian traditions. In Islamic religion, green is a color of great respect. Often, colors for religious space are chosen because they offer familiarity and comfort to members of the congregation. Philosophically, color sets a tone for the meeting space. Some of the most colorful combinations of stained glass available appear in churches, serving as inspiration. In other facilities, the color choices are more somber, reflecting a contemplative environment. Color can be used to draw focus to key functions or symbols within the meeting space by selective placement of contrasts.

While some religions hold fast to traditional use of color in their environments, others take a more contemporary approach. Harold Linton, in his book *Color in Architecture* (page 175), shares how he developed a very colorful, three-dimensional image of the Star of David for the Hodari Children's Library and Media Center at Temple Israel in West Bloomfield, Michigan. This approach communicated both the tradition of the religion and the forward thinking of the organization, whose library facility encompasses several high-technology tools. Color became a key concern for Christian Scientists and their designers during renovations of the publishing office near the Mother Church. Theirs is a thought-based religion in which members rely on contemplation and written communication. For them, inspirational work space needed order, beauty, and grace without suggesting a literal image of the church. The result of their design team's efforts to improve the reading room and work spaces is both unique and inspiring. (See Figure 13.15.)

▶ Educational Facilities

Some projects designed for public use are more challenging due to regulatory needs, which can make creative design solutions seem virtually impossible. Limitations in funding and size can leave us with a shortage of options for unique spatial experiences. In spite of this, several design teams have found new ways to enhance space through color-form combinations. Educational spaces are one of those applications where we continue to see new life through creative color application. Insights from educators suggest that when properly developed, a greater variety of coloration can enhance the acquisition of information and other thinking processes. We have already seen several examples of color in the educational environment that deliver a message or facilitate use in the context of the other issues discussed. As a reminder, here are some of those examples.

- Color and pattern can give **identity** to a complex educational facility, inside and out (Figures 7.5 and 7.6.), or refine an educational building form, giving it a preferable scale in a neighborhood context (Figures 3.12 and 4.4).
- Color is used to **stimulate** students by enhancing the public areas in ways that add interest,

FIGURE 13.13 The area of focus is quite clear in this assembly space. Contrast of value cues visitors about where major wall planes meet, and contrast of saturation is used to give seating clear edges. Visitors are able to orient themselves even when the light level is reduced during performances. *(Design by Miller Dyer Spears. Photo: Greg Premru.)*

FIGURE 13.14 In this music room, contrasts of value are used to readily identify changes in floor planes and wall surfaces and prevent missteps as users cross the room. The overall color is keyed to the age of the children—more subdued than might be used for younger students. *(Design by Flansburgh Associates, Inc. Photo: Greg Premru.)*

improve scale, and offer subtle cues to spatial functions (Figures 7.7, 7.15, 7.16, 8.9, 8.15, 8.23, and 9.13 through 9.17.)

■ Color character helps to establish appropriate **behavior** within the space (Figure 13.9) or to **direct** students within the space (Figures 3.10 and 3.11).

■ Color is integrated into space in ways that make it a **learning** tool. (Although examples have already been shown in Figures 12.10 and 12.11, we'll discuss this further in this section.)

Given that the most common space in an educational setting is the classroom, consider how color placement can help the users (Figure 13.16). Assume that the majority of time in class is spent facing the front to focus on a speaker or a visual presentation. During that time, the eye adjusts to the color of the front wall. After a while, the eye becomes stressed by the color of that large plane. If it's very light, the pupils are constricted for a long period of time and need something darker to flex them. If it's dark, they need some relief through dilation. To allow eyes relaxation from a surface of hue, an opposing color is needed so that alternative cones are used while those that have been stressed are relieved. Students need to change their view to give the eyes a rest. Closing the eyes for a moment may give stressed cones a rest, but by placing a different color (or value) on the side walls, the student can look away and get more effective relief quickly. When the view to the front is resumed, the eye is better able to focus because of the temporary experience. As an added advantage, the change in color of the wall planes makes it easier to register the size and shape of the room during its first use.

Facilities for Young Children

Color preferences vary predictably with the age of children. When assessing appropriateness of main colors for training facilities used by children, one might consider the results of some color-preference tests to appeal to the largest number of users. Keep in mind, however, that preferences will vary by location, especially between countries. What remains consistent is the tendency for **very young school children, such as those in preschool through kindergarten, to prefer highly saturated color.** As children age, the learning process becomes more complex, and concentrated focus is more the norm. To facilitate single-mindedness, colors with less strength (i.e., reduced saturation) become more appropriate. If the median age of the children using

an existing educational center changes, recoloring is one of the least expensive ways to improve that site for its new users. (Refer to Chapter 6, "Color Response," for color preferences by age group.) Most colorists believe that children up to the age of 5 remember color distinctions more frequently than form. This means that they have not yet developed a complex set of experiences to help them understand architectural form beyond what its applied color might suggest. At this stage they may develop strong hue preferences, and any hue of high saturation is preferred over subtle tones. Generally speaking, the reason very young children prefer intense colors of hue to more subdued versions is that they tend to be extroverts at heart, seeking interactive experience on all levels. Based on this information, there's been some tendency to use primaries or primary and

FIGURE 13.15 Color in this reading room and work space was developed to communicate the character of the religious organization it supports without relying on traditional religious imagery. *(Design by ADD Inc. Photo: © Lucy Chen.)*

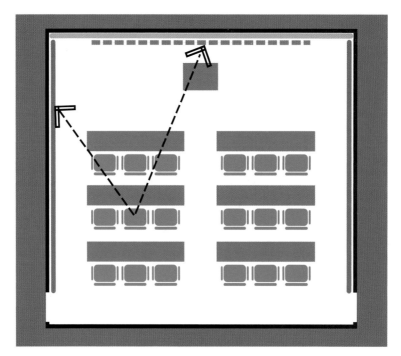

FIGURE 13.16   The most straightforward color enhancement for classroom function is a change in the color of the front wall.

secondary colors in full saturation in child-care centers, sometimes to the exclusion of other colors. Many contemporary educators and designers warn that this solution is overused. For example, Anita Rui Olds, who writes about the design of child-care facilities, points out that children do have difficulty concentrating on one thing when they are in the presence of visually demanding colors (*Child Care Design Guide,* page 228). Although they prefer the stimulation of contrasting hues, continuous exposure to strong contrasts such as a triad of primaries can be draining to children. Hyperactivity and exhaustion can result from exposure to too much coloration. As children approach the point of feeling inundated, their senses may shut down—the opposite response to what is needed for educational purposes. Olds's recommendations include contrast of hue and full-saturation color, but in combinations that facilitate education through an appropriate level of stimulation.

Appropriate Stimulation

The bright colors found in children's toys may be effective at grabbing and holding a child's atten-

tion, but they do not translate well as wall and furniture colors for an educational center. In a private residence, strong coloration is often useful in a child's bedroom or play area, but the situation is different in educational settings because several children must be accommodated at once. Colors that support children individually are stressful when used collectively in large proportions. To be clear, Olds does recommend less than full saturation of both warm and cool colors in child-care facilities for balance. To accommodate the young group's need for access to full-spectrum color without overstimulation, **balanced harmonies are recommended.** Since the triad of primaries is the strongest of harmonic combinations, this is not recommended in full saturation. A hexad of primaries and secondaries in full saturation is almost as forceful. An alternative is a hexad of six tertiaries or a tetrad with unique colors of hue to offer a balanced range of hues with more manageable intensity.

In addition, colors of reduced saturation are needed to give reasonable relief to strong colors of hue. In the example shown in Chapter 4, Figure 4.16, a hexad is combined with white, gray, and black to give some relief in a busy area. If a single color is intended to dominate, it can be softened through reduced saturation and the presence of its complement or its split complements. This approach allows children access to the richness they desire without the potential of overmotivation. The results are often more conducive to the needs of adult educators.

Loris Malaguzzi, who does research in this area, speaks to the complexity of color use in contemporary child-care facilities (*Children, Spaces, Relations: Metaproject for an Environment for Young Children*). Malaguzzi stresses the **inclusion of warm and cool colors in child-care applications.** Both Malaguzzi and Olds recommend the use of **neutral color as a backdrop in child-care centers** to reduce the difficulty that children have concentrating when surrounded by a bright environment. The idea is to let the children's artwork, toys, clothing, and other educational objects hold the strongest (most saturated) colors so they appear more important than the walls of the space itself. By limiting accents to key places, the space has more order, and color becomes a device for accentuating educational purpose. While the exclusive use of highly saturated colors can increase anxiety, their controlled presence in a space that offers some visual relief ensures visual balance. Elimination of strong color is not the solution—children need, and desire, the intensity of full-color stimuli. What's preferred is an environment that has some structure and offers a base in which colored objects can function.

Specific Hues

One concern in educational facilities is to reduce students' movement in the classroom to minimize distraction to each other. Color does impact human movement and thus can physiologically influence students. Pink is sometimes considered when addressing the special needs of teenagers in the classroom or principal's office. There are many documented cases where children or adults who were acting out ceased their disruptive behavior when moved into a pink room. (See Jain Malkin, *Hospital Interior Architecture,* page 56, or Jill Morton, *Color Voodoo,* page 3, for studies of psychological effects.) As we've noted, the effect serves the purpose only when used as a temporary solution. If used in the daily classroom, pink is not likely to make a group of students consistently passive.

Reduced surface saturation and cooler undertones are the recommended choice for sleep areas in schools for children under 6 years of age, just as high-chroma colors are suggested for activity areas. As children age, the particular tone, tint, shade, or hue mixture determines acceptance of a color for each specific age group. Lilac is seen as a very different color than purple, pink different from red. As children age, these distinctions become more discriminating. Teenagers in particular are susceptible to peer pressure in many areas, color being first among them. In general, older children prefer less saturated color, such as is shown in the example in Figure 13.14.

Texture

The visceral nature of a child's relationship with the environment suggests that we not limit color variation to the use of flat surface hue. Chromatic variation ideally includes solid-surface color (as in paint and fabric), translucent color (as in films, glass, and acrylic), and variable color (found in more organic materials like wood, gems, stone, or metals). Experts make a case for textural variation in child-care facilities as an extension of the connection children learn to make between color and form. When colors have varying tactile quality, they add to sensory knowledge and encourage greater exploration by the child. Greater sensation in the early years translates to more learning on a level that the developing child welcomes.

Teaching Tools

Since young children receive signals of color more intuitively than those of form, color is often incorporated as an educational tool. Seasonal displays, ceiling banners, or colored squares of flooring material are great devices to signal a shift in focus or the introduction of a new idea. Ro Logrippo suggests using colored squares organized like a calendar to introduce the spectrum itself. Other instructors use color to identify storage methodology and encourage cleanup. The idea is to assign one color each to specific functions—for example, red is the drawer for the red blocks, green is the drawer for the green-framed wooden puzzles. What is not suggested is assigning colors to individual children. This sets up a hierarchy of personal items, and since some colors are preferred, one child will get the preferred locker while another is assigned the so-called bad one. An alternative is to use stickers or other forms of the child's artwork to personalize storage containers.

Training and Meeting Rooms

Conference facilities are in many ways corporate classrooms for adults. They're frequently surrounded by other functions—informal gathering, refreshment service, or display. In larger conference facilities, color is often the device used to distinguish rooms from one another, much like hotel meeting rooms. Within the training and meeting rooms, some educators recommend neutral colors with bright accents; however, this is not the only solution possible. Monochromatic schemes with a change of value and contrasts of hue offer equally effective alternatives, as do schemes of medium saturation with temperature contrast. The goals are the same as for any other educational classroom—the sharing of information and stimulation of learning processes. As a learning environment, the rules of thumb for conference and meeting rooms are similar to classroom settings, with a few additions.

- **Simplify** the color combination to articulate the form and hierarchy of the room without unnecessary distraction.
- **Integrate** color consistently with the architecture by coloring each plane or change in form consistently from edge to edge.
- **Offer relief** for the eye from concentrated use by varying the room's sidewall color from the front wall color.
- Provide **training tables** that are light to medium in value, with reduced saturation to prevent afterimages when users shift their view from the table to the front of the room and back.
- Position any highly saturated **accent colors in more remote areas.** For example, use them in the refreshment area or at an entrance in the back of the room to reduce distraction during presentations.

Audiovisual Issues

Generally, the use of audiovisual tools in presentation complicates color selection in one respect only. That is, the positioning of extremely light surfaces, which reflect a significant amount of light, can be managed to minimize the reflection on any rear-screen projection or video monitor surface. When the shape of a wall plane, a ceiling soffit, or other feature registers in the visual screen, it's distracting to the presentation. The most common way to reduce this is to use a medium-value color on the side and rear walls or to reduce the light level in the room through dimmers. In addition, the face of the screen must be flat and positioned well below the ceiling plane or tilted down slightly away from the ceiling. In rooms where this is difficult to control, a nonwhite ceiling plane can be used.

As **videoconferencing** becomes more readily available in training and meeting spaces, the impact of color video imaging becomes more apparent. This situation takes a little more effort to resolve properly. Let's assume that several people are gathered around a table, with one camera facing them. Issues of color selection revolve around the desire to make their faces clear by distinguishing them from the wall behind while rendering the skin tones in a pleasing manner. These are the steps illustrated in Figure 13.17.

- Most human skin tones have a yellow or pink (light red) undertone. The **wall behind the participants** is best if cool in color—anything in the green to blue range, such as turquoise or aqua—since it will complement most people's skin. When seen on the receiving end of the video image, faces will stand out more clearly from the background.
- **Warm light** that reaches faces renders skin tones best, including any reflected light from ceiling surfaces. This means that both the light source and the surface from which indirect light is reflected need a warm color.
- **Light fixtures** should also be positioned to be diffuse or to light from across the table. If they are positioned directly above the users' heads, long shadows will occur on their faces, which will be exaggerated in the video image.
- Videotaping requires a significantly higher light level over conventional meeting space—up to about 150 footcandles compared to 60 footcandles. This implies a lighter value on **major surfaces** in the room to reflect as much light as possible.
- Large-scale **patterning** is not recommended in a room where videoconferencing will occur.

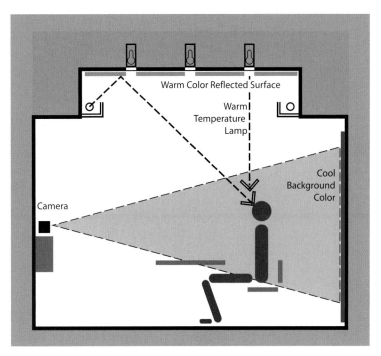

Warm Color Reflected Surface

Warm
Temperature
Lamp

Cool
Background
Color

Camera

FIGURE 13.17 This diagram illustrates one way color and lighting can accommodate videoconferencing effectively.

Small-scale patterns may read cleanly on tape, or register as a halftone, but large patterns can be distracting in the video image.

■ CONCLUSIONS

If we consider the common thread of the use groups covered in this chapter, we realize that successful color application can be reduced to some very simple guidelines. The design of retail, restaurant, hotel, religious, and educational facilities is on some level an effort to manage people in a public setting through visual cues in the space. To use color to its advantage in these commercial projects, the following steps are applied.

- **Establish the image** by identifying the target audience and setting up an expectation. When the facility is large, consider color as an organizing or orienting device.
- **Communicate the form** of the space to aid in overall orientation, to facilitate spatial use, and to enhance personal experience.

- **Support the function.** That means using color to sell the product, to enhance consumption, to increase comfort, to inspire revelations, or to augment learning.
- When appropriate, **use color to influence the character** of the space in terms of behavior, such as the length of stay or the volume of conversation. When possible, use color and lighting to enhance the appearance of key elements, such as food, products, people, or presentation material.
- Consider the implication of **continuous use** and select coloration that supports appropriate levels of maintenance.

Commercial projects in general offer unique color opportunities by virtue of their scale and exposure. It's very rare that hundreds of people will experience a well-done residential space, but such exposure is quite common in commercial applications. The challenge is to find solutions that effectively reach as many of those people as possible.

Through a discussion of each application in detail, we're able to see their common elements.

We also have the benefit of seeing successful ways in which color has been used—even exploited—to get people to respond as intended by designers and their clients. In the next chapter, another group of commercial applications is explored for successful color use. In these cases, the issue is not how we facilitate leisure pursuit for the users, but rather how we help them be productive. As with the areas previously discussed, the design process remains constant. What changes is the intended use of the space, which by necessity changes the appropriate colors and forms. In these cases, we work toward improvement in our quality of life as it is measured in workplace performance and improved health.

Commercial Applications

Commercial applications are those that support business functions. They include many of the project types already discussed such as hospitality, retail, educational, and elder-care facilities. In addition, commercial projects include corporate office space, industrial processing and manufacturing facilities, research laboratories, and medical treatment centers. Each area has its own set of design criteria, and each project involves its own decision-making process. While some of these processes are fairly straightforward, others involve greater participation from individuals with technical experience, and many make use of extensive committees.

Ultimately, design decisions are driven by business needs. By the end of the twentieth century, two such motivators had measurable impact on designed space. They were the competition for customers' attention and the emphasis on productivity. Increased use of positive imagery is evident at educational campuses, elder-care centers, and medical facilities as these organizations learn to compete for business in the way that retailers and hoteliers always have. More recent movements have put corporate entities in the position of learning to capitalize on spatial attributes as they vie for their customers' attention. Together with increased competition comes smaller margins and tighter control on the bottom line. Since worker reliability is a key part of that control, particularly in corporate, industrial, and medical settings, design solutions that support consistent worker participation are also prized.

Color applications with the most immediate impact on our health and well-being are those found in the workplace. We recognize the value of color as a tool to enhance work space from a psychological standpoint. In addition, we are aware of conditions that benefit worker performance, just as we acknowledge conditions that are detrimental to worker productivity. The goal is to use color as an environmental design tool to support physical and mental occupations to the best of our ability. The cumulative effect of these decisions can improve not only vocational performance, but also the individual well-being of office, manufacturing, and health care workers. The value of even a small positive impact in this regard is measurable and cumulative, particularly in the discipline of health care. In recognition of the impact color selection can have on the quality of workers' lives, this final chapter is dedicated to effective color use in the places that impact our health and well-being the most—our offices, factories, laboratories, and medical centers.

CORPORATE

In the corporate sector, competition for outstanding employees is considerable. During periods of reduced unemployment, employers must be more proactive about employee work environments. According to a recent American Society of Interior

Design (ASID) survey taken of people looking for work, 22 percent of respondents listed the quality of the physical environment as a key component in deciding whether to take a job, compared to 11 percent who listed location. Physical space tied as the second selection criterion, with the primary criterion understandably being salary. (This information was presented at the DesignBoston conference, November 15, 2000.) If those seeking employment have become less concerned about location and more focused on the quality of the space in which they work, then design contributions have a measurable benefit to business. Positive coloration adds relatively little to new construction costs. It's simply a matter of sound choice.

Interior work space is, of course, a human-made environment. As such, it needs a sound degree of stimulation and variation in order to avoid desensitizing its inhabitants. In nature we are accustomed to changes in color according to value, temperature, and saturation. We also expect to see patterning, shadows, and a variety of other conditions that add to the complexity of outdoor space. Ideally color variation serves as a reasonable substitute for nature, offering some outward stimulation, a level of complexity, and visible variation within the built environment. The more effective our solutions, the easier it is for users to continue working within them for long periods of time.

▶ Making an Impression

In a perfect world, the office environment supports two simultaneous functions: constructive interaction of the occupants and focused concentration by each individual. These would appear as to be contradictory if the functions didn't frequently occur in separate areas. Color decisions are often organized according to the distinctions between these two types of space. Interactive space involves company identification and image setting, as well as enhancement of desired group behavior. Areas of concentration are supported by sensitivity to particular tasks and protection of proper vision. Successful color assignments in the ideal office environment do both things. They encourage interaction and support individual taskwork.

Let's start with the interactive areas. Our notions about a corporation are often formed on arrival at the company's building or reception area. Since color registers in the mind's eye before all else, it's the key design element to informing the visitor and creating that first impression. The message delivered by color may be overt or subtle, but it almost always establishes some sense of what the company represents. The most successful concepts are those tied to the corporate image rather than to the products provided or the services currently offered. Products and service will change over time, often within the life of the office installation. The long-term values of the company are less flexible, offering the best representation of company image. Consider the example in Figure 14.1, a consulting firm whose service is to help companies generate business over the Internet. Their space tells a positive, progressive story through strong use of geometric form and very contemporary colors. Notice how the shape of the ceiling recesses and the use of reflected color expand the scale of the luminaries and add significant warmth to the space.

Taste and Trends

Taste comes in many forms and is subject to local influence. When we talk about taste with company representatives, linguistics can get in the way. People often use the same words to describe very different impressions, as one person's boldness is another's subtlety. The process of unraveling long-term corporate values leads to more timeless designs for companies whose product is devoid of fashion trend. The colors selected for the law firm space shown in Figure 14.2 reflect the client's desire to incorporate greater color saturation. However, the architectural colors are limited to a fairly neutral palette compared to those found in many technology company headquarters. This solution is more likely to withstand the test of time, communicating an appropriate image for the type of business it supports, yet distinguishing the company from its competitors.

In some cases, there's good reason to associate a company with trendy colors, such as a public relations agency, a cosmetic manufacturer, or a fashion consultant. Color palettes tied to current trends fall out of fashion quickly. Today's latest trend will look dated more hastily than a color combination that bridges several phases of popular color. To

FIGURE 14.1 The visual expression of this company through its office space suggests a group of forward-thinking professionals. *(NerveWire—Bergmeyer Associates, Inc., architect. Photo © Lucy Chen.)*

address images for more trend-based companies, the most fashionable colors are often located on easy-to-replace surfaces, such as painted walls or mobile furniture. More permanent surfaces, such as a stone floor or built-in woodwork, can be assigned colors in the palette that are less iconic and draw attention to the trend colors by contrast.

Behavioral Influence

Since people readily respond to their environment, color can be used to inspire employees or impress visitors. It can move the occupants toward orderliness or chaos simply by imposing an impression of one or the other through consistency of the environmental design. An apparently disorganized environment will breed chaotic behavior or thought; but a consistent overall color tone with systematic placement of color accent will enable the visitor to identify cues that aid in way finding and signal key locations for support functions. In the main reception area shown in Figure 14.3, designers used a change in color and materials to express a strong visual image for this professional-services firm. The bold, complex combination suggests the myriad activities that converge in the focal space shown. As we walk through the office beyond, much smaller references to these colors and materials confirm that we're still in the same space, but without the same level of complexity.

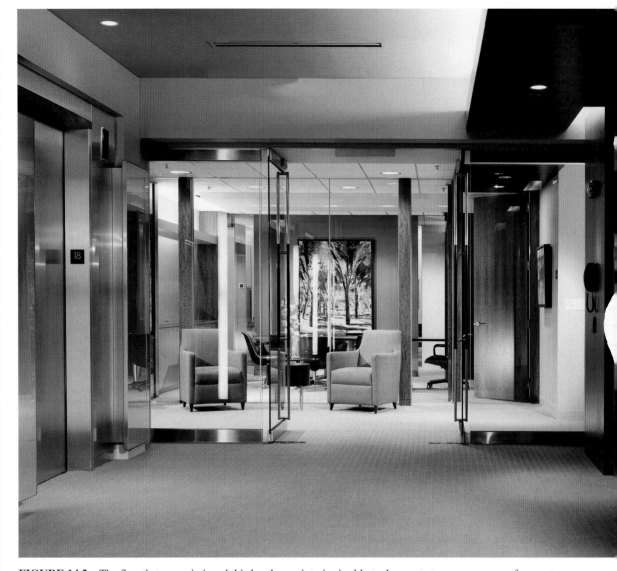

FIGURE 14.2   The firm that commissioned this handsome interior is able to demonstrate an awareness of current trends without being driven by them. Designers addressed the company's need to express itself in more contemporary color while maintaining an image appropriate to legal consulting. *(Design by CBT/Childs Bertman Tseckares Inc. Photo: © Edward Jacoby.)*

Even the level of interaction desired for employees will be influenced by the selection of spatial color. Just as people speak more loudly in an acoustically louder space, the more visually stimulating the space, the more interactive the users are likely to become. Spaces designated for think-tank or war-room functions often have more color contrasts than areas of concentration. Lunchrooms are a popular place for the most stimulating coloration in the office, as shown in Figure 14.4. The eating area

shown here is contained in the same law office as the reception area shown in Figure 14.2. Colors placed physically between the two spaces are adjusted to make a transition within the office suite.

▶ Supporting Taskwork

Too much color contrast is stressful to an office worker. So is too little. When color is overly complex, it is just as disruptive as noise or crowded physical conditions. The eye becomes fatigued from too much adjusting to accommodate changes in their various forms. In the absence of color variation, the eye has limited visual stimulation. This causes an equally adverse reaction. When faced with white, the pupils contract to limit the amount of light reflected through the lens. As darker colors come into view, the pupil stretches to a more open position to let light in. Since functioning in the eye is a muscular process, the eyes get tired when they work too hard, and fatigue results in headaches or heaviness around the eyes. Without color variation to cause flexing in the eye, sensory deprivation sets in and the eye loses its ability to function properly due to prolonged fixation. The symptom of this is irritability. Both conditions are adverse to productivity. **The ideal is an organized design with some variation and a sense of hierarchy so that areas of focus are clear, but the eye also has a place to rest.** Consider it good visual ergonomics, just as adjustable chairs and keyboards are used to protect other muscles in the body.

White seems to be the most overused color in rooms that house office-bound workers. There are several reasons for this. Neutral colors are often chosen when occupants cannot agree on choices of hue, so no one is offended. There also remains a lingering presumption that brighter space is more desirable from a task standpoint because it reflects more light. Nothing is lighter in value and more light-reflective than the color white. The disappointing aspects of an all-white environment are monotony, the obvious existence of dirt, discoloration, and exaggerated shadows, and ongoing opportunities for glare. All-white environments are very rare in nature.

The remedy is to include a bright color placed at some distance from the corporate worker. If it's

FIGURE 14.3 Color in this corporate office suggests a confident group of professionals through a complex use of materials with intrinsic color and the singular red-orange background. *(Interior design by GHK. Photo: Peter Paige.)*

FIGURE 14.4   The bright coloration evident in the lunch area cues employees that open conversation is appropriate in this area. *(Design by CBT/Childs Bertman Tseckares Inc. Photo: © Edward Jacoby.)*

positioned at a 90-degree angle relative to the user's computer monitor, by turning the head 90 degrees the user can allow the eye to focus at the distant plane for a moment, and then resume concentration. When concentration is resumed in this circumstance, the relaxed cones are no longer stressed and the eye muscles return more readily to the closer focal point. **By providing a mix of colors within the area of concentration, visual relief is offered to the employee.** Variations in hues and saturation levels are more consistent with the natural environment and offer the physical stimulation needed for positive physiological response. To ensure that a color combination will be nondisruptive, the colors can be selected in a balanced harmony, with the most intense selections placed out of the immediate line of sight to the object of concentration.

Value Contrast

The rule of thumb for optimum value range within office task areas is a ratio of 3 to 1, meaning that the darkest value should be no more than 3 times the value of the lightest color. For the purpose of evaluating color ratios, let's assume that lighting distribution is uniform and that all colors can be measured according to their *light reflectance value* (LRV), the amount of light reflected back into the space from a finished surface, which for practical purposes is usually between 5 percent (black) and 90 percent (white) for interior surfaces. Say a medium blue of about 40 percent LRV is used with a pale yellow at 80 percent LRV. The ratio of the darkest to lightest would be 80:40, or 2:1. (To evaluate the LRV of organic finishes, such as wood or stone, select a paint color that closely approximates the color.) The following additional steps are recommended to eliminate the conditions that cause eyestrain, and consequently headaches, nausea, and the symptoms of tension.

- Where large amounts of direct **daylight** will enter the space, such as east-facing windows, use a light wall color to reflect it further into the space while at the same time reducing strong value contrast. This sets the baseline for other values in that area.
- Limit contrasts immediately in the line of sight in the position of concentrated work. For

example, if **workstations** are enclosed with panels higher than 45 inches and white documents will be posted on them, limit the panel's color selection to at least 75 percent light reflectance. (See Figure 14.5.)

- Select a **work-surface** color within a reasonable range of value to the material most often viewed on it. Black desktops are effective at establishing image in a showroom display, but they're dangerous to the eye in an office situation. Moderately patterned surfaces are recommended, since they will diffuse light and reduce the possibility of glare. The ideal light reflectance for horizontal work surfaces in a nonpaperless society is considered to be 30 percent to 50 percent.
- Some concentrated tasks are tiring to the eyes because of voluntary **eye movement.** When a computer user must shift his or her vision repeatedly between a vertical screen and horizontal drawing or report, the eye muscles will be strained. (Vertical positioning of the document eliminates this concern.) The condition is compounded if the color on the monitor contrasts highly with the printed media. By adjusting the color of one or the other (successive) contrast will be reduced.

Hue Contrasts

For individuals who must work indoors without direct daylight for the best part of the day, there is a greater need for full-spectrum color and light. Colors of hue, even if subtle, are more desirable than gray or other truly neutral color to ensure moderate stimulation and to establish order in a space. In these cases, **contrasts of hue are preferred, with emphasis on balanced harmonies.** Few would dispute the notion that better working conditions lead to an increase in productivity. The less energy lost by an office worker adjusting to compensate for a distracting environment, the more efficient the worker may become. Spectral balance can be expressed in the pursuit of virtually any aesthetic color solution, although cool hues are considered by some experts to be preferable for tasks of intense concentration.

The presence of strong colors within the line of sight causes an involuntary reaction in the eye as pupils adjust and cones are stressed or relieved. The

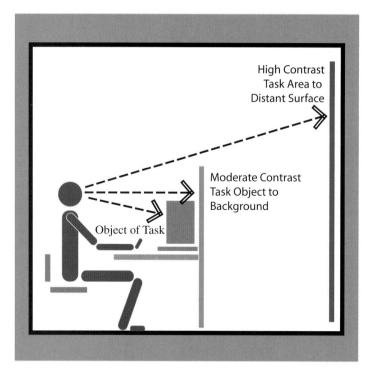

FIGURE 14.5   This diagram shows the relationship between the object of the task, the immediate background, and a distant background. As long as the distant background is not within the user's immediate line of sight, it will offer relief when he or she looks up.

constant adjustments will tire normal eyes. This means that the placement of very bright color (high value, high saturation) immediately within the worker's line of sight would be distracting to the eye. As it shifts rapidly from the object of concentration to the background, the pupil is forced to adjust constantly. The best location for a **strong contrast** is in a different plane than the task view, or above workers so that they must either look up or stand. Figure 14.6 shows an excellent example of this approach. In order to concentrate on printed documentation, the majority of which involves white paper, office occupants need **moderate contrast** within their immediate line of sight. Close work involves prolonged convergence, which also causes eyestrain without the help of environmental color. For ongoing relief within the line of sight for concentrated tasks, muted variations of one color or a combination of neutrals work well. The following guidelines for hue contrasts (hue, simultaneous, temperature, etc.) are offered.

- Avoid the use of a single color in any office scheme by incorporating a complement, a pair of split complements, or some other color variation to offer **visual relief.**

- Provide stronger colors of hue and a greater range of contrasts in areas intended for interaction so that they can offer **relief** from concentrated tasks. This is known as *optical relaxation.* By doing so, the occasional movement can provide much needed relief to eye muscles.

- Color **temperature** may be used to influence use of space. Attention will be drawn outward to the environment to a greater degree if the overall tone of the space is warm and the surface values are high (light). Comparatively speaking, most individuals focus inward in a space with lower brightness levels and cooler surface coloration.

- During concentrated tasks, high contrasts within the user's peripheral vision are exaggerated. The closer the edges of a worker's enclosure, the stronger their impact. This means that end caps and trim pieces of **workstation componentry** with little contrast to the surfaces are less distracting to worker performance.

- Use caution when **patterns** occur in areas of concentration. A checkerboard fabric pattern or a busy wallpaper pattern will read through paper tacked to its surface. Either can cause vibration when positioned behind a computer monitor. Similarly a work surface with large, irregular patterning may be distracting to one's sense of equilibrium.

- Locate **patterning** or some color contrast in a position appropriate for occasional distance viewing from the individual work space. If the user can look away and adjust the eyes without leaving the work space, he or she will do so more frequently. Distant viewing is about 15 to 20 feet away from the user to provide the needed relaxation.

Lighting

There seems to be more and more evidence supporting the benefits of full-spectrum color and light in our daily lives. When humans spend significant amounts of time in direct daylight, we are exposed to full-spectrum color through the benefit of sunlight. Without access to this benefit, full-spectrum color can be realized only by selection of color within the synthetic environment. This is a special challenge when designing space in which people work continuously without access to daylight. Ideally, lighting selected for work space would have the highest CRI rating possible within budgetary constraints.

It is difficult, if not impossible, to address functional issues of color without at least considering the impact of lighting and brightness levels in the context of color selection. Conditions of visual ergonomics are set as much by brightness levels established through lighting as by surface color.

FIGURE 14.6 In this example, designers made use of beneficial contrasts such as greater hues above eye level, lighter values at task surfaces, and patterning at the floor. Office workers have the benefit of limited visual distraction coupled with beneficial visual relief without leaving their workstations. *(Design by ADD Inc. Photo: © Lucy Chen.)*

Commercial Applications

The point is to integrate these two means in a way that provides appropriate stimulation and interest. Some basic steps taken in the development of the lighting will ensure positive perception of the proposed color scheme and offer the user protection from eyestrain.

- Specify full-spectrum light to the degree possible. This means choosing lamps with the highest **CRI rating** available for conditions of the space.
- Where lighting will be reflected from large surfaces, such as indirect pendants or wall-mounted fixtures, keep the color of the surfaces in the 80 to 90 percent **range of reflectance.** (Other wall surfaces can comfortably be in the 40 to 60 percent range.)
- **Eliminate glare** by sufficiently shielding light sources and windows (shades), by limiting the number of specular (highly reflective) surfaces, by controlling the direction of artificial light (as with parabolic lights), and by carefully positioning light sources relative to the surfaces upon which they will reflect. This last condition suggests that in task areas where a significant light level is needed, the user will want to adjust the primary light source so that its position does not cause glare or other reflection into the eyes.
- Visibility of characters on a monitor is greatly reduced by **too much illumination.** To prevent against this condition, maintain light levels of 15 to 35 footcandles for tasks that do not involve paperwork, and 35 to 50 footcandles for tasks involving a transfer of data from paper to monitor.
- Limit the use of semigloss or **gloss paints** on wall surfaces that will reflect light.
- In **computer workrooms,** consider reducing the light reflectance of surfaces. For example, the ceiling could offer a 60 percent level of reflectance, the walls 40 percent, and the floor 20 percent. This would still be in the 3 to 1 ratio of lightness levels, but the overall result is a reduction in reflected light. Note in this case the equipment is a key component to the tasks at hand and may need to be in a color that does not contrast significantly with the wall beyond.

■ INDUSTRIAL

Employees who spend their productive time supporting manufacturing and utility functions deserve as much visual clarity as possible to aid in legibility and manual dexterity. Color has become the most effective means to this end. It's been identified as a critical component of safe industrial facilities since World War II. At that time, colorist Faber Birren proposed selective color use to identify life safety features in the workplace. His methods employed colors of high hue contrast to separate elements within complex architectural structures and lesser contrasts to support tasks that are mechanically performed. In more recent years, color consultant and environmentalist Frank Mahnke has provided environmental color expertise, adding to the collective wisdom concerning safety in the workplace.

▶ Concepts

Industry is about creating something of value through systematic employment of human labor. Color can be used to articulate those systems and to improve on the large size and complex form of industrial facilities. Appropriate color use in and around large-scale industrial architecture suggests three potential benefits: communication of the type of work being performed, identification of the business image, and improvement in morale of the people associated with the facility. When unusual, bright colors are applied to equipment, piping, ducts and shafts, and other elements, industrial architecture becomes unique and explainable (see Figure 14.7). The facility breaks away from the stereotypical gray of yesteryears, which served simply to hide dust and dirt by mimicking them in appearance.

Sometimes spectral assignments are illustrative. An example would be a gradual shift of surrounding color as the flow of a material progresses from a raw state to a finished product. They can also be used to make comparisons, such as to distinguish between areas of key activity and elements of a supporting nature. Color has been used to express the mechanical systems necessary for the industrial activity. Smoke exhaust may be housed in one color, piping for water in another, passages, stairways, and elevators used by people in yet another. If water is being processed, the piping

FIGURE 14.7 Color selection can be used to express the activity contained within piping, ducts, or containers, as suggested in this contemporary industrial facility. *(Architect/engineer: Symmes Maini & McKee Associates. Photo: © Christopher Barnes.com.)*

containing processed water can be colored in one temperature before processing and in another after treatment. For a manufacturing plant, contrasting color can draw attention to anything that has moving parts, serving as a warning to stand back. Where the manufacturing process generates dust, this is most effective if the colors on key components are strong enough to be distinguishable through the dust.

▶ Practical Applications

The issues of lighting and color in task areas of an industrial setting are similar to those in task areas of business. Employee safety and efficiency are best protected by the prevention of visual eye fatigue. This means limiting glare while maintaining a light level appropriate to the task. It also means removing extreme conditions of value contrast from within the line of sight in the immediate task area. And it means placing alternatively colored surfaces at a distance to encourage relaxation by offering relief from pro-

longed fixation of the eye on close objects. The rule of thumb to keep in mind is that each color of material being processed and each piece of equipment used will be seen in the context of the surrounding colors. That said, here are a few recommendations about color placement.

- In areas where there are several **large-scale machines,** their collective color will have the impact of a wall of color. In this case, less saturated tones work best, particularly those that are light in value if prolonged taskwork will occur nearby.
- Contrast is needed between the materials being assembled and the **equipment or workbench** in use. A moderate value contrast or a temperature contrast will suffice. (See Figure 14.8.)
- Contrast is also needed between the equipment and its **background** and between the object of focus and its background. If the equipment is available only in gray, the wall beyond might be in a moderate color of hue in a slightly

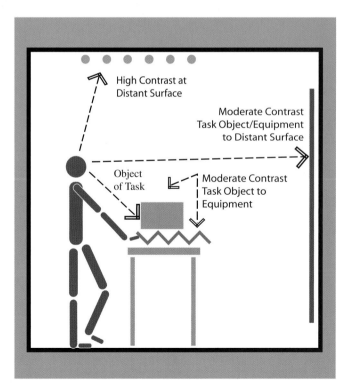

FIGURE 14.8 In manufacturing and processing task areas, moderate contrasts within the immediate area ease vision, while higher contrasts at a distance offer relief.

FIGURE 14.9   Color assignments in this large-scale clean room help to organize the space, reduce apparent scale, and identify functional aspects below the floor level. *(Architect/engineer: Symmes Maini & McKee Associates. Photo: John Yereance.)*

lighter or darker tone so that its edges register easily at the periphery. (See Figure 14.8.)

- In areas where precision work is performed, **patterning** should also be limited; otherwise, the complex forms can make concentrated focus more difficult. Conversely, in areas where more monotonous assembly procedures are performed, color patterns can offer a welcome source of visual interest.

If the work area is in an open space, a shield can be set up just beyond the task area to limit view and provide a place to control contrasts with the material at hand. Dull or matte surface textures are best to avoid glare from reflected light. In factories where **dye work** is handled, white backgrounds should be avoided. The reason is that workers will see afterimages of the objects they handle projected against a white wall, and in the extreme, frequent afterimaging can cause nausea.

Where **large-scale equipment** or moving machinery is used, the value of the equipment color shouldn't contrast in an extreme way with the wall behind it; otherwise, contrast fatigue may result. While the worker is focused on a particular mission, the eyes will adjust to a contrasting object or surface within peripheral view. This is as distracting as peripheral sound or movement, particularly if the background is bright.

Other positive approaches include reserving bright colors for **levers** or **buttons** to attract the eye to key components of machinery and using color to key workers to **functional building elements**. In the example in Figure 14.9, color is organized on the floor tile to communicate what happens below the floor level of a clean room and to give order to a large environment. When working with large equipment, darker colors are recommended on the **base** or **platform** compared to the color of equipment it supports. Otherwise, the equipment will risk appearing too heavy for its support, psychologically speaking.

Workplace Synesthesia

The condition of synesthesia lends itself to some key concerns in industrial applications. Workers who are subjected to continuous loud noise, who are exposed to extreme temperature, or who function in the presence of distinct odors can find relief through environmental color. As discussed in Chapter 6, "Color Response," humans have a physiological response to colors that is involuntary. Because of these strong connections, color choice can improve the individual's work conditions through selections that counteract response to the undesirable circumstance. The most obvious model is **temperature.** If a work environment is maintained at a low temperature, warm wall colors such as red or orange can be used to counteract its effect to a small degree; the impact of a warm environment can be reduced slightly by the dominance of blue, blue-green, green, or white. **Humidity** is another area of strong color association. Yellow, yellow-brown, tan, and beige have a strong association with dryness; cool colors, such as blue, green, and hues in between suggest wetness or dampness. The implication is that dry conditions can be compensated for by green-blue coloration and damp spaces by yellows from clear to neutral.

Scents are another condition of **synesthesia.** Manufacturers who work with fragrances recognize the strong association some colors have with certain smells, as do some managers of aromatic industrial facilities. For example, the presence of red is known to alter our ability to recognize perfume. Like concepts of temperature and humidity, consistencies in synesthetic associations have been documented for some time. (See, for example, *Color Light Sight Sense: An Elementary Theory of Color in Pictures* by Moritz Zwimpfer, section 427.) Reds and pinks, apricot, and rich medium-brown reinforce sweet sensations; yellow, green-yellow, and warm green increase the effect of sour taste or smell. In their text *Color and Light* (page 109), Mahnke and Mahnke go one step further and suggest that the presence of specific colors cannot only enhance the effect of a particular smell, but they can decrease the effect of an unpleasant odor. If color is an effective counterbalance for undesirable aromas in the workplace, then environmental color offers us a tool for effective olfactory management. For example, in an environment filled with a sour smell, the presence of a reddish-purple color is believed to decrease its impact. In a chocolate factory, the dominant presence of green, blue-green, green-blue, or blue can counterbalance the intensity of the sweet smell. Light blue is the color of choice to decrease a musky smell, while greenish-brown is likely to enhance musk.

The Mahnkes also offer synesthetic solutions to workplaces consumed by **sound.** In spaces consumed by high-pitched sound, an olive-green environment is believed to effectively reduce the disruption from a psychological standpoint, while yellow is likely to enhance it. For muffled sound, light colors are recommended, as dark colors will support the acoustic sensation. Obviously, such choices do not obliterate physical conditions. The sound of machinery, the smell of melting wax, and the chill of cold storage do not disappear because of effective color selection. What we can do is evaluate colors for their associative impact on undesirable work conditions and use that insight to improve the work environment.

Safety Standards

Color is often used to flag life safety features in industrial space. Faber Birren, in association with DuPont, developed a system of bright colors that could attract attention immediately for quick recognition. The purpose was to set up uniform color standards in industry to reduce the risk of accidents. Each functional device was assigned a particular color. Recommendations initiated by Birren were subsequently adopted by the American National Standards Institute (ANSI) as Safety Color Standards. While not all of Birren's proposed standards are used by the general public, those that are include red for fire-protection devices, orange for some electrical hazards, and yellow for platform edges. In addition, major facilities have developed some of their own standards to accommodate specific production conditions and preferential work flow. Unfortunately, although such standards may be well recognized at each facility by workers within the same company, they may not be as obvious to firefighters, police, or local tradespeople.

The Commission Internationale de l'Eclairage (CIE), which translates as the International Commission on Illumination, is working toward an international standard for industrial safety colors. In 1964, using the science of colorimetry, CIE established a set of color standards that can be calculated within tight spectral limitations. Through this system, which applies to both additive and subtractive color measurement, standards for life safety and other colors can be articulated with universal consistency. In time, our societies may well reach consensus on color standards for life safety, just as other building codes have evolved to be more universal. Whether established corporately or governmentally, the key to success of any life safety color standards lies in their clarity within the environment. This means that colors for architectural elements, equipment, and large-scale production tools need to be adjusted for value, saturation, and hue character to distinguish them from designated life safety colors.

▶ Research Labs

There are some spaces in which researchers and technicians must concentrate on visual samples and instrumental measurement, and color can be critical to functional observation. Needless to say, the ideal environment for these lab spaces involves lighting with the highest CRI possible to minimize reduction in color clarity for the material being observed. Beyond this, functional color has more to do with the particulars of the labs themselves, be they wet rooms, dry rooms, or dark rooms. Each material being examined demands different color conditions to enable its viewing. For instance, tissue culture labs have different color needs than robotic labs; blood labs function differently from DNA facilities.

Traditionally, labs have been colored in extremely light neutrals, such as tan, gray, or white, assuming that this enhances analytical work. While these colors are unlikely to interfere with concentration, when used exclusively they risk causing sensory deprivation to workers over long periods of time. For some time, blue was thought to be a more effective lab color because it is believed to augment meditative thought. However, recent observations suggest that the most effective coloration for labs, as with many work spaces, is to include a balanced spectrum of hues. Some tonal color of moderate satu-

ration will elicit a positive response without distraction, particularly if there is a moderate contrast with sample containers. As with other applications discussed in this chapter, stronger colors presented at a distance, or on less critical surfaces such as furnishings or doors, will offer visual relief without interfering with the work. The only caveat is that large planes of color within immediate view of the lab bench should not be highly saturated, since bright color in this case may reflect on materials being tested and analyzed, preventing accurate observation. In laboratories where color discrimination is critical, neutral gray walls are preferred. As with other work space, the goal here is to offer zones of focus and relief. Positioning is fundamental to making labs more humane without interfering with productivity. Here are a few recommendations.

- **Floor color** in this application is less effective when small patterns are used. Less small-scale patterning allows technicians to see small objects, especially bits of broken glass.
- In most labs, light to medium color at the **workbench top** is easier on the eyes than traditional black or charcoal because of the reduced contrast with paper and other materials.
- In large laboratory centers, color is needed for **way finding.** Color coding is used to identify departments, functional distinctions, or simply one's place within a building, such as the north wing. (An example of this is illustrated in Chapter 7, Figure 7.4.)

▪ HEALTH CARE

Medical facilities are among the most complex use groups. Due to the large scale of many medical complexes, design must offer cues to direct people and to define functionality—public zones, patient areas, technical labs, and controlled environments. It can also enhance a variety of experiences, serving those who provide medical care on the premises, employees who administer and maintain the facility, and infrequent visitors who are being treated or who know someone being treated. We realize how much the needs and expectations of such a user group must vary when we consider who it includes: doctors, nurses, medical practitioners, emergency personnel, lab technicians, facility administrators, financial staff, maintenance staff, food-service professionals, inpatients, outpatients, women in labor, intensive care patients, and the family members, friends, and loved ones of patients. To complicate matters further, these spaces must function 24 hours a day, seven days per week, unlike many commercial applications.

If these conflicting demands do not offer enough design challenge, consider the need for comforting and reassuring patients. The effect of a positive attitude in the healing process has been well documented by practitioners. Each patient looks for support through connections to the things that offer consolation. For some it's a sense of hominess; others find that the presence of nature grounds them so they can manage treatment. Designers of medical facilities and their clients have been challenged in recent years to provide that grounding, particularly in light of the competition between health care providers to attract us as consumers. The results demonstrate that these extra efforts are worthwhile, as feedback from patient satisfaction surveys indicates hospital staff and patients are positively impacted by design improvements (for evidence, refer to articles from the *Journal of Healthcare Design,* 2002). This suggests that insight from experienced members of the medical community can offer sound criteria for interior color.

▶ Color and Health

It's commonly believed that some behaviors of inhibition or repression result in medical afflictions. Some prolonged mental conflicts can lead to identifiable illnesses. High blood pressure, stomach ulcers or indigestion, asthma and colitis (inflammation of the colon) are the better-known conditions. Together, these demonstrate the strong physiological connection between mental and physical health. Comparatively speaking, some colors have demonstrated a greater impact on health and well-being due to involuntary human response. When selecting specific color for use in medical applications, it helps to separate what we know to be learned responses (those that result from trends and societal peer pressure) from physiological ones. The potential for negative physiological associations may suggest that some colors be modified slightly when

used in a treatment center so they don't compromise the health and well-being of the patient.

Perception

Experts in the field of design for health care concur that monotonous environments devoid of color variation can cause sensory deprivation. In order to sustain consistent physiological functionality, the brain needs exposure to a changing environment and some source of physical stimulation. A lack of such stimulation is essentially a detriment to the healing process. (For an assessment of the state of design in medical application, refer to Jain Malkin's text, *Hospital Interior Architecture.*) In addition, properly applied variable color will help users to orient themselves, particularly within the context of larger-scale environments. In years past, white was the color of choice for all visible surfaces to express a sense of cleanliness—a desirable trait at the time. As expectations have changed, the overuse of white has come to suggest a clinical appearance, which is undesirable in the current health care climate. Patients now look for a homelike environment, similar to what they seek in a hotel. This implies a greater use of balanced color, harmonic color combinations, and moderate value contrasts in areas of long-term and acute care. Higher value contrasts are less appropriate since they become tiring to the eyes more quickly. It also suggests consideration of the local community culture, since colors that represent patients' cultural values and local tradition will make them feel more at home.

Changes in the business approach to health care and the need in many areas to remain competitive have led a trend toward the design of environments that are more supportive and therapeutic. This often includes increased access to daylight and additional textural variation in materials. The combination of outdated color with any indication of wear suggests to patients a lack of attention, which is detrimental to a positive health care image. Consequently, color is used to accentuate the positive and ensure confidence by communicating the image of competency, expediency, and personal care. This means using more clear colors as opposed to muddy tones and choosing color that is reasonably up-to-date to send appropriate messages. For example, Figure 14.10 shows a hospital

FIGURE 14.10 This hospital cafeteria is an example of the positive, consumer-driven imagery being developed for today's medical facilities. *(Designed by TRO/The Ritchie Organization. Photo: © Edward Jacoby.)*

cafeteria that has the punch and sparkle of a café or retail space, using materials that tolerate continuous high maintenance.

Colors of Hue

While neutralized versions of any hue can add value to most types of medical space, in full saturation the inherent character of each hue has some bearing on its appropriate location. We've already noted that the presence of **red** in high-saturation levels will increase the heart rate and respiration rate, making it energizing to the viewer. This may suggest application in areas of physical therapy or at the ends of long circulation paths for patients who are encouraged do some form of motor activity as a part of recovery. Keep in mind that tints, tones, and shades of red, such as pink, rose, and maroon, have the effects of true red, allowing for more unique solutions. **Orange** is one of the color ranges frequently used in health care applications because of its tonic effect (*The Grid*, fall 1998). This includes peach, apricot, pumpkin, and spice tones, which are considered cheerful and emotionally positive, as well as flattering to most skin tones—a condition that, as we've noted elsewhere, makes patients feel better about themselves. The key is to take advantage of this condition in areas where it is beneficial to patients without being detrimental to the diagnostic process. Caregivers depend on accurate visual inspection of a patient's skin tone as a diagnostic. Artificially enhanced skin may be misleading and thus undermine treatment.

When used in small amounts as an accent color or in moderate saturation, **yellow** is a good stimulator. The sense of cheeriness normally associated with yellow can have value in many areas of a health care facility. However, in large amounts it is a risky color to use in some health care applications. While orange casts a positive glow onto the skin, yellow does just the opposite. Too much reflected yellow can make skin tone appear jaundiced. Yellow can also induce vomiting in a patient who is already nauseated from treatment. Beth Kuzbek, an experienced interior designer who is well versed on issues of health care, tells of a problem that surfaced in a radiation treatment center (Boston Design Symposium, IPC Design Institute). In this case, patients sat in a recently renovated recovery room that was rendered in cool tones,

such as blue, with a purple accent wall. Yellow had been carefully avoided. When caregivers noticed an increase in patient vomiting compared to prerenovation recoveries, carpet backings, adhesives, and paint surfaces were quickly analyzed for noxious fumes. None of these turned out to be offenders, which meant that some other condition was detracting from patient wellness. Kuzbek surmised that in the absence of any yellow within the space, patients were experiencing yellow afterimaging in their mind's eye from the purple wall—enough to have the same effect as facing a yellow wall. After the purple wall was repainted, the incidence of patient nausea was statistically reduced.

Cool colors are slightly less stimulating than their warm counterparts and may be beneficial in areas where visitors are prone to anxiety, such as emergency rooms or intensive care units. **Green** is exceptionally popular because it's considered emotionally calming, and some believe that it works as a sedative to the nervous system. Our societal association of green with nature may also have a secondary benefit for some patients. As the complement of red, the color of blood, it serves a functional purpose in the surgical units of many facilities, eliminating the green afterimage of the organ being repaired. **Blue** is believed to be the most calming, at least in reduced levels of saturation, and often finds its way into areas intended for respite. Its disadvantage is an association with cold temperature, which may be disadvantageous in exam areas. **Violet** (or purple) is among the least common colors found in interior applications, especially in health care facilities, although some consider it a healing color. Its ability to read warm or cool depending on the colors surrounding it give it flexibility for use in more complex color compositions.

General Illumination

The use of full-spectrum lighting in patient care areas is at least as important as it is in work areas. Lighting level and quality have a greater impact in the medical facility than some other forms of commercial space due to the demands of 24-hour occupancy. Those working the night shifts are more sensitive to the quantities and intensities of light around them because they're deprived of access to daylight for longer periods of time. The alternative is full-spectrum lighting, which can be provided by either incandescent or fluorescent sources. Jain Malkin, an interior designer and space planner who specializes in health care, tells us in *Hospital Interior Architecture* (page 36) that the results of full-spectrum lighting have included less depression, less stress, and improved mood for night-shift personnel. In addition, the quality of indirect lighting is believed to be better than that of direct lighting from overhead.

The physical connection between light and health has been demonstrated scientifically. In humans, a *pineal gland* the size of a pea, located in the center of the brain, serves as a light meter for the rest of the body. It's activated by information received in the eyes and transmitted via the *hypothalamus*. The pineal gland is responsible for regulating daily body functions, called *circadian rhythms,* by manufacturing the hormone *melatonin*. When the body is not exposed to daylight during the day, the system of body function and regularity is disrupted. As patients and night-shift workers lose their sense of orientation to night and day, they become depressed. In the extreme, they suffer from ICU psychosis, which is associated with disorientation. It's because of this that attention to lighting becomes more critical in health care environments. Given the difficulty in staffing second and third shifts, attention to these environmental improvements should provide positive cost-benefit results to management of the medical facility.

▶ Organizational Issues

In any large architectural complex, a variety of functional areas have different criteria for coloration. The medical facility is one of these. To establish conditions that make each functional area most effective, spaces can be separated into three categories during programming: (1) **public spaces,** which are used by outpatients, family, and friends of patients in treatment and by others who either provide a service or depend on a service offered by the medical establishment; (2) **patient care areas,** such as patient rooms, recovery areas, exam rooms, and therapy rooms; and (3) **utilitarian space,** which includes areas used by medical personnel (for surgery, emergency treatments, tests, and lab work) and processing areas (for radiation therapy,

X rays, MRIs, etc.). To program color for medical applications, functional areas are separated into these three groups. Since the purpose of color varies in each category, so must the criteria for color selection.

Public Areas

Public spaces in a medical facility need to communicate clear messages quickly. Within the architectural framework, color can help to orient visitors and patients. It can be sequenced according to building section, vertical level within a building, the relationship of north, south, east, and west, or the various disciplines housed within (emergency treatment area, maternity, etc.). The design and color of the space should help orient a visitor regarding which is the main walkway and which are access routes to specific functions—the hierarchy concept. Some areas need emphasis, such as the central information desk, the nurses' station, and the emergency room. Others, particularly the medical supply room, the family counseling area, and the staff locker rooms, need to be camouflaged. Ideally, colors seen in combination will cue the visitor by drawing attention to some functional areas and minimizing access to others. With each functional area, colorists may want to ask themselves what level of visual acuity is needed. Warning signs and instructions for emergency situations need to be immediately recognizable. The color of the signal devices should contrast most with the colors of the environment. This often suggests a strong color such as red—unless the environment incorporates red, violet, or orange consistently, in which case green or yellow may be the better choice.

Once a level of access is established, the next functional concern is the amount of time visitors, patients, and staff will spend in the space and thus be exposed to its surface colors. The longer the stay, the more complex the coloration may be. Hard colors in more dramatic contrasts serve as excellent attention-getting measures for focal areas. The same colors become tiresome very quickly in a waiting or recovery area. In a space of prolonged use, more subtle contrasts, more complex combinations, and the use of patterning or texture have the greatest value. Greater variety of color adds to the medical environment by offering a distraction where needed and enhancing functionality. Medical facilities with positive coloration typically resolve the following issues well.

- A **continuous theme** binds the facility together well as long as the palette includes enough of a color range to address the specific criteria of each functional area.
- The more monotonous the space, the more difficult it will be for the user to judge distance. In the case of a **complex building form,** color contrasts can be used to articulate the form and eliminate any optical illusions. If a uniform color is too light, glare from the lights can also distort public perception. If large reflective surfaces are used, they, too, can distort perception of form.
- **Corridors** in a large medical complex can be quite long. Color breaks that make use of obvious contrasts can reduce the impression of length and the monotony of the passage, as demonstrated in Figure 14.11. The combination of a very light wall and a very dark wall is not recommended because it can be disorienting to some medical conditions and treatments, just as the combination of two colors that are similar can be lost to view. A little contrast can have a big impact.
- Areas designed to address the needs of the **elderly** need more contrast and more saturated color to be effective with respect to conditions of the aging eye. (See Chapter 12, "Residential Applications," to review issues regarding senior citizens.)

Patient Care Areas

Traditionally, there have been two schools of thought regarding patient rooms. One advised that a stimulating color, (warmer tone or higher saturation) belongs on the wall at the head of the bed and that a calming color (lower saturation or cool in tone) belongs on the wall the patient faces. The idea is that patients have a calming environment during the time of respite and see a source of stimulation when they get out of bed and move around. The second approach is to place the more stimulating color where the patient can see it from the bed, as a motivator, and to keep the wall color at the patient's head in low to medium saturation to aid diagnosis. Of

course, the current drive to make hospitals feel like residences or hotels eliminates both approaches for the simple reason that an accent wall of any kind says "institution" to the patient. In view of the fact that most people use one color or pattern all the way around their living spaces and bedrooms, continuous color used in combination with patterning has become the norm for patient rooms. More colors of hue are being used, especially in combinations that offer spectral harmony. The proposal in Figure 14.12 shows one such solution.

Other considerations for the patient room are matters of judgment. There may be several pieces of equipment built into the bed area, offering a change of material and color. The presence of accents and patterning also offers patients a positive distraction from their current situation. Colors that are more flattering to skin tones can be strategically placed in the patient bathroom, rather than at the headboard, to enhance personal appearance without impeding diagnosis. If indirect lighting is used, the least desirable color for the reflecting surface in a patient area is green, since it tends to make skin tones pallid. A few other points are worth consideration relative to patient areas.

- The key functional area remains the **nurses' station.** A strong contrast here, or some directional patterning in the major floor or wall surface, can direct someone to help at a moment's notice. In the example in Figure 14.13, designers used a clever combination of color and form change to draw attention to the nurses' station and adjacent waiting area.
- Patients in **exam areas** often spend a fair amount of time looking up. This suggests that in addition to the obvious need to eliminate exposed lamps, some patterning or overall tone of hue at the ceiling level is beneficial as a focal point.
- Soft color combinations are preferred over hard ones in patient **recovery areas.** Hard colors can be disturbing to some patients and can become tiresome for patients who must view them over a long period of time. (See Chapter 7, Figures 7.1 and 7.2, for a comparison of hard and soft combinations.)
- **Tired eyes** will be more subject to conditions of simultaneous contrast and figure-ground reversal. Consider the functional needs of each

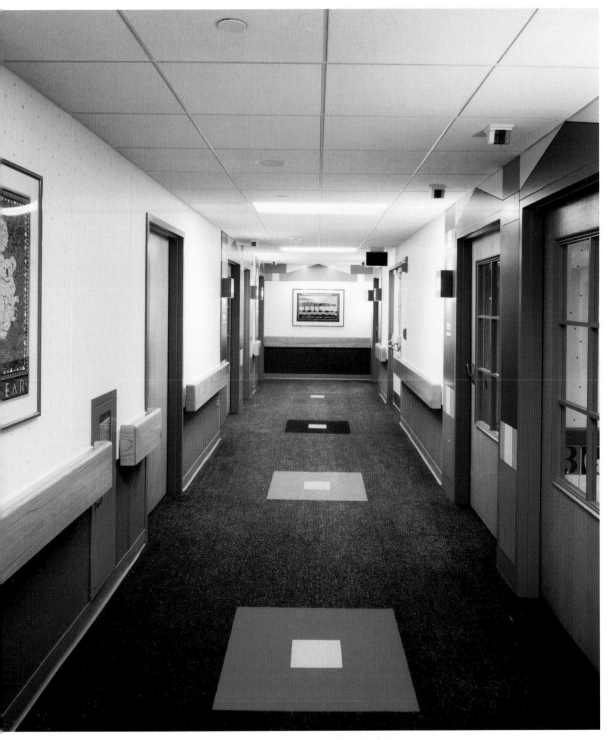

FIGURE 14.11 Creative color selection and placement in the pediatric wing of this medical facility offer positive imagery coupled with function (door openings highlighted, signage keyed, etc.). The result is a corridor length that's visually broken by contrasting colors. *(Designed by TRO/The Ritchie Organization. Photo: © brucetmartin.com.)*

area in terms of colors and pattern positions in light of these potential conditions.

Utilitarian Space

In many cases experienced medical staff can supply historical data to suggest color preferences that support the business of medicine. For instance, a registered nurse with 20 years' experience noted that the babies in her neonatal unit seemed more stressed in the recently renovated space. It was her impression that the new wall colors were appealing to young parents, but were not as soothing to the babies. Many caretakers in recovery areas are able to articulate ways that specific colors appear to be more supportive than others for their area of specialization. Some are offered here.

- In **physical therapy rooms** and other spaces where activity is promoted, a higher level of saturation is recommended for its ability to stimulate. Any hue will do. The saturated color may be used alone, in combination with others, or in combination with neutral colors. Alternatively, less saturated colors in contrasts of hue, extent, or value work well.

- Strong color contrasts are recommended for environments that serve as **therapy rooms for children** with physical disabilities. This can take the form of large-scale patterns, game boards, or characters in the wall treatment, vinyl flooring, or carpet. Even wheelchairs can be enhanced by applying coverings in playful, contrasting colors.

- Diagnosis of **children's medical** conditions, as well as behavioral problems, depends on a stimulating environment. Practitioners often must observe the way children interact with their surroundings to draw conclusions about their general state of health. To facilitate this, colorful graphic surfaces are beneficial, particularly those placed within the physical realm of the child. Alternatively, textural changes, such as mirror, glass windows, or tack walls have been used.

- Some **test areas,** such as EKG and EEG areas, are likely to cause agitation or stress in patients. This may be minimized through the use of low to moderately saturated colors, cool tones, and the visual distraction of some colorful art.

FIGURE 14.12 The color combination developed for this patient room evokes qualities of a residential approach through its moderate saturation and complementary hue combination. *(Rendered by Anna Mahan.)*

- In areas where a person is likely to become depressed, such as the family **waiting area** outside emergency surgery, warmer tones and some contrasts can offer temporary distraction.

- In a **consultation room,** many types of behavior are exhibited, depending on circumstance. In this case, a balance of temperature and moderation of hue, without full neutrality, is worth considering.

- Low levels of light and cool tones are suggested for **intensive care units** (ICUs) due to the nature of the activity in those areas. Green is particularly popular among practitioners.

- In an **operating room** (OR), the surgeon's eyes are subject to successive contrast from looking at intensely red blood and exposed body tissue. Here, green or bluish-green, its complement, is required to neutralize the effects of afterimaging. When the surgeon looks up from his or her work, the cool tone offers relief to cones that register red. Focus on the surgery can be immediately resumed. In this environment, a light reflectance of 30 to 40 percent is suggested for the walls.

- The feedback regarding **maternity wards** seems to be varied. Some recommend monochromatic schemes in cooler tones for a strong sense of harmony. Others suggest warm tones since women tend to feel cool at higher temperatures than men, contrasts to offer some

FIGURE 14.13 Strong color contrast at the floor in a space of otherwise subtle contrast helps to signify functional areas within the patient zone. *(Designed by TRO/The Ritchie Organization. Photo: © Edward Jacoby.)*

distraction, and patterning to serve as objects of focus.

As we noted in Chapter 6, color therapy is another practice that will impact some key color decisions. *Color therapy* is the practice of exposing a patient to colored light or environmental color to treat specific conditions or to enhance recovery when combined with other treatments. Some medical practitioners, behaviorists, and providers of alternative medicine claim to have used this approach with success beyond the therapies practiced in mainstream medicine. As the practice of color therapy increases, practitioners who use its methods can offer insights into particular color uses that aid in treatment. Given the limited statistical evidence available at this time, there is no simple set of colors to embrace for therapeutic spatial solutions. The suggestion here is to ask medical personnel involved some probing questions to unearth solutions that have already proved beneficial.

Diagnosis

Skin tone of the patient is critical in treatment and recovery areas. The color of one's skin will vary according to what foods have recently been consumed, the patient's energy level, and the light of the environment. However, a change in skin tone is a strong indicator of the health of the patient. This is why patients are asked not to wear makeup when they are scheduled for surgery. It shields the natural skin tone. For example, a bright red skin tone can indicate carbon monoxide poisoning. Blue or purple skin can suggest a lack of oxygen in the bloodstream. Babies' skin is the most reflective and therefore the most affected by surrounding color. Lighting with a high CRI level is recommended here. In neonatal wards (for premature babies), doctors and nurses watch for jaundice by checking the skin tone. A large presence of either yellow or blue walls in moderate to high saturation could make it more difficult to ascertain this condition quickly. Therefore, large planes of highly saturated color are not recommended in patient diagnosis and recovery areas.

In addition to skin tone, doctors rely on the color of the eyes, body fluids, and tongue as indicators for diagnosis. Redness of the eyes may be an indication of conjunctivitis or alcoholism. A greenish tinge to the skin suggests anemia, and a red-

dened tongue combined with yellow skin implies the anemic condition has reached a dangerous level. A patient's color perception may also be affected by a medical condition, such as the sense of yellow vision when jaundiced or following some types of poisoning, or blue vision, which results in some cases of alcoholism. All of this suggests that **lighting should be consistent from room to room within a recovery area, and saturated colors should be limited in diagnosis and recovery areas.**

Mental Health

While most experts seem to agree that some basic emotional response to color can be reliably predicted, some remain skeptical when it comes to detailed analysis and conclusions concerning the treatment of various conditions through color, at least for serious mental illnesses. Scientists have identified the part of the brain that receives the electromagnetic energy of color as the pituitary and pineal glands, which are found in the hypothalamus. These are also the organs that regulate secretions in the bloodstream (the endocrine system), controlling emotional responses such as aggression. Many believe it's possible that the variation in electromagnetic energy received in the form of color can result in changes in the signals carried from the brain to nerves and muscles. The degree to which this enables practitioners to use colors as a tool is the source of some debate. The study of environmental color in mental health is difficult because the details of architectural design are so complex; it's impossible to separate issues of form, color, texture, and lighting from each other. To isolate color unconditionally as a behavioral modifier, all other variables must be eliminated.

Since the most beneficial environment in general is believed to be one that feels most homelike to the patient, variations in color and lighting are preferred, as long as there is a balance of unity and complexity. Patients will feel less vulnerable in an environment of comfortable (balanced) colors, just as they feel more comfortable in clothing that is familiar. In the case of mental health facilities, here are some additional thoughts from multiple sources.

■ Eliminate an institutional look as much as possible through color selection and placement.

Those places appropriate to more **creative color** application are the recreation rooms, lounges, and occupational therapy rooms.

- A color that is preferred by a patient of extreme behavior may not necessarily be the color that offers benefit in terms of managing behavior. If the facility as a whole offers some **variety of color** (hues and combinations), professionals can take advantage of those variations to manage patients based on their own observations.

- When color is used to **enhance behavior,** the effects of an overall shift in environmental color are immediately therapeutic. For example, low saturated color can be used in a quiet room to calm agitated children. This suggests that color may be used effectively in some mental health clinics in transition spaces if the practitioner sees a benefit.

- Limit **visual patterns,** particularly in large-scale mental health facilities. Figure-ground patterns and large areas of very saturated color are not desirable in the patient rooms of psychotic patients due to their perceived imposition.

■ CONCLUSIONS

Due to the complex nature of any health care facility, not all considerations can be addressed in this text. Fortunately, several good references, which include meaningful color advice, are now available on health care as an area of design specialization. In light of their complexities, health care spaces can be challenging from a color standpoint. Through experience and shared results, we're able to manage the color tools at hand—contrasts, harmonies, balance, and association—to effect emotional, functional, and healthful results. Fortunately, we can recognize color characteristics for what they are and use our tools to create unique spaces. We're no longer limited to dogmatic solutions from past eras.

If the field of color therapy continues to gain momentum and credibility, it's likely that those of us in the design community will have more practical information, not only for health care applications, but also for the well-being of all our clients. What's needed now are double-blind studies to determine scientifically how we can manage the vibrations of electromagnetic waves, especially those we recognize as color, for therapeutic means. Practitioners in the field are just beginning to scratch this surface. Their success in part is a matter of faith that each electromagnetic vibration has a specific purpose in the physiology of the human body and that some of us will benefit from exposure to specific vibrations as a means to manage illness or impairment. If the successes of those therapies are documented with measurable consistency, we as designers will have color tools of greater impact than we ever thought possible. In the meantime, the best advice is to evaluate new color information in the context of personal experience. If new insights presented by others are consistent with your own experience as a designer, then they may be useful in practice, assuming there is evidence to support them. If results offered are clearly inconsistent with personal experience, my advice is to hold out for more evidence before embracing those new ideas as fact. Our strength as designers in the future will depend on collaborating documentation of effective color use and an openness to new possibilities.

Glossary

accidental colors   Term used by Chevreul to describe afterimages and color sensation experienced subjectively.

achromatic   Lacking any hue.

acid colors   Jarring tones such as chartreuse green, bitter yellow, or fluorescents.

additive color   Colors created by light, as opposed to pigment.

afterimage   A colored shape that appears to float in front of the eye after viewing extreme changes of light or a high-saturation color.

adjacent colors   Colors that are close to each other on the color wheel (e.g., green, green-blue, and blue). Synonymous with analogous colors.

analogous colors   Colors that are close to each other on the color wheel (e.g., green, green-blue, and blue). Synonymous with adjacent colors.

anodized   A finish on metal surfaces created by electrochemical treatment. The result is a hard, protective oxide film.

anomalous trichromatism   A condition of color deficiency in which the individual recognizes three primary colors, but a full range of color matching is not possible.

antiquing   Any artificial process that causes a surface to appear old, such as scuffing of paint, cracking a veneer, or abrading leather.

balance   The state of a composition when there is an appropriate amount of both unity and complexity of the design.

blackbody   A material that absorbs all the radiant energy (light) falling on it. In physics this is considered an absolute substance—one that does not exist on earth. Approximate blackbodies, which reflect less than 2 percent of incoming radiation, are used for color testing.

blond wood   Light wood, beige in tone, such as holly or birch, or created by adding a white pigment.

camouflage   The manipulation of color to make one thing blend into another, such as animals who blend with surroundings to hide from predators.

cast   The hint of one hue in another.

chiaroscuro   The technique of rendering images using light and dark shades as highlights and shadows to create the illusion of three-dimensional form.

chinoiserie   Chinese-like decorative, picturesque motifs applied to traditional furniture.

chroma   A synonym for saturation. Also used to distinguish hue, as in a specific chroma.

chromatic   Characteristic of a clearly identifiable hue.

chromacity   The comparative quality of a color based on its hue and saturation level, without concern for its relative value.

chromotherapy   The use of color sources for healing purposes; also known as *color therapy.*

color blindness   The term used to describe any physiological color deficiency.

color circle   Any circular diagram that shows colors of hue organized sequentially according to the spectrum of light.

colorfast   Used to describe a material that will retain its color characteristics when exposed to light.

colorimetry   The science of measurement and analysis of color.

colorways   The various color combinations in which a material is produced, usually applied to textiles.

concept   The basic idea or beginning of a design.

cones   The cells of the human retina that recognize chromatic color (hue) when light is present. The name comes from the shape of the cells.

contrast   The amount and type of difference between two or more colors.

complex colors   Colors that are created by combining more than one color of hue. Complex colors may involve texture. They are usually more difficult to describe concisely.

complexity   The amount of contrast of colors or the range of differences between them. This is what stimulates interest.

complementary colors   Colors that are directly opposite each other on the color circle.

crocking   The process of dye rubbing off a printed or dyed fabric, occurring most often in deep-colored fabrics with a pile.

dichromatism   A condition of color deficiency in which the person can distinguish color only in terms of value and a range of two colors—either red to green or yellow to blue.

digitize   The method of converting color into electronic signals so that it can be reproduced by computer technology. This is accomplished by breaking it down into small points of color, a process that occurs with digital photography and scanning.

dyad   A pair of complementary colors.

ebonize   To make black.

eglomise   Painted art form done on the reverse side of glass, which may include both pigment and gold leaf.

enamel   A solid, glossy coating created by fusing colored glass film to metal.

embossing   The process of pressing a design into a material (e.g., fabric or paper) by passing it through hot engraved rollers.

essential nature   The basic methodology by which color is assigned to its form and materials.

extent, extension   The relative strength of a color, or its ability to draw the eye. Greater extension is caused by lighter value increased saturation, or increased area.

faux finish   Applied finishes developed to create the impression of natural materials or to create other illusions of texture, age, or concealment.

film color   A large area of a single color that appears to take space independent of the form to which it is attached.

fluorescent   A condition of colors that makes them bright and luminous.

focus   The first thing the eye is drawn to (e.g., a model's face, an entry door, or the direction of travel).

fugitive   Condition in a color medium that causes it to fade from exposure to light.

fusion   The process of creating an image of one color by blending two or more colors in small increments. This is the process of color printing and the effect that occurs with textural paints.

gilding   The process of applying gold leaf or gold dust as ornamentation on architecture, furniture, and accessories.

glaze   An applied finish on ceramics that hardens after firing; a thin film of transparent paint or varnish; a smooth, polished finish applied to fabrics such as chintz.

gloss, glossy   A shine or luster on any surface. Light color with a glossy surface tends to look lighter in value, dark to look darker.

gouache   An opaque, water-based paint.

greige   A neutral grayish-beige color.

ground color   The base or background color upon which other colors are applied.

harmony   A state of compatibility in color hues. This occurs when colors are either similar to each other (i.e., within a 45-degree radius on the color circle) or, when used in combination, they create a balance of color hue along a diameter of the color circle.

hexad   A combination of six colors that form three pairs, equally spaced from a common diameter. The polygon so formed is a hexagon.

high tone; high key color   Color that is light in value.

hue   The relative position of a color on the color circle; the redness, blueness, or yellowness of a color.

intensity   The purity of a color, or the degree of hue characteristic of a color.

illumination   The colorful scrolls, arabesques, foliage, and so forth of medieval time that were hand-painted on manuscripts using pigment and gold and silver dust.

illusion   The act of using color to make one see something that does not exist. For example, one color can be made to look like two, a color may appear transparent, or a wall may be painted to look like a fireplace.

illusionary color   Use of color to create that which is nonexisting. This can include color transparencies or trompe l'oeil.

intrinsic color   A consistent method of organizing color, which makes placement of each color dependent on the materials used.

light reflectance value (LRV)   The amount of light that is reflected by a surface color, measured as a percentage. For practical purposes, the working range of LRV in interior applications is 10 to 90 percent.

luminance   The amount of light reflected from a surface, measured in candela per square meter.

luster   A glowing effect in a surface color, usually caused by oil or metallic particles in its composition.

matte   A finish with no gloss to shine.

metameric   A phenomenon that occurs when two colors appear the same under a particular light condition and different under another. This can be caused by a difference in texture or by the color formula of two different light sources.

monochromatic   A combination of colors in one hue.

monochromatism   A condition of color deficiency in which only achromatic vision is possible.

muted   Used to describe a color that is soft and restrained or dulled from fading.

nanometer   The unit of measure for comparing electromagnetic wavelengths, of which visible colors are a subset.

neutral   A condition of color that appears to have no discernible hue (i.e., gray, white, or black).

optics   The science of light and color perception.

optical color mixing   A condition in which an object appears to be only one color until close inspection reveals the combination of much smaller pieces of varying colors that make up the initial tone. The most common application is dots of color on printed media, which the eye blends into a picture.

palette   Any combination of colors organized for a purpose, as in a painter's palette, a room palette, or a reference palette.

patina   A surface appearance that is the result of natural aging of a surface, such as oxidization of copper, softening or fading of paint, yellowing of paper, or smoothing of leather upholstery.

photometer   A tool used to measure quantity of light.

Purkinje effect   The condition that causes the apparent strength, or brightness (saturation and value), of colors to shift in changing light levels. In more intense light levels, a person sees warmer colors as having greater strength or brightness. In low light levels, cooler ones appear brighter.

process colors   The three colors cyan, magenta, and yellow that are used in combination with black to create the full spectrum of print media.

primary colors   The three basic colors that can be combined to form all others. In pigment, they are red, yellow, and blue. In light, they are red, green, and blue. And in print media, they are cyan, yellow, and magenta.

psychedelic color   A group of highly saturated colors, including fluorescents, that were popular during the 1960s.

rods   Those cells in the retina that are used in low light conditions to perceive color.

safety colors   A group of colors specified by the Occupational Safety and Health Administration (OSHA) to identify hazardous zones and materials.

saturation   The degree or strength of hue in a color; intensity.

scale   A sequence of colors that vary according to one characteristic (e.g., a tone scale where gray is added to a color in increasing amounts).

secondary colors   The three colors created by mixing each of two primary colors. In pigment, they are orange, green, and purple. In light, they are yellow, cyan, and magenta.

sfumato   An Italian word meaning "smokelike." It is used to describe soft, hazy-looking, textural color created in wall paint with glazes, artist's oil paint, or pastels. Sfumato was originally associated with Leonardo da Vinci in the fifteenth century.

shades   Colors of hue mixed with black.

simple color   Any color that is easily identifiable.

simultaneity   The effect one intense color has over another due to the eye's tendency to find the strong color's complement. Simultaneous contrast can also occur between two equally strong colors, which will each affect the other directly.

spectral colors   The colors red, orange, yellow, green, blue, indigo, and violet, which are visible when white light is passed through a prism.

spectral power distribution (spd)   A graphic indication of a light source's ability to render the full range of visible color. SPD references are provided by lamp manufacturers for their products.

split complement   A combination of three colors in which two colors are equally spaced around the color circle from the third color's complement.

stencil   A pattern created by applying paint over a sheet of metal that has been precut with a design; the precut sheet itself.

subtractive color   Pigmentary color; the color of any solid material, including paint or dye.

successive contrast   The visual influence of colors on each other when viewed separately after short periods of time.

synethesia, synaesthesia   A condition in psychology where one type of sensation evokes a secondary one. Physiologically speaking, its is the sensation felt in one part of the body when another part is stimulated.

synthetic color   Color created by artificial methods (e.g., synthetic dyes and pigments) rather than obtained from organic means.

temperature   The apparent warmness or coolness of a color. Warm colors range from yellow to red on the color circle. Cool colors range from purple to green.

tint   Colors of hue mixed with white.

tone   Colors of hue mixed with gray.

triad   Three colors equally spaced around the color circle (e.g., orange, green, purple).

tetrad   Four colors positioned around the color circle such that they form two pairs of colors that are complementary.

transparency   The condition in which one color appears to be visible behind another.

tristimulus values   Numerical reference for color quality based on its reflectance under a standard set of conditions.

trompe l'oeil Illusionary imagery applied by paint, usually to a flat surface. The term is French, meaning "to fool the eye."

undertone A color applied underneath another, or within a visual mix, to give depth to the overall color. The result is a range of colors that are harmonic because of a common underlying hue.

unity The commonality of colors; the appearance of similarity, which creates comfort.

value The lightness or darkness of a color.

visual color mixing The process of mixing colors that occur in the eye rather than in the medium, such as in textile weavings and four color printing.

volume color The fluidic color that exists in conditions of fog, smoke, some atmospheric conditions, liquids and gases, and in air containing particulate matter.

weight A term used to describe color psychologically (e.g., a dark color is perceived to be heavier than a light one).

Bibliography

Albers, Josef. *Interaction of Color,* Yale University Press, London, 1975.

Anderson, Mary. *Colour Therapy,* The Aquarian Press, Thorsons Publishing Group, Northamptonshire, England, 1990.

Aria, Barbara. *Nursery Design: Creating a Perfect Environment for Your Child,* Bantam Books, New York, 1990.

The Athenaeum Library of Nineteenth Century America, *Exterior Decoration: A Treatise on the Artistic Use of Colors in the Ornamentation of Buildings,* The Athenaeum of Philadelphia, Philadelphia, 1976.

Aves, Melanie, and John Alves. *Interior Designers' Showcase of Color,* Rockport Publishers, Inc., Rockport, MA, 1994.

Barr, Vilma, and Charles E. Broudy. *Designing to Sell,* second edition, McGraw-Hill, New York, 1990.

Birren, Faber. *Color Psychology and Color Therapy,* University Books, Inc., New Hyde Park, NY, 1961.

———. *Color: A Survey in Words and Pictures,* University Books, Inc., New Hyde Park, NY, 1963.

———. *Color for Interiors Historical and Modern,* Whitney Library of Design, New York, 1963.

———. *A Grammar of Color: A Basic Treatise on the Color System of Albert H. Munsell,* Van Nostrand Reinhold Company, New York, 1969.

———. *Color & Human Response,* Van Nostrand Reinhold Company, Inc., New York, 1978.

———. *The Textile Colorist,* Van Nostrand Reinhold, New York, 1980.

———. *Color Perception in Art,* Schiffer Publishing Ltd., West Chester, PA, 1986.

———. *Creative Color: A Dynamic Approach for Artists and Designers,* Schiffer Publishing Ltd., West Chester, PA, 1987.

———. *Principles of Color,* Schiffer Publishing Ltd., West Chester, PA, 1987.

———. *Light, Color & Environment,* second revised edition, Schiffer Publishing Ltd., West Chester, PA, 1988.

Brawley, Elizabeth. *Designing for Alzheimer's Disease: Strategies for Creating Better Care Environments,* John Wiley & Sons, Inc., New York, 1997.

—————. "Elizabeth Brawley on Alzheimer's," *The Grid,* a newsletter for medical designers published by InPro Corporation, Muskego, Wisconsin, spring 1999.

Brusatin, Manlio. *A History of Colors,* Translated by Robert H. Hopcke and Paul Schwartz, Shambhala Publications, Inc., Boston, 1991.

Burnham, R. W., R. M. Hanes, and C. James Bartleson. *Color: A Guide to Basic Facts and Concepts,* John Wiley & Sons, Inc., New York, 1963.

Butterfield, Suzanne. *Color Palettes,* Clarkson N. Potter, Inc., New York, 1998.

Byrne, Alex, and David R. Hilbert, *Readings on Color, Volume 1: The Philosophy of Color,* The MIT Press, Cambridge, MA, 1997.

Chevreul, M. E. *The Principles of Harmony and Contrast of Colors,* based on the first English edition of 1854, as translated from the first French edition 1839, Van Nostrand Reinhold Company, New York, 1967.

Dean, Jenny. *Wild Color: The Complete Guide to Making and Using Natural Dyes,* Watson-Guptill Publications, New York, 1999.

Delamare, Francois, and Bernard Guineau. *Colors: The Story of Dyes and Pigments,* Harry N. Abrams, Inc., New York, translated 2000.

De Grandis, Luigina. *Theory and Use of Color,* Harry N. Abrams, Inc., New York, 1984.

Dolye, Michael E. *Color Drawing,* Van Nostrand Reinhold Company, New York, 1981.

Duttmann, Martina, Friedrich Schmuck, and Johannes Uhl. *Color in Townscape,* translated from German by John William Gabriel, W. H. Freeman and Company, San Francisco, 1981.

Eiseman, Leatrice, and Lawrence Herbert. *The PANTONE Book of Color: Over 1000 Color Standards; Color Basics and Guidelines for Design, Fashion, Furnishing. . . . and More,* Harry N. Abrams, Inc., New York, 1990.

Eiseman, Leatrice. *Colors for Your Every Mood,* Capital Books Inc., Sterling, VA, 1998.

Elliott, Inger McCabe. *Exteriors,* Clarkson N. Potter Inc., New York, 1993.

Esten, John, and Rose Bennett Gilbert. *Manhattan Style,* Little, Brown and Company, Boston, 1990.

Faulkner, Waldron. *Architecture and Color,* John Wiley & Sons, Inc. New York, 1972.

Fehrman, Kenneth R., and Cherie Fehrman. *Color: The Secret Influence,* Prentice-Hall, Inc, Upper Saddle River, NJ, 2000.

Fisher, Mary Pat, and Paul Zelanski. *Color,* second edition, Prentice-Hall, Upper Saddle River, NJ, 1994.

Fry, Mary G., Patricia Lambert, and Barbara Staepelaere. *Color and Fiber,* Schiffer Publishing Ltd., West Chester, PA, 1986.

Gage, John. *Color and Culture: Practice and Meaning from Antiquity to Abstraction,* Little, Brown and Company, Boston, 1993.

—————. *Color and Meaning: Art, Science, and Symbolism,* University of California Press, Berkeley and Los Angeles, 1999.

Garthe, Mary. *Fashion and Color,* Rockport Publishers, Inc., Rockport, MA, 1995.

Gerstner, Karl. *The Forms of Color,* translated from German by Dennis A. Stephenson, The MIT Press, Cambridge, MA, and London, England, 1986.

Goethe, Johann Wolfgang. *Theory of Colours,* first published in 1810, translated from German by Charles Lock Eastlake, Frank Cass & Co., Ltd., London, 1967.

Gwynn, Kate, and Annie Sloan. *Colour in Decoration,* Frances Lincoln Ltd., London, 1990.

Halse, Albert. *The Use of Color in Interiors,* McGraw-Hill Book Company, New York, 1968.

Holtzschue, Linda. *Understanding Colors: An Introduction for Designers,* Van Nostrand Reinhold, New York, 1995.

Hope, Augustine, and Margaret Walch. *The Color Compendium,* Van Nostrand Reinhold, New York, 1980.

————. *Living Colors,* Chronicle Books, San Francisco, 1995.

Hunt, R. W. G. *Measuring Colour,* second edition, Ellis Horwood Limited, West Sussex, England, 1991.

The IESNA Lighting Handbook: Reference & Application, Illuminating Engineering Society of North America, New York, 2002.

IPC Design Institute, Boston Design Symposium, Boston, August 28, 1997.

IPC Design Symposium 1, audiotaped proceeding from presentations to the design community published by IPC Design Institute, Milwaukee, 1997.

Issett, Ruth. *Color on Paper and Fabric,* Hand Books Press, Madison, WI, 1998.

Itten, Johannes. *The Art of Color: The Subjective Experience and Objective Rationale of Color,* Van Nostrand Reinhold Company, New York, 1973. Originally published in Germany under the title *Kunst der Farbe,* 1961, translated by Ernst von Haagen.

Jacobson, Egbert. *Basic Color,* based on *The Color Primer* by Wilhelm Ostwald, first published in German in 1916, Paul Theobald, Chicago, 1948.

Journal of Healthcare Design, proceedings from a series of symposiums on health care.

Kaufman, Donald, and Taffy Dahl. *Color: Natural Palettes for Painted Rooms,* Clarkson N. Potter, Inc., New York, 1992.

————. *Color and Light: Luminous Atmospheres for Painted Rooms,* Clarkson N. Potter, Inc., New York, 1999.

Khouw, Natalia. *The Meaning of Color for Gender,* ColorMatters-Research, www.colormaters.com/khouw.html, 2003.

Kobayashi, Shigenobu. *Color Image Scale,* Kodansha, Ltd., New York, 1990.

————. *Colorist: A Practical Handbook for Personal and Professional Use,* Kodansha, Ltd., New York, 1998.

Kuehni, Rolf G. *Color: Essence and Logic,* Van Nostrand Reinhold, New York, 1983.

Ladau, Robert F., Brent K. Smith, and Jennifer Place. *Color in Interior Design and Architecture,* Van Nostrand Reinhold, New York, 1989.

Ladd-Franklin, Christine. *Colour and Colour Theories,* Arno Press, New York, 1973.

Lambert, Patricia, Barbara Staepelaere, and May G. Fry. *Color and Fiber,* Schiffer Publishing, Ltd., West Chester, Pennsylvania, 1986.

Lambert, Patricia. *Controlling Color,* Design Press, New York, 1991.

Laurence, F. S. *Color in Architecture,* National Terra Cotta Society, New York, 1924.

Linton, Harold. *Color Consulting: A Survey of International Color Design,* Van Nostrand Reinhold, New York, 1991.

————. *Color Forecasting: A Survey of International Color Marketing,* Van Nostrand Reinhold, New York, 1994.

————. *Color in Architecture: Design Methods for Buildings, Interiors, and Urban Spaces,* McGraw-Hill Companies, Inc., New York, 1999.

Logrippo, Ro. *In My World: Designing Living & Learning Environments for the Young,* John Wiley & Sons, Inc., New York, 1995.

Luke, Joy Turner. *The Munsell Color System: A Language for Color,* Fairchild Publications, New York, 1996.

Lüscher, Max. *The Lüscher Color Test,* translated and edited by Ian A. Scott, Washington Square Press, New York, 1969.

Malkin, Jain. *Hospital Interior Architecture,* Van Nostrand Reinhold, New York, 1992.

Malaguzzi, To Loris. *Children, Spaces, Relations: Metaproject for an Environment for Young Children,* Domus Academy Research Center, Milan, Italy, 1998.

Mahnke, Frank H. *Color, Environment & Human Response,* Van Nostrand Reinhold, New York, 1996.

Mahnke, Frank H., and Rudolph H. Mahnke. *Color and Light,* Van Nostrand Reinhold, New York, 1993.

Marberry, Sara, and Laurie Zagon. *The Power of Color: Creating Healthy Interior Spaces,* John Wiley & Sons, Inc., New York, 1995.

Maycock, Susan E., and Sarah J. Zimmerman. *Painting Historic Exteriors: Colors, Application and Regulation,* Society for the Preservation of New England Antiquities, Boston, 1998.

Maynard, Micheline. "Automakers' Color Guard Not Spinning Its Wheels," *USA Today,* Monday, October 26, 1998.

Miller, Mary C. *Color for Interior Architecture,* John Wiley & Sons, Inc., New York, 1997.

Mirko, Mejetta, and Simonetta Spada. *Interiors in Color: Creating Space, Personality and Atmosphere,* Translated by Anthony DeAlteris, Whitney Library of Design, an imprint of Watson-Guptill Publications, New York, 1983.

Mitton, Maureen. *Interior Design Visual Presentation,* John Wiley & Sons, Inc., New York, 1999.

Morton, Jill. *ColorVoodoo,* electronic text published by Colorcom, Honolulu, 1998.

Moss, Roger W. *Century of Color: Exterior Decoration for American Buildings, 1820–1920,* The American Life Foundation, Watkins Glen, NY, 1981.

"New Construction: Kin On Healthcare Center," *Design '99,* A publication of nursing homes providing long-term-care management, March 1999.

Olds, Anita Rui. *Child Care Design Guide,* McGraw-Hill, New York, 2001.

Osram Sylvania. *Lightpoints: Understanding the Science and Technology of Light,* manufacturers' literature, Westfield, IN, 2001.

Perritt, Mitzi R., Sandra L. McCune, and Joyce E. Nuner, "Programming for Alzheimer's Disease: A New Perspective," *ISdesignNET,* published by Interior Design Educators Council, 2002. (Web site October 29, 2002 www.isdesignet. com/magazine/June%2700/idec.html.)

Peterson, L. K., and Cheryl Dangel Cullen. *Global Graphics: Color: A Guide to Design with Color for an International Market,* Rockport Publishers, Inc., Gloucester, MA, 2000.

Pile, John. *Color in Interior Design,* McGraw-Hill, New York, 1997.

———. *Interior Design,* second edition, Harry N. Abrams, Inc., New York, 1988.

Poling, Clark V. *Kandinsky's Teaching at the Bauhaus: Color Theory and Analytical Drawing,* Rizzoli International Publications, Inc., New York, 1986.

Poore, Jonathan. *Interior Color by Design: A Design Tool for Architects, Interior Designers, and Homeowners,* Rockport Publishers, Rockport, MA, 1994.

Porter, Tom. *Architectural Color: A Design Guide to Using Color on Buildings,* Whitney Library of Design, an imprint of Watson-Guptill Publications, New York, 1982.

Priester, Gary W. *Looking Good in Color,* Ventana Press Inc., Chapel Hill, NC, 1995.

Quant, Mary, and Felicity Green. *Colour by Quant,* Octopus Books, Ltd., London, 1985.

Ragan, Sandra L. *Interior Color by Design: A Design Tool for Architects, Interior Designers, and Facility Managers,* Rockport Publishers, Rockport, MA, 1995.

Rodemann, Patricia A. *Patterns in Environments: Perception, Psychology, and Practice,* John Wiley & Sons, Inc, New York, 1999.

Rood, Ogden N. *Modern Chromatics: Student's Text-book of Color with Applications to Art and Industry,* Van Nostrand Reinhold Company, New York, 1973.

Sharpe, Deborah T. *The Psychology of Color and Design,* Nelson-Hall, Inc., Chicago, 1974.

Stierlin, Henri. *The Spirit of Colors: The Art of Karl Gerstner,* translated from German by Dennis A. Stephenson, The MIT Press, Cambridge, MA, and London, England, 1981.

Stromer, Klaus. *Color Systems in Art and Science,* Regenbogen Verlag Klaus Stromer, Konstanz, Germany, 1996.

Swirnoff, Lois. *Dimensional Color,* Birkhauser Boston, Inc, Cambridge, MA, 1989.

———. *The Color of Cities: An International Perspective,* McGraw-Hill Companies Inc., New York, 2000.

Torrice, Antonio F., and Ro Logrippo. *In My Room: Designing for and with Children,* Fawcett Columbine, New York, 1989.

Varley, Helen. *Color,* editor, Marshall Editions Limited, The Knapp Press, Los Angeles, 1980.

Wagner, Carlton. *The Language of Color,* a videotape and correspondence course published by The Wagner Institute for Color Research, Chicago, 1988, 1993.

Wagner, Carlton. *The Color Response Report,* The Institute for Color Research, Chicago.

Walker, Morton. *The Power of Color,* Avery Publishing Group, Garden City Park, NY, 1991.

Wilcox, Michael. *Blue and Yellow Don't Make Green,* North Light Books, Cincinnati, revised edition, 1994.

Wright, Angela. Colour Affects, web site www.colour-affects.co.uk, London, United Kingdom, 2003.

Zwimpfer, Moritz. *Color Light Sight Sense: An Elementary Theory of Color in Pictures,* Schiffer Publishing Ltd., West Chester, PA, 1988.

Index

Barr, Vilma, 230
Bauhaus school, 19, 35, 71, 112, 197
Behavioral effects of color, 255–256, 276, 277
Bezold, Wilhelm von, 23, 142
Bezold effect, 142, 170
Binocular area, 10–11
Birren, Faber, 76, 85, 91, 95, 128, 262, 266
Black:
    as absorbed wavelengths, 14
    as contrast, 34, 35
    to create shades, 5
    as neutral, 67, 83
    in printing, 30
Blackbody, 150
Blind spot, of eye, 10
Block printing, 167
Blue:
    as additive color, 13
    chakra, 94
    characteristics of, 79–80
    in child development, 223
    in color therapy, 93, 159, 270
    as primary color, 4, 31
    as receding color, 129
    as subtractive color, 14, 18
Blue and Yellow Don't Make Green (Wilcox), 18
Boutique color, 193
Brass, 179
Brawley, Elizabeth C., 214, 216, 218
Brick, 174, 175
Bridge colors, 201
Brightness (brilliance):
    defined, 7–8
    and depth perception, 123
    peripheral, 132
Bronze, 179
Broudy, Charles E., 230
Brown:
    European preference for, 202
    as neutral, 82–83
Business competition:
    as design driver, 253
    in health care, 268

Calcimine paints, 197
Calvert, Diane, 202
Carbon black, 14
Carpets:
    complex color in, 170–171
    dye methods for, 168–169
    oriental, 162, 169
    pile, 170
Cast, within color, 195

Cataracts, 212
Ceilings:
    color of, 195, 210
    in conference facilities, 250
Center of Health Design, 214
Ceramics, 175–176
Chakras, 93, 94
Check rolling technique, 167
Chevreul, Michel-Eugène, 20, 45, 47–48, 156, 163, 164, 167
Chiaroscuro, 34
Child Care Design Guide (Olds), 248
Children:
    educational facilities for, 67, 247–250
    residential design for, 219–225
Children, Spaces, Relations (Malaguzzi), 249
Chroma:
    in color contrasts, 49–51
    in color models, 28
    defined, 6–7
    and depth perception, 130
    human response to, 86
    lack of, 35, 81
    with scotopic vision, 146
    (*See also* Saturation)
Chromacity, 7, 124, 126
Chrome, 179
Chromotherapy, 93
CIE System, 25, 190, 267
Circadian rhythms, 271
Clark, Linda, 9
Classifying color, 102
CMYK color matching, 30
Cold cathode lamps, 154
Color:
    attributes of, 3, 19 (*See also specific attributes*)
    boutique approach to, 193
    children's response to, 96, 219–220, 225
    complementary (*see* Complementary colors)
    creating, 155
    and depth perception, 124–135
    in design concept, 105
    as educational tool, 249–250
    effect of light level on, 148, 149
    experimenting with, 30–32
    in first impressions, 92, 254
    in form articulation, 135–144
    form-driven, 112–120
    hard versus soft, 106
    health affected by, 268
    human range of, 11
    human response to (*see* Color response)
    mood enhancement with, 99
    nature of, 121

ABOUT THE AUTHOR

JEANNE KOPACZ, IIDA, IFMA, NCIDQ certified, is a principal with Bryer Architects, LLP, in Cambridge, Massachusetts. She has 25 years of design experience, primarily with architectural firms. In addition, Ms. Kopacz teaches at the New England School of Art & Design, Suffolk University, for whom she developed such courses as *Color for Interiors*; *Interiors Contracts and Marketing*; *Commercial Studio II*; *Codes and Construction*; and *Materials and Finishes*. She serves on the advisory board to NESA&D and participates in the Principals Roundtable of IIDA, New England Chapter.